THE POLITICAL ECONOMY OF FEDERAL POLICY

THE POLITICAL ECONOMY OF FEDERAL POLICY

ROBERT H. HAVEMAN
ROBERT D. HAMRIN
The University of Wisconsin

Harper & Row, Publishers
New York Evanston San Francisco London

THE POLITICAL ECONOMY OF FEDERAL POLICY

Standard Book Number: 06–042691–8 (Clothbound)
06–042692–6 (Paperback)

Library of Congress Catalog Card Number: 72–8259

CONTENTS

Preface ix

PART I. INTRODUCTION

Private Power and Federal Policy **3**
Robert H. Haveman

PART II. PRIVATE POWER AND THE PERFORMANCE OF GOVERNMENT

Introduction 11

A. SOME PERSPECTIVES ON GOVERNMENTAL POLICY

Perverse Incentives and the Inefficiency of Government **15**
Charles L. Schultze

Cutting Government Back to Size—Eight Guidelines **23**
Milton Friedman

The Economic Origins of Political Power in America **26**
Timothy Bates

B. FEDERAL POLICY AND THE PRIVATE SECTOR

A Citizen's Guide to the American Economy **33**
Ralph Nader

Government Policy as the Source of Vested Power **43**
Walter Adams

Government as Promoter, Sustainer, and Subsidizer of "Private Enterprise" **47**
Gaylord Shaw

The Vested Oracles: How Industry Regulates Government **52**
Lee Metcalf

PART III. FEDERAL TAXATION POLICY

Introduction 63

The Rich, the Poor, and the Taxes They Pay **67**
Joseph A. Pechman

The Problem of Tax Loopholes (or: My Eighteen Years in a Quandary) **74**
Paul H. Douglas

Tax Expenditures and Tax Reform **82**
Stanley S. Surrey

Toward a Progressive Federal Tax System **92**
Joseph A. Pechman

PART IV. FEDERAL MILITARY SPENDING

Introduction 97

A. THE MILITARY BUDGET—ITS SIZE, STRUCTURE, AND DETERMINATION

A Profile of the Defense Budget **100**
Richard F. Kaufman

A Comprehensive National Security Budget **104**
U.S. Congress, Joint Economic Committee

The Ultimate Cost of the Vietnam Conflict **107**
James L. Clayton

Military Power and the Military Budget **112**
John Kenneth Galbraith

The Factors Behind Rising Military Expenditures **117**
Charles L. Schultze

B. THE MILITARY-INDUSTRIAL COMPLEX

The Pervasive Economic Impact of the Military **127**
Seymour Melman

A Profile of the Military-Industrial Complex **135**
Richard F. Kaufman

C. WEAPONS PROCUREMENT

The Economics of Military Procurement **145**
U.S. Congress, Joint Economic Committee, Subcommittee on Economy in Government

The Problem of Cost Overruns **159**
Frederic M. Scherer

Reform of Pentagon Procurement or Gilbert Fitzhugh's Golden Fleece **166**
A. Ernest Fitzgerald

PART V. FEDERAL CIVILIAN SPENDING

Introduction 177

A. AGRICULTURAL POLICY

U.S. Farm Policy: Who Gets the Benefits **182**
Charles L. Schultze

B. NATURAL RESOURCES AND ENVIRONMENTAL POLICY

The Water Giveaway: A Critique of Federal Water Policy **191**
Mason Gaffney

Clean Rhetoric and Dirty Water: The Failure of Federal Water Pollution Control Policy **198**
A. Myrick Freeman, III and Robert H. Haveman

The System of Government Subsidies to the Oil Industry **207**
Walter J. Mead

C. TRANSPORTATION POLICY

U.S. Maritime Policy: Subsidizing Waste and Inefficiency **215**
Leonard A. Rapping

White Elephants, Waterways, and the Transportation Act of 1966 **220**
Robert H. Haveman and Paula Stephan

The Federal Highway Program **226**
Louis M. Kohlmeier

D. URBAN AND SOCIAL POLICY

Evaluating Efficiency and Equity in Federal Urban Programs **231**
Anthony Downs

Incentives for Inefficiency in Medicare and Medicaid **238**
Vincent D. Taylor

Federal Housing Policy and the HUD Bureaucracy **243**
Howard E. Shuman

PART VI. FEDERAL REGULATORY AND INFORMATION POLICY

Introduction 253

The Regulators and the Regulated **256**
Louis M. Kohlmeier

Economic Analysis and Regulatory Decisions **261**
Nicholas Johnson

Efficiency and Regulatory Policy: Issues of Compliance, Disclosure, and Accountability **267**
Ralph Nader

Government Secrecy and the People's Right to Know **273**
Ralph Nader, Gary Sellers, Reuben Robertson, John Esposito, Harrison Wellford, James Turner, and Robert Fellmeth

Corporate Secrecy and the Need for Financial Disclosure **283**
Willard F. Mueller

INDEX **293**

PREFACE

Some of the most pressing public issues being debated today concern the nature and functioning of government. Clearly the role and effectiveness of the public sector is receiving more attention now than at any other time in United States history. Who is it that really makes public sector decisions and what motivates them? Why do some groups appear to have so much more power and influence over government decisions than do other groups? Can government serve the "public interest" when in area after area it seems to be serving special interests? Is it possible to eliminate wasteful and inequitable government programs and replace them with programs which are both equitable and efficient? It is questions such as these which have motivated this book.

The "political economy" perspective which has guided the choice of essays to be included in this volume is discussed in the introductory essay, "Private Power and Federal Policy." A quote from that essay summarizes this perspective:

> Inefficient and inequitable public policy exists because powerful vested interests . . . have been able to exploit citizens in their roles as taxpayers and consumers. The ability of vested interests to accomplish this extortion is rooted in their power to influence congressional votes, regulatory decisions, and administrative rulings. By means of their economic power, their familiarity with the channels of government decision-making, their knowledge of the details of policy issues, and, most importantly, their ability to organize and orchestrate the views of their members, vested interests gain, enhance, and stave off opposition to programs and policies which provide them subsidies or confer protected economic positions on them. These "welfare programs" for special interest groups are visible in . . . governmental taxing and spending policies, the decisions of regulatory bodies (covering everything from power generation to interest rates to radio

and TV broadcasting to the use of environmental resources), and the imposition of tariffs and import quotas.

The essays included in this volume illustrate and illuminate this theme. They are critical in tone and, taken together, they present a somewhat dismal view of what government does and how government does it. Their purpose is to educate and inform, in the belief that the improved perception of what government is, what government does, and who controls government will lead to more effective public policy and more democratic government.

It is anticipated that this volume will be of use to students in political science, introductory economics, and public finance courses—indeed, to students in any course which focuses on public policy and the nature of public decisions. While most of the essays have been written by economists and focus on the efficiency and equity effects of government policies, they are not technical in nature.

We would like to express our thanks to many people who have commented on the contents of the volume and on some of the essays included in it. They include John Akin, Ralph Andreano, Timothy Bates, Joseph Heffernan, Robert Lampman, Russell Lidman, Eugene Smolensky, and Burton Weisbrod. Clearly they should not be held accountable for the choice of essays, the political economy theme which binds the essays together, or the contents of any of them. To those who argued a different view of the nature of the public sector than the one represented here, we can only note that reasonable men can disagree. We would also cite the important influence which the work of the Joint Economic Committee (and especially its Subcommittee on Priorities and Economy in Government) has had on the development of the theme of the volume and the choice of essays. Indeed, many of the papers included here originally took the form of testimony before that Committee. Finally, we would thank Linda Bielski and Beverly Neupert for their clerical and editorial assistance in the preparation of the manuscript.

Robert H. Haveman
Robert D. Hamrin

I. INTRODUCTION

PRIVATE POWER AND FEDERAL POLICY

ROBERT H. HAVEMAN

During the early 1970s, many American citizens expressed and apparently felt a deep malaise regarding many of the institutions which, a scant decade before, they generally accepted as an intrinsic part of a growing and dynamic society. Governments at all levels, but particularly the federal government, have become viewed by many citizens as inaccessible, unresponsive, and wasteful. The corporate sector—"big business," in particular—has become feared because of the growing proportion of the nation's wealth which it controls and because of its seeming insensitivity to broader social concerns not reflected in private profit calculations. Institutions of higher education, and law enforcement, judicial, and religious institutions—among others—have experienced similar decreases in public respect and confidence.

Finding an explanation of this malaise is not a simple matter. Perhaps it is a natural accompaniment of growing affluence and higher levels of educational attainment. The more one has and knows, the more one comes to expect. Perhaps it is the result of the Vietnam War in which many citizens saw their country and its institutions pursue a set of objectives and a pattern of behavior with which they had little or no sympathy. Perhaps it is a function of sheer size, of a tendency for large institutions to develop bureaucracies which set their own goals and behavior irrespective of those who are affected by the decisions which are made. No matter what the explanation, few would deny the current lack of trust in many of the nation's major institutions.

This book addresses the malaise which afflicts the nation's dominant political and economic institution—the federal government. The essays which it contains present a variety of perspectives on and insights into the operation of the federal government. Without exception, these articles are critical in nature. Taken together, they present a fairly dismal picture of what government does and how government does it. Because this choice was a deliberate one, it deserves some explanation.

Robert H. Haveman is Professor of Economics at the University of Wisconsin, Madison, Wisconsin.

The first and primary rationale for the contents of this book is a professional one: It has to do with both the analytical perspective of economics and the evaluative studies of government policies made by economists. First, let us examine the perspective. Although something of an oversimplification, it is legitimate to claim that, among the social sciences, economics has developed the most comprehensive set of criteria for evaluating the effectiveness of economic policies, whether such policies are pursued by businesses, consumers, or governments. These criteria center on the concepts of efficiency and equity.

In the case of the efficiency criterion, economists strive to measure the benefits of a decision to whomever they accrue and to compare them with the costs to whomever they accrue. When the benefits to society exceed the costs, the economist concludes that the decision is at least an efficient one. In a similar vein, economists tend to focus on the incentives for private behavior which are implicit in public policies and other institutional arrangements. The question which is asked is: Do these incentives generate wasteful and uneconomic behavior or do they encourage efficiency in the allocation of the nation's resources?

However, decisions and incentives which satisfy this efficiency criterion may not satisfy an equity criterion. To be sure, there is no single equity criterion, as each man is likely to have his own peculiar preferences concerning what the distribution of income and wealth should be and how government decisions should affect these distributions. Nevertheless, it is fair to say that most people tend to look with skepticism at governmental decisions that yield benefits which accrue primarily to the rich or impose costs which are borne most heavily by those in lower-income classes.

Stemming from these notions of efficiency and equity, a set of norms has been established which yields fairly consistent judgments among economists concerning the extent to which a policy or government is or is not in the "public interest." Hence, to most economists a policy or program which generates benefits which exceed costs *and* which tends to equalize the distribution of income by the way in which the benefits and costs are distributed is judged to be in the public interest. A policy or program which is neither efficient nor equitable tends to be judged as contrary to the public interest. Those satisfying one standard but not the other are in no-man's-land and the economist searches for means to improve the efficiency without sacrificing the equity characteristics of the policy, or vice versa.

Employing analysis which reflects this perspective, economists have made numerous studies of federal government programs and policies. In nearly all of these studies, the efficiency and equity characteristics of the program are the matters of central concern. In reading these studies, one is left with a dominant impression that serious problems of inefficiency and inequity afflict program after program and policy after policy. Indeed, the pervasiveness of the inefficiency and inequity is, in my view, sufficient to reject the hypothesis that the documented performance shortfalls are extreme observations in a distribution with a quite satisfactory average. While the reasons offered for these inefficiencies and inequities are legion and, at an intellectual level, understandable and remediable, one is hard pressed to come away from a reading of these analyses feeling that the malaise toward government evidenced by so many is without basis. The professional rationale for this book, then, is both to convey the efficiency-equity framework of the economist and to share more widely those economic studies of government which document the efficiency and equity shortfalls of governmental performance.

There is also another, less professional, motivation for this book and rationale for the articles selected. It stems from a desire to understand why inefficient and inequitable governmental policies have come to exist and, more importantly, why they seem so resistant to improvement and reform. In particular, it stems from a desire to understand the role and influence of vested interest groups in the determination of these governmental policies. This question is obviously a basic one. Indeed, much of the writing of political economists from Adam Smith on has been devoted to seeking an answer to it. Many insights have been suggested and numerous points of view developed.

One answer to the question of how government

functions has been provided by the "pluralist" point of view. Although advocates of this position observe the presence and operation of powerful vested interests who curry special governmental favors, they claim that the public interest is generally furthered in a political process in which such groups struggle with each other for power, influence, and a share of the benefits disbursed by government. The excesses of any one bloc are largely offset by the "countervailing power" of other vested interest groups. Moreover, in the pluralist view, the composition of coalitions of vested interest groups is, in a dynamic setting, fluid and everchanging. Hence, the ability of any one group to persistently bias government in its favor is limited and over the long run the public interest is served.

While this thesis may well describe the operation of certain segments of the political system, it seems inconsistent with the observed operation of major areas of public policy. For example, the strength and durability of the military establishment, i.e., career officers, military contractors, and committed congressmen, does not seem to jibe well with the notion of fluidity implicit in the pluralist position. Also, the not unlikely possibility that certain segments of the population have relatively more representation by major vested interests and greater and more persistent participation in the process of shifting coalitions than do other segments is not satisfactorily addressed by the pluralist point of view.

Finally, perhaps the most telling critique of the pluralist point of view relates to its implicit assumption that interest groups countervail. In a setting in which the size of the pie to be allocated is fixed, rivalry and competition are to be expected and the power of opposing interests might well be neutralized. However, in a setting in which the size of the pie is expandable rather than fixed, accommodation rather than opposition among interest groups is to be expected. In such a setting, accommodation among organized groups can improve the position of each of them through an expansion in the size of the pie which they divide. If vested interests include only a portion of the nation's population, while those who contribute to the size of the pie include virtually all citizens, the effect of such accommodation is to redistribute income from citizens generally to those represented by organized interests. Such a situation describes the struggle over allocation of the federal budget. If the budget is flexible upward over time, mutually accommodating organized interests can maximize their combined well-being by shifting the costs onto citizens generally, who, in their role as unorganized and disparate taxpayers, are unable to effectively protect their own interests.

A second perspective on the functioning of government is represented by a growing group of radical political economists. In their view, it is the unequal distribution of wealth and power in the United States which produces inefficient and inequitable government. Because we have failed to adequately limit disparities in income and wealth and because we have not controlled the mechanisms by which economic power is translated into political power, those with wealth dominate political decisions as well as economic decisions. As a result, government becomes just one more vehicle to maintain and sustain the economic power of those who already have it.

In this view, government policy cannot be expected to be efficient or equitable until the fundamental relations of wealth and power are altered. Carrying this notion back one step further, this point of view asserts that the relations of wealth and power are intrinsic parts of the capitalist system. This has been expressed as follows: "Under modern capitalism, the state must not only protect and enforce private property, but it must also intervene directly in an increasing variety of ways in the functioning of the economy in order that the privileges and hegemony of private capital not be eroded. Thus control over the state apparatus becomes increasingly important for the capitalist class, and the links between private business and the state become ever closer."[1] Because of the dependence of the state on the capitalist system, that system must be overthrown before a humane, efficient, and equitable state can be erected.

While the insights of this perspective are not to

[1] Richard C. Edwards, Michael Reich, and Thomas Weiskopf, *The Capitalist System: A Radical Analysis of American Society* (Englewood Cliffs, N.J.; Prentice-Hall, 1972, p. 192.

be taken lightly, it is not the point of view which serves as the rationale for this volume. The purpose of documenting inadequacies in the performance of government is not to set the stage for revolution and the destruction of capitalism. Rather it is to illuminate the facts of and causes for inefficient and inequitable governmental performance, to convey this understanding to those concerned with the operation of government in a democratic society, and to alert those who are not yet concerned. Political and economic reform, then, is the objective and the stimulation of a clearer perception of how government really works is accepted as a prerequisite for such reform.

The basic perspective of this volume has already been hinted at. It is that inefficient and inequitable public policy exists because powerful vested interests, groupings of limited subsegments of the population, have been able to exploit citizens in their roles as taxpayers and consumers. The ability of vested interests to accomplish this extortion is rooted in their power to influence congressional votes, regulatory decisions, and administrative rulings. By means of their economic power, their familiarity with the channels of government decision-making, their knowledge of the details of policy issues, and, most importantly, their ability to organize and orchestrate the views of their members, vested interests are able to gain and sustain programs and policies which provide them subsidies or confer protected economic positions on them. These "welfare programs" for special interest groups are visible in the disbursement of subsidies implicit in government taxing and spending policies, the decisions of regulatory bodies (covering everything from power generation to interest rates to radio and TV broadcasting to the use of environmental resources), and the imposition of tariffs and import quotas.

Citizens, in their capacity as taxpayers and consumers, have a stake in the decisions made in all of these areas. While any given citizen may be specially favored by one or another governmental program, he must also, in his role as a taxpayer, pay the cost of all other governmental programs, programs which provide special benefits to other people and groups. Hence, he has a special set of concerns which he holds in common with all other taxpayers. For example, it is in the collective interest of taxpayers that governmental spending, taxing, and regulatory decisions meet an efficiency norm, i.e., that they generate social benefits in excess of social costs. It is in their collective interest that governmental decisions which provide subsidies to one or another group meet some established and accepted standard of distributive justice. It is in their collective interest that governmental decisions be open and explicit with the efficiency and equity results visible for all to clearly see.

In today's system of political economy, citizens in their capacity as taxpayers and consumers confront major obstacles in exercising their vested interest in governmental efficiency, equity, and openness. Because they are unorganized, uninformed on the technical details of public issues; and, without a specially designated spokesman to advance their case in the process through which tax laws are written, spending programs developed, and regulatory decisions made, their interests tend to be submerged and often ignored. For example, certain aspects of federal tax policy involving the depletion of minerals (particularly, oil), are almost certainly both inefficient and highly inequitable (in that they yield huge windfalls to oil companies and their owners). The effect of this policy is to artificially raise the taxes paid by other taxpayers and to generate a misallocation of resources in the oil industry.[2] Although this legislation has existed since 1913, those who bear the cost of this subsidy—the taxpayers—have been unable to muster the political strength to eliminate this program or even reduce it substantially. As a group they are large in number, unorganized, and generally uninformed on the intricacies of this policy. Because each of them bears only a small share of the total cost of the policy, there is little incentive for any one of them to spend the energy, time, and resources to

[2] The inefficiency and overdevelopment of the oil industry generated by the depletion allowance offsets a part if not all of the price decrease which the allowance might be expected to generate.

organize opposition to the policy. As a result, in deliberations on this issue, they have no one who stands to argue their position and to lobby for it. On the other hand they are confronted by a tightly organized group of oil companies—small in number, well financed, and most knowledgeable in the technical matters surrounding the issue and each receiving a substantial share of the subsidy provided. A hired lobbyist serves as the industry spokesman at every congressional hearing on the issue, contacts individual congressmen and senators, and makes substantial financial contributions on the industry's behalf to cooperative elected officials.

Implicit in this evaluation of the role of vested interests is the proposition that the political system is deficient in that it does not adequately account for a major, perhaps dominant, set of interests and concerns. Numerous characteristics can be cited as contributing to this deficiency. These include the concentration of legislative power because of the congressional seniority system, the incentives for cooperation between vested interests and legislators due to the dependence of elected officials on campaign contributions, the cabinet system which thrusts agency heads into the role of advocate for the interest groups which are agency clients, and the practice of reserving specific governmental positions for representatives of special interest groups.

While all of these malfunctions play a role, two of them seem particularly important in a context in which decision-makers in both the executive and legislative branches can be realistically viewed as behaving so as to further their own self-interests.

Because reelection is in most cases of prime importance to elected officials, the tendency to trade support on certain issues for campaign financing is a most serious problem. In this age of mass media, the need to obtain the several hundred thousand dollars required to be a serious contender for a major congressional race often tends to make alliance with certain vested interest groups both attractive and necessary. As Sen. Russell Long has stated, "It would be my guess that about 95 percent of campaign funds at the congressional level are derived from businessmen. At least 80 percent of this comes from men who could sign a net worth statement exceeding $250,000."[3] This then is one primary mechanism by which vested power is able to bias public decisions against the interests of citizens in their role as taxpayers.

A second characteristic of the political process works hand-in-glove with the expense of running for political office. It is the complexity and technical nature of so many public issues and the tendency for consideration of them to be surrounded by complicated legislative maneuvers and legal documents whose real purposes are not easily discerned. In such a situation, an elected official's support of a piece of special-interest legislation is *not* likely to be costly to him in terms of loss of constituent support. Few constituents are sufficiently well informed to evaluate, much less challenge, the reasons offered by an elected official in defense of this vote or that action. On the other hand, an "inappropriate" vote which offends some well-financed and powerful interest may mean the loss of large campaign contributions in a pending election.

The conclusion which follows from this is that the complexity of public policy issues, the low level of citizen knowledge regarding the intricacies of these matters, the high costs of seeking elective office, and the self-interestedness of public officials interact to transform economic power into political power. And as a result, powerful and well-organized vested interest groups are able to influence public sector decisions and bend government to serve their interests.

The resulting bias of public decisions against the interests of citizens in their role as taxpayers comes even more clearly into perspective when the formal structure of the federal decision-making process is considered. Legislation is controlled by a number of highly specialized congressional committees. For example, public works appropriations must pass the public works committees and agricultural appropriations are determined by the agriculture committees. Not surprisingly, elected officials who see their personal interests served by

[3] *Congressional Record*, April 4, 1967, p. 54582.

an alliance with a particular interest group tend to gravitate toward the relevant committee. Vested power, therefore, tends to be automatically represented at the committee level by the very nature of the committee system. Because legislation on a specific subject either dies or assumes its final form in a specialized committee, powerful interests often need to sway only a handful of additional committee members in order to control program structure and appropriations. At the extreme, control of legislation at the committee level can be obtained by winning the allegiance of one man, the committee chairman, who, because of the seniority system, may dominate legislation in particular fields for decades.

One final point remains to be made. It has to do with the observed tendency of federal policymakers to resist efforts to probe into the functioning of government. If the analysis of the role of vested interests in the determination of public decisions and the resulting inefficiency and inequity of many governmental decisions is correct, this response should not be surprising. After all, such probing can only have the result of exposing alliances of policymakers and vested interests and the effect of such alliances. And in their defensiveness, policymakers are not without weapons. Perhaps the chief weapons are those of secrecy and obfuscation. The less that people know or understand about what government does or how government does it, the more secure are they, their programs, and their special interest clients. Secrecy, subsidy, and inefficiency breed on one another.

This book, then, deals with the role of organized vested power in determining the structure and content of governmental decisions and with the efficiency and equity consequences of this power. It presents neither a formula for action nor a recipe for reform. Its main purpose is to educate and to inform; accepting the proposition that the improved perception by increasing numbers of citizens of what government is, what government does, and who controls government will ultimately lead to more effective and more democratic government. This problem, its basis in the operation of democratic government, and the dilemma which it poses was clearly stated as follows:

> Government is omnipresent—regulating, subsidizing, allocating—and it is highly susceptible to manipulation by well-organized groups (which are not necessarily big-business groups). It is in the nature of democratic (and perhaps of any) government that a numerous, durable, articulate, and focused interest group, able to organize financial and field support for political campaigners, to propagandize, to draft and shepherd bills through legislatures, to maintain continuous contact with regulatory officials, and to mobilize voters, will wrest privileges and benefits from government and thwart efforts to control its behavior. Consumers, citizens, taxpayers constitute too diffuse and amorphous a group to compete in this league. . . . The very democratic structure that we so highly—and rightly—prize facilitates the plundering of taxpayers and consumers by interest groups able to use the powers of government for their own ends.[4]

[4] Richard A. Posner, "Power in America," *The Public Interest*, vol. 25 (Fall 1971), pp. 119–121.

II. PRIVATE POWER AND THE PERFORMANCE OF GOVERNMENT

INTRODUCTION

Concern with the inefficiency and inequity of government, fear of the power of vested interests, and distrust of bureaucracy are issues of long duration. However, during the 1960s interest in these traditional concerns grew significantly. Many came to seriously question government's ability to improve its economic performance and its ability to respond to changed national priorities. While the events of the 1960s fostered increasing dissatisfaction with the performance of government, it also stimulated widespread probing into the functioning of government. Through the activities of citizens groups, public-interest lawyers, and the consumer, environmental, and antiwar movements, the spotlight of public attention became focused on the public sector. People began to ask very pointed questions about what government does, how government does it, and who government does it for. And much was learned.

While to some, government is simply unresponsive, deeper probings suggested that government might be overly responsive—to at least some people. Numerous instances came to light which indicated that organized, powerful, and well-financed interest groups had little trouble getting government to respond to their desires. Moreover, there were growing indications that government inefficiency and inequity are not so much a result of bureaucratic bumbling and a lack of information and professional expertise as they are attributable to the ability of private vested power to mold, shape, and bend government into its own service. Indeed, some went so far as to suggest that the control of government by powerful interests has resulted in governmental and public policy being the major source of private power and privilege. As one writer stated: "Government, working through and in alliance with 'private enterprise,' becomes the keystone in an edifice of neo-mercantilism and industrial feudalism."[1] By the early 1970s widespread concern with the structure and functioning of the public sector and its relationship to the private sector became an important question in political discussions.

The papers in this section deal with the problems of governmental inefficiency and inequity and with the role of private interests in effecting this result. The first grouping of papers focuses on the problems of public-sector inefficiency and inequity and the causes of these problems are discussed from three positions. These three papers represent a sampling of economic perspectives on the functioning of government. While they span the range of economists' views, they do not form a comprehensive discussion of economists' views on this matter.

In the first paper, Charles L. Schultze focuses on the role of incentives which have become built into the structure of public programs. These incentives, he argues, induce inefficient and wasteful decisions by both private citizens and governmental policy-makers. While the paper is persuasive in its claim that improved governmental performance requires alteration in the structure of public policy incentives, it does not deal with the question of why the incentives which are documented came to be.

The second paper is by Milton Friedman. "It is past time," he states, "to cut the government back to size." In suggesting how to achieve this, he lists eight guidelines which should serve as the basis for revised governmental policy. While the Friedman paper is written from an admittedly conservative perspective, many of his conclusions coincide with those of others holding quite different persuasions.

The final paper presents a critique of governmental performance from the perspective of a radical political economist. In the view of Timothy Bates, it is the basic distribution of wealth and income in the United States which generates an unequal distribution of power. Through the exercise of political power, those with wealth come to dominate government. By controlling governmental decisions, powerful interests insure protection of their own privileged status. The result is governmental inefficiency and inequity. Improving governmental performance awaits a fundamental alteration of the distribution of income and wealth in the society.

The second grouping of papers in this section has a somewhat different theme. These papers focus on the interrelationship between government and private vested interests. Collectively they suggest that while, from one perspective, government may appear inefficient and unresponsive, from another perspective government appears to be most efficient in responding to the demands of vested power. These papers deal with both the privileges bestowed by government on

[1] Walter Adams, "The Military-Industrial Complex and the New Industrial State," *American Economic Review*, vol. 58 (May 1968), p. 653.

private interests and, in turn, the power which these interests have to make government serve their ends.

The first paper in this grouping is by Ralph Nader. In it, Nader presents his perspective of the American economy and the role of government in it. He delineates six "subeconomies" which are categories of corporate and governmental operation, each of which results in the abuse of consumers and taxpayers. "In each case, the consumer's dollars are inexcusably wasted or his taxes misused." His analysis suggests that "corporations, by their control of both the market and government, have been able to divert scarce resources to uses that have little human benefit or are positively harmful."

A related theme is explored in the second paper. There, Walter Adams presents the position that government, having become captured by business, "creates and institutionalizes power concentrations which tend to breed on themselves and to defy public control." In his discussion, he defends his view by discussing a number of public decisions. Adams calls for the decentralization of power and the elimination of governmental interference in workably competitive markets.

The final two papers detail the interrelationship of government and private vested power. The first piece, by Gaylord Shaw, documents the theme suggested in the Adams paper—that government is the supporter, sustainer, and subsidizer of private power. Shaw summarizes the results of a study which estimated the volume of federal government subsidies to private business. He states that the level of business subsidy is about $30 billion a year and discusses the circuitous routes by which this subsidy finds its way to the business sector.[2] The final paper, by Sen. Lee Metcalf, presents the other side of the coin. Not only does government subsidize and support private business, but the "vested oracles" of industry control government. Senator Metcalf defends this assertion by analyzing the role of government-appointed, business advisory committees in the making of public policy. In his view, "The pervasive influence of these committees marks the emergence of the American corporate state, where dominant political power is officially and quasi-officially invested in the massive industrial and financial conglomerates."

[2] Since the appearance of the Shaw paper, the Joint Economic Committee of the Congress released its own study of the volume of subsidies provided by government. Because of a somewhat different definition of subsidy, the committee report concluded that the total volume of subsidies equalled $63 billion annually.

A. SOME PERSPECTIVES ON GOVERNMENTAL POLICY

PERVERSE INCENTIVES AND THE INEFFICIENCY OF GOVERNMENT

CHARLES L. SCHULTZE

INTRODUCTION

Efficiency in public spending has two aspects. Under the more usual definition, we judge public programs to be efficient if they achieve their objectives with the minimum possible costs. But, in a more fundamental sense, efficiency also requires that the particular objectives which public programs pursue are themselves a meaningful reflection of public needs and goals. A program may be well run, and highly efficient under the first definition, but still waste national resources if it pursues the wrong objectives. We might, for example, be highly efficient in building waste treatment plants to handle industrial water pollution, but still have a very inefficient program if building waste treatment plants is not the best way to deal with industrial pollution. Or we might be quite efficient in constructing flood control public works, but still have an inefficient program if those public works protect investments which should never have been made on the flood plains in the first place. The efficiency of our maritime subsidy program must be judged not only on whether it uses the minimum possible budgetary funds to create a U.S. flag fleet and a U.S. shipbuilding capacity of a particular size, but it must also be judged on whether or not a fleet and a shipbuilding capacity of that size are truly needed in the interests of U.S. national security.

In short, questions of efficiency relate not only to the carrying out of public programs once they have been created, but also to the design of programs and the specification of their objectives. As a consequence incentives must be considered not merely in the context of efficient program execution, but also in the process of specifying public objectives.

Excerpted and reprinted from Charles L. Schultze, "The Role of Incentives, Penalties, and Rewards in Attaining Effective Policy," in U.S. Congress, Joint Economic Committee, *Economic Analysis and the Efficiency of Government,* Part 3, Hearings of the Subcommittee on Economy in Government, September and October 1969.

Charles L. Schultze is Senior Fellow at The Brookings Institution, Washington, D.C., and Professor of Economics at the University of Maryland, College Park, Maryland.

There are two major areas for the application of incentives in the formation of public policy: First, the creation of incentives for private decision-makers to pursue public goals; and, second, the creation of incentives for public officials to execute public programs effectively and efficiently.

PROVIDING PUBLIC INCENTIVES FOR PRIVATE DECISION-MAKERS

Many public programs seek to modify, in quality or quantity, the outcome of private production and investment decisions. Urban development programs, air and water pollution controls, and flood protection are examples. Yet too often, by concentrating solely on the public sector side of a joint public-private problem, public programs produce distinctively inefficient results.

Flood protection is a case in point. Since 1936, the federal government has spent some $7 billion on flood protection projects. Expenditures on such projects currently run about $500 million per year, with another $100 to $150 million per year spent on disaster relief to flood victims. Flood losses, nevertheless, are high and rising, and recently have averaged in excess of $1 billion per year.

National policy toward flood protection is straightforward: build flood protection works primarily at public expense and assist states, localities, and private citizens to recoup against flood losses. Where it can be shown that potential projects would prevent losses whose value exceeds the cost of the project, then these projects become eligible for public financing, subject always to the availability of funds in the Corps of Engineers' budget and the normal vicissitudes of pork-barrel politics.

Once the flood plain is developed, the standard benefit-cost calculation well often shows that the construction of flood prevention works is worthwhile in terms of expected damage avoided. But in many instances, the optimum policy would have been not to have invested so heavily in the flood plain to begin with. The differential advantage of flood plain location over the next best alternative location is often worth less than either the cost of flood protection works or the expected value of flood damages. Since states, local communities, and individual beneficiaries typically contribute only a fraction of the cost of federal flood protection works (ranging from 5 to 60 percent and averaging 25 percent), there has developed a set of incentives for uneconomic use of flood plain lands. Development occurs in flood plains. Either in response to or in anticipation of floods, strong and often successful pressure is brought to bear for federal flood protection. In many cases, floodproofing of individual buildings would be much cheaper than building flood control public works. But the costs of floodproofing are borne by the individual owner; the cost of public works is not. Once federal works are constructed, further development occurs, beyond the protected areas. The resulting encroachment on the flood plain itself raises expected flood heights, increases the expected flood damage to prior investments, and leads to still further pressure for flood protection works.

Public policy toward flood damage protection ought not to be expressed solely—or even primarily—in terms of criteria for the construction of flood protection public works. Rather, it should be formulated in terms of encouraging rational use of the flood plains. We should be seeking a policy which induces public and private investment in the flood plains only if the advantages of locating there are greater than those of alternative sites by an amount which exceeds the expected value of flood damages or the cost of preventing those damages. The present policy, which concerns itself almost solely with public projects, not only fails to consider the establishment of incentives for economic private investment in flood plain lands, it sets up a series of monetary and political incentives which induce distinctly uneconomic investment decisions.

If, on the other hand, the government adapted a policy of requiring that flood plain investments be covered by mandatory flood insurance, whose premiums were actuarially scaled to the danger of flood damage, such rational location would be encouraged. Investors would have to weigh the potential advantages of the site against the insurance costs. The economic benefits of proposed flood protection works could be measured by the reduction in premiums thereby made possible. Moreover, since the reduction in premiums would be larger than the costs of the project—in order to pass the benefit-cost test—the beneficiaries could more easily be charged a larger proportion of the project than is now the case. If federal flood control works were required to pay more of their own way than is now the case, flood plain investors would also be induced to compare flood protection works with floodproofing of individual buildings on their true merits. Right now, the federal government pays the cost of flood protection works; the individual investor pays the cost of floodproofing. Small wonder that the former is more favored than the latter. Finally, were beneficiaries to pay the cost of flood protection, there would be less pressure for the construction of uneconomic projects.

In brief, consideration of flood control suggests a fundamental restructuring of public policy objectives and the creation of a set of incentives—through mandatory insurance premiums and user charges—which will provide incentives to private investors for rational investment policy in flood plain lands.

I have spelled this example out in some detail. Time does not permit me to develop further illustrations in such detail, but let me mention a few other instances where public policy needs to concentrate on the development of private incentives.

1. In the case of water pollution control, public policy concentrates on building waste treatment plants and using the police powers to stipulate water quality standards. Yet, many studies have shown that the most effective way of reducing industrial pollution is not by cleanup pollution once it has been created, but by changing internal production processes to reduce the amount of pollution created in the first place. The amount of water used and returned to the stream per tons of steel produced, for example, varies tremendously depending on the production process used. The volume of pollution created in paper production also varies sharply from one process to the other. Charging industrial pollutors an "effluent charge," whose size depended upon the amount of pollutants discharged, would provide powerful incentives to reduce pollution and at a lower cost than a program which concentrated solely on constructing waste treatment plants.

2. Hospital costs have been rising at a very sharp rate—over 15 percent per year for the past 3 years. The federal government itself, through medicare and medicaid, pays a substantial fraction of total hospital costs. And it does so by reimbursing hospitals for the care of patients on a full-cost basis, hospital by hospital. Every incentive is created to escalate hospital costs, since the higher costs are passed directly to the government, and efforts to achieve lower costs do not benefit the hospital. Moreover, hospitals are, in effect, free workshops for doctors, and like any professional group, doctors are anxious to add every conceivable device, gadget, and convenience to their workshop, particularly when the costs are borne by third parties. It seems to me imperative that we develop "incentive reimbursement formulas" which provide incentives to hospitals to reduce costs, and which do not guarantee a passthrough of any and all cost increases. Developing such formulas will not be easy, since we must insure that hospitals are not rewarded simply for cutting back the quality of medical care, but only for true increases in efficiency. But I am convinced that such formulas can be developed. Experiments with such incentive reimbursement schemes have been authorized by the Congress, and a few are now underway.

3. Our current maritime subsidies, which directly and indirectly cost some $500 million per year, seem to have been designed to insure the minimum possible efficiency in our merchant marine. While, in my own view, the case for the subsidy is dubious at best, at least if we must have it, it should be structured to create an efficient merchant marine. The basic operating subsidy that we now pay essentially makes up the difference between American and foreign operating costs. Any productivity gains result in lower subsidies—inefficiency leads to higher subsidies. Not only does the overall subsidy remove any incen-

tives for efficiency, its detailed composition discourages the kind of merchant fleet which is most appropriate for the American economy. The subsidy brings each element of American costs into line with foreign costs—labor, repairs, and maintenance, etc. But the comparative advantage of American ships lies in higher speed—that is, American ships' fuel costs are no higher than foreign costs, but labor costs are much higher. Consequently, American ships should be designed for high speed, quick turnaround time, catering to high-value cargo. But the subsidy system removes any incentives for pursuing this comparative advantage. To make matters worse, while the subsidy is partly justified as a means of providing a competitive weapon against potential discrimination, our cargo preference laws have resulted in the fact that almost half of the value of export cargoes carried by U.S. ships are noncompetitive preference cargoes, leaving only half of our capacity to compete in the competitive world market. Even accepting the need for a subsidy program, we have designed one which is guaranteed to produce decreasing relative efficiency in the American merchant marine compared to its foreign competitors.

4. Both the federal government and state governments have struggled for years with the problem of planning urban development. Almost every form of federal assistance to municipalities is conditioned on some kind of a planning requirement —comprehensive plans, functional plans, planning processes, social renewal plans, workable programs, and so on down the litany. But, all too often, the plans are more breached than observed. And in large part this occurs because the system of rewards and penalties at work in connection with urban investment is not merely neutral to but runs precisely counter to the goals and objectives of the plan.

One major aspect of urban development plans is zoning for differential intensity or other differences in use. The purpose may be esthetic, it may be to control development along lines conducive to efficient urban transportation, or it may have other purposes. But the principal characteristic of zoning is that it reduces the potential rent on specific parcels of land below the rent which could be earned without zoning restrictions. Under the most favorable conditions, this characteristic would make zoning hard to enforce. But this problem is substantially increased by the present tax system. The return to investment in physical improvements will not generally vary with zoning changes—the landowner will capture the gains from such changes. And while physical improvements yield an annual return subject to normal tax rates, the potential rewards from securing a change in zoning can be realized as capital gains, and will be taxed at much more favorable rates. As a consequence, the energies and capital of real estate developers are channeled into land speculation and into massive efforts to secure favorable changes in zoning codes. Other things being equal, this kind of activity yields returns which pay less than half the tax securable by investment in physical improvements. Small wonder that "year 2000" plans in most metropolitan areas quickly succumb to the relentless pressure of land developers.

In a similar vein, the owner of slum property hoping for a rise in land prices, has every incentive when faced with a tradeoff between improving his property and extending his holdings of existing property to favor the latter. Improvements yield a return subject to normal tax rates. The yield from the acquisition of additional property can be taken as capital gains. The availability of capital gains tax treatment on capital gains from the sale of land, shifts in the margin of tradeoff between improvements and extension of holdings in favor of the latter.

More generally, the availability of highly favorable tax treatment for those who speculate in land, tends to work counter to most of the objectives contained in urban plans. A change in the tax system would not itself automatically channel urban investment in socially desirable directions —there are a host of other factors which influence such investment. But certainly the system could be made more neutral with respect to planning objectives, rather than being highly counterproductive as it now is.

5. User charges are a special aspect of incentive policy. Most of the potential applications are not new to economists. The use of prices as a rationing

device, however, often seems alien to the public policymaker.

One of the most dramatic examples is the current agitation over congestion and delays at major air terminals. It is easy to predict that limited facilities will be rationed by congestion, when prices charged for facilities are either extremely low (as in the case of general aviation) or unrelated to the degree of congestion. I will not pursue this example in detail, except to note that in the case of air traffic, the administrative problems of levying congestion charges are far less than in the more classic case of highways (despite Professor Vickrey's ingenious suggestions for the application of congestion charges to highways).

There is one major area of federal programs in which user charges might well be profitably employed to change current *political* incentives for the better. At the present time, a large part of federal water resource investment is devoted to projects whose major beneficiaries are identifiable, but who pay little if any of the cost of the projects. In the case of navigation projects, there are no charges levied on the barges which use the waterway. Beneficiaries of federal irrigation and flood control projects typically pay only a small fraction of the cost. Moreover, there is little evidence that the benefits are distributed primarily to lower income groups, and much evidence to the contrary. But the availability of substantial subsidized benefits, primarily available to the "establishment" in the affected communities, sharply increases the political pressure for the authorization of marginal projects, and for the maintenance of very liberal benefit-cost criteria (low interest rates, liberal rules for defining and evaluating benefits and so forth). Adoption of more stringent rules on user charges would probably reduce sharply the political incentive to maintain uneconomic project evaluation criteria and to lobby for very marginal projects.

INCENTIVES FOR PUBLIC OFFICIALS

The use of incentives to increase the efficiency of public programs need not be confined to the provision of incentives for private producers or investors. Even where programs are carried out solely within the public sector, it is vital to try to create incentives for efficient and effective performance.

Several general means for providing incentives are available:

First, we can sometimes provide the spur of private competition to stimulate the performance of public officials. In providing public support to higher education, for example, we must choose between giving direct aid to institutions of higher learning and giving aid directly to students. The choice between the two will depend upon many considerations. But one of them should surely be the impact of the form of support upon incentives for performance. If assistance is given to students, then colleges and universities must, in effect, "earn" the subsidy to higher education by attracting students. Surely this provides greater incentives for performance than if the bulk of the assistance were directly provided to them by the government.

In a similar vein, we should experiment with providing parents of children eligible for Headstart programs with Headstart vouchers and let them choose the particular Headstart program to which they wish to send their child. Again, this would require operators of various Headstart programs to compete for the customer, rather than having a monopoly position as a chosen instrument in each locality. More generally, in our concern over the quality of education for the disadvantaged of the central city, we should at least experiment with providing some educational assistance directly to parents and let them choose among competing enrichment or remedial education programs. Alternatively, we might also experiment with letting private—profit or nonprofit—educational enterprises compete with each other and with the public school systems in providing educational enrichment programs under Title I of the Elementary and Secondary Education Act.

More generally, it would be worthwhile, I believe, to confront monopoly public enterprises with the threat of competition where this is possible, even though the number of cases where this is applicable may be relatively limited. There is nothing like a bit of competition to stimulate new ideas, to shake up encrusted bureaucracies, and to produce more effective programs. Because this is a relatively novel and untried approach, we might start not with full-scale programs, but rather with a number of small-scale experiments.

In the great majority of cases, it is probably true that we cannot provide competition as a means of introducing incentives for effective and efficient performance into public enterprises. But there are other means of achieving the same end.

In some cases we can improve performance by developing better measures of performance, so that the success or failure of federal agencies and public officials can at least be judged on relevant criteria. As one example, consider some of the loan programs of the federal government. Many of these programs, rightly or wrongly, have the supposed objective of providing loan capital to small enterprises which are too risky for investment by commercial lenders. The Small Business Administration is a case in point. Measures have not been developed, however, which can be used to judge the performance of various regional loan offices in terms of overall program objectives. Defaulted loans, on the other hand, are easily identified, and a significant default rate is sure to invite congressional questions. Loan officials, therefore, tend to avoid risky loans. As a consequence, far from meeting their original objectives, the programs end up, in many cases, simply in making loans of commercial quality at less than commercial rates. It is difficult to expect public officials to pursue the basic objectives of a program unless they are judged on the basis of performance measures which have some relevance to those objectives.

Another means of promoting efficiency in public enterprises is to make sure that the budgets of those enterprises are charged with all the costs which they incur. Until recently, for example, military installation commanders were not charged in their budgets for the use of military personnel. They were charged for other items of cost or at least many other items of cost. Quite naturally, they tended to use as much as possible of the "free" resource—that is, military personnel—while economizing on civilian personnel, equipment, and the like.

In a similar vein, the Defense Department is not charged with the cost of the atomic warheads for its nuclear weapons. The Defense Department levies requirements upon the AEC, which then has no option but to request the necessary funds from Congress. Given a limited budget, and I would hope it would be limited, any set of rational planners will tend to overuse the free resource. If the Defense Department were forced to "buy" its nuclear warheads from AEC, then one could be more confident that the mix between nuclear and nonnuclear forces reflected considerations of relative effectiveness, rather than simply the fact that nuclear warheads are "free" to military planners.

To pursue the same thought further, our $500 million a year maritime subsidy is justified primarily on grounds of national security. But its costs are not reflected in the defense budget. If its costs were charged to defense, so that military planners had to judge whether that $500 million could or could not produce more for the national security if used elsewhere, we might get a more objective assessment of the worth of the program. One might be even more radical by suggesting that the cost to consumers of the oil import quota program—justified on national security grounds—also be included in the defense budget.

In short, providing proper incentives for efficiency requires that those who make decisions about the use of resources get charged for the cost of those resources. Unless we do this, the supposedly "free" resources—which are not really free to the economy—will inevitably be overutilized.

A very particular kind of incentive problem arises in the case of federal grant-in-aid programs, which constitute a very large part of recent federal social legislation. Presumably the purpose of the grant is to increase the resources devoted to a particular objective. (If the purpose of the program were to ease state and local overall financial burdens, revenue sharing or some form of tax credit would be much more appropriate.) But, as a matter of fact, little attention is paid to the problem of whether federal grant funds, designed to achieve a particular purpose, add to the resources currently being spent for that purpose by state and local governments or simply substitute for funds that otherwise would have been spent by those governments.

Various "maintenance of effort" provisions have been written into federal grant programs, but we know little about their effectiveness. In some cases, there may be other approaches to maximizing "additivity." Title I of the Elementary and Secondary Education Act, for example, provides funds to *school districts* to be used for increasing the resources devoted to the education of poor children. But the larger and more diverse the income levels in the school district, the more difficult it is to determine the extent to which federal funds have actually increased resources devoted to the purposes of the program. Allocation of federal funds to units smaller than the school district (neighborhood areas, individual high schools with their associated junior and elementary schools, etc.) might help to increase the additivity of federal funds.

But my point is not so much to describe "solutions" as to point to a major problem. To the extent that the federal grant-in-aid system continues to be the major tool of social legislation, we need to do substantial research on the factors which determine additivity and to experiment with various devices to maximize additivity.

A similar problem arises in the case of federal transfers-in-kind to individuals and institutions. To what extent does the transfer-in-kind increase the consumption of the particular good by the recipient, or merely substitute for funds which otherwise would have been spent on that good, thereby freeing up income for other consumption. More accurately expressed, we need to know the extent to which transfers-in-kind change a recipient's consumption patterns from what they would have been if the same resources had been transferred through a cash grant.

Evidence seems to suggest that low-income housing subsidies and food stamps do increase recipient's consumption of the goods in question beyond what they would have been under cash grants. But there are other cases which are distinctly questionable. The federal government's college housing program is a case in point. Under this program about $300 million in loans, at 3-percent interest, are made to public and private universities for the construction of college housing. For public universities, who have access to tax-exempt bond financing, the value of the interest subsidy is relatively modest, amounting to about $6 to $7 per month for each student housing in the newly constructed facility. Some 45 to 50 percent of the students at publicly supported universities come from families with income of $10,000 or more. Of those who board on campus, the proportion from upper income families is probably higher yet. At these income levels, it is hard to believe that a subsidy of $60 to $70 per year has any significant effect on the quantity or quality of education demanded, although it might have some small impact on the number of those who choose to board rather than commute. In the case of public universities, therefore, the transfer-in-kind probably has little effect in raising the consumption of the particular good, and is, in effect, a disguised *cash* subsidy heavily favoring upper income groups.

More generally, federal grant-in-aid and transfer-in-kind programs need to be reviewed in terms of the additivity question, and techniques devised to maximize incentives for grant recipients to use the funds for the purpose intended.

CONCLUSION

I have tried to give representative illustrations of the various ways in which incentives can be used to increase the efficiency and effectiveness of public programs. As these illustrations have indicated, there are a number of quite different aspects to the incentive problem. In some cases a consideration of incentives suggests major revisions in the objectives of particular public programs. In other cases, incentive considerations call for changes in budgetary procedures. In still others, incentives for improved performance can be increased by a better measurement of program performance.

More generally, we need to give more attention to how we can induce both public and private decision-makers to pursue voluntarily courses of action which effectively and efficiently bring about the attainment of public goals. This is the meaning of the term "incentives" as applied to public programs. There is no single way in which the idea can be applied. Rather, it is an aspect of social behavior which should be taken into account at every stage of public policy formulation.

CUTTING GOVERNMENT BACK TO SIZE-EIGHT GUIDELINES

MILTON FRIEDMAN

Much of the present widespread feeling of malaise in this country arises from the contrast between governmental promise and governmental performance—the contrast between the wide-ranging responsibilities that government has grasped or had thrust on it and its failure to discharge those responsibilities effectively. This malaise has grown slowly. Its origins go back at least three decades. But in recent years, reinforced by dissatisfaction over the Vietnam War, it has become a veritable flood. The initial widespread willingness to take it for granted that there is a governmental cure for every social problem has reinforced the disillusionment that set in when adoption of the recommended cure was followed by a deepening of the problem. This has been the outcome in area after area, whether it be agricultural policy, public housing, urban renewal, welfare programs, regulation of railroads, or the war on poverty. And the final blow has been the failure of government—distracted by ever more ambitious undertakings—to perform its basic function of protecting the persons of its citizens from violence and their property from theft and destruction.

Excerpted and reprinted from a statement of Milton Friedman in U.S. Congress, Joint Economic Committee, *Economic Analysis and the Efficiency of Government,* Part 3, Hearings of the Subcommittee on Economy in Government, September and October 1969.

Milton Friedman is Paul Snowden Russell Distinguished Service Professor of Economics at the University of Chicago, Chicago, Illinois.

We urgently need a new governmental policy, an end to ill-considered expansion in all directions, a beginning of retrenchment and curtailment. It is past time that we started to cut the government back to size, particularly the federal government. That is the only true route to economy in government.

As we move toward a new government policy, we would do well to consider eight broad guidelines for governmental activities. I shall first state them boldly, then illustrate them a bit, though necessarily still dogmatically and cryptically.

1. The basic function of government is to make and enforce general rules governing individual behavior. Changes in such rules are frequently the most effective way to resolve problems without further government intervention.

2. When in doubt whether to go farther, stay out and let private actions prevail.
3. If government does go farther, the least harmful measure is generally to finance specified activities, openly and directly, without administering them, directly or indirectly.
4. When government does finance, it is best to finance intended beneficiaries, not producers.
5. If government not only finances but also administers an activity, it should always permit competition in order to have a private yardstick.
6. Also, it should buy the resources it uses on the market and not commandeer them.
7. Whenever government produces a product or service, it should if possible charge the user his pro rata cost, not give the item away.
8. Only as a last resort should government finance, administer, and deliver free of charge.

Let me illustrate these guidelines by applying them to a number of specific examples.

Schooling

The clearest example of a governmental activity currently in category 8—that is, an activity which the government not only finances and administers, but also delivers free of charge—is schooling. This is predominantly a local rather than federal activity, but the federal government has been increasingly involved.

At the elementary and secondary level, government (1) enforces compulsory schooling, (2) finances schooling from general tax revenue, (3) administers the schools, (4) makes the schooling available without specific charge. The result, particularly in large cities, has been technologically backward schools, a bureaucratic maze, community dissatisfaction, and burgeoning costs. Private competition (guideline 5) is permitted but under a severe handicap—parents who send their children to governmental schools pay nothing in addition to school taxes; parents who send their children to private schools must pay full costs—except as they are beneficiaries of the charity of others.

The least extensive reform that would yet enormously improve matters would be to apply guidelines 4 and 7: Let each community use its present schooling funds to give the parent of every child a voucher to cover his appropriate share of these funds. The voucher could be used for schooling and only for schooling but at any approved school, governmental or private. Government schools would charge a fee and would have to cover their costs from their receipts. This would decentralize schools, widen the opportunity available to currently disadvantaged children, and promote a major improvement in efficiency and quality of schooling.

On the higher educational level, the failure to adopt guidelines 4 and 7 has produced one of the most disgraceful scandals of our time—albeit one that tends to be shielded by the self-interest of those of us who are the beneficiaries. Almost every governmentally run institution of higher schooling gives a substantial scholarship to anyone who is admitted, regardless of his present or future income or his parents' present or future income. The result is that we impose heavy taxes on the poor and unschooled to provide large subsidies to the present or future well-to-do and schooled. Every young man or woman who has the ability and the desire should be able to attend a college or university suited to his talents, provided that he or she is willing to pay the costs, either currently or out of the higher income that the schooling will make possible.

The way to achieve this objective is to apply guideline 7—charge full-cost fees—and guideline 4—make governmental funds available to needy students—preferably by loans along the lines of the proposed Economic Opportunity Bank—rather than to educational institutions.

Post Office

The post office illustrates the partial fulfillment of guideline 7 but the complete violation of guideline 5. Guideline 5, you will recall, is the availability of competition. Permit private competition and the present postal mess would be transformed. There would be an incentive for private institutions to introduce new and efficient techniques, and the government post office would have to keep pace or go out of business. Equally important, it would become clear who is being subsidized and how much, and we might be able to go the next step—of adopting guideline 4—and give the subsidy directly to the persons it is intended to help, rather than to reduce the price of the service to all consumers of it.

It is important to recognize two levels of efficiency: in production and consumption. Let production be however efficient, if what is produced is given away without charge, it will be wasted by the consumers. Subsidized postal service is one example. Schooling, already discussed, is a second. If college is available without cost to the student, youngsters will go to college who attach no value to it.

Welfare

Welfare illustrates how great an improvement could be obtained by applying guidelines 3 and 4 —give direct and open subsidies to intended beneficiaries. The negative income tax is an application of these guidelines. By comparison with the present system of attempted detailed administration and supervision, it would give the truly needy more assistance in a more dignified fashion; provide an incentive for persons now on relief to get off the welfare rolls; reduce governmental bureaucracy; and promise future financial relief.

Oil

The broad applicability of these guidelines is illustrated by the relevance of the same items to oil as to welfare. The alleged objective of our scandalous collection of special measures about oil—prorationing, depletion, oil import quotas, and still others—is the preservation of an oil reserve for time of national emergency. It would be far cheaper—and far less corrupting politically—to subsidize this objective directly—if indeed any subsidy is necessary—than to continue our present policies.

Rent Control in New York

An excellent example of guideline 2—stay out if possible—is the continuance of rent control in New York City after World War II. Other cities had the wisdom—or luck—to let rent control lapse when federal control lapsed. New York is still stuck with the consequences of its lone decision. It is the only major city in the country that has a "shortage" of housing in the sense of more applicants for rent-controlled apartments than there are apartments available, that has under-the-table payments, and incredible red tape. More important, much of the deterioration in the physical character of New York City in the past two decades is the not-so-indirect consequences of rent control. And there is no end in sight.[1]

New York's experience illustrates the main virtue in guideline 2. The problem is not so much that governments choose the wrong thing to do. Of course, they do, but so do individuals and perhaps as frequently. The key problem is rather that once government undertakes something, it almost never lets go. A private individual or enterprise will be forced, by limitation of resources and power, to terminate an unsuccessful enterprise. Not so a government. Rent control in New York City was to be a temporary expedient. Again, our present agricultural price support program, also intended to be temporary, is almost uniformly regarded as a mistake. If it were not on the books, yet by some miracle all members of Congress recognized as well as they do now how it would work, I doubt that there would be a dozen votes for it in the House and Senate combined. Yet it apparently cannot be repealed.

Many more examples could be added. However, these are, I hope, enough to suggest the direction in which these guidelines would lead us, and to give some flavor to the principles in terms of which a believer in freedom would seek to reverse the trend of recent decades toward ever greater control of individuals by government.

[1] Ed. note: In 1971, New York City did modify its rent control policy, permitting rent increases as dwellings change occupancy.

THE ECONOMIC ORIGINS OF POLITICAL POWER IN AMERICA

TIMOTHY BATES

The political process is viewed with cynicism and distrust by a large number of American citizens. While people perceive that government is failing to cope with the social and economic problems of the 1970s, they feel powerless to act and unable to institute constructive, corrective action through the channels of government. Individually, the typical citizen has, in fact, no voice in government. Even collectively, the typical citizen-taxpayer group has little influence on public decisions. As a group, citizen-taxpayers are uninformed and underrepresented in the political game through which government decisions are made. In sharp contrast, the monied elite, the possessors of economic power in America, tend to be well represented in government decision-making circles. "The state is the executive committee for the ruling class," thundered Karl Marx a century ago. Expanding on Marx's theme, Woodrow Wilson stated (with Franklin D. Roosevelt later concurring), "The masters of the government of the United States are the combined capitalists and manufacturers of the United States. It is written over every intimate page of the record of Congress, it is written all through the history of conferences at the White House, that the suggestions of economic policy in this country have come from one source, not from many sources. . . . The government of the United States at present is a foster child of the special interests."[1]

This essay will argue that American political power is derived from economic power. The severe problems of the political-economic system will be viewed as mere symptoms of a deeply fundamental malaise—the grossly unequal distribution of wealth and power in our society.

THE STRONGHOLDS OF ECONOMIC POWER IN AMERICA

As evidence of the high degree of concentration of overall personal wealth in America today, con-

Timothy Bates is Assistant Professor of Economics at Kenyon College, Gambier, Ohio.

[1] Woodrow Wilson, *The New Freedom* (Garden City, N.Y.: Doubleday, 1913), pp. 57–58.

TABLE 1. Distribution of Personal Private Wealth, December 31, 1962 (Percentage of total dollars of equity in specified assets held by households—grouped by level of net asset holdings)

Size of net asset holdings	Percent of households	Total wealth[a]	Own home	Auto	Business, profession (including farms)	Liquid	Investment assets: All	Investment assets: Publicly traded stocks	Miscellaneous assets
Up to $4,999	44.0	2	4	17	—	6	—	—	—
$5,000–9,999	15.7	5	12	15	3	7	1	1	1
$10,000–24,999	23.0	18	36	30	9	23	7	3	3
$25,000–49,999	10.7	18	24	19	18	25	11	7	5
$50,000–99,999	4.3	14	11	10	18	17	15	14	5
$100,000–199,999	1.2	8	5	4	7	8	11	10	2
$200,000 and up	1.2	35	8	5	44	13	54	65	83
All households	100.0	100	100	100	100	100	100	100	100

[a] Because valuation was arbitrary or impossible, the following assets were excluded from consideration: equity in life insurance, retirement funds and annuities, household equipment and furniture, clothing, sports equipment, boats, jewelry, collections of coins, stamps, art, etc.

Source: Dorothy Projector and Gertrude Weiss, *Survey of Financial Characteristics of Consumers*, Board of Governors of the Federal Reserve System, Washington, D.C., pp. 136, 151.

sider the following figures. The information summarized in Table 1 comes from the most comprehensive and reliable data source on the distribution of America's private wealth, the Federal Reserve System's survey of household net asset holdings.[2]

Of the 57.9 million United States' households in 1962, 44.0 percent had net asset holdings of less than $5,000, and held, as a group, 2 percent of America's private wealth. At the other end of the scale, a mere 700,000 households, only 1.2 percent of the population, held over $200,000 in net assets each—a whopping 35 percent of the nation's private wealth. These statistics, though, understate the extent to which the monied elite, herein preliminarily defined as those families worth more than $200,000, exercise control over the private sector of the economy. To focus more clearly upon the possessors of economic power one must examine the composition of wealth holdings. The lesser wealth holders (the vast majority of Americans) own automobiles, small amounts of equity in mortgaged homes, and small-to-moderate sums of liquid assets. Top wealth holders, on the other hand, own investment assets in sufficient volume to effectively control most of corporate America. While families having net assets of less than $25,000 hold, as a group, 62 percent of the automobiles and 52 percent of the residential equity, they own a mere 4 percent of the publicly traded corporate equities. In contrast, the top wealth holders own 54 percent of the investment assets, 65 percent of the publicly traded stocks, and 83 percent of the miscellaneous assets. This miscellaneous assets category, not to be taken lightly, represents a cool $60 billion in wealth—primarily beneficial interests in assets held in trust. These trusts typically consist of corporate blue-chip stocks which are, in turn, under the control of the monied elite. While the asset holdings of most Americans assume inert forms, typically cars and houses, the asset holdings of the wealthy convey economic power and control.

The economic aggregates cited thus far have, however, understated the economic strength of the top property holding class. Family foundations, the exclusive domain of America's super-rich citizens, hold billions in corporate equities but are excluded from the personal wealth statistics. Established to protect family fortunes from steep inheritance taxes, these philanthropic foundations typically operate as essentially tax-free holding companies for the heirs of inherited wealth.[3] For

[2] Dorothy Projector and Gertrude Weiss, *Survey of Financial Characteristics of Consumers*, Board of Governors of the Federal Reserve System, Washington, D.C.

[3] The Du Ponts, for example, have set up at least 18 foundations which serve a variety of family interests. Two

motives unrelated to benevolence the tax-averse ultra-wealthy have created thousands of these "philanthropic" creatures in the last 50 years. While only 18 foundations existed in 1910, over 50,000 foundations exist in 1972. In a gesture of questionable generosity, Henry Ford (who openly opposed public benefactions) escaped inheritance taxes by bequeathing his estate to the Ford Foundation. This mighty foundation-holding company, today worth over $3 billion, enables his heirs to retain effective control of the third largest industrial corporation in America—the Ford Motor Company.[4]

Through trusts, foundations, direct ownership, and top management posts, the wealthy effectively control America's corporate sector. Significantly, this top layer, as a group, would have little more power if it directly owned 100 percent of the investment assets. Complete ownership might indeed mean less power for the monied elite because they would probably lose the support and admiration of many small stockholders, those "people's capitalists" who hold, say, 10 shares of General Motors, 5 shares of IT&T, or a small interest in some mutual fund.

Digressing briefly from the main topic, a bit of basic clarification is needed regarding the relationship between ownership and control in the modern American corporate sector. A number of recent studies have concluded that giant corporations are not controlled by their owners; control is in the hands of top management—the top executive officers.[5] These chief corporate officers—executive vice presidents, presidents, and board chairmen—are most easily identified by their six-figure salaries which, at the top tiers, often exceed $500,000 annually. The fact that many large corporations are controlled by top management rather than stockholders is *not* inconsistent with the proposition that the wealthy control America's corporate sector. In this context, the issue of ownership versus control dissolves because, as Baran and Sweezy assert, managers are simply an important elite within the wealth-holding class, "Far from being a separate class, they constitute in reality the leading echelon of the property-owning class."[6] Data collected by the Federal Reserve's survey on household wealth support the Baran and Sweezy position: it strongly suggests that the management elite of America's giant corporations—the highest income earners in the nation—are heavily represented in the very highest tiers of the wealth-holding class, earlier defined as including families worth more than $200,000.

By assuming that chief officers of the largest corporations individually received 1962 pre-tax incomes of at least $100,000 (the vast majority were paid more than twice that sum), one can spot where the corporate elite appears on the scale of private wealth ownership. Not surprisingly, Table 2 reveals that virtually all of the nation's top income earners are also among the nation's top wealth holders, indicating that the corporate king-

---

of their foundations, Longwood and Winterthur, with over $120 million in assets, are devoted to maintaining certain Du Pont estates as public botanical gardens. The larger Nemours Foundation is designed to inherit the assets of various family trusts when the beneficiaries die, thus retaining control of the trust assets and avoiding estate taxes. Through direct ownership of 30 percent of Christiana Securities, Inc., which owns 29 percent of the Du Pont Corporation and by controlling the stock portfolios of family foundations, the Du Pont family retains effective control of the corporation bearing its name. Congressman Wright Patman estimated, in 1962, that at least 45,124 foundations were nominally operative in the U.S.

[4] Although the Ford family owns only 11 percent outstanding common stock of Ford Motor Company, they directly control 39 percent of the voting power because family stock carries 3.49 votes per share and nonfamily stock carries one vote per share. The largest shareholder, however, is the Ford Foundation which has Benson Ford and Henry Ford II sitting on its board of trustees. The Ford family's dominance of Ford Motor is therefore above challenge from rival factions of stockholders because the family can produce a majority of votes in a showdown situation. Through myriad interlocking trusts, foundations and other assorted gimmicks, wealthy families often manage to control investment assets and enterprises that they do not own directly.

[5] The displacement of ownership control by management control was first documented by A. A. Berle and Gardner C. Means in *The Modern Corporation and Private Property* (New York: Macmillan, 1933). In *The Power Elite* (New York: Oxford University Press, 1956), C. Wright Mills popularized the notion of management control, which has, more recently, been picked up by Harvard economist, John Kenneth Galbraith.

[6] Paul Baran and Paul Sweezy, *Monopoly Capital* (New York: Monthly Review Press, 1966), p. 35.

TABLE 2. Percent of Households Earning Incomes of More than $100,000 in 1962, Classified by Holdings Wealth[7]

Less than $100,000	$100,000–199,999	$200,000–499,999	$500,000 and up
–	1%	5%	94%

pins are a leading group in the rank of America's largest wealth holders.

Clearly it would be unreasonable to assert that all families with wealth holdings exceeding $200,000 exercise control over the American economic system. Nearly 9 percent of the family heads in this wealth-holding group are no longer active in business. Others are headed by playboys, wealthy widows, and other assorted noninfluentials. Nevertheless, by focusing upon the 700,000 families holding $200,000 or more in wealth one can isolate the controlling class of the American economic system. Members from this elite group of families own or control most investment assets, manage America's trusts and foundations, direct the major corporations and, in general, run the private sector of the American economy for their own benefit. This ruling elite, consistent with economists' model of the economic man, directs the allocation of vast economic resources, domestically and internationally, for narrow, self-serving purposes which are often at odds with a sane and humane society.

DERIVING POLITICAL POWER FROM ECONOMIC POWER

As rational economic men, members of the property-owning class that directs America's private sector support public policies which will maintain or improve their position and oppose those which will do otherwise. Because of the structure of the political system, the amount of wealth controlled by an individual or group affects its ability to influence government policy. Not surprisingly, the American political system is quite responsive to the interests of the monied elite, the possessors of economic power, who make up no more than one percent of the U.S. citizenry.

The average citizen-taxpayer has, of course, the right to vote for candidates seeking elective government office who will best represent his interests. In a properly functioning democratic system, it is through the electoral process that nonmonied citizens seek to guarantee that governmental decisions reached by their elected representatives will reflect the general interest. Government officials who are required to gain the support of others in order to exist would be very cautious, one would suspect, about ignoring the welfare of these citizen-taxpayer constituents. To assert that the citizens collectively cannot alter public decisions is to assert that the electoral process is seriously malfunctioning.

To defend such an assertion the process by which public decisions are reached must be understood and this requires a theory of government. While many conflicting theories of government exist, a sizable body of literature has appeared in recent years which explains the performance of government by examining the motivation and behavior of government decision-makers. This theory of government, which I shall refer to as the Self-Interested Policy-Maker Model, hypothesizes that policymakers each try to maximize their own self interest, their personal utility. The notion of the public servant guided by the public interest is emphatically rejected.

Economic theorists postulate the existence of rational consumers maximizing utility for themselves subject to the constraint imposed by their budgets; consistent with both this conventional economic interpretation of behavior *and* the Self-Interested Policy-Maker Model, the elected public official can be viewed as maximizing his personal utility subject to the constraint of losing the next election. In less formal terms, elected officials are viewed as individuals who wish to maximize their own well-being, which is derived from wealth, recognition, power, leisure, etc. Because staying in office is a requisite for attaining these, officials will

[7] *Survey of Financial Characteristics of Consumers, op. cit.*, p. 98.

tend to do what is necessary to get re-elected. One obvious necessity for re-election entails raising money to finance a campaign. In this age of mass media, political campaigns have become so costly that obtaining adequate financing is generally contingent on the support of vested interest groups. As former President Eisenhower observed, in 1968, "We have put a dollar sign on public service, and today many capable men who would like to run for office simply can't afford to do so."[8]

The expense of running for public office clearly is the mechanism by which the concern for the public interest of many political candidates is undermined. Running for office, especially at the national level, typically requires hundreds of thousands of dollars and, therefore, candidates must be rich or they must persuade others to finance their campaign. Where does all of the money come from? Fund raisers, noted the *Wall Street Journal*, "depend on wealthy contributors who give $500 or more."[9] Chairman of the Senate Finance Committee, Sen. Russell Long, has authoritatively stated that virtually all campaign funds at the congressional level come from businessmen. "Businessmen contribute," Long stated, "because the Federal Corrupt Practices Act prohibits businesses from contributing. Funneling contributions is a simple and safe way for a business to accomplish what it cannot do directly."[10]

To illustrate the nature of this inherently corrupt campaign contribution process, Senator Long outlined these details for the benefit of nonbelievers:

> Many businessmen contribute to legislators who have voted to exempt their businesses from the minimum wage. Businessmen contribute to legislators who have fought against taxes that would be burdensome to their businesses, whether the tax increase was proposed as a so-called reform, a loophole closer, or just an effort to balance the Federal budget. . . . Drug companies are often able to sell brand name drug products at anywhere from twice to 50 times the price of identical nonbranded products for welfare and medicare patients if the companies can prevail upon government to permit their drugs to be prescribed and dispensed by their private brand names rather than by the official or generic name of the product. Executives of drug companies will contribute to legislators who vote to permit or bring about such a result. . . . Many industries are subsidized. This includes the merchant marine, the shipbuilders, the sugar producers, the copper producers and a host of others. Executives of such industries contribute to those who help keep them in business. This list is merely illustrative; it could be elaborated upon and enlarged to include many more.[11]

"A vote in the U.S. Senate is of such great effect and influence," states former Sen. Albert Gore, "that any person who is willing to sell his soul can have handsome financing for his campaigns."[12]

Obtaining the financial backing of business interests, then, is an essential element of almost every congressman's political life. While the public interest can usually be ignored because of the complexity of most issues and the lack of constituent knowledge, an "inappropriate" vote that offends some well-financed power bloc may mean large contributions for one's opponent in a forthcoming election.

In a very real sense, most legislators are robbing their constituents; they are stealing the right of the voters to have someone in Congress who represents citizens generally instead of representing America's wealth-holding classes. In the June 11, 1965 issue of the solidly bourgeois *New York Herald Tribune*, a well-known veteran Washington lobbyist outlined his *modus operandi* for bribing legislators: "Anyone who wants any legislation buys it with cold, cold cash. I don't mean you go up to a Senator and ask him if he'd like to make $5,000 by voting for your bill. . . . What you do is arrange to meet him alone somewhere—but not at his office. I almost never go up on the Hill, except maybe to show friends around.

"You don't tell him what you want. He knows. You tell him you understand he has a tough campaign coming up—or he has had a tough campaign—and you'd like to help cover the costs. Then you leave an envelope with cash in it. The real reason you are giving the money is never

[8] Morton Mintz and Jerry S. Cohen, *America, Inc.* (New York: Dial Press, 1971), p. 155.

[9] *Wall Street Journal*, September 20, 1960.

[10] *Congressional Record*, April 4, 1967, p. 54582.

[11] *Ibid.*

[12] *America, Inc., op. cit.*, p. 157.

mentioned. Of course you can't do this with all Congressmen. But generally it takes only a couple of votes in subcommittee to swing a bill one way or another. After you've been here awhile you know who to deal with."[13]

The required disclosure of certain personal financial information in 1969, sheds light on how members of Congress manage to use their elective positions, particularly their committee appointments, to maximize personal well-being. Over 20 percent of the House members revealed personal stakes in financial institutions, usually in hometown banks. On the House Banking and Currency Committee, however, 12 members (nearly one-half of the committee membership) disclosed interests in banks or savings and loan associations. Representative Del Clawson had such an interest but did not list it. Representative Seymour Halpern, the committee's third-ranking Republican, revealed debts of over $100,000 to banks and other creditors; this burden included a $40,000 loan made by First National City of New York—without collateral and at the prime interest rate. Committee Chairman Wright Patman stated that the banking lobby has offered large amounts of bank stocks and bank directorships to committee members, immediate loan service to freshmen congressmen, campaign contributions, and mass mailing to stockholders on behalf of certain political candidates.[14]

Most congressmen are attorneys by profession and most of them maintain highly lucrative "affiliations" with law firms in their home districts. Some of America's largest corporations are attracted to law firms in such out of the way places as Portsmouth, Ohio, where the firm known as Kimble, Stevens, Harsha, and Harsha attracts corporate clients like Phillips Petroleum and Ashland Oil. One of the two Harshas, Representative William Harsha, has sponsored legislation to limit imports of fuel oil. On June 22, 1964, Harsha led the House fight against the Mass Transportation Act, denouncing the measure as "nothing more than a tool to drive private transportation systems out of existence." He failed to add that his law firm represented the Greyhound Bus Lines.[15] In a study of 50 law firms with partners who are elected to Congress, Jack Anderson and Drew Pearson found that these firms "represent the vested interests of America: the banks, the insurance companies, gas and oil interests, great corporations."[16]

Former FBI agent Thomas Dodd of Connecticut, censured for diverting campaign contributions into his pocket for personal comforts, provides an interesting, rare glimpse of a truly enterprising senator in operation. Among the conflict of interest charges brought against Dodd by his former employees, a partial list is presented below; he had:

1. Dropped a planned investigation of the movie industry after taking a contribution from the Motion Picture Association;
2. Taken money from the firearms industry, and thereafter cooled his opposition to interstate shipment of guns;
3. Taken a gift from Westinghouse's lobbyist while sitting on a judiciary subcommittee probing price-fixing in the electrical industry;
4. Threatened to investigate the television industry but, after taking money from a major member of the industry, dropped the matter;
5. Taken money from insurance companies while supposedly investigating them;
6. Sought favors for a number of groups and individuals who had contributed to his seemingly bottomless need for money.[17]

Not wishing to truly investigate his misconduct, the Senate simply censured Dodd for misusing contributions and ignored the more serious charges against him. In commenting on Dodd's money-taking practices, Senator Long of Louisiana can-

[13] Ferdinand Lundberg, *The Rich and the Super Rich* (New York: Bantam Books, 1969), p. 624. Lundberg's fascinating book and a related study, Gabriel Kolko's *Wealth and Power in America* (New York: Praeger, 1962), are highly recommended to the serious reader.

[14] *America, Inc., op. cit.*, pp. 208–209.

[15] *Ibid.*, pp. 225–226.

[16] This book, *The Case Against Congress: A Compelling Indictment of Corruption on Capitol Hill* (New York: Simon and Schuster, 1968), is filled with stories of political skulduggery.

[17] *The Nation*, vol. 204, no. 26, June 26, 1967, p. 805.

didly declared that "half the Senate" was in the same boat.

While most legislators are simply furthering their own self-interest by "selling" their votes to some collection of monied interests, a few elected officials do, no doubt, actually resist the monetary touch. Not only is it unnecessary to have all of them serving as protectors of wealth but, indeed, the whole operation looks more legitimate if there are a few honest dissenters on hand. But in general, the interlocking effects of self-interested public officials, cohesive monied interest groups, the complexity of most issues, and the disparateness of taxpayers are reflected throughout the operation of the political system. The interest of the typical taxpayer-citizen is submerged before a parade of special interests. America's citizens acquiesce in the tax laws whose basic provisions they only partially perceive and whose special provisions and loopholes they often fail to understand. After contributing their taxes to the pool—now almost $200 billion every year—they stand by helplessly while a number of business interests hover like vultures, to divide up the jackpot.

Government subsidizes business on a grand scale and taxpayers foot the bill. In the process, congressmen entrepreneurs gain prestige and reelection. Subornation of the political process by monied interest groups has become, in fact, the very essence of modern American government.

Obviously, the world is more complex than any single theory about it. The proposition that political power is the foster child and servant of economic power is discussed here because it serves to explain both the observed nature of most public sector decisions and the continued inequitable distribution of American wealth, income, and power.

The primary factor facilitating the transformation of economic power into political power is the self-interested behavior of elected officials. The steep costs of campaigning for elective office serve the dual functions of thwarting the potential candidacy of public-spirited citizens and insuring that successful candidates will be continually dependent upon wealth holders for financing in future campaigns. The federal government's formal decision-making structure is rife with institutional arrangements which help well-organized, handsomely financed pressure groups to direct and control government policy.[18] America's monied elite owes much of its success in influencing government, though, to the limited knowledge that voters have of most issues, particularly complex economic issues. When the results are added up, the public interest has been submerged beneath a multitude of decisions which serve the interests of the elite that owns and operates America. This is why the net effects of government operations fail to meet any reasonable standard of equity or economic efficiency; this is why government fails to serve the people.

[18] The introductory chapter in this volume outlines how two of these institutional arrangements, the seniority system and the specialized nature of the committee system, facilitate the transformation of economic power and political power. In an interesting book by former Sen. Joseph S. Clark, *Congress: The Sapless Branch* (New York: Harper & Row, 1964), a Senate insider describes in detail how the reactionary Democratic-Republican Establishment in Congress controls the institutional machinery of the legislative branch. This powerful coalition of Southern Democrats and assorted agrarian conservatives derives most of its power from its minute control over committee appointments. The aim of this inner clique is, according to Ferdinand Lundberg, to "cater to favored ultra-acquisitive interests and to frustrate the general non-acquisitive interests." (Lundberg, *op. cit.*, p. 586.)

B. FEDERAL POLICY AND THE PRIVATE SECTOR

A CITIZEN'S GUIDE TO THE AMERICAN ECONOMY

RALPH NADER

This year the gross national product of the United States will exceed one trillion dollars, while the economy will fail to meet a great many urgent human needs. This contrast between the statistics of growth and the fact of economic deprivation in America has become more and more evident to the public during the past decade—especially in such dramatic cases as that of the medical care industry, which has received vastly higher payments from both the government and patients, while the quality of medical care itself remains unchanged or has become worse. Indeed, the quality of life is deteriorating in so many ways that the traditional statistical measurements of the "standard of living" according to personal income, housing, ownership of cars and appliances, etc., have come to sound increasingly phony.

Nevertheless the methods used to understand the economic system have remained rigid ones. The current analyses of and arguments about "national income levels," "inflation," and "government spending" do little to trace the precise ways in which the operations of the economy affect the life of the consumer. Nor do such analyses make political judgments or assign responsibilities so as to effectively change the consumer's situation. We have all heard arguments about the need to change national priorities in allocating public funds for defense, health, education, welfare, pollution control, etc. But such proposals have so far failed to take account of the ways in which portions of reallocated public funds may be siphoned off or misused before any are used for the purposes originally intended.

Meanwhile, the impact on our lives of the largest economic force of all, the corporate economy, has been badly neglected. Most formal inquiries into a more just and efficient use of national wealth have failed to measure how the citizen's dollars are being wasted and depreciated in the marketplace and his taxes converted into corporate property and income. Instead these studies

Reprinted with permission from *The New York Review of Books* © 1971 NYREV Inc.

Ralph Nader is associated with the Center for the Study of Responsive Law in Washington, D.C.

focus mainly on "aggregate consumer spending" without asking specifically what consumers receive in return.

What are needed now are analyses of the corporate economy that will do what economists for the most part have failed to do: show how corporations, by their control of both the market and government, have been able to divert scarce resources to uses that have little human benefit or are positively harmful. Such studies will have to take account of facts that economists now tend to ignore because they find them untidy or because they cannot fit them into prevailing economic theory. But as they are carried out, they will show the folly of pouring more dollars into the sieve of an irresponsible corporate system.

To encourage more inquiry into the institutionalized abuses of unchecked corporate power, I would like to outline some of the major categories in which the abuses fall and to give a few of the many possible examples of how they work. I call these categories "sub-economies." In each case, the consumer's dollars are inexcusably wasted or his taxes misused. To some extent these categories have been arranged so that they overlap or converge in order to avoid isolating phenomena artificially and to emphasize the economic realities underlying policy questions. As economic measurements become more precise, new categories will evolve, and these in turn will be replaced by others.

THE INVOLUNTARY SUB-ECONOMY

By this I mean the billions that consumers would not have paid if they knew or could control what they were getting, or if corporations observed elementary standards of honesty, safety, and utility in producing and selling the things that are bought. Consumers are now spending billions of dollars for products sold under false pretenses: meat and poultry that are adulterated with fat and water; patent medicines, mouthwashes, and "aids" to beauty and diet that do far less than they are said to do or nothing at all. Both the Food and Drug Administration and the National Academy of Sciences have compiled lists of drugs, patent medicines, and mouthwashes that are valueless for the purposes they advertise and often harmful as well, as in the case of certain antibiotics.

Worthless drugs alone cost consumers $1 billion a year. The Federal Trade Commission estimates that another billion is wasted on fraudulently sold home improvements or repairs. Last February, Sen. Philip Hart of Michigan had this to say about worthless auto repairs:

> American consumers spend 25 to 30 billion dollars a year on auto repair. Various studies on the quality of the work were presented to us. They rated the poor, unneeded, or not done work at amounts ranging from 36 percent to 99 percent. Even taking the low figure, that means consumers are wasting 8 to 10 billion dollars that they lay out for auto repair yearly.

Equally flagrant is the short-weighting, short-counting, and short-measuring of consumer purchases that were the subject of a report in the *Wall Street Journal* last month. "The pennies add up fast enough," the *Journal* said, "that estimates by state officials of the total U.S. loss from short-weighting start at $1.5 billion a year and rise to as high as $10 billion a year."

All these expenses—and I could list many more —were clearly involuntary: The consumers did not get what they thought they were paying for.

Quite as serious are what might be called "secondary consumer expenditures": The consumer may get something he wants, such as a car, but its defects are such as to force him to incur more costs. The fragile recessed bumpers of most automobiles are a case in point. Collisions at under ten miles per hour have been costing $2 billion a year for damages that could easily have been avoided if these cars had had effective bumpers.

What might be called the "accident injury industry," composed of companies and professionals providing insurance and medical, legal, and repair services, is now being paid about $12 billion a year. When emergencies occur these services are of course needed; but in fact many of them would not have to be paid for at all if cars were sensibly and safely designed, as could be done without increasing the overall cost of making cars. Nor would a large proportion of auto repair costs be as expensive or even necessary if key parts were not so inaccessible and fragile, or so constructed that a small defect requires replacement of an entire large unit of the car.

By now some of these involuntary expenditures imposed by the auto industry have become fairly familiar. Less well understood is the way in which many different products, including packaged food, soft drinks, and gasoline, are sold through incredibly expensive advertising of their brand names for which the consumer must bear the cost, but for which he receives nothing of additional value. The staff of Senator Hart's antitrust committee estimates, moreover, that deceptive packaging and promotion in the food industry alone are causing consumers to lose $14 billion a year, for example, by pushing the large "economy"-sized boxes of food that in fact cost more per unit than medium-sized boxes. Of course such expenses would not be involuntary for consumers who could set up their own experimental kitchens and prowl the supermarkets with scales and slide rules. But most families are simply duped.

Until recently the involuntary subeconomy I have been describing has been the main concern of the consumer movement. The movement has had some limited success in improving regulatory action against deceptive sales practices and the safety standards of some products, notably cars, and in encouraging private litigation. Its main achievement has been to create an awareness among consumers that they are being gypped and endangered. But it has yet to devise the economic and political machinery that will counterbalance or deplete the power of corporations to impose involuntary expenditures. Meanwhile, however, the drive for consumer justice is extending its emphasis to less visible parts of the corporate economy where political influence, corporate back-scratching, and the structure of industry itself all work to victimize the public, as we shall see by examining other sub-economies.

THE TRANSFER SUB-ECONOMY

It is in the transfer sub-economy, for example, that the prices for goods and services may rise unconsciously as they move from the supplier of raw materials to the manufacturer, and then to the wholesaler, the retailer, and the consumer. The announcement of a price increase by the steel, aluminum, and copper industries concerns the White House economists far more than would a sudden increase in retail prices. It is not simply that a rise in the price of steel will cause a rise in the price of steel products. The economists know that such increases will escalate sharply as they pass from one shared monopoly or oligopoly of steel buyers and sellers to another, until they reach the consumer who may well have to buy his car or stove from an "exclusive dealer." To the extent that such price rises are unchecked by effective competition, consumer bargaining, public exposure, or government antitrust standards at each stage of the economic process, it becomes easier to transfer costs all along the line.

At the moment, to take another example, air, rail, and truck cargo thefts are rising to epidemic proportions, causing losses of hundreds of millions of dollars each year. Most of these losses are being passed on to consumers who do not realize that they are paying for the cost of such pilferage and yet would be unable to challenge it in the courts or anywhere else if they did. Thus there is little pressure on the corporations to increase efforts to stop pilferage, instead of transferring the costs to the consumer.

Sometimes pressures can be mounted to stop transfers of costs to the consumer. For years the insurance industry failed to encourage programs for fire and auto safety, preventive medicine, and pollution control, which would have helped to prevent huge losses from taking place. It preferred to pass on these costs to its unorganized and generally uncomplaining policy holders in the form of higher premiums.

Recently, however, premiums for car insurance have become so high that many people cannot pay them, and those who can are becoming angry. At the same time, the public generally has been made more aware of auto safety. The insurance companies, more eager now to lower the damage claims for minor crashes, have decided at last to change their policies. They have lately been sharply critical of the auto industry for making overpowered engines and useless bumpers—and the auto manufacturers are beginning to respond. It now looks as if more functional bumpers may soon be replacing the ones I mentioned earlier; and by adding a surcharge to the insurance rates for high-powered "muscle cars," the insurance companies are driving down the sales of these absurd machines.

The lesson of this story is that we can no longer depend, as classic market theory held, on consumer response alone to encourage efficiency and competition that will result in higher quality. In a complex multilayered economy it is necessary that countervailing economic power be brought to bear at each level of the buying and selling process, however remote from the consumer. This is the only way to prevent excessive transfers of costs and to encourage efficiency and innovation.

We are very far from such a situation now. When railroad and trucking groups obtain rate increases from the all too compliant ICC, the large supermarkets and other retail chains rarely say a word; they calmly transfer the new costs on to the consumer. Since most of the railroads and truckers raise their rates uniformly, the supermarkets have no choice among competing transport services; and so the consumer is forced to pay the bill.

THE CONTROLLED MARKET SUB-ECONOMY

Both sub-economies I have mentioned so far are facilitated by the controlled market sub-economy. By this I mean the thousands of arrangements that make it possible for corporations to avoid competition over the price, quantity, and quality of things made and sold, so that the value of what buyers receive is often outrageously distorted, by comparison with what the value would be if the market was not controlled.

Many of the practices in this sub-economy are violations of the antitrust laws that have become both familiar and tolerated: price fixing, product fixing—for example the auto industry's entrenchment of the internal combustion engine—shared monopolies, etc. They also include other barriers to entry into the market such as excessive restrictions on occupational licenses, oil import quotas, the tying up of patents, and other devices that blatantly serve special economic interests while causing consumers and workers to suffer losses.

How much do they lose? The Federal Trade Commission has estimated that if highly concentrated industries were broken up by the antitrust laws into more competitive companies so that the four largest firms in any industry would not control more than 40 percent of that industry's sales, prices would fall by 25 percent or more. This estimate applies to such major industries as autos, steel, copper, aluminum, containers, chemicals, detergents, canned soups, cereals. Nevertheless the figure represents only a small proportion of the unjustifiable costs to the consumer that result from the controlled market.

It is not just a question of price fixing. Concentrated industries can for years resist the innovations that would make them more efficient. The basic oxygen furnace was not used by the big steel firms until 1963, 13 years after it was developed by a small Austrian steel company. The controlled market, moreover, blocks the individual or small business inventors who are still the source of so many of the really new techniques in our society.

Such inventors find that their chances of entering the market or selling their work to established companies are dim when their ideas would not only serve the consumer but also disturb existing capital commitments or ways of doing business: thus we cannot have a humane and efficient transportation system, nor can we buy engines that cause less pollution, can openers that prevent tiny metal fragments from falling into the can's contents, safer power lawn mowers, and countless other inventions that exist but are not produced. Think of the benefits to the consumer if the computer industry vigorously developed a computerized consumer information system to make more intelligent choices possible in the marketplace. Or of the uses to which Comsat might be put if it were freed from the heavy hands of the AT&T monopoly complex that controls it.

But the major corporations will go to fantastic lengths to avoid competition over value. The merchandising in the supermarkets attempts to substitute elaborate games of chance, trading stamps, coupons, and other gimmicks—for all of which the consumer finally pays—for decisions based on the price and quality of the goods themselves.

The price and quality of goods and services are also distorted by what might be called "mini-monopolies." Millions of consumers throughout the country have little choice except to use the only bank or finance company or pharmacy in their town. In company towns they must use the company store. Many specialty markets, such as hospital equipment or drugs, are monopolized by one or a few firms, making competition all the more impossible. Even the legally sanctioned monopolies, such as public utilities, usually manage to regulate the public agencies that are supposed to regulate them. The effect on the consumer is the same as if these businesses were private monopolies illegally controlling the market.

Another example of the controlled economy that we all live with—and for the most part tolerate—is the manipulation of zoning by corporations so as to control the use of land. Zoning boards were originally supposed to bring the exploitation of land under democratic control. In most cases, in fact, large corporations and other powerful real estate interests are able to pressure zoning authorities into granting land restrictions, or obtaining "variances" from existing regulations, that are profitable to them. One frequent result is "snob" zoning designed to exclude people who would depress land values or inhibit speculation.

CORPORATE SOCIALISM SUB-ECONOMY

Such an example brings us to the corporate socialism sub-economy which includes both (a) corporate pressure on government to unjustifiably transfer public funds and privileges to corporate control and (b) withholding of proper payments and other obligations from the government by the corporations that owe them.

The tax system has become, to a disgraceful degree, an indirect subsidy to corporations and other privileged groups. Many of the glaring tax loopholes that slip through Congress each year are in effect huge payments by the government of money it would otherwise have received: for example, the depletion allowances for oil and minerals, the tax dodges allowed to the real estate, timber, and cattle industries, the uses of the capital gains tax that favor the very rich. Thanks to the oil depletion allowance, among other loopholes, the Atlantic Richfield Oil Company, to take an extreme example, had a net income of $797 million, while paying no federal tax, whatever, from 1962 until 1968, when it paid at the rate of of 1.2 percent.

These "tax expenditures" by the federal government have their local counterparts in the gross underpayment of property taxes by mineral companies, real estate developers, and commercial and industrial property owners. A preliminary estimate shows that local taxpayers are paying a subsidy of at least $7 billion a year to such interests when they allow them to evade property taxes. Of course municipal and county services such as schools, roads, hospitals, and garbage disposal also suffer as a result.

As we might expect, Texas provides excellent examples of such underpayment of property taxes. A recent survey by University of Texas Law School students shows that under-assessment of the value of oil and gas properties belonging to Texaco, Shell, and Atlantic Richfield in one part of west Texas caused county taxes for homeowners and small businessmen to be 33 percent higher than they should have been. Over a period of 7 years, a county school board in the region lost $7 million in taxes that it should have collected. Another inquiry by law students showed that in Houston, Texas, industrial and commercial properties are assessed at about 13 percent of fair market value, while residential property is assessed at 31.94 percent.

In Gary, Indiana, the tax situation is shocking. Mayor Hatcher, in an attempt to meet the city's financial crisis, has ordered all city agencies to cut their budgets, including the budget for education. The big company in Gary is U.S. Steel. Between 1961 and 1971 its property assessment only rose from $107 million to $117 million, although during that period the company installed $1.2 billion worth of capital improvements. U.S. Steel refuses to allow the city authorities to examine its books and it refuses to apply for building permits, as required by city law, because this would reveal the size of its taxable investment.

U.S. Steel is able to get away with all this because it exerts raw corporate power in a company town. It is not in any way unusual. Timber companies in Maine, mine owners in Appalachia, paper mills, and chemical plants in cities and towns that depend on them for employment—all flagrantly evade the constitutional provisions in their states for equal treatment under property taxes.

Before national priorities can even be determined, it is crucial that Congress and the public know how much money is being spent by the government through the tax system. Tax expenditures now amount to roughly $45 billion a year but there is no systematic way of knowing precisely how much is being spent for what purposes. Some tax expenditures have worthy aims, such as the deduction for contribution to pensions, but it is rarely considered whether such deductions are the most desirable or easy ways to achieve these aims. Others, such as deductions for medical expenses, seem useful but are in fact regressive, allowing the same percentage of deduction to rich and poor alike. Others, as we have seen, are merely subsidies for the rich, particularly the capital gains tax and the allowances for accelerated depreciation of property.

What is needed, first of all, is an annual federal tax expenditure budget which will show exactly how much money the government loses for each tax privilege that is granted and just where that money goes instead. Recently there has been bipartisan support for such an analysis. Senators Javits and Percy have sponsored a bill to include a tax expenditure analysis in the annual budget report. Senator Chiles has introduced a similar bill. The Joint Economic Committee is now making its own analysis of tax expenditures and is publishing its findings. There is some hope that an annual tax expenditure budget may become a reality during this session of Congress.

But a tax expenditure budget will be only a beginning of a reform of the tax system, for the pressures from private interests and from the executive itself to increase tax subsidies are bound to continue. Under the Constitution Congress supposedly has the power to control priorities through the tax system, but this power is being eroded. Recently, for example, the Treasury Department without any Congressional authorization issued its new proposals—the "ADR system"—for allowing depreciations for tax purposes. This system would allow fast write-offs of business equipment without any relation to the useful life of such equipment—the traditionally accepted measure of depreciation for tax purposes.

ADR would mean a tax subsidy to business of over $3 billion a year—more than Nixon's welfare reform proposals (which would cost $2.1 billion). More than a dozen tax authorities, including the former commissioner of Internal Revenue and experts from the Harvard, Yale, and Pennsylvania law schools, have stated that this multibillion-dollar tax break is an illegal use of presidential power. It remains to be seen whether the Congress or the courts will declare it invalid.

The direct subsidies paid for agriculture, shipping, business promotion, and "research" are quite as important—and as much neglected by Congress—as the indirect subsidies paid by the tax system. The Department of Agriculture, for example, is now spending over $4 billion each year for its subsidy programs. Who evaluates these payments and the reasons for making them? As it happens, big corporate farms receive the lion's share and Congress does not question the inequities that result.

Agriculture is only one sector of this sub-economy where hard questions must be asked if the public usefulness of *existing* tax dollars is to be improved. The inflated contract and procurement practices of the government are another. Thanks to Senator Proxmire and others, the public has at least begun to learn of the waste and mismanagement in defense contracting, and the consequent multibillion-dollar "cost-overruns" that have become commonplace—e.g., the $2 billion overrun paid Lockheed for the C5A. But who is looking into the waste in other government contracting—from the leasing of buildings at inordinate cost to the billions of dollars paid for research in "think-tanks" and advice from private consulting firms such as A. D. Little, Booz Allen, and hundreds of lesser known outfits, not to mention the hundreds of studies done for HUD, HEW, DOT? Many of these studies are worthless, expensive, used mainly to delay policy decisions and to get the agencies who commission them off the hook. Others are wholly ignored.

If only the grossest forms of waste and corruption in federal, state, and local procurement practices were investigated and eliminated many billions of dollars would be saved and political life itself would get a badly needed shake-up, especially in local politics where procurement procedures are generally antiquated and enmeshed in the spoils system. Over a decade ago the Blatnik subcommittee of Congress uncovered extensive corruption in highway building programs in states throughout the country; during the last 2 years officials in New Jersey were arrested for receiving kickbacks from construction contracts and the purchase of supplies. It would be hard to find a state in which similar (if sometimes less egregious) procurement practices involving bribery, campaign contributions, wasteful patronage, and corruption of officials are not costing millions to the taxpayers.

Some idea of how much money is being wasted in local procurement can be gained from a recommendation made to the states 2 years ago by the General Services Administration, the purchasing and housekeeping agency of the federal government. The GSA suggested that state and local governments cooperate in setting up systems of centralized purchasing direct from manufacturers, thus bypassing the 20 to 30 percent mark-up of the wholesalers. If they did this, they would save between $6 and $7 billion a year.

This recommendation was not followed, nor did the GSA pursue it. The wholesalers' trade association immediately launched a campaign against it in Congress, and the Bureau of the Budget suppressed this somewhat unexpected display of good sense by the GSA. The wholesalers' association has plenty of political muscle and uses it on all levels of government.

The great illusion of the public is that it is protected by the conscience of public officials, when in fact aggressive monitoring of these officials and those they deal with is constantly needed. Even tax funds used directly for medical care are funneled unscrupulously to prosperous doctors and drug companies, or to hospitals that use them for unauthorized purposes. Herbert S. Dennenberg, the Insurance Commissioner of Pennsylvania, stated recently that the "Medicare Program is resulting in the American people being overcharged billions of dollars a year"—a conclusion that has been confirmed by congressional inquiries and independent studies.

THE COMPULSORY CONSUMPTION SUB-ECONOMY

Unlike the other aspects of the economy that have been discussed here, the compulsory consumption sub-economy is not part of any recognized system of economic exchange—but it has grave economic effects. I am referring to the compulsory consumption of environmental pollution and compulsory exposure to occupational health and safety hazards. These reduce the *quality* of the GNP and thus diminish the value of the citizen's dollar, even when they do not directly compel people to pay for medical treatment, for example. We are just beginning to calculate the billions of dollars that pollution costs in damages to health, in cleaning costs, and in damage to property, resources, and agricultural crops. Air and water pollution are each costing at least $14 billion a year. (The yearly damage to California crops alone from air pollution runs to $45 million a year.) The costs to the unborn, or to the environment in the future, have not even been estimated.

Safety and health hazards on jobs in factories, foundries, mines, and other work places are also a form of compulsory consumption. They now cause three times as many injuries as street crime: 15,000 sudden deaths last year, uncounted thousands of deaths resulting from occupational disease, 2.5 million disabling injuries, several million cases of less serious injuries and illness. (These figures are necessarily inadequate—how does one estimate when a case of black lung disease becomes bad enough to be included in the statistics of a given year?)

Clearly the forced consumption of pollution—gases, chemicals, coal and cotton dust—is a silent and sometimes invisible form of violence which compels people to pay insurance, medical, and other costs, including the loss of wages. The polluting corporations inflict these burdens on workers when, for only a fraction of the money they force others to pay, they could have prevented much of the pollution in the first place. (This is patently true in the case of dust control in coal mines, textile mills, and foundries, for example, where a small investment would prevent brutal physical damage to workers.)

The power of corporations to pollute, in short, is far too great for them to exercise responsibly. General Motors, by virtue of the engines it designs and the plants it operates, has been responsible for over 30 percent of the estimated tonnage of U.S. air pollution. Is there any city street where the citizen can escape the pollution of GM engineering when he breathes? Between 1967 and 1969 GM spent $250 million to change its slogan on billboards, dealers' signs, and other promotional material to read "GM Mark of Excellence." With the same funds it could have easily developed a workable nonpolluting engine.

We may expect two developments to occur if certain industries in both the compulsory and the controlled sub-economies are successfully challenged in the market and by public protest. First, many industries would be displaced or diminished as superior technologies are invented and sold on their merits. Cleaner and cheaper sources of energy for cars and power plants, for example, will increasingly pose the threat of displacement to large industries. So will safer and more effective nonchemical methods of pest control eventually diminish the chemical pesticides industry.

Second, new services are already emerging to show businesses how to reduce telephone, utility, and insurance bills, for example. These services give advice that the big companies should be providing themselves. They also show how to avoid dealing with middlemen who now stand between the producer and seller of a product or service, thus reducing costs now passed on to the consumer. Recently a small company was started to give advice to users of Xerox machines on how to save money by buying ink, paper, and other items independently, rather than through the Xerox company; and on how to obtain the most efficient service with the best combination of reproduction machines, something the Xerox company itself fails to point out.

These, it should be said, are just the kinds of changes that are called for by the theory of capitalism; they are what Joseph Schumpeter, perhaps the leading theoretician of the capitalist economy, had in mind when he wrote of the "creative destruction" of inferior or obsolete industries under capitalism. But in fact, such developments are being discouraged and suppressed by politically entrenched corporate institutions.

THE EXPENDABLE SUB-ECONOMY

The expendable sub-economy is composed mostly of poor people who are being excluded from the services of the economy at large. It is not simply that the poor pay more: they are not being allowed to buy. In Washington, Baltimore, New York, in fact in every large city, insurance and banking firms commonly "red line"—or refuse to do business with—people in the poor districts. What has happened is that *Fortune's* Five Hundred largest corporations have decided that they have less and less need for the business of the poor. But by cutting off the funds needed for housing, for financing small business, and for municipal bonds in the low-income areas of the cities, the banks and other lenders are causing the deterioration of the urban economy and injuring the well-being of millions of people.

The government, moreover, has become a willing partner in such discrimination. It provides fast tax write-offs for airplanes, computers, bulldozers, and trucks, causing loan money to flow in these directions and not toward loans to the poor and those who have more urgent needs. It provides tax inducements for slum landlords who are allowed to depreciate slum property at an accelerated rate and to pay capital gains taxes on profits from sales—a process which is quickly repeated by the next slum landlord.

The federal government artificially restricts the money supply in order to control inflation. It should ensure that all segments of the borrowing public be given equitable treatment so far as restrictions on borrowing are concerned. Several methods are available to accomplish this. One is to provide for different Federal Reserve Board requirements for different kinds of loans. Such reserve requirements specify the percentage of their demand deposits which banks must set aside at the District Federal Reserve banks. For example, the FRB could require a reserve requirement of 5 percent against residential loans and one of 20 percent against nonproductive corporate loans, such as loans to conglomerates to acquire yet another company. Reserve requirements can be used in this way to encourage loans to sectors of the economy badly in need of funds.

Another method would be to link certain kinds of deposits to certain kinds of loans. For example, savings and loan association deposits are now required by law to be used heavily for housing loans. Banks have similar deposits—so-called "time deposits" by individuals. In return for the benefits they receive from the federal ceilings on interest rates, as well as from other government programs, the banks could be required to make time deposits available when there is a shortage of funds for home mortgages and home construction.

Like so many of the other economic forces I have dealt with here, the banking system needs systematic surveillance and is not getting it. Banks in New York City, for example, often encourage industrial mergers which result in deposits being transferred to New York from regional or local banks all over the country. These regions find their local banks drained of funds, unable to extend credit, and the local economies suffer as a result.

Not long ago the large New York conglomerate called Teledyne Inc., a customer of the First National City Bank, bought up the Monarch Rubber Co. in Hartville, Ohio. The banks in Canton, Ohio, lost Monarch's deposits and its $2.5 million pension fund to First National City. Money that should have been available for local borrowing was siphoned off to New York. The usual solution in such cases is for the local businessmen to appeal to Washington to come to the rescue—at the taxpayer's expense.

Apologists for the present corporate system will argue that the sub-economies I have described so generally here are justified because they support industries, create jobs, generate income. But it should be clear that their operations and the kinds of needs they satisfy are, to a great extent, neither desirable nor socially responsible; in many cases they are not legal. A safer traffic system would no doubt weaken the accident-injury industry, and that is as it should be. For most of this century there has been declared a national consensus in favor of competition, as well as numerous laws designed to encourage it, but both have been for the most part betrayed. When they have not, the benefits for the citizen have been dramatic.[1] Indeed each of the sub-economies I have described subverts values that are deeply rooted in American life.

What has been tragic is the general failure to understand how this has occurred. Fundamentally new ways must be found to make both government and corporations accountable. We should pursue the suggestion already made by some social critics for a "social accounts system" which would enable government and citizens to evaluate whether programs of education, medicine, and transportation, for example, were improving or

[1] Last year a new supermarket chain broke into the complacent food market of Washington, D.C., long dominated by three major chains. This episode and a detailed FTC report on monopolization of food prices in the Washington, D.C., area, according to an FTC report, saved Washington consumers $40 million in reduced prices in 1 year.

deteriorating in quality. (The current inclusion of such activities in the GNP has nothing whatever to say about their quality.)

Similarly computers should be made directly available to the citizen, and should be accessible both at shopping centers and by telephone. Such a cheap and simple source of information, which would give advice on the quality of products and of government and private services, could do much to squeeze the waste and deception out of the economy and give value to the dollar.

Sen. Philip Hart has estimated that of the $780 billion spent by consumers in 1969, about $200 billion purchased *nothing* of value. By nothing of value he meant just that: over $45 billion was drained away by monopolistic pricing, for example, and over 6 billion by oil import quotas which drive up the prices of fuel oil and gasoline. His estimate, and it is only a preliminary one, shows how crucial is the need to evaluate how corporate and government wealth is being used—or misused—for individual and social purposes.

Such evaluations simply have not been made in our corporate political economy—not by our blinkered economists, certainly, and not by the government or the corporations themselves. Indeed the corporations have effectively blocked both the government and independent researchers from collecting and analyzing such information. Even the data on pollution must be fought for if it is to be extracted from corporations by government agencies and individuals bringing law suits. The task of the consumer movement now is to gather and analyze and disseminate this type of information by demanding it from the three branches of government and by mounting private actions by consumer groups to publicize it. Such information is the currency of economic democracy, the first tool for changing the perception of citizens and society itself.

GOVERNMENTAL POLICY AS THE SOURCE OF VESTED POWER

WALTER ADAMS

In *The New Industrial State,* Galbraith finds that the giant corporation has achieved such dominance of American industry that it can control its environment and immunize itself from the discipline of all exogenous control mechanisms—especially the competitive market. Through separation of ownership from management, it has emancipated itself from the control of stockholders. By reinvestment of profits, it has eliminated the influence of the financier and the capital market. By brainwashing its clientele, it has insulated itself from consumer sovereignty. By possession of market power, it has come to dominate both suppliers and customers. By judicious identification with, and manipulation of, the state, it has achieved autonomy from government control. Whatever it cannot do for itself to assure survival and growth, a compliant government does on its behalf—assuring the maintenance of full employment; eliminating the risk of and subsidizing the investment in research and development; and assuring the supply of scientific and technical skills required by the modern technostructure. In return for this privileged autonomy, the industrial giant performs society's planning function. And this, according to Galbraith, is inevitable because technological imperatives dictate it. The market is dead, we are told; and there is no good reason to regret its passing.

In this paper, I shall eschew a dreary and repetitive recital of the voluminous evidence that negates the Galbraith version of a crude technological determinism. . . . I shall also spare the reader any comments on the virtues of private planning—the proposition that what is good for General Motors is good for the country. Instead, I shall offer an alternative (and, hopefully, more realistic) explanation of the source of private economic power.

Excerpted and reprinted from Walter Adams, "The Military-Industrial Complex and the New Industrial State," *American Economic Review* (May 1968), pp. 652–665, by permission of the American Economic Association and Walter Adams.

Walter Adams is Professor of Economics at Michigan State University, East Lansing, Michigan.

My hypothesis—the obverse of Galbraith's—holds that industrial concentration is not the inevitable outgrowth of economic and technical forces, nor the product of spontaneous generation or natural selection. In this era of big government, concentration is often the result of unwise, man-made, discriminatory, privilege-creating governmental action. Defense contracts, R and D support, patent policy, tax privileges, stockpiling arrangements, tariffs and quotas, subsidies, etc., have far from a neutral effect on our industrial structure. In all these institutional arrangements, government plays a crucial, if not decisive, role. Government, working through and in alliance with "private enterprise," becomes the keystone in an edifice of neomercantilism and industrial feudalism. In the process, the institutional fabric of society is transformed from economic capitalism to political capitalism.

My hypothesis is best explained in Schumpeterian power terms. According to Schumpeter, the capitalist process was rooted, not in classic price competition, but rather "the competition from the new commodity, the new technology, the new source of supply, the new type of organization—competition which commands a decisive cost or quality advantage and which strikes not at the margin of the profits and outputs of existing firms but at their very foundations and their very lives." The very essence of capitalism, according to Schumpeter, was the "perennial gale of creative destruction" in which existing power positions and entrenched advantage were constantly displaced by new organizations and new power complexes. This gale of creative destruction was to be not only the harbinger of progress but also the built-in safeguard against the vices of monopoly and privilege.

What was obvious to Schumpeter and other analysts of economic power was also apparent to those who might suffer from the gales of change. They quickly and instinctively understood that storm shelters had to be built to protect themselves against this destructive force. The mechanism which was of undoubted public benefit carried with it exorbitant private costs. And, since private storm shelters in the form of cartels and monopolies were either unlawful, unfeasible, or inadequate, they turned increasingly to government for succor and support. By manipulation of the state for private ends, the possessors of entrenched power found the most felicitous instrument for insulating themselves against, and immunizing themselves from, the Schumpeterian gale.

It requires no exaggeration to argue that modern technology and the inherent dynamism of Schumpeterian competition are such that, in the absence of governmental interference and protection, some of the bulwarks of concentrated power could be successfully eroded. Governmental policy toward the petroleum industry is a case in point. Under the antitrust laws, it is a per se offense for private firms to fix prices or allocate markets, yet in the name of conservation the government does for the oil companies what they could not legally do for themselves. The process is familiar. The Bureau of Mines in the Department of Interior publishes monthly estimates of the market demand for petroleum (at current prices, of course). Under the Interstate Oil Compact, approved by Congress, these estimates are broken down into quotas for each of the oil-producing states which, in turn, through various prorationing devices, allocate "allowable production" to individual wells. Oil produced in violation of these prorationing regulations is branded as "hot oil," and the federal government prohibits its shipment in interstate commerce. Also, to buttress this government-sanctioned cartel against potential competition, oil imports by sea are limited to slightly more than one million barrels a day. Finally, to top off these indirect subsidies with more visible favors and to provide the proper incentives for an industry crucial to the national defense, the government authorizes oil companies to charge off a 27½ percent depletion allowance against their gross income. In all, the industry has been estimated to receive special favors of $3.5 billion (according to Milton Friedman) and $4.0 billion (according to Morris Adelman)—in addition to having a government-sanctioned cartel provide the underpinning for its control of markets and prices.

Another case in point is the military-industrial

complex, where the morganatic alliance between government and business is even clearer, bolder, and more positive. Here government not only permits and facilitates the entrenchment of private power but serves as its fountainhead. It creates and institutionalizes power concentrations which tend to breed on themselves and to defy public control. The scenario of events should be familiar. The "mad momentum" of an international weapons race militates toward large defense expenditures (currently at an annual rate of $75 billion). This generates a demand, not only for traditional, commercial, shelf items like food, clothing, fuel, and ammunition, but also for the development and production of sophisticated weaponry. Lacking a network of government-owned arsenals, such as produced the shot and cannon in the days of American innocence, or having dismantled the arsenals it did have, the government is forced to buy what it no longer can make. It becomes a monopsonistic buyer of products which are not yet designed or for which production experience is lacking. It buys at prices for which there is little precedent and hardly any yardsticks. It deals with contractors, a large percentage of whose business is locked into supplying defenses, space, or atomic energy needs. It confronts powerful oligopolists in a market where technical capability rather than price is the controlling variable—in an atmosphere shrouded by multilateral uncertainty and constant warnings about imminent aggression. In the process, government becomes almost totally dependent on the chosen instruments, i.e., creatures of its own making, for effectuating public policy. Lacking any viable in-house capabilities, competitive yardsticks, or the potential for institutional competition, the government becomes—in the extreme—subservient to the private and special interests whose entrenched power bears the governmental seal.

This unique buyer-seller relationship, which defies analysis by conventional economic tools, lies at the root of the military-industrial complex and the new power configurations generated by it. The complex is not a conspiracy between the "merchants of death" and a band of lusty generals, but a natural coalition of interest groups with an economic, political, or professional stake in defense and space. It includes the armed services, the industrial contractors who produce for them, the labor unions that represent their workers, the lobbyists who tout their wares in the name of "free enterprise" and "national security," and the legislators who, for reasons of pork or patriotism, vote the sizable funds to underwrite the show. Every time the Congress authorizes a military appropriation, it creates a new constituency (i.e., propaganda machine) with a vested interest in its perpetuation and aggrandizement. Thus, the current proposal for an antiballistic-missile system, the "thin" variety of which would cost $5 billion and the "thick" variety $40 billion, and which would probably be obsolete by the time it was completed, has been estimated to involve 28 private contractors, with plants located in 42 states (i.e., 84 senators), and 172 congressional districts. Given the political reality of such situations and the economic power of the constituencies involved, there is little hope that an interaction of special interest groups will somehow cancel each other out and that there will emerge some compromise which serves the public interest. There is little assurance that the corporal's guard of auditors in the General Accounting Office or Galbraith's scientific-professional elite or a handful of disinterested university analysts will constitute a dependable and adequate force of countervailing power. The danger remains that the "conjunction of an immense military establishment and a large arms industry," against which President Eisenhower warned, will become a Frankenstein threatening to control the contract state which brought it into being. The danger persists that power will be coalescing, not countervailing—that the political cloakroom will displace the economic marketplace.

It would be facile to conclude that the military-industrial complex and the new industrial state represent a price which society must pay—and inevitably so—because of national defense considerations or because of technological inexorability. But this would be to miss the point—to ignore the crucial political component in the institutional arrangements at issue. The military-industrial complex is only a special case illustrating the power problems inherent in the new industrial state. Both are created, protected, privileged, and subsidized by the state. Both represent a form of private socialism—a type of social planning through fragmented, special-interest chosen instruments operating in the "private" sector. Both represent a blending of private economic power and public political power. Both are reminiscent of the Elizabethan monopoly system and its abuse, corruption, favoritism, waste, and inefficiency—an *imperium in imperio*, without demonstrable public benefits, and without any built-in safeguards for the public interest. In sum, to the extent that they are creatures of political power and not the product of natural evolution, there is nothing inevitable about their survival and nothing inevitable about the public policies which spawn and preserve them.

We may note that the problem at hand is not one of technological determinism which would militate toward fatalistic acceptance of the status quo. Nor is it rooted in the ineffectiveness of what Galbraith calls the charade of antitrust. Instead, it is largely a political problem of governmental creation, protection, and subsidization of private privilege. If this diagnosis is indeed correct, then public policy alternatives are available and a reasonably competitive market is more than a utopian policy objective.

Let me offer two general policy recommendations:

1. Most important is government noninterference in markets which in the absence of such interference would be workably competitive. In the words of Adam Smith, it may be difficult to "prevent people of the same trade from sometimes assembling together," but government "ought to do nothing to facilitate such assemblies; much less to render them necessary." While assuring effective enforcement of the antitrust laws, government should abjure the role of the mercantilist state in sanctioning and legitimizing private privilege. One can only speculate on the quantitative benefits of such measures as the abolition of tariffs in concentrated industries, the deregulation of surface transportation from ICC control, or the elimination of the honeycomb of governmental supports for the petroleum price and power structure.

2. In those areas where competition cannot be allowed full sway or where government cannot avoid active participation in the economic game, the basic guidelines point to preserving the maximum amount of power decentralization feasible. This may require positive encouragement of institutional competition from whatever source available and, at the very least, the preservation of effective yardsticks by which to measure and control monopoly performance. In the national defense sector, for example, government must rebuild and preserve its in-house competence for R and D, systems engineering and management, and contract evaluation. In short, the government cannot surrender the yardsticks essential for the discharge of its responsibilities to the public. . . . And the public must recognize that the servants of the military-industrial state cannot be allowed to become its masters—either in the name of "free enterprise" or under the guise of promoting the "national security."

What I have said here is not likely to please those who rationalize the status quo by invoking some deterministic inevitability. I do not claim that what I have said is particularly new or startling. I do believe, however, that it is true and that, as Dr. Johnson said, men need not so much to be informed as reminded.

GOVERNMENT AS PROMOTER, SUSTAINER, AND SUBSIDIZER OF "PRIVATE ENTERPRISE"

GAYLORD SHAW

Private enterprise in America collects roughly $30 billion a year in government subsidies and subsidy-like aid, much of it hidden or disguised. The $30 billion is an estimate. No one, in the government or out of it, knows exactly what the figure is. There is no full list of subsidy programs. But a government-wide study disclosed evidence that the total is at least $28 billion a year, and may run as high as $38 billion.

Contrary to the conventional wisdom that private business is free of federal handouts, the study showed that it collects aid in many forms: cash payments, tax breaks, bargain-basement loans, technical guidance, low-cost services, and grants routed through state and municipal middlemen. Assistance ranges from massive to miniscule; from a $100 million loan guarantee for the Penn Central Railroad to an $18,000 advance for the Horse Heaven mercury mine in Oregon; from $4.4 million in subsidy checks for a single California farm to $20,000 in technical assistance for Grandmother's Bakery in Chicago. Federal aid for private enterprise is more than twice what the government spends for all its welfare programs; three times what it spends for strategic nuclear forces; ten times what it spends to control pollution; fifteen times what it spends to fight crime.

The 2-month study excluded nonbusiness aid to individuals, families, and organizations, and probably did not detect all the concealed business benefits that flow through the fine-print regulations of more than 200 separate federal programs. It is impossible to calculate the total amount of aid to business. "There's no system of accountability for federal subsidy programs," said Sen. William Proxmire, chairman of Congress' Joint Economic Committee, which is trying to compile a list of programs. "Nobody knows what programs exist, their purposes, what they cost or what their benefits are."

In opposing the administration's bill to guarantee up to $2 billion in loans for failing businesses,

Excerpted and reprinted by permission of the Associated Press.

Gaylord Shaw is a researcher and reporter for the Associated Press, Washington, D.C.

including Lockheed, Proxmire argued that it would set a dangerous precedent, one that would "destroy the foundations of our free enterprise system." Secretary of the Treasury John B. Connally disagreed. "The government has done it before," he said in one exchange with Proxmire at a committee hearing. "We sometimes kid ourselves it is a free enterprise system, but it is not all that free. Much of it lives under regulation, much of it under subsidy."

"Our economy is neither free nor enterprising," Douglas Grymes, president of Koppers Co. Inc., a major chemical and steel product firm, said in a speech to fellow industrialists. "The truth is that free enterprise has indeed disappeared," said Grymes, urging business to "accept the government as an important, indispensable and . . . welcome partner."

President Nixon advocates government-business cooperation in building "a modern free enterprise system—not managed by government and not ignored by government but helped by a government that creates the climate for steady, healthy growth."

The word "subsidy" rarely appears in his public announcements. "Subsidy is a sensitive word around here," said a White House economist. "It carries a bad connotation." Others in government avoid the word, too. It does not, for example, appear in the extensive index of the 935-page *Catalog of Federal Assistance.*

To chart the scope of subsidies and similar aid to private enterprise, the AP study examined tax laws and the details of federal programs administered by 61 different agencies. It found:

1. Backdoor subsidies for business and industry from tax breaks, incentives, allowances, and exemptions are so complex that government tax experts can only guess at their size. Best guesses: Somewhere between $9.5 billion to $15 billion annually.
2. Farming, the nation's largest industry, got direct and indirect subsidies of between $6 billion and $9 billion in 1970, depending on your definition of a subsidy. Direct payments alone have increased fivefold in a decade, to $3.8 billion in 1969.
3. No breakdown is available in the number and value of government loans to profit-making concerns, but this fiscal year [1971] the total of outstanding loans—direct, guaranteed, and insured—will reach $250 billion, six times the outstanding installment credit advanced by all commercial banks.
4. Transportation got the first federal subsidies 182 years ago and still ranks among the biggest recipients: $450 million a year to keep the maritime industry afloat; $63 million to keep local service airlines flying; and $172 million over 5 years to help commuter railroads buy 875 new passenger cars.
5. Defense contractors have custody of $14.6 billion worth of taxpayer-owned property, and can use government equipment for commercial work at least 25 percent of the available time. "Many contractors would experience severe economic hardship or even bankruptcy if commercial use was not permitted," said a Pentagon spokesman. There is no estimate on the dollar value of this type of aid.
6. In attempting to better the balance of payments, government agencies last year supplied loans and insurance with a face value of $6.8 billion to companies doing business overseas. It also offers a wide range of technical assistance to exporters, and substantial tax breaks for firms with foreign operations.
7. Private industry benefits substantially from research financed by tax dollars. For example, a Nevada mining company extracted gold from a half-million tons of previously worthless carbonaceous ore after federal researchers developed a new refining process.
8. For those interested in exploring for gold, silver, or 33 other minerals, Uncle Sam will advance up to $250,000, and you do not have to pay it back unless you make a strike.

These are some, not all, of the areas in which government pumps cash into private enterprise. Almost every government program benefits business in one way or another. For example, money spent on social welfare, such as the JOBS program to train unskilled blacks, pays all training expenses, plus half of the employee's salary during training, thus underwriting the labor costs of participating firms.

In the study, the estimates of business subsidies of 116 programs were excluded among these programs offering cash subsidies, to help members of minority groups who want to open their own businesses; federally subsidized housing programs, aimed at helping individuals, but a boon also to the construction industry and real estate developers; public works such as hydroelectric dams and irrigation projects that spin off business benefits in low rates for electricity and water. And then there are government services operated at a loss with taxpayers making up the difference. A prime example is the postal service. Subsidies for businesses with the Founding Fathers. The special aid passed by the First Congress in 1789 set up a shipping system similar to some of today's subsidies. Since then, federal subsidies have expanded, in fact if not in name. "There is ample willingness to take benefits from government," says Professor C. Lowell Harris of Columbia University, "but there is strong preference for forms of subsidies which help conceal the nature of the receipt."

One way to disguise a subsidy is to insert a few lines of fine print in Subchapter A, Chapter 1, Title 26, Code of Federal Regulations—the income tax law. A Treasury Department study found that special concessions reduce the government's tax take by at least $40 billion a year. Some economists estimate that $15 billion of this benefits private enterprise, but Deputy Assistant Secretary of the Treasury John Nolan says that figure is too high. "About $9.5 billion of the $40 billion is business related," he said. Whatever the total, corporate taxes are reduced $2 billion a year through the $25,000 surtax exemptions; $350 million by tax breaks for firms doing business overseas, and $325 million by special concessions allowed mineral firms for exploration and development costs. And, there is the much publicized depletion allowance on natural resources, a $1.3 billion item each year.

"Tax aids have the outward appearance of involving no government costs," said Assistant Treasury Secretary Murray L. Weidenbaum, but "there is a real cost to the government in terms of foregone revenue and to the economy as a whole in terms of the increased share of current national output available to the beneficiary of the particular tax aid." Once a tax concession is born, it has a tendency to expand. An example is the mineral depletion allowance. It began as a temporary measure in World War I, became permanent for oil and gas in 1926, was expanded to metal mines, sulfur, and coal in 1932, and to other minerals in 1942, 1943, 1947, 1951, and 1954. Finally, after periodic congressional slugfests, the allowance was trimmed slightly in 1969.

Farm subsidies have undergone similar expansion. Conceived in the early days of the New Deal, they reached their peak in the 1950s and 1960s when agricultural production outran demand, resulting in crop surpluses and sagging prices. Now, the Agriculture Department operates 82 separate programs to aid farmers. The most expensive programs—$3.3 billion in 1970—are intended to prop up prices of three major crops: wheat, feed grains, and cotton. Other direct payments go to producers of such diverse crops as sugar ($80 million for 46,000 growers) and mohair wool ($10 million for 13,000 producers), while tobacco, tung nuts, and other crops are bolstered by the government's Commodity Credit Corporation through loans or purchases. In 1970 nine farms got subsidy payments of more than $1 million each. This year a $55,000 per farm limit was imposed on cotton, wheat, and feed grain subsidies. Many large farms promptly skirted it by splitting their cropland into smaller segments held in the names of other family members.

Direct subsidies are but a portion of the aid available to the farm industry. To help farmers market their crops domestically, the department churns out 20 million releases at an annual cost of $7.5 million, including the *Honey Market News*, a 12-page monthly publication prepared by a staff of 18 for 1,250 beekeepers and a few hundred honey handlers at a cost of $50,000 a year. To help farmers sell their crops in other countries, the department runs a $12 million-a-year overseas market development program that financed, among other things, a cattle trade fair in Mozambique and television spots to advertise cotton garments in Austria. It also includes cost-sharing promotion agreement with more than 60 private groups, such as the California Prune Advisory Board, and $9,800 spent in 1969 to finance a tour of wheat-producing states by the "Japanese Noodle Industry Team" representing both the Japan Wet Noodle Association and the Japan Dry Noodle Association.

The Agriculture Department runs more than a score of loan programs. The granddaddy belongs to its Rural Electrification Administration. Set up in 1935, when 9 of every 10 farms had no electricity, it has made $7 billion in 2-percent interest loans to nonprofit electric cooperatives. Today, when 99 percent of all farms have electricity, it still is making loans at a $360 million-a-year clip, increasingly to benefit suburban housing subdivisions. Virtually all electrical loans go to co-ops, but two-thirds of low-cost loans under a sister program to provide telephone service in rural areas go to profit-making private companies: $1.2 billion to 629 companies over the past two decades.

Recent years have seen a significant shift in Uncle Sam's loan portfolio. The level of direct loans has remained relatively stable, but the annual volume of guaranteed or insured loans nearly doubled between fiscal 1970 and fiscal 1972. One reason is that most indirect loans don't show up in the federal budget and thus don't require congressional approval each year. Governmental loan programs provide "more favorable terms than many borrowers can obtain from other sources, and often provide access to credit that might not otherwise be available to them on any terms," said a special analysis prepared this year by administration economists. "Lower interest rates, longer maturities and higher loan-to-value ratios are the most common favorable terms," said the document. Excluding administrative costs and losses, the analysis concluded that the loans amounted to $1.2 billion annually in interests subsidies; or, calculated another way, a capitalized value subsidy of $6.4 billion. It's impossible to determine how much of this goes to individuals, such as college students, and how much to private business. But dozens of major programs are beamed directly at business enterprises.

Perhaps the best known are offered by the Small Business Administration. The bulk of SBA's 145,000 outstanding loans, with a face value exceeding $2.5 billion, have gone to small enterprises, but a number of recent loans have financed local outlets for such national franchise chains as McDonald's, Burger King, and Western Auto. Such giants as General Motors, Bank of America, and Chase Manhattan Bank have gotten SBA aid in forming small business investment corporations which, in turn, make loans to small firms.

Low-cost government loans, as Penn Central has discovered, are no guarantee of business success, and neither are cash subsidies, as the maritime industry knows from experience. When the S.S. *Santa Paula* sailed last year for Curacao and other Caribbean ports, the 300 tourists sipping drinks in the Techo bar or dining off blue-rimmed china had Uncle Sam as a financial angel at the rate of $402.30 per passenger. The money was part of a $220 million subsidy given each year to American shipowners to make up the difference between U.S. and foreign costs for crew wages and other operating expenses. That same factor, higher costs, is the basis for $230 million paid this year in construction subsidies for ships built in American shipyards. That adds to an annual cash flow of $450 million, but despite that assistance, the maritime industry is still in serious trouble. It has all but lost its passenger business. In the past 18 months, the ranks of U.S. passenger liners has dwindled from 19 to 4.

Like the merchant marine, railroads have a long history of subsidies. A century ago the government gave 70 railroads 187 acres in land grants. More recently, the Interstate Commerce Commission guaranteed $244 million in loans to railroads from 1958 to 1963. A new flurry of help for the railroad has come in the last 2 years. In 1970, Congress established the semiprivate National Railroad Passenger Corporation, dubbed Amtrak, in an effort to salvage intercity passenger service, making privately owned railroads eligible for $300 million in loans or loan guarantees.

In addition to Penn Central's rescue loan, the Transportation Department has been pumping $10 million a year in subsidies into the firm for its experimental high-speed Metroliner in the heavily traveled Boston–New York–Washington corridor. And, by filtering $172 million in grants through state and municipal agencies, the department has helped five railroads, the Long Island, Penn Central, Illinois Central, Jersey Central, and Reading buy 875 commuter cars. Similarly, the Urban Mass Transportation Administration works through municipal middlemen to aid dozens of private bus lines. For example, officials in Worcester, Massachusetts, this spring got a $500,000 federal grant to buy 34 buses which will be leased, at $1 a year, to the private Worcester Bus Company.

Like others in the transportation industry, airlines have been running into financial difficulties. Last year, the Civil Aeronautics Board increased by 60 percent, to $58.6 million, the subsidy paid nine "feeder airlines" essentially to maintain needed air service at communities which would otherwise represent loss operations. The biggest payment, $10.5 million, went to Howard Hughes' Air West Airlines. Larger companies, such as American and United, do not receive direct subsidies, nor do international carriers, although Pan American has hinted it may seek aid for flying into cities where losses are high but service is considered important to U.S. interests. CAB chairman Secor Browne told Pan Am Officials at a private meeting May 28 that he would support a subsidy keyed to the national interest. "If we have to go somewhere for political or historical reasons," Browne said, "let the government pay for it."

There's no ready gauge of benefits reaped by private enterprise from the $16.7 billion the government spends annually for research. But some yardsticks can be found. For example, a private company can buy from the government, for $14, any one of 102 computer programs developed at a cost of up to $1 million each. In another field, the Horse Heaven mine got $18,000 this year to explore for mercury in Oregon's Cascade Range from the Geological Survey's Minerals Discovery loan program, which advances to private firms or individuals up to $250,000 of the costs of exploring for any of 35 minerals. "We don't finance grubstaking or prospecting expeditions," said Harold Kirkemo, the program's chief, but records indicate that only 41 of 184 projects financed under the 12-year-old program have paid off, the required 5 percent royalties have amounted to only $350,000, and in 73 cases, the government has written off as lost more than $1 million.

In the name of bettering the U.S. balance of payments, a half dozen agencies actively promote overseas business ventures by financing export sales, clearing the way through loans and insurance for U.S. investment abroad, and delivering technical assistance and guidance. For the same reason, the U.S. Export-Import Bank last year authorized loans, guarantees, and insurance totaling $4 billion to help foreign companies finance large purchases from American firms. Twenty-five American manufacturers made sales of $40 million or more on the basis of such government financing. Heading the list is Boeing Co., with sales valued at $3.8 billion, followed by McDonnell-Douglas at $2.7 billion.

The Commerce Department has a full division assigned to help pinpoint overseas markets, along with a special high-level office especially to help the business community make fullest use of all government resources. Thomas Drumm, the ombudsman heading the new office, said he hasn't compiled a listing of all the types of assistance available to private enterprise, or the dollar value of the aid. "It's so big," he said, that "it's just beyond the comprehension of anyone."

THE VESTED ORACLES: HOW INDUSTRY REGULATES GOVERNMENT

LEE METCALF

The main complaints about the more than 1,500 advisory committees to the federal government have been directed at the ones that don't do anything significant, or never meet. Such groups as the Tea Tasters and the International Screw Thread Commission have been dodging flak from budget-minded critics who say there is no reason for the $75 million a year the government puts out for these and like ventures.

The nation might be better off, however, if the healthy, active, and influential advisory committees, especially those from industry, would adopt the ways of their inactive companions. For in the realm of advisory committees, the ones that don't say anything seem to be much less detrimental and costly to the public interest than those that do.

Industry advisory committees exist inside most important federal agencies, and even have offices in some. Legally, their function is purely as kibitzer, but in practice many have become internal lobbies—printing industry handouts in the Government Printing Office with taxpayers' money, and even influencing policies. Industry committees perform the dual function of stopping government from finding out about corporations while at the same time helping corporations get inside information about what government is doing. Sometimes, the same company that sits on an advisory council that obstructs or turns down a government questionnaire is precisely the company which is withholding information the government needs in order to enforce the law.

The industry advisory groups enjoy a favored position over other nonindustry special interests and even public interest groups. If the environmentalists, for instance, asked to sit in while government policy was being made and to have free access to the files of the Environmental Protection Agency, they would be scoffed at. But this is exactly the position the nation's largest companies enjoy inside the Defense Department, the Department of Com-

Reprinted from Lee Metcalf, "The Vested Oracles: How Industry Regulates Government," *The Washington Monthly* (July 1971) pp. 45–53. By permission of *The Washington Monthly*.

Lee Metcalf is U.S. Senator from Montana.

merce, and elsewhere. Because of their quasi-official status, advisory councils are aware of potential policy changes and interagency dissensions that may help them oppose government actions.

As early as February, 1962, President Kennedy, concerned about the use and abuse of government advisory committees, issued an executive order "prescribing regulations for the formation and use of advisory committees." Among the requirements Kennedy imposed were: (1) annual publication of the names of members (and their affiliations) of all advisory committees; (2) a full-time salaried officer or employee of the government chairing each committee; and (3) verbatim transcripts of all industry advisory committee meetings.

But each of these requirements carried a most convenient escape clause: the requirements could be dispensed with if the head of the department or agency felt that they "would be unduly costly or impracticable" or "would interfere with the proper functioning." Not surprisingly, in case after case, the agency heads, usually at the prodding of the advisory group itself, found that the waiving of these requirements was "in the public interest."

To combat the excesses of these committees, I introduced a bill in the 91st Congress to diversify the representation in the advisory groups in the Office of Management and Budget, at least. Eventually the bill died, but a more comprehensive one has been introduced in the current Congress, and hearings are now in progress.

Advisory committees proliferated in the early postwar years, when the public romance with private industry still blurred the collusion between government and corporations. Today, the advisory system still acts as if that climate were unchanged. Many do not even bother to create the appearance of impartiality, as was the case with the Civil Aeronautics Board Finance Advisory Committee, established in 1970 along with similar groups for consumer affairs and for labor. Airline finances are not merely the concern of banks and business; nevertheless, the committee was made up purely of men from those institutions. The committee even dispensed with the pretense of meeting in the CAB offices and convened for the first time at One Chase Manhattan Plaza, in the office of James P. Mitchell, chairman of the committee and also Chase Manhattan's vice president in charge of airline finances. The bank is the major creditor for five of the nine local service carriers and a major stockholder in two airlines. No wonder the committee dealt with the serious liquidity problem of the carriers and with Mitchell's suggestion for a large federal ante into the airlines' kitties to help them pay their bills.

Five weeks after I publicly cited the CAB case as an example of the partiality of advisory bodies, the CAB disbanded the committee. The rapidity with which they backed down may be evidence of the flimsy rationale for the entire industry advisory structure. But most committees continue to function.

Take the National Industrial Pollution Center Control Council. President Nixon created it in April, 1970, to advise the President and the chairman of the Council on Environmental Quality, through the secretary of commerce, on industrial pollution problems.

The President apparently felt that council effectiveness demanded the recruitment of the world's most renowned experts on pollution, for he set about naming representatives of companies that have the greatest experience in spewing filth and poison into our environment. He manned the council with 63 top executives of major polluting companies, including the chief officers of airlines and electric utilities, and producers and manufacturers of steel, automobiles, detergents, coal, petroleum, chemicals, beverage containers, and paper and wood products. The President charged the pollution advisory group with collecting data and evaluating "programs of industry relating to the quality of the environment." Not one member of the council represents conservation groups, consumers, universities, or other public interest groups.

Obviously, the National Industrial Pollution Control Council must be placed in the category of the rabbit sent to fetch the lettuce. The analogy certainly befits Bert S. Cross, chairman of the board and chief executive officer of Minnesota Mining and Manufacturing. At the time of Cross' designation as council chairman, his company had been under order for four years by the Wisconsin Department of Natural Resources to stop discharging sulfurous wastes into the municipal sewers of Prairie du Chien.

The pollution council conducts its meetings in a fashion quite unlike anyone conditioned by industry's environmental advertising would suppose. The October 14, 1970, meeting was not publicly announced. Several environmental and consumer organizations had heard rumors of the pending meeting and presented themselves at the Commerce Department that morning, requesting admission. They were denied entrance. Their request for a transcript of the industrial polluters' meeting was turned down, as were reporters' requests that the officials hold a postmeeting press conference.

The agenda for that meeting suggests why the environmentalists were barred. While only 10 minutes were allotted to Russell Train of the Council on Environmental Quality for discussion of the national pollution standards, one hour and 45 minutes was set aside for an exploration of tax breaks and incentives to promote pollution control.

The appearance of the environmentalists at the doors of the meeting apparently embarrassed both the administration and the council. The next gathering, in February, 1971, convened in the State Department building, where security regulations prohibit entry of nonemployees without special arrangements.

The February meeting added a new twist to the previous format. The industrialists were whisked over to the White House to stand on the lawn with the President and witness the effectiveness of new air pollution abatement equipment on commercial jetliners. First, a Boeing 727 took off from National Airport. Rising into view over the Jefferson Memorial, a trail of heavy, black smoke belched from the three jet engines. Another 727 quickly followed, trailing a remarkably smaller, less dense plume of exhaust.

The President and his visitors, official protectors of the environment that they are, delightedly hailed this demonstration as an example of the great, voluntary strides of industry in controlling pollution. But a member of my staff also observed the demonstration, coming away less impressed than the President and his polluters' council. My aide's feeling was that if the first plane had flown at as low a speed and climbed at as slight an angle as the second 727, it too might have significantly reduced its exhaust emissions.

THE POLLUTERS' COUNCIL

This little episode on the White House lawn demonstrates the industrial pollution council's function as a massive, government-established public relations arm of the world's worst polluters. Little more than one year after its inception, the council has published approximately 25 reports printed at public expense by the Government Printing Office, including a "Casebook of Pollution Cleanup Actions." These cleanup actions are "drawn from published accounts of individual company environmental accomplishments throughout American industry"—most of them reprinted from such highly unimpeachable sources as industry trade association publications and house magazines.

To be sure, each report carries the disclaimer that "it does not necessarily represent the views of the Department of Commerce or any other Government agency." Indeed, the research and writing of these reports is carried out entirely by industry. But the corporate polluters have now decided they will pass these reports to senators, congressmen, and the public as government pamphlets on the scientific facts of pollution.

Mike Manatos, associate director of governmental relations (a fine euphemism for lobbyist) at Procter and Gamble, pleaded in a recent letter to me that the idea that phosphates in detergents pollute is a "misguided notion." He was sure I wanted the "real rights and wrongs," so he provided me with "a new Commerce pamphlet which gives the full story."

The "new Commerce pamphlet" was, in fact, neither new nor commerce's. Published in October, 1970, and superseded by a March, 1971, report, it did not represent the views of the Commerce Department, but rather only of the council of polluters.

By May, 1971, portions of the October pamphlet discussing the chemical, NTA, were scientifically and legally incorrect. These discrepancies were rectified in the March report on detergents, but Procter and Gamble neglected to mention the council's March report, passing off the earlier pamphlet as Commerce's "full story."

The detergent report was not just an unfortunate mistake or an embarrassing oversight, but rather the logical result of the council's methods of operation and stacked membership. The detergents subcouncil consists of eight industry members, including the president or chairman of Procter and Gamble, Lever Brothers, Purex, and Calgon. Moreover, the subcouncil operates by the stated council rule that it "does not regard its assignment as including a responsibility to obtain, weigh, and reflect all other viewpoints as well, except to the extent that sound business advice regarding industry policies and programs so require."

The National Industrial Pollution Control Council is the President's one official advisory council on industrial pollution. The Administration's lack of enthusiasm for more balanced bodies is evidenced by comparing how quickly it staffs such industry committees—named either by the President or the heads of federal agencies—and how slowly it mans more representative councils, like the Advisory Council on Environmental Education. Established by Congress as part of the 1970 Environmental Education Act, this Office of Education advisory group provides guidance on environmental education programs. In setting it up, Congress required balanced membership, to include academic, scientific, medical, and legal representatives, as well as at least three ecologists and three students. Yet nearly nine months after its inception, the council has not met. In fact, it has no members, Health, Education and Welfare Secretary Elliot Richardson having completely failed to comply with the congressional directive.

Even when the President conformed with a congressional mandate setting up a broadly based advisory committee on railroads, the result was simply another panel stacked with businessmen. In creating the National Railroad Passenger Corporation, Congress set up a 15-man financial advisory group. The law requires that these 15 members consist of six from investment, commercial banking, and railroads; two from the Treasury Department; and seven from "the public in the various regions of the Nation."

On December 1, 1970, the Department of Transportation announced the administration's choices for this advisory body. All 13 nongovernment members came from business. The President did not appoint seven representatives of the public, and did not even bother to dig up a tamed, retired academician for window dressing.

SLOW-TALKING POLLUTER

Until last year very few people were aware even of the existence of such committees. My first experience with them and their influence came about six years ago, when I suggested that the Federal Power Commission ask the major utilities whether they gave money to specified right-wing organizations. The FPC pleaded that such an inquiry was impossible without Budget Bureau (now the Office of Management and Budget—OMB) approval. Budget, I learned, had to call the question form to the attention of something called the Advisory Council on Federal Reports, which in turn would buck the proposed form to one of its utility industry advisory committees.

This revelation sparked me to take a closer look at the operations of the Advisory Council. It dates back to 1942, when the Congress was inundated with small businessmen's pleas for legislation controlling the flood of forms and questionnaires resulting from wartime rationing and wage-price controls. In short order, Congress overwhelmingly enacted the Federal Reports Act of 1942, instructing Budget to coordinate governmental collection of information.

The director of Budget turned to officials of industry for advice on administering the new law. The industrialists promptly established the privately financed and operated Advisory Council, consisting of 16 committees on banking, broadcasting, chemicals, equal employment, fats and oils, meat packing, natural gas, oil, railroads, trade, and utilities. Subsequently, when federal agencies sent a proposed questionnaire to Budget for its evaluation and approval, the bureau listed the questionnaire on "birdwatcher sheets" mailed to a few dozen industry and association representatives. If something on the sheets caught the corporate birdwatcher's eye, he would inform Budget of the need for a meeting of the industry advisory committee with the government agency responsible for the proposed form, and Budget would cordially comply.

The procedures, still followed in today's OMB, bring some strange results. For instance, a critical national inventory of industrial water wastes was delayed more than seven years by a filibuster of OMB and the advisory committees. In June, 1964, officials of the Public Health Service launched negotiations with 27 men from the various industry advisory committees, reviewing a health service inventory form designed to catalogue the composition, volume, and locations of water-contaminating industrial wastes. The advisory group, including representatives of such industrial giants as U.S. Steel, Consolidated Coal, and American Paper and Pulp, challenged the inventory on the basis that the data would find its way into the hands of the news media and opportunistic politicians. Further, they charged the survey—which was voluntary—would garner incomplete, outdated, and misleading information. Besides, they lamented the frightful costs to industry and the revelations of trade secrets that allegedly would result. After wrangling over the form for seven hours, the advisory committee adjourned, failing to resolve its conflict with the Public Health Service.

In 1968—four long years of mounting pollution after the initial advisory committee meeting—a new team of concerned bureaucrats tried to get the industry group to accept the inventory. The government environmental protectors faced several veterans of the meeting held several years earlier. Industry rehashed the old argument. The Budget Bureau again did not approve the inventory, thus awarding the decision to the polluters.

By last year, growing attention to this issue from Congress, the press, and Ralph Nader had created a public image problem for the Administration, forcing it to do something, if only to create the illusion of action. So it initiated a pilot, voluntary inventory. Just a few firms in each state, including, in many cases, small operators rather than big polluters, are asked to send in information. The result is that we still don't know who pollutes what, where, and how much.

THE INTIMATE CAUCUS

OMB, of course, is not legally required to accept the objections of the industry advisory committees. But industry wins out because of its power and its experts, who can cajole and even intimidate government officials into seeing and doing things industry's way. Peter Petkas, an attorney with Nader, last year described a September, 1970, meeting he attended of the Communications Industry Committee of OMB's advisory council. The meeting, called to discuss a Federal Communications Commission questionnaire probing the effects of conglomerate ownership of broadcasting facilities, was packed with representatives of CBS, NBC, ABC, Westinghouse Broadcasting, and other communications corporations. The industry representatives, as Petkas put it, "quite literally put [the FCC man] through the wringer. For the first few hours he held his ground. . . . As time wore on he was more willing to accept industry criticism and to offer to make changes accordingly." As examples of the wearing-down process, Petkas cites an hour-and-a-half discussion as to which company official should sign the questionnaire and whether it should be notarized, and a three-hour bemoaning of NBC's difficulty in locating the necessary information in its files.

The discussion frequently focused on questions that OMB and industry claim are not supposed to be considered by the advisory committees. Petkas recounted industry inquiries concerning "agency policy, the depth of support among the commissioners for carrying out the survey, and the names of commissioners who were responsible for instigating it."

OMB had made no attempt to notify the FCC in advance of industry allegations and objections to the questionnaire, and, after eight hours of sometimes heated discussion, the advisory committee had reviewed merely five of the 17 questions on the form. The meeting then adjourned with the agreement that issues remaining between the industry people and the FCC be ironed out in "intimate caucus." When Petkas suggested that he might attend the "intimate caucus," he was bluntly uninvited by the committee's industry chairman and assured by the OMB reviewing officer that this closed, informal meeting between an OMB advisory committee and the FCC was none of Petkas' or OMB's business. OMB, it was explained, could not assure Petkas' admittance.

Prior to introduction of the Senate bill on advisory committees, OMB discouraged public knowledge of its advisory meetings. Today, public interest representatives can be notified of, and sometimes participate in, these gatherings, albeit as observers rather than members. But these changes, forced because of the bad light in which congressional hearings placed OMB and its advisory committees, do not address the more serious implications of industry's dominance of these groups and its quiet exercise of governmental power.

FIVE-SIDED PROFITS

The commerce groups may make the polluters look good and the OMB advisory groups may keep government away from industry's files, but it is at the Pentagon where the real potential of industry expertise is realized, where corporations can advise the government on how to help them make more money off federal contracts.

The Defense Industry Advisory Committee (called merely the Industry Advisory Committee, or IAC, since 1968—they dropped the "Defense" in deference to growing public opinion against militarism) was established in 1962 by Secretary of Defense Robert McNamara. All of its members, except the deputy secretary of defense, who serves as chairman, are heads of corporations. And as of mid-1970, 12 of the 24 members were from among the top 40 defense contractors, their firms holding $6.12 billion in prime military contracts let last year.

When the IAC advises the Pentagon on defense profits, it advises from experience. It has negotiated both for changes in procurement rules and for higher profits, and its success can be measured by a recent General Accounting Office questionnaire that last year found an average 56-percent profit based on equity invested in 146 negotiated defense contracts examined.

The IAC, wanting to minimize its success in the area of profits, worked to convince the GAO to write another draft of its report, highlighting new information voluntarily and unselfishly provided by industry, showing a lower profit margin of 21 percent. The IAC prevailed—the final version of the GAO report deemphasized the government's independent conclusions and upgraded the industry's data showing the lower figures.

Such is the influence of the closed, secretive board, whose nine-year history is shrouded in mystery. Its rules forbid members to "issue or make public statements regarding the work of the council without prior approval of the chairman," and rarely does the Pentagon reveal anything about IAC activities.

There's something in the IAC both for the Pentagon and for industry. On the government side, it permits the Pentagon to prevent or resolve conflicts between contractors in private, where arrangements can be worked out without the danger that a disgruntled contractor will complain to Congress or the press. Rumors still abound that the IAC was specifically established to smooth rumpled feelings surrounding the award of the TFX contract to General Dynamics rather than Boeing. William M. Allen, Boeing's chairman, was a charter member of IAC, serving from 1962 to 1969.

On industry's side, contractors gladly exchange the right to publicly protest for the chance to get inside the Pentagon, where things can be worked out amicably among friends and there is always enough for everybody. Being inside gives the IAC a way to influence procurement rules before they are promulgated, to criticize troublesome government regulations, reporting forms, and audits, and to get advance information on Pentagon decisions so there is still time for industry to apply pressure. IAC members also enjoy what all other private citizens' groups are denied—top-secret briefings on the war, Soviet technology, domestic militants, and the administration's economic "game plan." Little wonder that some have tagged IAC as the "board of directors of the military-industrial complex."

The IAC had some influence on the changes in defense contracting that led to the cost-plus contracts and the lucrative overruns. And now it is moving to eliminate all competition between contractors as well. Arguing against the low profits that imperil national security, John Dresser, chairman of Dresser Industries, told the February, 1971, IAC meeting that actions must be taken to boost contractor earnings, that defense is inconsistent with haggling over the price, and that "the country will be best served without cutthroat competition."

Apparently, the Pentagon agrees. At the same meeting, Ron Fox, assistant secretary of army installations and logistics, referred to a memorandum issued by Deputy Secretary David Packard which outlined major Pentagon policy changes in contracting. The new guidance provides for more cost-plus contracts and less competition, which, according to Fox, "will probably increase the actual profit earning on defense contracts."

MINI-ARMS RACE

Most of the IAC's work is carried on by subcommittees, such as the one on military exports that dates back to 1962. This subcommittee, representing a large variety of companies, has as its prime objective the selling of the Pentagon abroad by promoting overseas military sales and mini-arms races. Small countries provide a lucrative market for second-hand arsenals, and the IAC subcommittee helps convince them they need to be the first on their continent to have a surplus destroyer or an obsolete jet. At a June, 1967, meeting, Henry J. Kuss, Jr., special assistant for International logistics, delivered to IAC the export subcommittee's recommendations for a joint industry/defense effort to expand the number of U.S. companies engaged in exporting weapons as well as the yearly volume of shipments overseas. Their approach seems not unlike a weapons' sale roadshow, including a more favorable policy on profits so as to stimulate export expansion; a combined effort by industry and the Departments of State, Commerce, and Defense to solicit foreign sales; and upgrading of "industrial-educational institutions" in the instruction of problems of military hardware export.

The IAC has also concerned itself with the possible threat to the defense industry from domestic unrest. After hearing the Army's Provost Marshal, Maj. Gen. Lloyd B. Ramsey, imply that the increase in the national crime rate and the jump in "student unrest and disobedience" are indicators of a conspiracy to disrupt production, Mark Shepherd, Jr., president of Texas Instruments and IAC member since 1969, took the floor. In a paper specifically endorsed by several council members, Shepherd advocated an immediate and far-reaching program to combat the radical threat to industry. His program involves giving industry access to federal records and criminal data, so a job applicant can no longer conceal arrests for "loitering, illegal picketing, and disorderly conduct"—misdemeanor charges Shepherd views as indicators of "potential militancy."

In his conclusions, "wholeheartedly endorsed" by W. P. Gwinn, chairman of United Aircraft, and W. F. Rockwell, Jr., North American Rockwell's chief, Shepherd said that federal agencies, including the FBI, should share their intelligence with industry, and that special FBI agents should work closely with industry "to identify potential militants." He also proposed the establishment of a "central repository of criminal data for the purpose of screening job applicants."

Lest silly, groundless fears of civil libertarians and other bleeding hearts allay the government from taking industry's recommended course, United Aircraft's W. P. Gwinn warned that industry would do it themselves. Said Gwinn, "It is conceivable that if the present restrictions on the release of such information to industry are not modified, industry may in effect have to establish an undercover organization of its own in order to protect itself."

ADVISE AND DECEIVE

But in reality this is what industry has already done through the vast and complex web of advisory committees. The growth of advisory groups in the last 30 years, and particularly in the last decade, has not benefited society through increased information and expertise in government. Rather, it has closed off the flow of information and reserved key governmental access points for the leaders of the corporate world. The widespread and pervasive influence of these committees marks the emergence of the American corporate state, where dominant political power is officially and quasi-officially invested in the massive industrial and financial conglomerates.

Clearly, we must eliminate this source of government by special interests. All unnecessary advisory committees certainly must go. And if some are indispensable, they should be open, representative bodies operating under adversary proceedings, thereby assuring that no interest will be officially enthroned. While not guaranteeing all societal interests equal political resources and influence, at least all interests will share an equal chance at information and access.

Prospects for such changes are not good. Even when diverse representation on advisory committees is legally mandated, the President puts himself above the law by either refusing to appoint the committees or stacking them with businessmen. In our present system, government by advisory committees, the public can have no more confidence in the advice of these panels than it has in the quality and reliability of the products of the industrialists who man them.

III. FEDERAL TAXATION POLICY

INTRODUCTION

The examination of federal economic policy and the forces which shape it must focus on the means by which government gains control over a share of the nation's resources. In the United States, the technique used to transfer resources from the private to the public sector is that of taxation. Through legislation, citizens agree to impose charges upon themselves, the revenues from which support government activities.

The federal government in the United States imposes taxes on individuals, corporations, foundations, and many of the activities in which they engage. The earning of income, the making of profits, the buying of certain products, and the bequeathing of assets are all activities which make one liable for taxes.

In all, the federal government collects about $200 billion in taxes—an amount equal to about 20 percent of the nation's trillion-dollar Gross National Product. Table 1 describes the kinds of taxes collected and the amount of revenue generated by each.

While the primary function of taxation is to raise revenue with which to provide public services, the system of taxes is also designed to achieve other objectives. The structure of taxes, for example, has substantial influence on how the society allocates its resources. By imposing taxes on an activity, government alters the incentives—the payoff—for engaging in the activity. Hence, a tax on the earning of income tends to decrease the quantity of labor supplied to labor markets. If the imposition of such a tax were the only economic change occurring in the economy, the ratio of labor to capital used in production processes would tend to

TABLE 1. Federal Taxes by Major Sources, Fiscal Year 1970 (in billions of dollars)

Sources	1970 actual	Percentage of total
Individual income taxes	90.4	46.7
Corporation income taxes	32.8	16.9
Social insurance taxes and contributions (trust funds)	45.3	23.4
Excise taxes	15.7	8.1
Estate and gift taxes	3.6	1.9
Customs duties	2.4	1.2
Miscellaneous receipts	3.4	1.8
Total Budget Receipts	193.7	100.0

decrease. Similarly, taxes imposed on sale of certain commodities, like the 7-percent excise tax on automobiles, tends to raise the market price of the commodity and discourage its sales and production. If government gives favorable tax breaks to certain industries or activities, investment in these industries tends to be high and disproportionate, and often uneconomic, volume of the nation's resources becomes devoted to that activity. The favoritism shown to the oil industry by the U.S. tax structure accounts for a good share of the excess capacity in that industry.

The level and structure of taxes can also play a role in the achievement of full employment and stable prices. Cutting the tax rates imposed on personal income, for example, leaves people with more income available for spending. The resulting increase in spending stimulates additional production and, hence, the creation of additional jobs, reducing the rate of unemployment. It was to achieve such macroeconomic objectives that President Nixon's message of August 1971 proposed that the excise tax on new automobile sales be eliminated, that the effective tax rate of personal income be reduced through an increase in exemptions and deductions, and that investment spending by businesses be subsidized through an investment tax credit.

Because taxes do alter and, indeed, determine the distribution of income and wealth in a society, consideration of tax revisions sets all of the organized vested interests into action. The National Association of Manufacturers and the Chamber of Commerce go to work to protect the existing provisions which subsidize business profits, to secure increases in the special provisions for business, or to develop loopholes in any additional taxes which might be imposed on business. The oil industry mobilizes to protect its sheltered position and other powerful interests strive to find someone to sponsor amendments which favor them with tax relief.[1] Wealthy people in general argue for continued favoritism for the kinds of special income which tend to accrue to them, e.g., capital gains income.

[1] In the 1969 tax reform effort, the story of the "Lockheed provision" became a national issue. A provision in that tax bill provided specific tax relief for aircraft manufacturers building planes of specifications such that only the Lockheed Corporation could qualify for the favor.

And, as we will see in this section, various vested interests have been effective in obtaining and maintaining special tax privileges.

In the taxation area, the stakes for winning are very high. A single percentage point preference in tax rates, a single exemption or special provision, a single carefully thought out tax shelter can mean millions of dollars in implicit subsidy and increased profits. Because of the complicated nature of the tax laws, complex and tortured arrangements are often devised by the powerful in order to protect their income and wealth position. A classic example of such a contortion was reported recently in a newspaper article entitled "Ghost Foundations Help Cut Oil Taxes."[2]

> Dozens of shadow foundations are being used as middlemen by banks and oil companies in deals through which mineral producers avoid $100 million a year in federal income taxes.
>
> The tax-exempt foundations are nonprofit charitable corporations, yet they give little or no money to charity.
>
> Instead, an Associated Press study shows, their main purpose is to serve as conduits in complex, multimillion-dollar transactions that allow mineral producers to . . . reduce or eliminate federal income tax liability, sometimes by creating self-induced paper losses.
>
> The transactions, legal under present law, involve carved-out production payments. In essence, a production payment is the right to future income from a mineral deposit such as an oil field. An oil company may carve out a certain percentage of that future production and sell it for immediate cash.
>
> Because the courts have held that production payments are "interests in land" and because national banks' land dealings are restricted by law, banks are leary of buying production payments outright.
>
> So instead of banks dealing directly with mineral companies, foundations—known in the trade as "straws"—are set up to buy the production payments. The foundations get the money from the banks through loans, with the production payment serving as collateral.
>
> Government officials said they don't know how many foundations are involved in such deals. But an Associated Press check of foundations in two states—Louisiana and Texas—turned up more than 30 foundations whose only assets were production payments. Most had directors or officers linked to banks or oil company law firms.
>
> These foundations handled $118,500,000 in production payments last year. They gave to charity $145,635—or little more than one-tenth of one percent of the money they handled.
>
> The charitable contributions are small, foundation officers said, because the foundations have little net income. All they earn is the fractional difference between the interest rates charged by the banks on loans to the foundations and the slightly higher interest equivalent paid by the oil companies on the money received from the foundations.
>
> An unpublished Treasury Department study shows production payment deals totaled $750 million in 1967 and $703 million in 1968, a threefold increase from 1965's total of $217.4 million.
>
> Treasury officials calculate that one tax dollar is lost for every seven dollars involved

[2] *Washington Post*, November 24, 1969, pp. 1, 9.

in the deals. Thus, they say, the transactions have cost the government more than $100 million annually in tax revenues in each of the last 2 years.

One federal official (stated), "Frequently, the only purpose is tax avoidance."

Representatives of banks and the mineral industry, who are lobbying against changes in the present tax law, deny that production payments are used primarily to avoid taxes.

An example of a bank-foundation-oil company arrangements can be found in New Orleans. There eight foundations list clerks and tellers of Whitney National Bank and members of the bank's law firm as directors.

The foundations carry such names as Thirteen-Hundred Foundation, Eleven-Hundred Foundation, Two-Twenty-Eight Foundation, Six-Twenty-Four Foundation and Six-Thirty-Five Foundation.

In 1967 and 1968, the Thirteen-Hundred Foundation handled production payments totaling $2,926,353. Its net income during that period was $273, and its sole charitable contribution was $25 to Phillips Memorial Methodist Church.

In 1968 another of the eight foundations, St. Charles, Inc., had a gross income of more than $4 million but made no charitable contributions because it showed a deficit of $10,000.

St. Charles' president is Rene A. Gatt, a teller at Whitney National Bank which made the loan. "Don't ask me about it, I really can't tell you much . . . I'm listed as president . . . but in name only," Gatt said.

He referred to a bank vice president, George P. Bywater, as "the one who sets up these things."

Bywater said he handled the foundation's paperwork but added "The bank doesn't own these foundations or control them. No bank officer is the director or anything."

As for the bank clerks and tellers listed as foundation directors, Bywater said, "These men are just individuals."

THE RICH, THE POOR, AND THE TAXES THEY PAY

JOSEPH A. PECHMAN

The distribution of income has always been a hotly debated subject. Whatever has happened or is happening to the distribution of income, some people will always assert that the rich are getting a bigger share of the pie than is "fair," while others will seek to show that this is not the case. Few people, however, bother to find out the facts and fewer still understand what they mean.

The same applies to the tax system. Everybody knows that there are loopholes in the federal tax laws, but few realize that there are loopholes for persons at all income levels. Even fewer have a clear idea about the effects on the distribution of income of closing the more controversial loopholes. And only the experts know the state-local tax structure is in more urgent need of reform than the federal structure.

Excerpted and reprinted from Joseph Pechman, "The Rich, The Poor, and The Taxes They Pay," *The Public Interest,* No. 17 (Fall 1969), pp. 21–43. By permission of National Affairs, Inc. and the author.

Joseph Pechman is Director of Economic Studies at The Brookings Institution, Washington, D.C.

This article is intended to put these matters in perspective by summarizing the available information. What has happened to the distribution of income before taxes in recent years, and how has the tax system modified it? What's wrong with the national tax system? What reforms are needed to make it a fairer system? What are the chances of getting these reforms? And, beyond such reforms, what would be the shape of a tax distribution that most Americans today might agree to be "fair"?

THE DISTRIBUTION OF INCOME

Despite the proliferation of sophisticated economic data in this country, the United States government does *not* publish official estimates of the distribution of income. Such estimates were prepared by the Office of Business Economics for a period of years in the 1950s and early 1960s, but were discontinued because the sources on which they were based were acknowledged to be inadequate. We have data from annual field surveys of some 30,000 households conducted by the Bureau of the Census, as well as from the annual *Statistics of Income* prepared by the Internal Revenue Service from federal individual income tax returns. But both sources have their weaknesses. Nevertheless, if used with care, the two sources provide some interesting insights.

Before turning to the most recent period, it should be pointed out that a significant change in the distribution of pretax income occurred during the Great Depression and World War II. All experts who have examined the data agree that the distribution became more equal as a result of (a) the tremendous reductions in business and property incomes during the depression and (b) the narrowing of earnings differentials between low-paid workers and higher-paid skilled workers and salaried employees when full employment was reestablished during the war.

The movement toward equality seems to have ended during World War II, at least on the basis of the available statistics. In 1952 the share of the top 5 percent was 20.5 percent and of the top 20 percent, 44.7 percent.

To trace what happened since 1952, we shift to the census data that provide the longest continuous and comparable income distribution series available to us. The best way to appreciate the trend is to look at the figures for income shares at five-year intervals:

TABLE 1. Before-Tax Income Shares, Census Data (in percentages)

Year	Top 5 percent of families	Top 20 percent of families
1952	18	42
1957	16	40
1962	16	42
1967	15	41

Source: Bureau of the Census. Income includes transfer payments (e.g., social security benefits, unemployment compensation, welfare payments, etc.), but excludes capital gains.

The figures indicate that the share of the top 5 percent declined slightly between 1952 and 1957, and has remained virtually unchanged since 1957; the share of the top 20 percent changed very little.[1] Correspondingly, the shares of the groups at the bottom of the income scale (not shown in Table 1) also changed very little throughout the period.

If the figures are anywhere near being right, they suggest two significant conclusions:

First, in recent years the very rich in our society have not enjoyed larger increases in incomes, as defined in the tax code, than the average income recipient. Although realized capital gains are included in our figures, they do not include nonreported sources, such as tax-exempt interest and excess depletion; correction for these omissions would probably not alter the results very much, because the amounts involved are small relative to the total of reported incomes. Even a correction for the undistributed profits of corporations wouldn't change the result very much because undistributed gross corporation profits have remained between 10 and 13 percent of total reported income since 1950.

Second, a change in the income distribution may have occurred in what are sometimes called the "middle-income" classes. These classes consist of most of the professional people in this country (doctors, lawyers, engineers, accountants, college professors, etc.) as well as the highest paid members of the skilled labor force and white-collar workers. The increase in their share of total income from 24 percent to 27 percent, if it actually occurred, represents a not insignificant improvement in their relative income status.

Clearly, this improvement in the income shares of the middle classes could come only at the expense of the lower 85 percent of the income distribution. But this is not the whole story. These figures contain only incomes that are generated in the private economy; they do not include transfer payments (e.g., social security benefits, unemploy-

[1] People with money always feel poorer than they are, and it might be useful to indicate what kinds of income we are talking about for these various categories. For the year 1967, a taxpayer was in the top 1 percent if his income (including realized capital gains) was over $43,000, the top 2 percent if his income was over $28,000, the top 5 percent if his income was over $18,000, the top 10 percent if his income was over $14,000, the top 15 percent if his income was over $12,000.

ment compensation, welfare payments, etc.) which are, of course, concentrated in the lower-income classes. Correction of the figures for transfer payments might be just enough to offset the increased share of the middle-income classes. If this is the case, the constancy of the shares of pretax income shown by the census data is fully consistent with the growth in shares of the middle incomes shown by the tax data. And, if this is the explanation of the constancy of the income shares in the census distribution, it means that the lower classes have not been able to hold their own in the private economy; large increases in government transfer payments were needed to prevent a gradual erosion of their income shares.

THE EFFECT OF TAXES

Since one of the major objectives of taxation is to moderate income inequality, it is appropriate to ask how the tax system actually affects the distribution of income and whether it has become more or less equalizing. We examine first the impact of the federal individual income tax, which is the most progressive element in the nation's tax system and for which data by income classes are readily available, and then we speculate about the effect of the other taxes in the system.[2]

The Federal Income Tax

While everybody grumbles about the federal income tax, few people realize that tax rates have been *going down* for about two decades. Even with the 10-percent surtax, the rates are lower today than they were from 1951 through 1963.

The structure of the tax has been remarkably stable during this entire period, despite all the talk about closing loopholes. The preferential rate on long-term capital gains was enacted in 1942; income splitting became effective in 1948; interest on state and local government bonds has never been taxed by the federal government; percentage depletion dates back to the 1920s; and the deductions allowed for interest charges, taxes, charitable contributions, medical expenses, and casualty losses date back to 1942 or earlier. The 1954 law introduced a 4-percent dividend credit, but this was repealed in 1964.

The single major victory for tax reform occurred in 1964, when the dividend credit and the deductions for state and local taxes other than income, sales, property, and gasoline taxes were eliminated. All told, these revenue-raising reforms amounted to about $750 million, and they were accompanied by revenue-losing reforms of $400 million (mainly the minimum standard deduction which benefitted only those with very low incomes).

Although this history is of considerable interest, it is not directly useful for an analysis of the effect of the tax on the income distribution. It must be remembered that most people moved up the income scale almost continuously throughout this period; under a progressive tax, they would be taxed more heavily as a result of this upward movement. There is a case for the argument that, as incomes rise, it is only "fair" that progressive tax rates—established on the basis of an earlier income distribution that was considered "fair"—ought to go down somewhat. The key question is: how much? Specifically, has the progressive taxation of increased incomes been offset by the reduction in tax rates, or has there been a "surplus" on the side of either income or taxation?

To answer this question, the effective tax rates were computed for the top 1, 2, 5, 10, and 15 percent of the income tax units (Table 2), but in this case the full amount of realized long-term capital gains, and also other exclusions, were included to arrive at a total income concept. The data show that, on this basis, average effective tax rates were substantially lower in 1967 than in 1952 for the top 1 percent, slightly lower for the next 1 percent, and roughly constant for the next 13 percent. Note also that the effective rate of tax paid in 1967 by the top 1 percent, whose before-tax income was

[2] Since the terms are often used loosely, it might be a good idea explicitly to define what *regressive, proportional,* and *progressive* taxation mean. A tax is *regressive* when it takes a larger proportion of a poor person's income than of a rich man's, *proportional* when it takes equal proportions of such incomes, and *progressive* when it takes a larger proportion of a rich man's income than of a poor man's.

$43,000 and over, was only 26 percent of their total reported income, including all their realized capital gains.

TABLE 2. Effective Federal Tax Rates on Total Income (in percentages)

Year	Top 1 percent of tax units	Next 1 percent of tax units	Next 3 percent of tax units	Next 5 percent of tax units	Next 5 percent of tax units
1952	33	20	16	14	12
1963	27	20	16	14	13
1967	26	18	15	13	12

Source: *Statistics of Income.* Total income is the sum of adjusted gross income and excluded capital gains, dividends, and sick pay.

It is a fairly simple matter to deduct the tax paid by each of these groups from their total income to obtain their disposable income. The results modify the conclusions we drew on the basis of the before-tax incomes in only minor respects. The shares of disposable income of the top 1 percent remain stable, and the shares of the top 2, 5, 10, and 15 percent go up from 1952 to 1967. Furthermore, the shares of the middle-income classes—the 14 percent between the top 1 and top 15 percent—rise from 23 to 27 percent on a disposable income basis, or about as much as on a before-tax basis (Table 3).

TABLE 3. Shares of Total Disposable (i.e., After-tax) Income (in percentages)

Year	Top 1 percent of tax units	Top 2 percent of tax units	Top 5 percent of tax units	Top 10 percent of tax units	Top 15 percent of tax units
1952	7	10	16	24	30
1963	7	10	17	26	33
1967	7	11	17	26	34

Source: *Statistics of Income.* Disposable income is total income less federal income tax paid.

We may conclude that the federal individual income tax has moderated the before-tax income distribution by roughly the same proportions since 1952. Thus, while tax rates at any given absolute income level have declined, the effect of progression has just about offset the decline, leaving the relative tax bite about the same in the top 15 percent of the income distribution.

It should be emphasized that the foregoing data omit large chunks of income that are received primarily by high-paid employees of large business firms. Tax-exempt interest and percentage depletion have already been mentioned. In addition, beginning with the imposition of the very high individual income tax rates and the excess profits tax during World War II, methods of compensation were devised to funnel income to business executives in nontaxable forms. The devices used are well known: deferred compensation and pension plans, stock option arrangements, and direct payment of personal consumption expenditures through expense accounts. There is no question that these devices are used widely throughout the corporate sector. But little is known about the amounts involved, and even less is known about the impact on the distribution of income.

The Corporation Income Tax

The corporation income tax was enacted 4 years before the individual income tax and it has been a mainstay of the federal tax system ever since. It produced more revenue than the individual income tax in 17 out of 28 years prior to 1941; today, it is the second largest source of federal revenue. The general corporation tax was reduced to 38 percent after World War II. It was raised to 52 percent during the Korean War and remained there until 1964, when it was reduced to 48 percent.

Some people have argued that a large part or all of the corporation income tax is shifted forward to the consumer in the form of higher prices. On this assumption, the corporation income tax is a sales tax—a very peculiar one, to be sure—and is therefore regressive. But the majority view among tax experts is that the corporation income tax comes out of corporate profits, as was intended, so that the tax is borne by shareholders. Despite the large post-World War II increases in the number of shareholders, stock ownership is still concentrated in the highest income classes. This means that the corporation income tax is, to some extent at least, a progressive tax.

Estate and Gift Taxes

In theory, estate and gift taxes are excellent taxes because they have little effect on incentives to earn income and, if effective, would reduce the inequality of the distribution of wealth that in turn accounts for much of the inequity in the distribution of income. In practice, the yield of these taxes is disappointing. Tax rates are high, but there are numerous ways to escape them. The result is that the federal government receives little of its revenue from these tax sources—about 1.7 percent in the current fiscal year. The effective rate of estate taxes on wealth passed each year from one generation to the next must be less than 10 percent; and the gift tax is even less effective. While these taxes are progressive, they have little effect on the distribution of wealth.

The Social Security Payroll Tax

We now turn to the features of the national tax system that, in combination, more than offset the progressivity of the federal income and estate and gift taxes. The social security payroll tax, which is levied at a flat rate on earnings up to a maximum of $7,800 under present law, was enacted in 1935 as the basic method of financing social security on the principle that the workers were buying their own insurance. This idea is doubtless responsible for the widespread acceptance of social security as a permanent government institution in this country; but the insurance analogy is no longer applicable to the system as it has developed. Present beneficiaries receive far larger benefits than the taxes they paid would entitle them to—a situation that will continue indefinitely as long as Congress raises benefits as prices and wages continue to rise. The trust funds have not grown significantly since the mid-1950s; the payroll taxes paid by the workers have not been stored up or invested, but have been paid out currently as benefits. When benefits promised to people now working come due, the funds for their payment will be provided out of tax revenues as of that future date.

Nevertheless, the insurance analogy has a strong hold on the thinking of the administrators of social security and the congressional tax-writing committees. Every time a benefit increase is enacted, the payroll tax rates (or the maximum earnings subject to the tax) are raised, in order to balance out the revenues and expenditures for the next 75 years on an actuarial basis. In a relatively short time, the trust funds begin running large surpluses, which then become the justification for another round of benefit increases by Congress. This requires a further increase in rates for actuarial reasons, payroll taxes are again raised, and so on.

As a result of this process, payroll taxes have been raised seven times since the beginning of 1960. The combined employer-employee tax was 6 percent on earnings up to $4,800 on January 1, 1960; this year the tax is 9.6 percent on earnings up to $7,800. Most economists believe that the burden of the employer tax, as well as the employee tax, falls eventually on the workers (either by substituting for larger wage increases or inflating prices). Thus, the federal government has been placing more and more weight on this regressive element of the federal tax system.

The federal income tax bill of the families and individuals who are officially classified as poor is less than $100 million a year, as compared with the $1.5 billion they pay in payroll taxes. The regressive feature of the payroll tax at the higher-income levels should be moderated immediately and ultimately eliminated entirely.

Several different approaches might be taken to achieve these objectives.

First, part or all of the payroll tax could be converted into a withholding tax for income tax purposes. No formal change in the payroll tax need be involved; at the end of the year, individuals would receive credit against their income taxes (or a refund if they are not income-tax payers) for the amount of payroll taxes paid.

Second, contributions from general revenues might be made, on the basis of a fixed formula, to the Social Security and other trust funds. Such a possibility was foreseen in the earlier days of Social Security.

Third, the Social Security system might be combined with a liberalized and modernized public assistance system or some variant of a negative income tax. The negative income-tax payments to the aged in such a system would be financed out of general revenues.

But whatever is ultimately done about the payroll tax as the basic revenue source for Social Security financing, the poor should be relieved of paying this tax as soon as possible. The principle of a minimum taxable level under the income tax —which was recently raised by the Congress to the poverty levels—should be carried over into the payroll tax. The Internal Revenue Service is already proficient at handling tens of millions of refunds per year under the income tax; the additional payroll-tax refunds would not be an excessive burden.

State and Local Taxes

Although the federal tax system is progressive on balance, the state and local tax system is highly regressive. The states rely heavily on sales taxes, while the local governments rely on property taxes. Personal and corporation income taxes account for only about 11 percent of state-local revenues from their own sources. This situation is disturbing because the state-local tax system is the growing element of the national system. Whereas the federal government has been able to reduce income-tax rates several times beginning in 1954, and has eliminated virtually all of its excise taxes, state governments continue to enact new taxes and to raise the rates of old taxes to keep up with their increasing and urgent revenue needs; meanwhile, local governments keep raising the already excessively burdened property tax.

Federal tax receipts have moved within the narrow range of 19 to 21 percent of the Gross National Product since 1951. By contrast, state-local receipts rose from 7.1 percent of the GNP in 1951 to 11.9 percent in 1968. Assuming that state-local taxes respond more or less proportionately to the rise in the national product (a reasonable assumption), the state and local governments must have increased rates by 68 percent in these 17 years to push up their tax yields to current levels. The net result is, of course, that a greater degree of regression is being built into the national tax system by the state and local governments as they continue to seek for more revenues.

Parenthetically, it might be observed that the "tax revolt" which was so much in the news in the late 1960s must have been a reflection of the increasing burden of state and local taxes.[3] The revolt is allegedly concentrated in the "middle-income" classes living in the suburbs. In this, there is a paradox: this group probably pays a smaller proportion of its income in taxes than the poor and near poor (see below), but the taxes they have been paying, or recently began to pay, are highly visible.

Summary of the National Tax System

It is not easy to arrive at an accurate estimate of the impact of the whole tax system at various income levels. Taxes are reported to different federal, state, and local governmental agencies. No single agency has the responsibility to compel reporting of taxes on a meaningful and consistent basis.

Recent estimates of this overall impact were prepared by the Council of Economic Advisers for the year 1965. They show the distribution of taxes by the income classes of families and unattached individuals, income being defined exclusive of transfer payments. The estimates for taxes and transfers separately, and in combination, are summarized in Table 4.

The following are the major conclusions that can be drawn from these and previously published estimates:

1. Since at least the mid-1930s, the federal tax system has been roughly proportional in the lower- and middle-income classes, and clearly progressive for the highest classes. Federal income tax data suggest that the preferential rate on capital gains, and the exclusion of interest on state and local bonds and other items from the tax base, have produced some regressivity for the very small

[3] The "tax revolt" came to a head in 1969, when the secretary of the treasury told Congress that 155 people in 1957 were paying no income tax even though they earned more than $200,000 that year. Twenty-one of the 155 people had incomes of over $1 million.

TABLE 4. Taxes and Transfers as Percentage of Income, 1965

	Taxes				
Income classes	Federal	State and local	Total	Transfer payments	Taxes less transfers
Under $2,000	19	25	44	126	−83[a]
$2,000–4,000	16	11	27	11	16
$4,000–6,000	17	10	27	5	21
$6,000–8,000	17	9	26	3	23
$8,000–10,000	18	9	27	2	25
$10,000–15,000	19	9	27	2	25
$15,000 and over	32	7	38	1	37
Total	22	9	31	14	24

a The minus sign indicates that the families and individuals in this class received more from federal, state, and local governments than they, as a group, paid to these governments in taxes.

Source: *Economic Report of the President,* 1969. Income excludes transfer payments, but includes realized capital gains in full and undistributed corporate profits.

group at the top of the income pyramid, say, beginning with incomes of $100,000 or more.

2. State and local taxes are regressive throughout the income scale.

3. The combined federal, state, and local tax burden is heaviest in the very bottom and top brackets, and lowest in the middle brackets. This statement is, of course, based on averages for each group and there are wide variations around these averages for specific individuals, depending on the sources of their incomes, the kind of property they own, and where they live.

4. The poor receive numerous transfer payments (e.g., Social Security, unemployment compensation, public assistance, etc.) that are financed by this tax system. The net effect of transfers as against taxes is distinctly progressive, because transfer payments make up such a large proportion of total income at the bottom of the income distribution—56 percent for those with incomes of less than $2,000 in 1965. (To some extent, this progressivity is overstated because the transfers do not always go to the same people who pay taxes, the best example being Social Security retirement benefits that are received only by retirees—many of whom are not poor—while $1.5 billion of the payroll tax levied to pay for these benefits are paid by the poor.) There is no reason in the abstract, why a nation should not levy taxes on and pay transfers to the same groups; but while the nation wages a war on poverty, it is surely appropriate to consider the possibility of providing additional financial assistance to the poor by *tax reduction* as well as through transfer payments.

THE PROBLEM OF TAX LOOPHOLES (OR: MY EIGHTEEN YEARS IN A QUANDARY)

PAUL H. DOUGLAS

By the summer of 1950, the attack by the North Koreans upon South Korea had plunged us into a full-scale Asiatic war. North Korea was being egged on and equipped by Red China and Russia, and the war was another effort by the Communist bloc to take over additional territory.

President Truman and the United Nations rose to the occasion and resisted this aggression, and it became necessary to raise large additional sums of money, running into many billions of dollars.

As the new tax bill moved onto the floor of the Senate, I became more aware of the injustices in the existing tax structure and of new abuses that were being added.

The longer the discussion of these bills went on the more convinced I became that the tax code was, in fact, permeated with favors to particular groups and individuals, and that it violated what seemed to be an elemental principle of equity, namely, that people with approximately equal net incomes should pay approximately equal taxes.

There were two general sets of facts that convinced me that there were great abuses within our federal tax system.

The first was that only about half of the total personal income in the country was subject to taxation, while the other half completely escaped being levied on. The basic exemption of $600 a person accounted for only a fraction of this latter amount. The remainder was income that most people believed was taxable, but that was exempted in reality by a series of devices.

Then we discovered and got the Treasury to confirm that in every year there were a considerable number of persons with annual incomes of over $500,000 who paid no taxes at all. As we gathered evidence we found this number would never fall below 25 and sometimes went above 30. We also found an even greater number with huge incomes who paid less than 10 or 15 percent.

We found that the averages paid by the groups

Excerpted and reprinted from Paul H. Douglas, "The Problem of Tax Loopholes," *The American Scholar* (Winter 1967–1968), pp. 21–43. By permission of the author.

Paul H. Douglas is former U.S. Senator from Illinois.

with incomes above $50,000 was only a fraction of the amount they were presumed to pay, and that the uppermost group with incomes over $250,000, who according to the schedules were presumed to pay nearly 90 percent, actually paid on the average only 25 percent or slightly less. The "effective" rate was therefore far less than the nominal rate.

All this, plus the evidence on specific "loopholes" or "truckholes" that enabled large quantities of income to slip through the tax net, still further convinced me that these abuses should be exposed and curbed.

Out of my experience of nearly two decades in the Congress I have distilled certain facts and conclusions. They show that our tax system is riddled with injustices that violate the simple principle, upon which I would think that all could agree, that people with equal net incomes should pay equal or approximately equal taxes. Whether we believe in progressive, regressive, or proportional taxation, can we not all agree on this elementary principle of horizontal justice?

But this experience of nearly two decades and our relative lack of success also plunged me ever more deeply in a quandary.

When the so-called "Ruml plan" for withholding a basic percentage of the federal income tax from wages and salaries was adopted by Congress, it did not apply the withholding principle to interest and dividends. Such income was, on the contrary, to be reported by the recipient and the taxes were to be paid by him.

The Joint Economic Committee hearings that I held in 1955 showed that while virtually all of the wages and salaries were reported, there were a big volume of interest and an appreciable portion of dividends that were not. It became possible to estimate the size of this gap from the reports published by the Securities and Exchange Commission and by the Treasury. The little liberal group in the Senate, therefore, began to advocate applying the withholding principle, or what the British term "payment at the source" to dividends and interest so that ownership would not receive any more favored treatment than employment.

In 1962, under President Kennedy and Secretary Dillon, the administration adopted this provision. It was clear that in 1959 about $1 billion dollars in dividends and $3 billion dollars in interest were not reported, with a consequent annual loss in taxes of between $900 million and $1 billion. These unreported sums amounted to 8 percent of all dividends and 34 percent of all interest. The proportion of wages and salaries not reported in 1959 came, on the other hand, to only 3 percent. This showed the greater efficiency of the withholding method.

The administration tax bill for 1962, therefore, contained a provision for the automatic deduction and transmission to the Treasury of 20 percent from the total sums credited to dividends and interest without specifying the individuals or their amounts, and then for the filing of claims for any excess to be made periodically by the recipients. The plan was simple and just, and was adopted by the House Ways and Means Committee and by the House itself. I prepared to support it in the Senate Finance Committee and, if necessary, on the floor of the Senate itself.

We had heard rumblings of opposition, but I must admit we were not prepared for the storm that followed. Suddenly, from all over the country, but especially from Illinois, thousands of protests poured into my office. By the end of a month, I had received over sixty-five thousand such letters and other senators had received about as many. Inquiry proved that these had been stimulated by the building and loan associations, whose main national body had launched the campaign from Chicago. The banks also helped in the letter-writing blitz.

These letters showed an extraordinary misconception of the tax. A large proportion hotly attacked the requirement for withholding as the imposition of a completely new and additional tax. They apparently thought that interest either was not income or was so sacred that it should not be taxed. This very fact was in itself eloquent proof of the widespread evasion or avoidance of the tax. It was in vain that in my initial answer I pointed out to these protesters that this was not a new tax but merely a better means of collecting an existing tax that had been widely evaded and avoided, and that their confusion was indeed ample proof of an existing failure to report.

All of my explanations were in vain. No one was convinced. The tide of angry letters continued to pour in. Virtually every senator received thousands, and many counted their letters in the tens of thousands.

The result was inevitable. By a vote of 11 to five, the withholding provision was stricken from the bill in the Finance Committee. Then, on the floor of the Senate, when I moved to restore the clause I was overwhelmingly defeated and mustered only 20 votes.

Here we were deserted by the administration, which evidently decided that the struggle was useless. During the entire battle, the academic profession of economists was all but silent, so that I felt that the issue had been allowed to die on an economic Berlin Wall without a hand ever being raised to help.

What then were the real reasons for this apparently illogical opposition? I think they were the following: A very large proportion of those who had savings accounts in the banks and shares in the building and loan institutions never drew out in cash the annual interest that accumulated on their accounts but allowed it to be added automatically to their principal. Many of these savers were sufficiently naïve not to realize fully that this increase in their capital holdings came from income. They seemed to think it came from spontaneous generation. The banks and building and loan associations, of course, knew what was happening, but they also realized that a large share of the growth in their savings deposits was due to the accumulation of compound interest, and they did not want to have this increment of growth diminished by the amount of the tax. They had the use of the funds of which the federal government was deprived, and they wanted to hold on to them.

I left this battle with a wry taste in my mouth.

My biggest and longest battle was, however, over the worst abuse of all, namely the 27.5 percent depletion allowance on gas and oil. Billions of dollars are at stake here, and a little explanation of the present tax procedures in the oil industry is appropriate. The oil industry already had certain tax favors that I did not question. For example, I did not raise any objection to granting the industry the right to charge off in the first year all the "intangible" drilling and development costs. These so-called "developmental costs" comprise from 75 to 90 percent of the total exploratory and drilling costs and were granted the fastest of all rates of accelerated depreciation—namely, a complete write-off in the initial year. Men in the industry who were secretly in favor of my stand (and there are a few) have repeatedly assured me that this is an even more important special favor than the depletion allowance itself.

I determined to concentrate on the 27.5 percent depletion allowance. This exempted from taxation 27.5 percent of all gross income in the oil and gas industry up to 50 percent of net income, and it did this without any limitation as to the length of time for which this exemption was to continue or the ratio of the tax rebate to the original investment.

This provision had been inserted in our tax laws during the 1920s when the corporation income tax was only 14 percent of net profits, and when the total amount of the tax privilege thus conferred was not overwhelming, say, about 7 percent of the profits. But it continued to be retained after the corporate tax had risen to 52 percent and when the depletion allowance could and commonly did cut in half the taxes paid by this rich industry. Moreover, it had spawned a series of similar exemptions: sulfur had been granted a 23-percent exemption, and a number of minerals, including coal, had been allowed a 15-percent depletion grant. This exemption had been further broadened by a 5-percent rate on clam and oyster shells, as well as on sand and gravel—although there was no danger of "dry holes" or unsuccessful explorations in these cases! Every mineral had come to be included.

We ultimately got the Treasury to tell us how much these exemptions amounted to, and their report was that in the late fifties and early sixties the total came to about $3.5 billion annually with the Treasury losing about $1.5 billion. Today it is undoubtedly much more.

Long before this, however, I had prepared a counterproposal which I tried out in committee and on the floor nearly every year.

This was to introduce a sliding scale allowance

that would amount to granting the existing 27.5 percent on the first million dollars of annual gross income but decreasing this to 21.2 percent on gross incomes of between $1 and $5 million and then having it fall to 15 percent on all incomes over $5 million. This would have yielded in the earlier years from $350 to $400 million a year in revenue, while in later years the gain would have been around $500 million annually. Today it would probably be still more.

I justified this differential between small and large operators on the ground that the smaller operators were not able to distribute their risks to the same degree as the big operators and companies. Their fewer drillings exposed them, therefore, to higher risks.

I must confess, however, that I also hoped that this compromise would help to split off the small operators from the huge companies and make it more possible to pass the measure. In this, I was disappointed. Although there were only two or three concerns in Illinois that had gross in excess of a million dollars, nearly all of the small operators lined up behind the big companies and in bitter opposition to me. They were the dominant economic interest in one congressional district covering the southeastern section of the state. Most of them insisted that I was proposing to cut their allowance to 15 percent, although this was, of course, not the case. No explanation was effective, although finally the more knowledgeable would privately admit that while they understood that they would not be hurt, for the sake of industry solidarity they must oppose the Douglas amendment and me personally. Despite all their efforts and the oil money that came into the state in the 1954 and 1960 election campaigns, I had been able to beat off their attacks, and had even carried the oil district. Their opposition continued, however, and in the Senate I had no such luck.

Despite all the propaganda and the pressures, there was a heroic group of senators who stood firm. Once we got as many as 38 votes, but later we slumped to 20. Calling for a roll-call vote was in a sense like marching brave troops into the valley of political death and reducing the number of public-spirited soldiers. Therefore, toward the end of the long bitter struggle, I would agree to a voice, rather than a roll-call, vote in order to shield our secret supporters.

Some of us have been effectively disposed of; more probably will be; but the issue remains. And as one who still believes (perhaps foolishly) that in a democracy no issue is settled until it is settled right, and that in the long run an educated public opinion will prevail, I remain guardedly hopeful. I am grateful to other senators, as we all should be, for keeping the issue alive, and I pray that they may succeed where others of us have failed.

The third great abuse lies in the field of the capital gains tax. Here the profits realized from the sale of a capital asset that has been held for longer than 6 months are taxed, when sold, at only one-half the income tax rate, but in no case at more than 25 percent. Moreover, the amounts not taxed are not counted as "taxable income," and hence do not appear in the statistics issued by the Treasury Department. Like the murdered victims of the criminal syndicate, they, with the oil and mineral depletion allowances, are given an anonymous burial so that even the buried bodies disappear.

Philip Stern estimated in 1962 that this favored treatment shrunk the tax base by $6 billion a year and cost the Treasury $2.4 billion annually. But this is only the beginning. An even greater leakage occurs when property is bequeathed. Let us take the case of a father who buys property for $100,000 during his lifetime, which by the time of his death is worth $1 million, or $900,000 more. His son inherits the estate and a year later sells this same property for $1,100,000. He will pay a capital gains tax only on the $100,000 that has accrued during his ownership, while the $900,000 gain inherited from his father not only will go tax free but will be unrecorded. Stern estimates that from $12 to $13 billion thus escape taxation every year and that the Treasury annually loses an approximate added $2.9 billion.

It was such injustices in the capital gains system (and not such incidental absurdities as giving capital gains treatment to the raising of cattle but not to chickens and turkeys) that most outraged me.

To deal with the untaxed capital gains during a testator's lifetime, I proposed collection at the time of ultimate sale, but, of course, with a deduction or tax credit given for all inheritance taxes paid in the meantime on the property. In other words, if a total inheritance tax of $50,000 had been levied on this property, this would be deducted dollar for dollar from the tax ultimately realized on the capital gains.

And if it be objected that to tax capital gains in years of bunched income would be inequitable, I constantly made it clear that I would agree to lengthen this period to any proper degree. This would reduce the total of the super-taxes that would be paid. But such conciliatory motions were overwhelmingly defeated in committee and on the floor.

Another persistent loophole is the exemption from federal taxation of the interest on the bonds of state and local governments. This exemption was first enacted because of the fear that such a tax would be held unconstitutional by the courts, and also by a desire to make the financing of capital improvements easier for the state and local governments. That it has helped in the latter direction is shown by the fact that while high-grade municipals are still much less safe than federal issues, their yield in March of 1967 was a full percentage point below the latter, namely, 3.5 instead of 4.5 percent. Without this tax advantage, the municipalities would probably have had to pay at least 4.75-percent interest and possibly 5 percent in order to float their loans. Since the total outstanding bonds issued by the state and local governments amount to approximately $100 billion, the total in interest that is saved for these bodies probably comes to somewhere around $1.25 to $1.5 billion a year.

Such tax-free issues, however, become tax havens or sanctuaries for men and women in the upper income and tax brackets. If the federal government were to pay in outright subsidy to the local government to compensate for these lost tax benefits, this would still net at least a half million dollars a year for the federal government. It might indeed net more since the interest rate, and hence the total interest payments on state and municipals, would rise. Assuming that the total interest could increase to $4.5 billion, at an average tax rate of 50 percent, this could net $2.25 billion or a billion dollars more than the compensating subsidy. Unless some such action is taken, the amount of lost income will probably increase as retired men and women of wealth seek these privileged sanctuaries.

The depreciation allowances on buildings are computed on the money cost of the property to the last purchase and not on the book value of the physical structure of the building itself. Thus if a man constructs an office building at a cost of $5 million, he can take accelerated depreciation for several years and use this as a credit against the net income from that property, or any other property that he may own. At 5 percent a year, he would thus get a credit of $250,000. If his net income from the building was $200,000, this would mean that he would pay no taxes and would have an additional credit, to be carried over, of $50,000. This could go on for at least 5 years, when the accelerated depreciation amounting to approximately $1.7 million would have to be greatly reduced. But office buildings enhance somewhat in value during the first year of occupancy, and it would be quite possible to sell the property for $5 million or more instead of the depreciated book value of approximately $3,300,000. The original owner would pay a capital gains tax only on the $1.7 million profit made from selling at above book value, although he had used his depreciation allowance to reduce his higher regular income tax rate.

The newcomer could, however, start taking his double depreciation on his $5-million purchase price instead of on the $3.3 million of book value. This, as a matter of fact, would be an important reason why he would pay the full $5 million.

After a few years a third comer might even be willing to pay $5 million, although the $3.4 million taken for depreciation might have left but $1.6 million of the original cost of $5 million.

This process could be kept up almost interminably, with the ultimate total amounts deducted for depreciation far exceeding the original cost. This practice also puts a premium upon a frequent change of ownership, which is especially injurious in the case of tenements. We would save many hundreds of millions of dollars of taxes if depreciation were to be computed upon the book value of the building rather than upon the purchase price paid, and so that the total taken could not exceed the original cost or possibly the original cost plus replacements. It is true that double depreciation in the early years was eliminated for housing in the 1964 act, but the so-called "sum of the years" method gives substantially the same result, and the earlier provision has since been restored. Since all this is computed on the money cost of the building to the present owner, this is a stimulus to frequent changes of ownership. And this in turn leads to added neglect.

The depreciation allowance is, moreover, divorced from the performance of any major replacement or repairs. It would be better if the average depreciation rate were to be lowered from 2.5 to 2 percent or less, thus assuming a life of 50 years or more rather than 40, for the structure, and then to provide additional allowances for those major repairs and replacements to the degree that they are made subject to a maximum allowance in any one year or over a span of years. This would be a mighty stimulus for owners to keep houses in repair and would lessen the tendency for them to deteriorate.

During our consideration of one of the major tax bills a seemingly innocent provision was inserted that later turned out to be a Trojan horse. This was to exempt from taxation all future "charitable" contributions if in 8 of the past 10 years 90 percent of the *taxable* income had either been given to charity or paid in taxes. There were two booby traps carefully concealed within this seemingly public-spirited provision that was represented as an encouragement to private charity. I confess I was fooled by them. The first is that it is only 90 percent of the *taxable* income that is counted, and not 90 percent of the real income. By exempting capital gains income and "depletion income," which is not taxed, the proportion of income actually given away can be, and frequently is, only a small fraction of the actual real income. It is therefore especially popular among the oil barons of the Southwest.

The second joker is that by creating "personal foundations" the donor can retain control of those properties that he is apparently giving away and have the income spent in accordance with his wishes and frequently to his profit.

Congressman Wright Patman has unearthed many of the abuses perpetrated by these "foundations." And it is significant that the unlimited charitable deduction ranks alongside the depletion allowance, the fast write-off of drilling and developmental costs, and the capital gains privileges as an important reason why so many men with huge incomes pay small taxes, or none at all.

I began my senatorial career in a quandary, and when I left, the quandary was even bigger than when I started. It was this: Can and will the people under the best system of government in the world, and with an able and high-minded Congress, ever be able to protect the public interest in tax matters and enforce equal justice for all?

I must admit that the 18 years have, on the surface, been disillusioning. We have made a few improvements during that time and may have saved a billion dollars or more a year, but the big loopholes and truckholes remain. Indeed, new ones have been opened, sometimes over our opposition and sometimes, as I have pointed out, without our knowledge. I daresay that there may be still other financial timebombs, presumably concealed in innocent-sounding verbiage, which will turn out to free still more income from taxation. The summing up that Philip Stern gave in his *The Great Treasury Raid* is substantially true today.

> For a raid of its magnitude, the time (high noon) and setting (the United States Treasury, a stone's throw from the White House) showed a breath-taking boldness of design and planning. From out of nowhere, it seemed, they appeared—old people and young, rich and poor, an oil millionaire here, a factory worker there, a real estate tycoon, a working mother, several well-known movie stars, some corporation presidents, even the chairman of a powerful congressional committee. It was a mixed lot, all right, that converged on the Treasury Building that high noon. Into the building they strolled, gloriously nonchalant. No one stopped them, not a guard looked up to question them. Quickly and quietly they found their way to the vaults; opened them noiselessly with the special passkeys each had brought with him. Like clockwork, with split-second timing, each went to his

appointed spot, picked up a bag and walked out as calmly as he had entered. At the exits the guards sat motionless. At precisely 12:04 it was all over. Each of the "visitors" had vanished into thin air.

So had forty billion dollars from the United States Treasury.

Despite all our efforts, the brutal fact must be admitted. We have largely failed.

Is the fault then in the structure of our economic life, "in our stars," so to speak, or in ourselves, that so little progress has been made?

It used to be said by some that the trouble with democracy is that the ablest and best educated men and women in the country do not take part in political affairs, but that if they would only interest themselves more in public matters they would set matters right.

But it has been the extremely able who have inserted these loopholes in the tax laws. The loopholes and even more, the truckholes, are defended against elimination or lessening by other extremely able men. The large hearing room of the Finance Committee seats 150 persons. When we considered a tax bill, the room was filled with prosperous lawyers, graduates of great universities and of the top-ranking law schools all working to hold what they and their clients had and to enlarge it.

One major trouble with our tax system is, therefore, precisely this: that these "best minds" in the country have largely worked to make it what it is. Not more than one out of every hundred citizens actively working on a tax bill is trying to represent the general interest. And in the halls outside the hearing rooms the lobbyists are as thick as flies, while the publicity men and noisemakers are busily at work in Washington and elsewhere. In the halls of academe, erudite professors train their students in the intricacies of the tax code so that their students may succeed in the private practice of law by helping wealthy clients avoid taxes and thus beat the government of the people.

All this raises the question whether this is a fundamental weakness of our democratic system, namely, that the producing and possessing interests are compact, powerful and well-organized, while the consuming and nonpossessing classes are busy with other things, and their interests diffused; and that while the people are numerically more numerous, they are collectively weak, ignorant, and unorganized. Does it follow that in a conflict between these two groups it is almost invariably the more powerful that wins?

As I watched the struggle and indeed took part in it for nearly two decades, I was struck with the similarity between it and the way the Spaniards were able to take over Mexico, Peru, and indeed all of Latin America, as narrated by William H. Prescott in his two classic histories, the *Conquest of Mexico* and the *Conquest of Peru.*

There were about thirteen million Indians in Mexico whereas there were only about five hundred Spaniards under Cortes. But the Spaniards wore armor, and they had gunpowder and powerful harquebuses, while the Indians were largely unarmed and unprotected. The Spaniards had horses, which gave them mobility, which the Indians did not have. They were, moreover, under tight discipline and moved as one, whereas the Indians were torn by internal dissension and overawed by the proud and arrogant newcomers.

So it sometimes seemed to me in these tax battles. A particular measure would mean millions to a few, but only a few cents to each of the two hundred million Americans. It was hard for the individual citizen to become informed. Even if he knew what was at stake, he was busy earning a living for his family and could not interrupt his work to defend his infinitesimal interest. Leisure, moreover, has its proper claims as well. So only a minute fraction can enlist in the common cause, and they can only do so at great risk to themselves. This in itself is a preventive to action.

Everywhere one finds powerful groups moving in to extract special privileges from our society, and they always seem to be able to attract to their cause skilled lawyers, technical experts, economists, publicity men and public relations practitioners, who then use their brains and wiles to promote the fortunes of their employers. Meanwhile the main mass of the general public and even of the academic profession stand by as mere spectators and allow without protest the power juggernauts to conquer. They behave indeed like so many city spectators who watch crimes being committed without raising a hand to defend the victims or lifting their voices to call the police.

To me this was and is a sign of the disintegration of a society that has lost sight of its common purpose.

This is what deepened my quandary.

The query is appropriate: where are the champions of the people? Where are the men, better and more effective than we who have tried and lost, coming from?

I do not know. But I am an optimist. I cannot believe that the people with all their weaknesses will allow the noble ship of democratic government to be taken over by these well-clad pirates with impeccable credentials. For if they do, there may ultimately be such disillusion with our form of government as to cause the people in frustration to abandon ship and to allow it to be taken over by a still worse group of tyrants, who will suppress our liberties and shut the gates of mercy on mankind.

TAX EXPENDITURES AND TAX REFORM

STANLEY S. SURREY

The present federal income tax is replete with tax subsidy provisions. Some were adopted to assist particular industries, business activities, or financial transactions. Others were adopted to encourage nonbusiness activities considered socially useful, such as contributions to charity. Moreover, suggestions are constantly being made that many of our pressing national problems can be solved, or partially met, through the use of income tax subsidies.

Since 1969 the list of these tax subsidies has grown larger with both the Treasury Department itself, forces within the Congress, and outside groups pushing new subsidies into the tax system. The major part of the permanent changes in the income tax provided by the 1971 act—both as to revenue and space in the tax law—involved new subsidies. Thus, the 1971 act introduced the following income tax subsidies: restoration of the 7 percent investment credit; a class life system for depreciation of machinery and equipment, currently based on the use of the thirtieth percentile experience as of 1962 (starting at the shorter pole); abandonment of a reserve ratio test requiring attention to a taxpayer's own experience, and with permission to the Treasury to grant a 20 percent shorter class life; a preferential treatment of income from exporting (DISC), which in practical operation will exempt one-half of that income from tax; 5-year amortization for the construction of facilities for employer on-the-job training programs and child care facilities; a large increase in the child care deduction, including household expenses; a tax credit to employers who employ persons certified by the secretary of labor as having been placed in employment under work incentive programs (WIN); a tax credit and deduction for political campaign contributions. It should be added, to indicate the extent to which the 1971 bill involved tax subsidies, that the Conference Committee on that bill rejected the follow-

Excerpted and reprinted from a statement of Stanley S. Surrey in *The Federal Subsidy System,* Hearings of the Joint Economic Committee, U.S. Congress, January 1972.

Stanley S. Surrey is Jeremiah Smith Professor of Law at Harvard Law School, Cambridge, Massachusetts.

ing Senate-passed subsidies: a system of credits and rebates for post-secondary school education; a tax credit for elderly persons for property taxes on their residences or rent constituting property taxes; an extra personal exemption for disabled persons; a 10 percent credit for investments in rural or central city job development assets.

The 1971 tax legislation was thus dominated by the aspect of tax subsidies. It is not a coincidental but a direct result of this influence that the 1971 Tax Act is one of the least creditable revenue measures in many a decade and one that considerably weakens the fairness and structure of the income tax. It can generally be said that less critical analysis is paid to these tax subsidies than to almost any direct expenditure program one can mention. The tax subsidies tumble into the law without supporting studies, being propelled instead by clichés, debating points, and scraps of data and tables that are passed off as serious evidence. A tax system that is so vulnerable to this injection of extraneous, costly, and ill-considered expenditure programs is in a precarious state from the standpoint of the basic tax goals of providing adequate revenues and maintaining tax equity. It is therefore imperative that the process and substance of these tax subsidies be reexamined.

THE NATURE AND EXTENT OF EXISTING TAX SUBSIDIES—THE TAX EXPENDITURE BUDGET

The Tax Expenditure Budget

The federal income tax system consists really of two parts: one part comprises the structural provisions necessary to implement the income tax on individual and corporate net income; the second part comprises a system of tax expenditures under which governmental financial assistance programs are carried out through special tax provisions rather than through direct governmental expenditures. The second system is simply grafted on to the structure of the income tax proper; it has no basic relation to that structure and is not necessary to its operation. Instead, the system of tax expenditures provides a vast subsidy apparatus that uses the mechanics of the income tax as the method of paying the subsidies. The special provisions under which this subsidy apparatus functions take a variety of forms, covering exclusions from income, exemptions, deductions, credits against tax, preferential rates of tax, and deferrals of tax. The Tax Expenditure Budget, included herein as Table 1, identifies and quantifies the existing tax expenditures. This Tax Expenditure Budget is essentially an enumeration of the present "tax incentives" or "tax subsidies" contained in our income tax system.

The list of these tax expenditures here used for the purposes of discussion (Table 1) is based on that drawn by the Treasury for the fiscal year 1969, but brought up to date. I have underlined with dashes the additions made by the 1969 reform act and with a dotted line those made by the 1971 act. The estimates are generally at 1971 levels, with various asterisks indicating reductions and increases. These notations are explained briefly in a footnote. These tax expenditures include both tax subsidies (or tax incentives) and individual welfare items (such as old-age assistance).

The items in this Tax Expenditure Budget total between \$55 to \$60 billion, equal to one-fourth of the regular budget. Yet most of these items seem almost to live a life of their own, undisturbed and unexamined. No agency studies or controls them. The Budget Bureau neglects them, for the items are not in its budget. The executive departments likewise are not concerned, for the items are not in their program. The Treasury is apparently not evaluating them, but rather is adding new and indefensible items. This is clearly no way to run a tax system and no way to run a budget policy.

Some Uses of the Tax Expenditure Budget

I turn now from the Tax Expenditure Budget itself to the uses to which such a budget may be put. For what purposes of tax policy is it a useful tool? For what purposes of expenditure policy is it a useful tool? What questions does it help us to

TABLE 1. Tax Expenditures: Fiscal Year 1971 (in millions of dollars)

By Budget Function		Expenditure
National Defense		
Exclusion of benefits and allowances to armed forces personnel		500
International Affairs and Finance		
Exemption for certain income earned abroad by United States citizens		40
Western Hemisphere trade corporations		50
Exclusion of gross-up on dividends of less-developed country corporations		55
Exclusion of controlled foreign subsidiaries		165
Exclusion of income earned in United States possessions		90
*** Partial exemption of export income (DISC)		170[a]
	TOTAL	570
Agriculture and Rural Development		
* Farming: expensing and capital gain treatment		820
Timber: capital gain treatment for certain income		130
	TOTAL	950
Natural Resources		
Expensing of exploration and development costs		325
* Excess of percentage over cost depletion		980
* Capital gains treatment of royalties on coal and iron ore		5
** Five-year amortization of pollution control facilities in pre-1969 plants		120[a]
** Five-year amortization of coal mine safety equipment		1[a]
	TOTAL	1,431
Commerce and Transportation		
*** Investment credit		3,600[a]
* Excess depreciation on buildings (other than rental housing)		500
Dividend exclusion		280
* Capital gains: corporation (other than agriculture and natural resources)		425
* Excess bad debt reserves of financial institutions		380
Exemption of credit unions		40
Deductibility of interest on consumer credit		1,700
Expensing of research and development expenditures		540
* $25,000 surtax exemption		2,000
Deferral of tax on shipping companies		10
** Five-year amortization of railroad rolling stock		105
*** Class lives for depreciation—20% reduction		2,400
	TOTAL	11,980
Community Development and Housing		
Deductibility of interest on mortgages on owner-occupied homes		2,800
Deductibility of property taxes on owner-occupied homes		2,900
* Excess depreciation on rental housing		255
** Five-year amortization of housing rehabilitation expenditures		330[a]
* Deferral of capital gain on sale to occupants of capital low-income housing		n.a.
	TOTAL	6,285

Explanation: The items underlined with dashes (– – –) were added by the 1969 act. The items underscored with dots (. . .) were added by the 1971 act. The items marked with a single asterisk (*) involve reductions under the 1969 act, as explained below. The items marked with a double asterisk (**) involve increases under the 1969 act, as explained below. The items marked with a triple asterisk (***) involve increases under the 1971 act. The items marked with a quadruple asterisk (****) involve de-

By Budget Function		Expenditure
Income Security		
Disability insurance benefits		130
** Provisions relating to aged, blind, and disabled: compiled cost for exemption for aged, retirement income credit, and exclusion of Social Security payments		2,950
** Additional exemption for blind		10
"Sick pay" exclusion		105
Exclusion of unemployment insurance benefits		400
Exclusion of workmen's compensation benefits		210
Exclusion of public assistance benefits		50
Treatment of pension plans:		
Plans for employees		3,075
Plans for self-employed persons		175
Exclusion of other employee benefits:		
Premiums on group term life insurance		440
Deductibility of accident and death benefits		25
Privately financed supplementary unemployment benefits		20
Meals and lodging		170
Exclusion of interest on life insurance savings		1,050
* Deductibility of charitable contributions (other than education)		3,550
*** Deductibility of child and dependent care and household expenses		145[a]
Deductibility of casualty losses		80
** Standard deduction		3,000
****	TOTAL	15,585
Health		
Deductibility of medical expenses		1,700
Exclusion of medical insurance premiums and medical care		1,450
	TOTAL	3,150
Education and Manpower		
** Additional personal exemption for students		500
* Deductibility of contributions to educational institutions		200
Exclusion of scholarships and fellowships		60
*** Five-year amortization of employer child care and on-the-job training facilities		n.a.
*** Credit for employment of public assistance recipient under WIN Program		25[a]
	TOTAL	785
Veterans benefits and services		
Exclusion of certain benefits		650
Aid to state and local governments		
*** Exemption of interest on state and local debt		2,300
Deductibility of nonbusiness state and local taxes (other than on owner-occupied homes)		5,600
	TOTAL	7,900
Election Process		
*** Credit and deduction for political contributions		90[a]
The 1968 Treasury Table contained the following:		
**Capital Gains—Individual Income Tax*		
Special provisions (increase in basis at death, exclusion of one-half of long-term gains; maximum tax rates of 25% on long-term gains)		5,500–8,500

creases under the 1971 act. The estimates marked with (a) are for fiscal years other than 1971, n.a. indicates not available.

Source: Statement of Hon. Murray L. Weidenbaum, assistant secretary of the treasury, reprinted in *Annual Report of the Secretary of the Treasury on the State of the Finances, Fiscal Year 1970*, p. 306–308, and table in *Congressional Record*, S18764, November 16, 1971 giving 1971 data.

formulate and ask? What questions does it help us to answer?

The Tax Expenditure Budget enables us to look at the income tax provisions reflected in that budget in a new light. Once these tax provisions are seen not as inherent parts of an income tax structure but as carrying out programs of financial assistance for particular groups and activities, a number of questions immediately come into focus. Once we see that we are not evaluating technical tax provisions but rather expenditure programs, we are able to ask the traditional questions and use the analytical tools that make up the intellectual apparatus of expenditure experts.

We thus can put the basic question of whether we desire to provide that financial assistance at all, and if so in what amount—a stock question any budget expert would normally ask of any item in the regular budget. We can inquire whether the program is working well, how its benefits compare with its costs, is it accomplishing its objectives—indeed, what are its objectives? Who is actually being assisted by the program and is that assistance too much or too little? Again, these are stock questions directed by any budget expert at existing programs. They all equally must be asked of the items and programs in the Tax Expenditure Budget.

The fact that the Tax Expenditure Budget summarizes an "expenditure system described in tax language" adds, however, a new dimension to these traditional questions. Each program in that budget is carried out through a special tax provision. The financial assistance which the program grants is thus determined through the effect of that special provision on the tax liabilities of the persons benefited. And also, since the persons benefited are only those within the ambit of the income tax system, the program's assistance is confined to taxpayers and does not extend to nontaxpayers. Individuals whose income amounts are below personal exemption levels, businesses that are losing money rather than making profits, organizations that are tax exempt, being nontaxpayers thus do not receive the assistance. As a consequence, before we analyze the tax expenditure program, we must first translate the tax language into expenditure results.

Thus, consider the tax expenditure program for housing represented by the deductibility of mortgage interest and property taxes paid on owner-occupied homes, listed as an item under Community Development and Housing. This is a program of assistance estimated at about $5.7 billion (fiscal 1971). The translation of the tax language in which the program is framed and the assistance provided—a *deduction* in computing taxable income—tells us first that the wealthier the individual the greater is his assistance under the program. This is because the higher the individual's income and thus the higher the individual's income tax rate, the larger is the tax benefit—the tax reduction—brought about by the deduction. A deduction of $100 in mortgage interest or $100 in property tax is "worth" $70 to a taxpayer in the 70-percent top bracket—i.e., is financial assistance of $70. But it is "worth" only $14 to a taxpayer in the first bracket of 14 percent. As a consequence of this method of providing assistance, about 70 percent of the $5.7 billion of this financial assistance for owner-occupied homes goes to individuals with incomes of over $10,000. The translation next tells us that an individual or family whose income is so low that they are not required to pay an income tax—their income being below their personal exemptions and low income allowance—does not receive any financial assistance, for deductions benefit only taxpayers and not nontaxpayers. The translation also tells us that there is no limit placed on the size or value of the homes to be assisted nor on the number of residences for which a taxpayer may receive assistance, for the deduction is simply in terms of mortgage interest and property taxes paid.

The process of translation thus gives us the contours of the tax expenditure program for housing—contours that are quite different from the housing assistance programs formulated in direct expenditure terms. But the contrast—and hence the nature of the task of analysis in expenditure terms—can only be appreciated after the translation is made. It is only then that we can really ask the crucial question of how does this tax expenditure program measure up as an "expenditure" program. For then we can restate the tax program as a direct expenditure program and ask whether such a program represents a desirable policy.

The translation and consequent restatement of a tax expenditure program in direct expenditure terms generally show an upside-down result utterly at variance with usual expenditure policies. Thus, if cast in direct expenditure language, the present assistance for owner-occupied homes under the tax deductions for mortgage interest and property taxes would look as follows, envisioned as a HUD program:

> For a married couple with more than $200,000 in income, HUD would, for each $100 of mortgage interest on the couple's home, pay $70 to the bank holding the mortgage, leaving the couple to pay $30. It would also pay a similar portion of the couple's property tax to the state or city levying the tax.
>
> For a married couple with income of $10,000, HUD would pay the bank on the couple's mortgage $19 per each $100 interest unit, with the couple paying $81. It would also pay a similar portion of the couple's property tax to the state or city levying the tax.
>
> For a married couple too poor to pay an income tax, HUD would pay nothing to the bank, leaving the couple to pay the entire interest cost. The couple would also have to pay the entire property tax.

One can assume that no HUD Secretary would ever have presented to Congress a direct housing program with this upside-down effect.

Other illustrations exist—in fact almost any of these tax subsidies is seen as woefully unfair or inefficient when cast as a direct expenditure program. Thus, the 1969 tax legislation contained a tax incentive for the rehabilitation of low-income housing, using the device of 5-year amortization of capital expenditures which otherwise would be depreciated over a longer period. This device, which was proposed by the Treasury Department, has these interesting effects for individual taxpayers: for a taxpayer in the 70-percent bracket, the benefit is the equivalent of a 19-percent investment credit (assuming an expenditure with a 20-year life and discount rate of 10 percent); for a taxpayer in the 20-percent bracket it is the equivalent of a 5-percent credit. In terms of interest costs on a loan made for rehabilitation purposes, the benefit of 5-year amortization is equivalent for the 70-percent bracket taxpayer to reducing an 8-percent interest charge to 3-percent; for the 20-percent-bracket taxpayer it is equivalent to reducing the 8-percent charge to 7 percent. Besides having this upside-down effect, the rehabilitation incentive is probably a waste of government money all around. It is not likely to increase the amount of rehabilitated housing over what would be accomplished through the existing HUD direct subsidy alone, so that the tax incentive will just make some wealthy people more wealthy.

It is tax incentives like this rehabilitation provision that produce the various "tax shelters" being marketed by investment houses for upper-bracket individuals. These tax shelters—through fast tax write-offs for investment in low-income housing, oil drilling, leasing of equipment, and farming—are responsible for many of the cases in which these individuals pay little or no income tax. The tax shelters are as inefficient as they are unfair. Thus the tax benefits for investment in low-income housing result in the Treasury's paying the investor $1 in tax benefits so that he will in turn pay the developer seventy cents—a 140-percent commission. But generous commissions paid by the Treasury are not unusual in this tax subsidy world. The Treasury also pays $1 in tax benefits to a top-bracket taxpayer who buys a tax-exempt bond so that he will pass along seventy-five cents in interest rate benefits to the state or city issuing the bond—a 133-percent commission.

These unfairnesses and inefficiencies cannot be escaped when the tax system is being used to pay the financial assistance provided by the government. A recent example is the 1971 act provision for political contributions. The $100 deduction (on a joint return) for political contributions, or alternative tax credit of one-half of the contribution up to a maximum credit of $25 (on a joint return), added in 1971, in effect bars individuals below the taxable levels from participating in the allocation of government funds to their candidates. Thus, the credit approach in effect means that if a taxpayer sends $25 to a candidate, then the government will also send $25 to the candidate—the effect of allowing a tax credit of $25 for a contribution of $50. But if individuals below these taxable levels—perhaps

25 to 30 percent of the electorate—contribute any money, the government refuses to match those funds.

The deduction for charitable contributions, the tax device used to provide government assistance to philanthropy, is another example. This deduction translated into direct expenditure terms would look like this, envisioned as an HEW program:

> We propose to establish a Division of Charitable and Educational Assistance which will distribute its funds as follows:
>
> Suppose a person calls and says: "I am too poor to pay an income tax but I am contributing $15 to my favorite charity. Will the government also help it?" The answer here will be: "We appreciate your sacrifice but we cannot use our funds in this situation."
>
> Suppose a person calls and says: "I am quite well-off and want to send a check for $3000 to one of my favorite charities. Will the Government also aid it?" The answer here will be: "We are delighted to be of assistance and are at once sending a government check for $7000 to that charity."
>
> Suppose a person calls and says: "I am really very wealthy with a considerable fortune in various stocks that originally cost me or my family very little. In fact, I will be selling about $2 million of stock to pay my income tax this year and to raise cash for other purposes as well. I think that a particular charitable institution deserves support and while I have decided not to contribute anything myself, I am calling to inquire whether the government will contribute to it." The answer here will be: "We understand the situation and will be delighted to contribute $2 million to that institution. We will of course say it is in your name. And, in appreciation of your suggesting this to us, we are sending you a check for $100,000, tax-exempt of course."
>
> Finally, if a person makes application to the Office for Private Foundations and says he is establishing a foundation which he will direct and manage, with the advice of his wife and one or two friends, and is contributing, say, $1 million in cash to it, then the government will send him funds in the amount of $2.3 million to be placed in the foundation, also under his control. (We have discontinued the system under which if the person paid his income tax or obtained cash for other purposes by selling appreciated stock, we would fund the entire foundation for him and then give him a payment, itself tax-exempt, for thinking of the idea.)

While this direct expenditure mechanism would mirror the tax expenditure approach, the latter was never consciously designed to operate in the manner that has emerged. Rather it grew up that way without the government or philanthropy really thinking through its implications.

This examination and translation of tax expenditure items would force the exploration of possible direct expenditure programs as alternatives to accomplish the same overall financial assistance goal. The exploration would seek to ascertain if such direct expenditure programs would be more desirable and effective vehicles for providing that assistance than the existing tax expenditure program. This process would probably be hastened if the tax expenditure items were placed in the regular budget and the funds involved charged to the agencies having the prime responsibility for the program objectives represented by the items. An agency so charged with these tax expenditure funds in its "budget" might well be prompted to see if it liked the results and is willing to stand behind them, in contrast with the present attitude of indifference to the tax expenditure item or perhaps even ignorance of the item of its effects.

THE VARIED APPROACHES NECESSARY TO REPLACE TAX EXPENDITURES WITH DIRECT GOVERNMENTAL ASSISTANCE

The fact that a tax expenditure program can be recast as a direct expenditure program really takes us to the heart of tax reform, for it opens up a new way to consider the entire subject. We can regard a major aspect of income tax reform as involving the reexamination of all of the tax expenditure provisions now contained in the income tax. We should start by examining the list of tax expenditures and seeking to decide which should go and which should remain. In a sense, that of course is what tax reformers have always done, whether they talked in terms of base broadening, elimination of preferences, or needed elimination of loopholes.

The tax expenditure analysis, however, really tells us why that traditional approach is not enough. The analysis helps us to understand why that approach can deal with some problems but why it fails to reach others, as indeed it did as recently as 1969. For tax expenditure analysis conceives of the special provisions—the preferences and loopholes—as government financial assistance comparable to that contained directly in the budget. So viewed, this aspect of tax reform becomes a review of budgetary programs.

The questions then become:

> Which tax programs—which tax expenditures—which tax incentives—which special tax provisions—can simply be dropped without substituting another form of governmental assistance, because on review it is seen that government policies and priorities do not require the expenditure of federal funds for the purposes involved in these items?
>
> Which tax programs cannot be simply dropped—because governmental policies and priorities do require the expenditure of federal funds for the purposes involved—but can be readily changed from tax expenditures to direct expenditures, in a way to achieve an improvement in equity and efficiency?
>
> Which tax programs, in the group which cannot simply be dropped, would have to meet special criteria regarding the structure of the substituted direct expenditure program, so that a change must await the development of the latter program?
>
> Finally, which tax programs function much more efficiently and effectively as tax expenditure programs than as direct expenditures so that any consequent loss in tax equity or strain on the tax structure must yield to the need for the use of the tax system in this special case to carry out a particular government policy?

An overall view of much of the task of tax reform, under this analysis, can therefore be obtained by examining the list of items in the Tax Expenditure Budget in the light of the questions posed earlier. A glance at the list and some general observations may here be helpful.

First, a considerable number of items in the tax expenditure list might be dropped without substituting any alternative program of financial assistance from the government. The additional revenue so obtained could be used for rate reduction, for other tax reduction purposes, or for budgetary purposes. In most of these instances tax history has resulted in a tax expenditure for a group or activity that has no present claim for such governmental assistance. Current budgetary priorities and policies would simply leave the matter to the judgments of the private sector. For these items the pace of tax reform progress is largely measured in political terms.

There are, thus, a number of items as to which it would seem appropriate that the proponents for retention of the tax expenditures should be called upon to make the case for their continuance. Thus, they should be required to demonstrate that, as a matter of national priorities and policies, they should continue to receive financial assistance for the activities involved, and if so, assistance of the magnitude now obtained. I would suggest the following items in the Tax Expenditure Budget (Table 1) could be explored from this standpoint to see if they fall in this first category:

- The items under *International Affairs and Finance*
- Farming under *Agriculture and Rural Development*
- The items under *Natural Resources,* except pollution control facilities and mine safety
- The items under *Commerce and Transportation,* except the investment credit, railroad rolling stock, and perhaps buildings
- Sick pay, interest on life insurance savings, casualty losses, under *Income Security*
- Deduction of gasoline, personal property, and similar taxes under *Aid to State and Local Government*

This listing is based on the previous legislative consideration of these items, and the relevant legislative debates, which largely appear to indicate that other factors, and not a considered congressional judgment that financial assistance is needed, are responsible for their continued presence.

The important point as to these items, however, is that if financial assistance is considered necessary, the items would then generally seem to fall in the next category, encompassing programs where direct financial assistance can readily be structured. Thus, for example, if it is decided that elimination of tax expenditures for natural resources should be accompanied by government assistance in oil and mineral exploration, the direct programs can readily be devised. The same can be said for tax expenditures for farming. Nevertheless, in the 1969 debates on these items the degree of tax change appeared to turn on vote counting and not on the aspect of an alternative assistance program.

Second, a number of tax expenditure items now provide financial assistance for activities as to which it is quite probable that the groups assisted could be expected to sustain the burden of demonstrating the appropriateness of financial assistance. However, analysis of the special tax provisions involved has demonstrated in a number of these situations serious inequities and inefficiencies in the use of the tax system to apply that assistance. Both tax and direct budgetary policy would thus appear to dictate a conversion of some or all of the funds involved from the "tax expenditure budget" to the regular budget. This could be accomplished by the concurrent removal of the special tax provision and the adoption of a direct expenditure program structure to provide whatever financial assistance is appropriate and in the form desired. Any amounts not so converted would simply remain part of general revenue receipts. Tax reform would thus in this category encompass a double-sided program: removal of the special tax provision and simultaneous adoption of a direct expenditure program using the funds made available by the tax change. In the past, tax reform proposals have generally dealt only with the first aspect, and for this reason have been vulnerable to objections by those benefited by the special tax provision that its continuance was vitally needed, as an incentive, subsidy, benefit, assistance, or whatever.

Nearly all of the remaining items in the tax expenditure list appear to fall in this category, with the exception of the few matters discussed later. We are here considering items in which the information of the direct expenditure program would in general not appear to be a difficult matter. Presumably straightforward grant or loan expenditure programs would usually be involved. In some cases somewhat comparable programs presently exist, though usually involving smaller amounts. The important task is to interest the administrative agency having cognizance of the particular field to concern itself with working out the direct expenditure program. It is really unfortunate that up to now these administrative agencies have largely left unexamined the tax expenditure items in their areas, allowing the tax funds to be spent without coordination with their own objectives and programs. In other cases, also unfortunately, they have uncritically joined the benefited groups in defense of the tax programs.

Third, the first two categories cover most of the items in the tax expenditure list. The few that remain appear to impose special requirements that must be incorporated into any alternative program of direct assistance, and thus to lift such programs out of the more usual run of federal assistance programs. In other words, the use of the tax system in these cases provides monetary assistance under criteria or circumstances which, if they must be duplicated in a direct program if it is to replace the tax expenditure, will necessitate some special structuring of that program. We can here include the following:

Exemption of interest on state and local obligations and deductibility of various state and local taxes, under *Aid to State and Local Government,* where the task as to the obligations is to devise a direct subsidy that state and local governments will consider to possess sufficient automaticity and freedom from federal control. The use of a taxable bond issue by state and local governments on which a significant portion of the interest cost is automatically paid by the federal government should here be a suitable approach.

Deduction of charitable and educational contributions, under *Income Security* and *Education and Manpower,* where the task is to devise a direct subsidy that continues private designation of the charitable donee and freedom from federal control. The thinking here is still in the initial stages, with some researchers exploring a system of direct matching grants.

Deduction and credit of political contributions, under *Election Process,* where the task is to devise either a direct subsidy that continues private designation of the political candidates, such as a matching system, or a system of direct government financing of political campaigns without reliance on private funds.

The tax assistance accorded to owner-occupied

homes and rental housing, under *Community Development and Housing*, and perhaps to buildings, under *Commerce and Transportation*. As to owner-occupied housing, the task is to devise a direct subsidy that can replace, for those homeowners for whom assistance is proper, the present tax incentives of the deduction for mortgage interest and property taxes. As to rental housing, the task is to devise an additional direct subsidy for low-income housing—perhaps a direct payment to the developer—to replace the present inefficient and over-generous tax shelter that now exists through the deduction of accelerated depreciation for new housing, 5-year amortization in the case of rehabilitated housing, and other real estate tax benefits. The research here seems to be gathering momentum and the problem could be solved if HUD and the Treasury would recognize their joint responsibilities for the solution.

In a special category, finally, we could probably place the 7-percent investment credit for machinery and equipment, under *Commerce and Transportation*. This is a tax subsidy of broad scope and high visibility, so that its purpose as an incentive is readily apparent. The more important task here is to develop the credit so that it can become a flexible economic tool to be used countercyclically to dampen business demand for credit and funds in a tight money period and to spur investment demand in a slack period. At the same time, care needs to be taken that the existence of this special credit does not become the continuing wedge for those urging the adoption of a whole flock of tax subsidies in other fields where the direct approach is clearly preferable. This has been its history in the past and while the necessary care was taken in the sixties, this so far has not been the case starting in 1969.

In conclusion, the pathways to reform of the present tax expenditure apparatus are reasonably clear. What is needed are research in some areas, the exercise of responsibility by the administrative agencies involved in other areas, leadership toward reform by the Office of Budget and Management and the Treasury Department, and political will to reform on the part of legislators.

TOWARD A PROGRESSIVE FEDERAL TAX SYSTEM

JOSEPH A. PECHMAN

The long list of needed revisions in our federal, state, and local tax system should convince anyone that the reforms now being contemplated will not make a significant change in the progressivity of the system. Congress could, if it wishes, increase the yield of the present tax system by $25 billion a year, an amount that would be sufficient substantially to relieve the tax burdens of the poor and low-income nonpoor and to lower tax rates clear across the board. Instead, the revenue gained from the Tax Reform Act of 1969—a Herculean effort by past standards—was in the neighborhood of $3 billion a year and much of this was used to reduce the taxes of the "middle"-income classes by what amounts to little more than a pittance, while the poor continue to bear much heavier tax burdens.

Excerpted and reprinted from Joseph Pechman, "The Rich, The Poor, and The Taxes They Pay," *The Public Interest,* No. 17 (Fall 1969), pp. 21–43. By permission of National Affairs, Inc. and the author. Copyright © by National Affairs, Inc., 1969.

Joseph Pechman is Director of Economic Studies at The Brookings Institution, Washington, D.C.

According to the Council of Economic Advisers, total taxes of those with incomes below $2,000 amounted to $7.3 billion in 1965, of which $4.2 billion were state and local taxes and $3.1 billion were federal. Those with incomes between $2,000 and $4,000 paid another $11.5 billion consisting of $6.8 billion federal and $4.7 billion state-local taxes. The total tax bill of $18.8 billion of those with incomes below $4,000[1] suggests what regressivity really means in a country collecting taxes amounting to about 31 percent of its GNP.

The classic objection against an attack on tax regressivity has been that there is simply not enough income in the higher classes to do the job. Would a substantial reduction in regressivity require confiscatory rates? To appreciate the magnitudes involved, suppose the federal government decided to refund all general sales, payroll,

[1] It will be recalled that the income definition we are using for 1965 excludes transfer payments. Hence, this $18.8 billion of tax is paid both by poor and nonpoor families and individuals. The poor alone pay about 30 percent of this amount.

and property taxes on housing paid by those who are officially classified as poor. (The remaining taxes are selective excise taxes levied for sumptuary purposes or in lieu of user charges, which could not be refunded in any practical way. After 1969, the poor have been paying very little federal income taxes.) These refunds would amount to about $4 billion—perhaps three-quarters of the total tax burden of the poor and one-sixth of the burden of those with incomes below $4,000—less than what this year's tax reform bill may give away in higher standard deductions and rate reductions.

It might be thought that such a proposal—to lift three-quarters of the tax burden of the poor—is too timid. Why not go further? That indeed could be done, but only as part of a larger redistribution of the tax burden. After all, it is both inequitable and politically impossible to create a noticeable "tax divide" between the poor (a fluid concept, in any case) and the rest of society. To make the tax system progressive, it would not be enough drastically to reduce the tax burden of the poor; the burdens of the near poor and others at the lower end of the income scale would have to be cut simultaneously. Indeed—again on principles of equity and political feasibility—the relief should be diffused upwards until it benefits, say, the lower half of the income distribution (or, more technically, those receiving less than the median income, which is now in excess of $9,000).

There are a number of ways of modifying the tax system to redistribute the tax burden in this way. The most straightforward—and perhaps even the most practical, given the federal system of government in this country—would be to give taxpayers credits against the federal income tax for a declining percentage of the major taxes they now pay to federal, state, and local governments, except for income taxes. Suppose we make refunds to the poor for the general sales, payroll, and property taxes they pay and permit others to claim credits against their federal income taxes for 75 percent of these same taxes if they are in the $2,000 to $4,000 class, 50 percent in the $4,000 to $6,000 class, and 25 percent in the $6,000 to $8,000 class. (Obviously, refunds would be paid to those with credits larger than their federal income taxes.)[2]

Let us further assume that the taxes paid by those with incomes between $8,000 and $10,000 remain the same, and that the revenues needed to pay for the relief below $8,000 would come from those with incomes above $10,000 in proportion to the taxes they now pay. Again, we need not be concerned with the details of how this can be done. It would certainly be more equitable to close the major federal income tax loopholes first and then raise whatever additional revenue is needed by an increase in the rates above $10,000. Either way, the ratio of total taxes to income for any specific income class could be set at the same figure, although the burden *within* each class would be distributed much more equitably if the loopholes were closed first.

It turns out that, in 1965, the credits (and refunds) would have reduced taxes for those with income of less than $8,000 by $19 billion, and this would have required an increase in the taxes paid by those in the $10,000 to $15,000 class from an average of 27 percent to 32 percent and by those above $15,000 from 38 percent to 46 percent, or an average tax increase of about a fifth. The resulting effective rates of tax in this system compare with the rates as they were in 1965 as follows:

TABLE 1. Taxes as Percentage of Income, 1965

Income classes	Present tax system (%)	Alternative tax system (%)
Under $2,000	44	13
$ 2,000–4,000	27	14
4,000–6,000	27	19
6,000–8,000	26	23
8,000–10,000	27	27
10,000–15,000	27	32
15,000 and over	38	46
TOTAL	31	31

Income includes capital gains, but excludes transfer payments.

A glance should convince anyone that this tax system would by no means eradicate taxes at the

[2] In practice, we would probably vary the credits for families of different size, but this is a refinement which need not concern us here.

lower end of the income scale. Most people would regard tax burdens of as much as 13 to 14 percent for those with incomes below $4,000 and 23 percent for those between $6,000 and $8,000 as much too high. Yet, the idea of relieving tax burdens for the lower half of the income distribution even in this relatively modest way is clearly impractical; Congress would face a revolt if it tried to raise taxes on incomes above $10,000 by an average of 20 percent.

Perhaps we exaggerate the difficulties by using 1965 figures? Incomes have risen substantially so that there is much more income to be taxed above $15,000. But state and local taxes have also risen and the degree of regressivity in the tax system has been aggravated. On balance, the rise in incomes has probably been more powerful, but not enough to alter very much the general conclusions that we have reached from the 1965 data.

The prospects for making the tax system progressive are more discouraging when one notes the way Congress usually behaves when it reduces taxes. On the basis of past performance, one can predict with certainty that Congress will not limit income tax reduction to the lowest income classes. In 1964, when federal income taxes were reduced by an average of 20 percent, incomes above $15,000 were given a tax cut of 14 percent. In 1969, much more than the revenue gained from closing the loopholes and repealing the investment credit was given away in tax-rate reductions. Of course, these actions reflect the pressures on the congressmen. The influence of the groups arrayed against a significant redistribution of the tax burden is enormous, and there is no effective lobby for the poor and the near poor.

It may be that, at some distant future date, the well-to-do and the rich will have enough income to satisfy not only their own needs, but also to help relieve the tax burdens of those who are less fortunate. In the meantime, the tax system will continue to disgrace the most affluent nation in the world.

IV. FEDERAL MILITARY SPENDING

INTRODUCTION

In recent years the military budget has been the focus of the most serious attacks on federal government policy. Indeed, the entire debate over national economic priorities has revolved around the appropriateness of an enormous and growing level of military expenditures in the face of serious social problems. Numerous reasons explain why military expenditures have been singled out as the primary example of government waste and inefficiency.

Clearly the most immediate of these reasons is the Vietnam War. That the general revulsion from government which it spawned became concentrated on the military budget is not surprising.

A second reason for the recent attack on the military budget is the series of revelations which indicate that inefficiency and waste of major proportions lies within the $80 billion budget. The mismanagement indicated by cost overruns of over $2 billion on a single weapons system (the C-5A cargo plane), the failure of numerous weapons systems to perform up to specification, and the growing evidence that the government buys "Cadillac" systems when less elaborate designs would be adequate if not superior has convinced taxpayers that military spending is out of control. Few citizens seem inclined to doubt the oft-repeated claim that the military could be leaner and more effective if $10 billion were cut from its annual stated budget.

Finally, because of the circumstances surrounding the revelations of military mismanagement and waste and because of the documentation of deliberate secrecy, propagandizing, and news management by the Pentagon, many people concluded that the budget wasn't the only thing about the military that was out of control.

These realizations have led to substantial inquiries into the structure and performance of the military and the basis for its control over such a sizeable chunk of the nation's resources. Studies have been made of the size of the military establishment and its pervasiveness in the American economy. Inquiries have been made into the process of decision-making in the Pentagon and the federal government and of the forces which seem to drive the military budget inexorably upward. Serious questions have been raised concerning the complex of interrelationships between military contractors, congressional committees, and the military itself, and their effect on the military budget and the uses to which it is put.

Much has been learned from these investigations of military spending, decision-making, and power. While many citizens realize that the military and its budget are large, few recognize the pervasive effect of the military on the United States economy, in all of its aspects. The following list provides some indication of the extent of its economic power.

- Except for the entire economy of the U.S.S.R., the system of military production managed by the Defense Department is the largest planned economy in the world.
- Property owned by the Department of Defense is valued at over $200 billion, which is equal to about 10 percent of total U.S. assets.
- The Department of Defense owns 39 million acres of land, used for military bases, test sites, and storage installations.
- In the late 1960s, the military had 3.5 million uniformed "employees" and 1.2 million civilian employees. They were located at over 2,250 locations, at home and abroad.
- It is estimated that an additional 3 million workers employed in private industry work directly on military production.
- Over 60 percent of all U.S. scientists, engineers, and technicians are employed on research and development efforts supported by the military.

These studies have also revealed much concerning the structure of the decision-making process which determines the size and allocation of the military budget. In particular, the complex web of interaction between military personnel, private contractors, and the members of congressional committees overseeing military spending has become clarified. The exercise of power—both political and economic—by corporations in the struggle for a share in the annual pot of $40 billion of production contracts is an illustration of industrial feudalism. While a handful of very large contractors whose primary source of revenue is defense contracts are highly visible in this process, it is less widely recognized that over 15,000 corporations possess prime military contracts. Their location in each of the 50 states and in the bulk of the 435 congressional districts goes far toward explaining the failure of the Congress to exercise significant restraints on the military budget. This is reinforced by the existence of over 100 members of Congress holding military reserve commissions who serve on various armed services and veterans affairs committees.

These same corporations have also learned to influence military decisions in the executive branch of government as well as in the Congress. The flow of contractor executives to high administrative posts in the Pentagon is now well documented, as is the reverse flow of former military officers to executive positions in the defense and aerospace industries. One recent study, for example, found over 2,000 former officers employed in major defense firms, with a heavy concentration in the specialized military contractors.

Finally, much has been learned regarding the nuts and bolts of the military contract system and the incentives for inefficiency and waste which are implicit in it. Obscure practices such as progress payments and change orders have become understood and the implicit contractor subsidies which they convey have become recognized. The tendency of the military to plan for the worst contingency, no matter how remote, and to insist on "gold-plated" weapons systems creates an atmosphere in which cost overruns become normal and budget growth inexorable. It is such an atmosphere that breeds contractual relationships like that between the air force and Lockheed for the C-5A airplane in which the total *profits* of Lockheed were a direct function of the *costs* incurred by Lockheed in producing the first few planes. This "golden handshake" contract rewarded inefficiency and waste with profits.

In Part IV, a number of the structural and performance characteristics of the military budget and the decision process which surrounds it are explored. These papers illuminate only the tip of the iceberg of issues in this area. Hopefully, reading them will encourage further efforts to understand the problems of governmental performance in this single dominant area of public decision-making.

A. THE MILITARY BUDGET—ITS SIZE, STRUCTURE, AND DETERMINATION

A PROFILE OF THE DEFENSE BUDGET

RICHARD F. KAUFMAN

The total amount of federal outlays in 1969 for military and nonmilitary purposes was $184.5 billion. How much went for defense? This question is not so easy to answer as one might think, mainly because it is government policy to create confusion over the federal budget. There is no way for anyone to learn how much money is spent for military purposes by simply reading the budget document. Military outlays of the Department of Defense were $77.9 billion in 1969.[1] But if we add the expenditures of other agencies which were intended for purposes of defense, the total would be much higher. For example, military-assistance funds spent by the Department of State amounted to $685 million. Expenditures by the Atomic Energy Commission, almost entirely for military purposes, were $2.5 billion. The costs of stockpiling materials deemed essential for reasons of national security, of the selective service system and of other minor defense-related activities total about $120 million. The outlays mentioned thus far bring the defense bill to $81.2 billion. Even the federal government formally recognizes this much.

Now consider some items that are not recognized as essentially for defense purposes. The cost of veterans' programs is largely the cost of old wars and old defense programs. Veterans' pensions, compensation, and insurance cost $7.6 billion in 1969. The interest on the national debt, most of which was borrowed in order to finance World War II, amounted to $15.8 billion and is another cost of old wars. The space program is closely intertwined with defense, primarily in the advancement of missile technology and the potential use of space and space platforms for military purposes. It cost $4.2 billion in 1969. Federal maritime subsidies, justified on the grounds that a healthy maritime industry is essential to national security, amounted to about $800 million. Even

[1] Figures for defense outlays are from *The Budget of the United States Government, Fiscal Year 1971.*

Richard F. Kaufman is Economist-Counsel for the Joint Economic Committee of the U.S. Congress.

a conservative apportionment of these costs and the costs of other programs that are advertised as necessary to national security, such as the oil-import program, would bring the total cost of defense to well over $100 billion. By this reckoning defense spending took at least 54 percent of all federal outlays.

However, let us take a closer look at the narrower meaning of defense spending, the expenditures of the Department of Defense, since it is these sums which support the more important segment of the defense industry and which stimulate related outlays, keeping in mind the fact that the related outlays have a profound impact on the nation.

The $78 billion spent by the Pentagon in 1969 accounted for about 42 percent of all federal spending and represented a per capita outlay of about $400. When we try to break down this budget into its constituent parts, we again run into difficulty. It can be done in several ways.

TABLE 1. National Defense (in millions of dollars)

Program or agency	Outlays 1969 (actual)
Department of Defense—military	
Military personnel	21,374
Retired military personnel	2,444
Operation and maintenance	22,227
Procurement	23,988
Research, development, and evaluation	7,457
Military construction	1,389
Family housing	572
Civil defense	87
Revolving and management funds and other	−1,534
Military trust funds	10
Deductions for offsetting receipts	−135
Subtotal, military	77,877
Military assistance	
Grants and credits sales	685
Trust fund	103
Subtotal, military and military assistance	78,666
Atomic energy	2,450
Defense-related activities:	
Stockpiling of strategic and critical materials	18
Expansion of defense production	166
Selective Service System	65
Emergency preparedness activities	11
Deductions for offsetting receipts:	
Proprietary receipts from the public	−138
Total	81,240

Source: *The Budget of the United States Government, Fiscal Year 1971.*

THE APPROPRIATIONS BUDGET AND THE IMPORTANCE OF ADVANCED WEAPONS

One way is to divide it up the way Congress does, by appropriation. The budget request submitted by the President to the legislative branch contains line items with sums of money alongside each one. When Congress finally appropriates for defense, it in effect fills in its own figures beside the line items, although for many years the tendency was merely to rubber-stamp the Presidential requests. Table 1 shows the appropriation budget for 1969.

It will be noted that the largest single item was $23.3 billion for procurement. Another large item —research, development, test and evaluation— amounting to $7.7 billion, is closely related. These two items represent the amount of money spent for the purchasing of weapons systems and other hardware. I will come back to them.

After procurement the next-largest items are military personnel, $21.9 billion, and operation and maintenance, $20.6 billion. Military-personnel outlays include pay and allowances, subsistence, and other costs such as the expenses of apprehending deserters and escaped military prisoners. (The budget document does not state whether the last expense has been rising in recent years, but one suspects it has.) Operation and maintenance expenditures pay for day-to-day costs of operating aircraft, naval and missile forces, troops in combat, forces providing airlift and sealift capability, logistics support, training, medical care, communications and intelligence activities.

Military construction totaled $1.6 billion and paid for the acquisition of land and construction of facilities such as those required to deploy the Safeguard antiballistic missile system (ABM), as well as medical facilities, service schools, troop housing and bachelor-officer quarters.

It should be seen from the discussion of the defense budget so far that the linchpin in the modern war machine is the expensive advanced weapons systems. It used to be that the principal cost of war was that of supporting masses of men who would wield their axes or fire their small arms in combat. We still support masses of men, in fact, larger numbers on a permanent basis than ever before. But the dominant expense is the cost of researching, developing, purchasing and maintaining the sophisticated weapons systems—the jet aircraft, and guided missiles and the nuclear-powered warships. The masses of men have become, for the most part, servants to machines.

For example, of the 3.5 million men in uniform in 1969, a little more than a million were in the navy and slightly less than a million were in the air force. Obviously most of these men were not trained to go on fixed-bayonet charges or to board enemy ships for hand-to-hand combat. (The Marines are a notable exception.) Their mission was mostly to operate multimillion-dollar ships, planes, and missiles and, when they were not in operation, to babysit for them. Further, a large if not predominant percentage of army personnel had a similar assignment, for the army has a substantial number of planes and missiles of its own. The ABM is an army program.

Similarly a significant proportion of the operation and maintenance expense goes toward the upkeep of major weapons systems. The 10-year operation-and-maintenance costs, for instance, of a modern airplane equal and sometimes exceed its procurement cost. That is, if a jet fighter cost $10 million to buy, it will cost another $10 million to operate and maintain for the 10 years following its purchase. Military construction . . . is in part devoted to the physical housing of manpower attached to weapons systems. Even civil defense, an army program, is related to electronic weapon systems, especially missiles, to the extent that it is supposed to defend against the all-out war that could be produced by the arms race in which we are a full participant.

The point here is that the largest part of the defense budget is directly related to or a by-product of the sophisticated weapons system. In this sense the production and acquisition of weapons is the moving force underlying defense expenditures.

THE PROGRAM BUDGET: STRATEGIC AND GENERAL-PURPOSE FORCES

A second way of looking at the defense budget is by program, a method advocated by former Secretary of Defense Robert S. McNamara, who was instrumental in shifting the emphasis of our defense strategy from nuclear "massive retaliation" under Eisenhower and John Foster Dulles to the concept of "balanced defense" and "flexible response" under John F. Kennedy and Lyndon Johnson.

Under the program budget the dollars spent are related to missions, the key ones being nuclear war (strategic forces) and conventional war (general-purpose forces). (See Table 2.) In 1969 $8.6 billion was spent for strategic forces, $30.7 billion for general-purpose forces. These figures are increased when other items in the program budget are properly charged to either strategic or general-purpose forces. For example, "airlift and sealift" is a general-purpose-force expense. It is sometimes maintained that the amount spent for

TABLE 2. Summary of the Department of Defense Budget Program (in billions of dollars)

Major military programs	Total obligational authority 1969 (actual)
Strategic forces	8.6
General-purpose forces	30.7
Intelligence and communications	5.8
Airlift and sealift	1.6
Guard and reserve forces	2.1
Research and development	4.7
Central supply and maintenance	9.4
Training, medical, and other general personnel activities	12.4
Administration and associated activities	1.3
Support of other nations	2.2
Total obligational authority	78.7
Of which:	
New budget authority	77.0
Prior-year funds and other financial adjustments	−1.7

Source: *The Budget of the United States Government, Fiscal Year 1971.*

conventional-warfare capabilities as compared with nuclear-warfare capabilities show that the costs of ICBMs and nuclear bombers are exaggerated out of proper proportion and that it is the cost of ground and naval forces and their deployment around the world that accounts for the bulk of defense expenditures.

A COMPREHENSIVE NATIONAL SECURITY BUDGET

U. S. CONGRESS JOINT ECONOMIC COMMITTEE

In order to understand what our federal spending priorities are, we need to have some confidence in the annual estimate of outlays for each category of spending, and we need to be assured that the categories themselves are properly identified. The category in the federal budget called "National Defense" presents serious problems on both counts. First, administration estimates for national defense expenditures are notoriously wide of the mark. The budget estimates for the current fiscal year, 1971, have already been sharply modified. Last year, the proposed budget for national defense in fiscal year 1971 was $73.6 billion. This year, the estimate has been raised to $76.5 billion, an increase of nearly $3 billion. In general, the tendency has been for the administration to overestimate prospective reductions and to underestimate prospective increases. In our judgment, the administration needs to do a better job of estimating the levels of expenditure for national defense.

Excerpted and reprinted from U.S. Congress, Joint Economic Committee, *1971 Joint Economic Report,* March 1971.

Second, the budget category "National Defense" does not fully identify all of the items of expenditure that should be included in that category; the definition of national defense found in the budget is so restrictive that the outlay figures do not adequately reflect the true costs of national security. Listed under the National Defense Budget at the present time are the following items: Department of Defense—Military, Military Assistance, Atomic Energy, Stockpiling of Strategic and Critical Materials, Expansion of Defense Production, Selective Service System, and Emergency Preparedness Activities.

It is apparent from this listing that some recognition has been given to the fact that it is important to itemize the defense-related expenditures and to distinguish them from those of the Department of Defense. In addition, however, are a number of programs which also make a direct contribution, in whole or in part, to national security or which would probably not be undertaken but for the requirements of national security. In this category are the Coast Guard, the Veterans' Program, the Department of State, the United States Information Agency, the Arms Control and Disarmament Agency, the Renegotiation Board, the National Aeronautics and Space Administration, the National Security Council, and expenditures for interest on the national debt. Although experts differ on the question of whether all of these programs should be considered defense-related, economists such as Arthur Burns have concluded that expenditures for international programs and for space research and technology "are mainly pursued in the interests of our national security," that the Veterans' program is entirely a legacy of past wars, and that interest on the national debt is preponderately a payment for past wars.

In our judgment, expenditures for defense and defense-related activities should be incorporated under the heading "National Security" and should contain the following types of information:

1. Total outlays of the Department of Defense for military purposes
2. Outlays for all other agencies or programs whose activities are related to current military programs
3. Outlays of all other agencies or programs justified on the grounds of national security
4. Outlays for all other agencies or programs in payment for past wars or military programs.

The more important reason for expanding the current breakdown of defense expenditures is to reflect as accurately as possible the full costs of national security, whether pursued through programs administered by the Department of Defense, the Department of State, or any other agency. Of course, it would be implied by identifying total national security expenditures that all of them are subject to the same sort of control by the administration or the Congress.

Table 1 is a breakdown of the National Security Program actual outlays for selected years from fiscal year 1965 to fiscal year 1970. Estimated outlays are shown for fiscal year 1971 and 1972. The administration's requested obligational authority for fiscal year 1972 is also shown.

This is admittedly an imperfect attempt to explain to the American taxpayer the full costs of national security, whether for past or present wars or defense.

The committee recognizes that others will question certain items contained in the national security program, that objections will be raised to parts of it, and that suggested changes will be proposed. Last year in our Annual Report, the Joint Economic Committee recommended that the full costs of past and current defense-related activities be included in the category of defense programs found in the budget document. No action was taken on this recommendation. We now hope that the national security program breakdown that we have offered will provoke widespread discussion and debate, and that the Office of Management and Budget will be moved to incorporate this concept in next year's budget.

TABLE 1. National Security Budget for Fiscal Years 1965–1972 (in millions of dollars)

	Outlays						
	1965	1968	1969	1970	1971 (est.)	1972 (est.)	Authority 1972
Defense, military assistance and defense-related activities:							
DOD military[1]	46,173	77,373	77,877	77,150	73,370	74,975	77,663
Military assistance[2]	2,469	1,237	1,355	1,186	1,823	1,827	2,052
Atomic energy	2,625	2,466	2,450	2,453	2,275	2,318	2,251
Space research and technology	5,093	4,721	4,247	3,749	3,368	3,151	3,270
U.S. Arms Control and Disarmament Agency	7	11	10	11	10	9	9
Renegotiation Board	3	3	3	4	4	5	5
National Security Council	1	1	1	1	2	2	2
Stockpiles	16	19	18	15	27	30	30
Expansion of defense production	60	51	166	−15	−167	−24	—
Selective Service	43	57	65	75	75	78	78
Emergency preparedness	17	12	11	4	10	9	7
Deductions for offsetting receipts	−124	−116	−138	−118	−278	−898	−898
Subtotal	56,383	85,835	86,065	84,515	80,519	81,482	84,469
Payments for past wars and defense program							
Veterans' benefits	6,080	6,882	7,640	8,677	9,969	10,644	10,991
Interest[3]	8,577	10,308	11,843	13,734	14,575	14,765	14,765
Subtotal	14,657	17,190	19,483	22,411	24,544	25,409	25,756
Programs justified on grounds of national defense:[4]							
Ocean shipping[3]	253	227	236	239	326	345	374
Impacted area school aid[3]	263	380	299	492	385	365	330
Subtotal	516	607	535	731	710	710	704
Total, National Security	71,556	103,632	106,083	107,657	105,773	107,601	110,929

[1] DOD Military excludes DOD civil outlays which totaled $1.2 billion in 1965; $1.3 billion in 1968; $1.3 billion in 1969; $1.2 billion in 1970; $1.4 billion in 1971 (est.); $1.5 billion in 1972 (est.); and $1.5 billion in new obligational authority for 1972.

[2] Includes Military Assistance Program (MAP), supporting assistance, credit sales, and part of the Food for Peace Program. Excluded are outlays for military assistance purposes funded through the Department of Defense.

[3] Includes 75 percent of the program.

[4] Portions of programs, other than those listed, have been justified in the past as essential to national security, including the National Defense Highway System, the airport program and others. The committee intends to further analyze this matter.

Source: Estimated from data in The U.S. Budget, various years.

THE ULTIMATE COST OF THE VIETNAM CONFLICT

JAMES L. CLAYTON

Except for World War II, the Vietnam conflict is by far the most expensive war in American history. This is true whether measured by initial costs or by ultimate costs. In terms of initial dollar costs, the Vietnam War, according to Department of Defense figures, will have cost $110 billion by the end of the next fiscal year. This $110 billion figure is already twice as high as the initial cost of the Korean War and more than four times higher than the original cost of World War I (see Table 1).

But the most striking thing about the cost of the war in Vietnam is that *the greatest costs are yet to come.* If history is an accurate guide in these matters—and we have no other—the expenditures of veterans' benefits over the next century will cost at least 50 percent more than the initial cost of the war itself. Twenty percent of our adult population are war veterans, and almost half our population is potentially eligible to receive some kind of veterans' benefits. The cost of their support (including dependents and survivors) in recent years has been between the third and fifth most expensive item in the federal budget, and since 1950 the annual average value of veterans' benefits has been increasing at a rate of 20 percent per decade. Add to those veterans' benefits the annual interest payments on debt incurred owing to the Vietnam War, and the ultimate cost of that involvement will probably be about *three times* its initial cost. This kind of accounting is seldom if ever mentioned in the debates about the war.

Measuring the monetary costs of any war is an extremely difficult but not impossible task. The Executive Office of the President has, however, made a valiant attempt to ascertain the costs of the Vietnam War since 1965. Its findings are printed in the 1970 *Budget of the United States Government*

Excerpted and reprinted from James L. Clayton, "The Ultimate Cost of the Vietnam Conflict," in *The Military Budget and National Economic Priorities*, Part 1, Hearings of the Joint Economic Committee, U.S. Congress, June 1969.

James L. Clayton is Professor of History at the University of Utah, Salt Lake City, Utah.

TABLE 1. How Veterans' Benefits Increase War Costs (in millions of dollars)

War	Original cost[1] (major national security expenditures)	Veterans' benefits to 1967[2]	Number of years following war veterans' benefits[3] Peaked	Ended	Estimated total benefits under present laws[4]	Veterans' benefits as a percentage of original war costs
American Revolution	100	70	([5])	128	70	70
War of 1812	93	49	68	131	49	53
Mexican War	73	64	43	116	64	88
Civil War (Union only)	3,200	8,567	60	113	8,580	260
Spanish-American War	400	5,256	51	—	6,000	1,505
World War I	26,000	39,854	49	—	75,000	290
World War II	288,000	76,767	—	—	290,000	100
Korean conflict	[6] 54,000	12,863	—	—	99,000	184

[1] Based on expenditures of the Departments of the Army and Navy to World War I and major national security expenditures thereafter. Usually the figures begin with the year the war began, but in all cases they extend 1 year beyond the end of actual conflict. See "Historical Statistics of the United States," 1960 ed., pp. 718–720.

[2] 1968 stat. abst., p. 266.

[3] Veterans' Administration, annual reports.

[4] To World War I estimates are based on Veterans Administration data. For the last three wars estimates are those of the Bradley Commission plus 25 percent (which is the increase in the average value of benefits since the commission made its report). See especially "Veterans' Benefits in the United States," President's Commission on Veterans' Pensions, 1956, pp. 110–117.

[5] Unknown.

[6] Assumes 5,700,000 men served an average of 19 months at $2,835 personnel costs per man-year, $2,723 operation and maintenance costs per man-year, and procurement costs totaling ⅓ the increase over previous years. Averages were based on the number of service men divided by the defense budget for each year.

(p. 74). According to these official estimates, in fiscal 1970 the Vietnam War will eat up 13 percent of all federal expenditures, and will have cost a total of $108.5 billion since 1965. But these figures do not tell the whole story. Actually, only about $100 billion of the federal budget is relatively controllable. The remainder is already committed or in trust funds. Of this $100 billion, no less than 80 percent is accounted for by the national defense. Since the Vietnam War accounts for 32 percent of the 1970 defense budget, in terms of what the government actually can spend in that year, the Vietnam War is really costing us 25 percent of all possible expenditures, not 13 percent as the official figures indicate. This 25-percent figure, it should be noted, is based on a projected deescalation in Vietnam costs estimated at $5 billion under 1969 costs. It is further assumed that the big increases are over. But that is what we were told in 1968 and costs *increased* $2 billion. If the war in fact continues at its present rate, almost a third of our federal disposable budget will be committed to Southeast Asia. If the war escalates, the ratio could easily go to one-half.

Focusing on short-run costs is not merely so informative, however, as looking at long-term war costs. The *pattern* of long-term costs clearly indicates that the largest money costs of war come long after the fighting stops. This fact is not widely appreciated today. The basic reason for this pattern is that veterans' benefits for our first five major wars—payments that are now virtually complete—have averaged more than three times the original cost of those wars. The projected increase in benefits for veterans for wars fought during the past century, although varying widely in their total impact, are equally large. To illustrate, the estimated original cost of the Civil War is $3.2 billion (Union forces only). This estimate is based on the expenditures of the Departments of the Army and the Navy for the years 1862 through 1866. Veterans' benefits for that war to 1967 have amounted to $8.6 billion, or an increase over the original cost of 265 percent. Projected veterans' benefits for World War I, World War II, and the Korean War—assuming today's laws and no increased coverage—will increase the original cost of those wars by 290

TABLE 2. How War Loans and Interest Payments Increase War Costs (in millions of dollars)

War	Original cost[1]	Estimated total costs of war loans: Principal	Estimated total costs of war loans: Interest	Interest payments as a percentage of original costs
American Revolution	100	[2] 64		(3)
War of 1812	93	[4] 109	[5] 16	17
Mexican War	73	[6] 49	[7] 10	14
Civil War (Union only)	3,200	[8] 2,600	[9] 1,172	37
Spanish-American War	400	[10] 200	[11] 60	15
World War I	26,000	21,400	[12] 11,000	42
World War II	288,000	[13] 215,000	(3)	(3)
Korean Conflict	54,000	[14] 10,000	(3)	(3)

[1] See Table 1, note 1.
[2] Treasury Department estimate in C. F. Childs, "Concerning U.S. Government Securities," (1947), p. 405.
[3] Unknown.
[4] See D. R. Dewey, "Financial History of the United States," (1939), p. 134; and Studenski and Krooss, "Financial History of the United States" (1952), p. 79.
[5] One-half of the annual increase of interest on national debt over $2,500,000 (average rate prior to war), 1816–1836.
[6] Childs, p. 30.
[7] One-half the annual increase of interest on national debt over $1,000,000 (average), 1845–1859.
[8] Ibid., p. 46.
[9] One-half the annual increase of interest on national debt over $4,000,000 (average) 1861–1891.
[10] Dewey, p. 467.
[11] Estimated at 3 percent per year for 10 years on the total balance since much of this debt was refinanced.
[12] The interest on World War I war debts in 1929 had reached $7,000,000,000, according to the Treasury Department, and was costing $663,000,000 annually. At the then current rate of payment, approximately $4,000,000 in additional interest would have been paid out. See John M. Clark, "The Costs of the World War to the American People" (1931), p. 297.
[13] Henry C. Murphy, "The National Debt in War and Transition" (1950), ch. 18.
[14] The U.S. public debt increased $16,000,000,000 between 1951 and 1954. It is assumed that $10 billion of this increase was owing to the Korean War.

percent, 100 percent, and 184 percent respectively.

It should be further emphasized that these benefits have acted as an enormous transfer payment to this sector of the population. Partly owing to educational subsidies, veterans are generally better educated than nonveterans. Their median educational level in 1967 was 12.3 years as opposed to 12.0 for the population as a whole. For post-Korean veterans the level was 12.6. The median 1966 income of war veterans who had completed college was $10,900. For nonveterans it was $9,510. The employment data for veterans also reflects this higher status, in part because of their educational attainments and in part because of laws favoring veterans' job security. Only 2.2 percent of veterans were unemployed in the first quarter of 1968, versus 3.8 percent for the civilian labor force as a whole. The incidence of poverty among veterans and nonveterans is even more striking. In 1966, 13.8 percent of all families had incomes below $3,000. Only 6.6 percent of veterans' families had incomes that low. For post-Korean conflict veterans that figure was 3.7 percent. Clearly, wars (and more especially their aftermath) can be profitable to those who have participated in them.

Next to veterans' benefits the interest costs on money borrowed to fight our major wars is the most significant long-range cost. Again, any attempt to measure actual interest costs is extremely difficult, if not impossible. Still, the patterns of interest costs are instructive. Overall, these costs have probably ranged from 15 to at least 40 percent of the original cost of the war itself.

Using the pattern of veterans' benefits paid out for the Civil War, World War I, World War II, and the Korean War as a guide, we may expect the Vietnam conflict to eventually cost us about 200 percent of the original cost, all other things being equal. This figure is conservative, however, because a much higher percentage of Vietnam veterans are using their educational

TABLE 3. The Ultimate Cost of the Vietnam Conflict* (in billions of dollars)

1. Original cost:	
(a) Major national security expenditures for the Vietnam Conflict, 1965–1970 (fiscal years)	108.5
(b) Cost of supporting American personnel in South Vietnam, 1954–1964, at $25,000 per man per year	1.5
Total	110.0
2. Veterans' benefits:	
(a) Low estimate, 100 percent of original cost	110.0
(b) Medium estimate, 200 percent of original cost	220.0
(c) High estimate, 300 percent of original cost	330.0
3. Interest on war debt:	
(a) Low estimate, 10 percent of original cost	11.0
(b) Medium estimate, 20 percent of original cost	22.0
(c) High estimate, 40 percent of original cost	44.0
4. Total:	
(a) Low estimate	231.0
(b) Medium estimate	352.0
(c) High estimate	484.0

* Assumed the war ends in fiscal 1970. Occupation costs were not included.
Sources: Tables 1 and 2.

benefits now than in previous wars, and life expectancy is increasing. Benefits also tend to be more inclusive with time and rise with the cost of living. The present cost of these benefits is about $130 per year per family, and this figure does not include mortgage guarantees or substantial state aid to veterans. Regarding interest costs and using the Civil War and World War I as guidelines, we may fairly expect interest rates of the Vietnam War to cost at least 20 percent of the original cost and possibly as much as 40 percent. In short, the cost of the Vietnam conflict, even assuming a major deescalation at the end of this year and a total withdrawal next year, will be about $350 billion (see Table 4).

It should be emphasized that this is a conservative figure and measures only the direct major monetary costs. The estimate does not include inflationary costs owing to the war, the loss of services and earnings by the 45,000 men killed in the war to date, the cost of resentment abroad, the depletion of our natural resources, the post-

TABLE 4. Cost of American Wars, by Rank (in millions of dollars)

War	Estimated initial cost[1]	Total veterans' benefits	Estimated interest on war loans	Estimated ultimate cost
World War II	288,000	290,000	[2] 86,000	664,000
Vietnam conflict	110,000	[3] 220,000	[3] 22,000	[3] 352,000
Korean conflict	54,000	99,000	[4] 11,000	164,000
World War I	26,000	75,000	11,000	112,000
Civil War (Union only)	3,200	8,580	1,172	12,952
Spanish-American War	400	6,000	60	6,460
American Revolution	100	70	[4] 20	190
War of 1812	93	49	16	158
Mexican War	73	64	59	147

[1] Major national security expenditures.
[2] Assumes an interest rate of 40 percent of original cost, on approximately the same rate of increase for the Civil War and World War I.
[3] Medium estimates, see Table 3.
[4] Assumes an interest rate of 20 percent of original cost.
Source: Tables 1–3.

ponement of critical domestic programs, the cost of the arrested training and education of our youth, the cost of suspended cultural progress of our nation—and nothing of the death and destruction to the South Vietnamese civilians in the war zone itself.

The estimated ultimate cost of the Vietnam War is so high it boggles the mind unless placed in perspective. How much money is $350 billion? Compared with other federal expenditures during the same period of time the war has been on (fiscal years 1960–1970), the war in Vietnam has cost 10 times more than Medicare and medical assistance, 4 times more than support for all levels of education, and 50 times more than was spent for housing and community development. We have spent several times more money on Vietnam in 10 years than we have spent in our entire history for public higher education or for police protection. Put another way, the war has cost us more than one-fourth of the value of current personal financial assets of all living Americans, a third again as much as all outstanding home mortgages, and seven times the total U.S. money now in circulation.

Looking back over the costs of wars in American history, there seems to be an evil nemesis dogging our destiny. Each of our major wars (the Civil War, World War I, and World War II) during the past century have initially cost about ten times more than the previous wars, if indirect as well as direct costs are included. The Civil War initially cost more than $3 billion, World War I $33 billion, and World War II about $381 billion. Since World War II, our major conflicts have tended to *double* in price. Korea cost $54 billion and Vietnam to date has cost $110 billion. Total federal expenditures, moreover, have tended to increase four to five times after each major war. In the case of Vietnam, government expenditures to date (1960–1969) have doubled. Unless we drastically reverse this trend and significantly reduce our current military expenditures, war will soon be too expensive to contemplate and governments too cumbersome to endure.

MILITARY POWER AND THE MILITARY BUDGET

JOHN KENNETH GALBRAITH

The importance of military spending in the economy—half the federal budget, about one-tenth of the total economic product, I need not stress. Though much attention is focused upon it, this bloodless economic side is not, I venture to think, the important feature. The important feature is the peculiar constitutional and bureaucratic arrangements which have come to govern this economic activity.

In our ordinary economic arrangements we think of the individual as instructing the market by his purchases and, the market, in turn, instructing the producing firm. Thus economic life is controlled. This the textbooks celebrate. And where public expenditures are concerned, the young are still taught that the legislature reflects the will of the citizen to the executive. The executive, in turn, effects that will.

Excerpted and reprinted from statement of John Kenneth Galbraith in *The Military Budget and National Economic Priorities,* Part 1, Hearings of the Joint Economic Committee, U.S. Congress, June 1969.

John Kenneth Galbraith is Professor of Economics at Harvard University, Cambridge, Massachusetts.

I have argued that with industrial development—with advanced technology, high organization, large and rigid commitments of capital—power tends to pass to the producing organization—to the modern large corporation. Not the consumer but General Motors tends to be the source of the original decision on the modern automobile. If the consumer is reluctant he is persuaded—to a point at least.

This part of my case has not escaped argument. Dissent raises its head everywhere these days. But where military goods are concerned one encounters little or no argument. Here, it is agreed, the historic economic and constitutional sequence is reversed. The citizen does not instruct the legislature and the legislature the Pentagon and its associated industries. No one wants to be that naïve. Vanity here becomes the ally of truth. It is agreed that the services and the weapons manufacturers decide what they want or need. They then instruct the Congress. The Congress, led by the military housecarls among its members, hastens to comply. The citizens play no role except to pay the bill. As I say, these matters are not subject to serious dispute, those with a special capacity to believe in fairy tales apart.

One must not think of the military power—the association of the military and the defense firms—in conspiratorial terms. It reflects an intimate but largely open association based on a solid community of bureaucratic and pecuniary interest. The services seek the weapons; the suppliers find it profitable to supply them. The factors which accord plenary power of decision to the military and the defense plants, and which exclude effective interference by the Congress and the public, are quite commonplace. Nothing devious or wicked is involved. The following are the factors which sustain the military power.

First, there is the use of fear. This, of course, is most important. Anything which relates to war, and especially to nuclear conflict, touches a deeply sensitive public nerve. This is easily played on. The technique is to say, in effect, "Give us what we ask, do as we propose, or you will be in mortal danger of nuclear annihilation."

Second, there is the monopoly, or near monopoly, of technical and intelligence information by the services, their suppliers, and the intelligence community. This monopoly, in turn, is protected by classification secrecy. This allows the military power to exclude the lay critic, including the legislator, as uninformed. But even the best scientist can be excluded on the grounds that he is not fully informed on the latest secret technology—or does not have the latest knowledge on what the Russians or the Chinese are up to. Here, too, the new administration has been very apt.

Third, there is the role of the single-firm supplier and the negotiated contract. These are largely inevitable with high technology. One cannot let out the MIRV to competitive bidding in the manner of mules and muskets. In fiscal year 1968, as the work of this committee has revealed, 60 percent of defense contracts were with firms that were the sole source of supply. Most of the remainder were awarded by negotiated bidding. Competitive bidding—11.5 percent of the total—was nearly negligible. With single-firm supply, and in lesser degree with negotiated supply, opposition of interest between buyer and seller disappears. The buyer is as interested in the survival and well-being of the seller as is the seller himself. No one will enter this Elysium to cut prices, offer better work, earlier deliveries, or cry favoritism if someone gets too much of that particular business. That is because there is no other seller. The situation, if I may be permitted to coin a word, is cozy.

Fourth, there is the fiction that the specialized arms contractor is separate from the services. The one is in the public sector. The other is private enterprise. As Professor Murray Weidenbaum, the notable authority on these matters, . . . as well as others have pointed out, the dividing line between the services and their specialized suppliers exists increasingly in the imagination. Where a corporation does all or nearly all of its business with the Department of Defense; uses much plant owned by the government; gets its working capital in the form of progress payments from the government; does not need to worry about competitors for it is the sole source of supply; accepts extensive guidance from the Pentagon on its management; is subject to detailed rules as to its accounting; and is extensively staffed by former service personnel, only the remarkable flexibility of the English language allows us to call it private enterprise. Yet this is not an exceptional case, but a common one. General Dynamics, Lockheed, North American-Rockwell and such are public extensions of the bureaucracy. Yet the myth that they are private allows a good deal of freedom in pressing the case for weapons, encouraging unions and politicians to do so, supporting organizations such as the Air Force Association which do so, allowing executives to press the case and otherwise protecting the military power. We have an amiable arrangement by which the defense firms, though part of the public bureaucracy, are largely exempt from its political and other constraints.

Fifth, this is a more subtle point. For a long period during the 1950s and 1960s, during which the military power was consolidating its position, military expenditures had a highly functional role in the economy. They sustained employment; they also supported, as no other expenditures do, a high technical dynamic. And there was no wholly satisfactory substitute. More specifically, a high federal budget, supported by the corporate and progressive personal income tax, both of which increased more than proportionally with increasing income and reduced themselves more than proportionally if income faltered, built a high element of stability into the system. And the scientific and technical character of this outlay encouraged the expansion of the educational and research plant and employed its graduates. It was long a commonplace of Keynesian economics that civilian spending, similarly supported by a progressive tax system, would serve just as well the goals of fiscal stability as military spending. This argument which, alas, I have used myself on occasion was, I am now persuaded, wrong—an exercise in apologetics. Civilian spending does not evoke the same support as does military spending on a large scale. And although it is now hard to remember, the civilian pressures on the federal budget until recent times were not extreme. Taxes were reduced in 1964 because the pressures to spend were not sufficient to offset tax collections at a high level of output—to neutralize the so-called "fiscal drag." And civilian welfare spending does not support the same range of scientific and technical activities, or the related institutions, as does military spending. On a wide range of matters—electronics, air transport, computer systems, atomic energy—military appropriations paid for development costs too great or too risky to be undertaken by private firms. They served as a kind of honorary nonsocialism.

Sixth and finally, there is the capacity—and this is a notable phenomenon of our time—for organization, bureaucracy, to create its own truth—the truth that serves its purpose. The most remarkable example in recent times, of course, has been Vietnam. The achievements of bureaucratic truth here have been breathtaking. An essentially civilian conflict between the Vietnamese has been converted into an international conflict with a rich ideological portent for all mankind. South Vietnamese dictators of flagrantly regressive instincts have been converted into incipient Jeffersonians holding aloft the banners of an Asian democracy. Wholesale larceny in Saigon has become an indispensable aspect of free institutions. One of the world's most desultory and impermanent armies—with desertion rates running around 100,000 a year—was made, always potentially, into a paragon of martial vigor. Airplanes episodically bombing open acreage or dense jungle became an impenetrable barrier to men walking along the ground. An infinity of reverses, losses and defeats became victories deeply in diguise. There was nothing, or not much, that was cynical in this effort. For, for those who accept bureaucratic truth, it is the unbelievers who look confused, perverse and very wrong. Throughout the course of the war there was bitter anger in Saigon and to a lesser extent here in Washington, over the inability of numerous people—journalists, professors and others—to see military operations, the Saigon government, the pacification program, the South Vietnam army in the same rosy light as did the bureaucracy.

An equally spectacular set of bureaucratic truths has been created to serve the military power—and its weapons procurement. There is the military doctrine that whatever the dangers of a continued weapons race with the Soviet Union, these are less than any agreement that offers any perceptible opening for violations. Since no agreement can possibly be watertight, this largely protects the weapons industry from any effort at control. There is the belief that the conflict with communism is man's ultimate battle. Accordingly, no one would hesitate to destroy all life if communism seems seriously a threat. This belief allows acceptance of the arms race and the production of the requisite weapons no matter how dangerous. The present ideological differences between industrial systems will almost certainly look very different and possibly rather trivial from a perspective of 50 or a 100 years hence if we survive. Such thoughts are eccentric. There is also the belief that national interest is total, that of man inconsequential. So even the prospect of total death and destruction does not deter us from developing new weapons systems if some thread of national interest can be identified in the outcome. We can accept 75 million casualties—preferably not including ourselves—if it forces the opposition to accept 150 million. We can agree with Sen. Richard Russell that, if only one man and one woman are to be left on earth, they should be Americans. Not from any particular part of the country, just Americans.

We can make it part of the case for the Manned Orbiting Laboratory (MOL) that it would maintain the American position up in space in the event of total devastation from Maine to California. Such is the power of bureaucratic truth that these things are widely accepted. And being accepted they sustain the military power.

What now should be our response? How do we get the power under control?

Our response must be in relation to the source of power. Again for purposes of compressing this discussion, let me list specific points:

1. Everyone must know that fear is deployed as a weapon. So we must resist it. I am not a supporter of unilateral disarmament. I assume that the Soviets also have their military power sustained by its bureaucratic beliefs. But we must look at the problem calmly. We must never again be stampeded into blind voting for military budgets. These, as a practical matter, are as likely to serve the bureaucratic goals of the military power and the pecuniary goals of the contractors as they do the balance of terror with the Soviets. And we must ascertain which.

2. That part of the military budget that serves the balance of terror can be reduced only with negotiations with the Soviets. As Charles Schultze and others have pointed out, however, this is a relatively small part of the military budget. The rest serves the goals of the military power and the interests of the suppliers. This can be curtailed. But it can only be curtailed if there is a vigorous reassertion of congressional power. Obviously this will not happen if sycophants of the military retain the final word on military appropriations. The Congress has the choice of serving the people in accordance with constitutional design or serving military interests in accordance with past habit.

3. Informed technical and scientific judgment must be brought to bear on the foregoing questions. This means that the Congress must equip itself with the very best of independent scientific judgment. And the men so mobilized must not be denied access to scientific and intelligence information. I believe that on military matters there should be a panel of scientists, a Military Audit Commission, responsible only to the Congress . . . to be a source of continuing and informed advice on military needs—and equally on military non-needs.

4. We must, as grown-up people, abandon now the myth that the big defense contractors are something separate from the public bureaucracy. They must be recognized for what they are—a part of the public establishment. Perhaps one day soon a further step should be taken. Perhaps any firm which, over a 5-year period, has done more than 75 percent of its business with the Defense Department, should be made a full public corporation with all stock in public hands. No one will make the case that this is an assault on private enterprise. These firms as I said before, are private only in the imagination. The action would insure that such firms are held to strict standards of public responsibility in their political and other activities and expenditures. It would exclude the kind of conspiracy to protect capital gains that was recently uncovered in the Lockheed case. It would help prevent private enrichment at public expense. In light of the recent performance of the big defense contractors, no one would wish to argue that it would detract from efficiency. And the 75-percent rule would encourage firms that wish to avoid nationalism to diversify into civilian production. Needless to say, the 75-percent rule should be applicable to the defense units of the conglomerates. Perhaps to press this reform now would direct energies from more needed tasks. Let us, however, put it on the agenda.

5. Finally, it must be recognized that the big defense budgets of the 1950s were a unique response to the conditions of that time. Then there were the deep fears generated by the cold war, the seeming unity of the Communist world, and, at least in comparison with present circumstances, the seeming lack of urgency of domestic requirements. All this has now changed. We have a wide range of tacit understandings with the Soviets; we have come to understand that the average Soviet citizen—in this respect like the average American voter—is unresponsive to the ideas of nuclear annihilation. And as all philosophers of the commonplace concede, we have the terrible urgency

of civilian needs—of the cities, the environment, transportation, education, housing, indeed wherever we look. It is now even agreed as to where the first danger to American democracy—if there is one—lies. It is not from the U.S.S.R., China. The first danger is from the starvation of our public services, particularly in our big cities, here at home.

One final point. Our concern is not with inefficiency in military procurement. Nor is it with graft. These divert attention from the main point. And I would like to suggest this is not a crusade against military men—against our fellow citizens in uniform. Soldiers were never meant to be commercial accessories of General Dynamics. It would horrify the great captains of American arms of past generations to discover that their successors are by way of becoming commercial accessories of Lockheed Aircraft Corporation.

The matter for concern is with the military power—a power that has passed from the public and the Congress to the Pentagon and its suppliers. And our concern is with the consequences—with the bloated budgets and bizarre bureaucratic truths that result. The point is important for it suggests that the restoration of power to the Congress is not a sectarian political task. It is one for all who respect traditional political and constitutional processes.

THE FACTORS BEHIND RISING MILITARY EXPENDITURES

CHARLES L. SCHULTZE

SOME SPECIFIC CAUSES OF RISING MILITARY EXPENDITURES

Barring major change in defense policies, military spending for non-Vietnam purposes will surely rise significantly over the next 5 years. There are five specific factors working toward an increase in military expenditures.

Military and Civilian Pay Increases

There are now 3.5 million men in the armed forces. In addition some 1.3 million civilian employees, about 4.5 percent of the federal total, work for the Department of Defense. As wages and salaries in the private sector of the economy rise, the pay scales of these military and civilian employees of the Defense Department must also rise. The military and civilian pay raise scheduled for this coming July 1 will add some $2.3 billion to the defense budget. If we assume, conservatively, that in succeeding years private wage and salary increases average 4 to 4.5 percent per year, the payroll costs of the Pentagon will rise by about 1.5 billion each year.

The Future Expenditure Consequences of Already Approved Weapons Systems

A large number of new and complex weapons systems have been approved as part of our defense posture; the bulk of the spending on which has not yet occurred.[1] Some major examples are:

- The Minuteman III missile, with MIRVs; cost, $4.5 billion.

Excerpted and reprinted from statement of Charles L. Schultze in *The Military Budget and National Economic Priorities*, Part 1, Hearings of the Joint Economic Committee, U.S. Congress, June 1969.

Charles L. Schultze is Senior Fellow at The Brookings Institution, Washington, D.C., and Professor of Economics at the University of Maryland, College Park, Maryland.

[1] For most of the systems listed below, the decision to procure the item has already been made. In a few cases, such as the navy VSX antisubmarine plane, procurement has not yet been approved, but development is well along, and official statements of Defense Department officials have already indicated that the system is most likely to be approved.

- The Poseidon missile, with MIRVs; cost, including conversion of 31 Polaris subs, $5.5 to $6.5 billion.
- The Safeguard ABM system, with a currently estimated cost, including nuclear warheads, of some $8 billion, plus hundreds of millions per year in operating costs.
- The F–14 navy fighter plane in three versions; the 1970 posture statement indicates that the entire F–4 force of the navy and Marine Corps may be replaced by the F–14. If so, the total investment and operational cost of this system over a 10-year period should be well in excess of $20 billion.
- A new F–15 air-to-air combat fighter for the air force.
- Three nuclear attack carriers at a currently estimated cost of $525–$540 million each.
- 62 new naval escort vessels, at an investment cost of nearly $5 billion.
- A number of new amphibious assault ships.
- A new Navy antisubmarine plane, the VSX, at a cost of $2 to $2.5 billion.
- A new continental air-defense system, including a complex "lookdown" radar and an extensive modification program for the current F–106 interceptor.

These do not exhaust the list of new weapon systems already a part of the approved defense posture. But they do give some idea of the magnitude of the expenditures involved.

Cost Escalation

The weapons systems costs given for each of the systems listed above represent current estimates. But, as this committee is well aware, past experience indicates that final costs of complex military hardware systems almost always exceed original estimates.

A study of missile systems in the 1950s and early 1960s revealed that the average unit cost of missiles was 3.2 times the original estimates.

The nuclear carrier *Nimitz* now under construction, was estimated in 1967 to cost $440 million. One year later the estimate was raised to $536 million. No new estimates have been released but given the rapidly rising cost of shipbuilding, it is almost certain that this latter figure will be exceeded.

In January 1968 the Defense Department proposed a plan for building 68 naval escort vessels at a total cost of $3 billion. In January 1969 the estimated costs of that program had risen to $5 billion.

The cost of modernizing the carrier *Midway* was originally given as $88 million, and the work was scheduled to be completed in 24 months. In January 1969 the cost estimate was double, to $178 million, and the time estimate also doubled, to 48 months.

The air force's manned orbiting laboratory (the MOL) was originally announced by President Johnson at a cost of $1.5 billion. The latest estimate was $3 billion.

In many cases the rising unit costs of these systems forces reevaluation of the program and a reduction in the number purchased. The F–111 program is a classic case in point. Consequently the *aggregate* costs of the procurement budget do not rise by the same percentage as the inflation in *unit* costs. Nevertheless, cost escalation does tend to drive the total military budget upward.

Weapons Systems Under Development, Advocated by the Joint Chiefs of Staff, but Not Yet Approved for Deployment

In addition to weapons system already approved, there are a large number of systems, currently under development, which are being advocated for deployment by the Joint Chiefs. Among these items are:

- The AMSA—advanced manual strategic aircraft —a supersonic intercontinental bomber designed as a follow-on to the B–52. President Johnson's proposed 1970 budget requested $77 million for advanced development. Secretary Laird proposed an additional $23 million to shorten design time and start full-scale engineering development. This $10 million will be supplemented by $35 million of carryover funds. The investment costs of the AMSA, if procurement decision is made, are difficult to estimate, but it is hard to see how they could be less than $10 billion.
- The new main battle tank is now in production engineering. Depending on the number purchased, a procurement decision will involve investment costs of $1 to $1.5 billion.

- A new advanced strategic missile in super-hard silos is being advocated by the air force.
- A new attack aircraft, the AX, is under development for the air force.
- The navy is proposing a major shipbuilding and reconversion program to replace or modernize large numbers of its older vessels.
- A new continental air defense interceptor, the F–12, is being advocated by the air force.
- A new underwater strategic missile systems (the USMS) is under development for the navy.

In the normal course of events, not all of these new systems will be adopted in the next 5 years. But, in the normal course of events, some will be.

Mutual Escalation of the Strategic Arms Race

The United States is currently planning to equip its Minuteman III and Poseidon missiles with multiple independently targeted reentry vehicles (MIRVs). MIRV testing has been underway for some time. The original purpose of MIRVs was as a hedge against the development of a large-scale Soviet ABM system, in order to preserve our second-strike retaliatory capability in the face of such development. Recently, however, Pentagon officials have indicated that we are designing into our MIRVs the accuracy needed to destroy missile sites—an accuracy much greater than needed to preserve the city-destroying capability of a retaliatory force. Secretary of Defense Laird, in recent testimony before the Armed Services Committee, for example, asked for additional funds to "improve significantly the accuracy of the Poseidon missile, thus enhancing its effectiveness against hard targets."

Putting MIRVs with hard-target killing capabilities on Poseidon alone will equip the U.S. strategic forces with 4,000 to 5,000 missile-destroying warheads. Viewed from Soviet eyes the United States appears to be acquiring the capability of knocking out Soviet land-based missile forces in a first strike. It might be argued that the difficulties of attaining a hard-target killing capability on our MIRVs are so great that the objective will not be realized for many years, if ever. But without attempting to evaluate this observation, let me point out that what counts in the arms race is the Soviet reaction to our announcements. And, like our own conservative planners, the Soviets must assume that we will attain our objectives.

SOME BASIC FACTORS BEHIND RISING MILITARY BUDGETS

While this discussion presents some of the specific reasons why the defense budget will expand sharply in the next 5 years, it does not address itself to the underlying forces which threaten to produce this outcome. In the first half of the 1960s the military budget ran at about $50 billion per year. With those funds not only were U.S. strategic and conventional forces maintained, they were sharply improved in both quantity and quality. Both land- and sea-based missile forces were rapidly increased. Similarly dramatic increases in the general purpose forces were undertaken. Fourteen army divisions, undermanned, trained primarily for tactical nuclear war, and short of combat consumables were expanded to over 16⅔ divisions, most of them fully manned. Equipment and logistic supply lines were sharply increased. The 16 tactical air wings were expanded to 21. Sea-lift and air-lift capability were radically improved.

In short, on $50 billion per year in the early 1960s, it appeared to be possible to buy not only the maintenance of a given military capability, but a sharp increase in that capability. By the early 1970s, taking into account general price inflation in the economy plus military and civilian pay increases, it would take $63 to $65 billion to maintain the same purchasing power as $50 billion in 1965. Yet, . . . even on conservative assumptions the non-Vietnam military budget is likely to approach $80 billion by fiscal 1974—$15 to $17 billion more than the amount needed to duplicate the general purchasing power the pre-Vietnam budget had—a budget which already was providing significant increases in military strength. Why this escalation? What forces are at work?

While there are a number of reasons for this increase, I would suggest that four are particularly important.

First, the impact of Modern Technology on the strategic nuclear forces: During most of the 1960s the primary goal of our strategic nuclear forces was the preservation of an "assured destruction capacity"—the ability to absorb an enemy's first strike and retaliate devastatingly on his homeland. In turn this capability provided nuclear deterrence against a potential aggressor. In general this could be described as a stable situation, in part because of the technology involved.

But the development of MIRVs, and more critically the development of guidance systems which are designed to make them accurate enough to "kill" enemy missiles on the ground, changes this balance. Now a single attacking missile, with multiple warheads, can theoretically take out several enemy missiles. The advantage to the first attacker rises sharply. Strategic planners on both sides, projecting these developments into the future, react sharply in terms of the danger they perceive their own forces to be facing. Add to this the development of ABM, which—however initially deployed—raises fears in the minds of enemy planners that it can be extended to protect cities against his submarine-launched missiles, and escalation of the strategic arms race becomes increasingly likely.

The impact of changing technology on strategic arms budgets, therefore, is one of the driving forces which changes the prospects of post-Vietnam military expenditures from what they might have seemed several years ago.

The second major factor in driving arms budgets up is the propensity of military planners to prepare against almost every conceivable contingency or risk. And this applies both to force-level planning and to the design of individual weapons systems. Forces are built to cover possible, but very remote, contingencies. Individual weapons systems are crowded with electronic equipment and built with capabilities for dealing with a very wide range of possible situations, including some highly unlikely ones.

If military technology were standing still, this propensity to cover remote contingencies might lead to a large military budget, but not to a rapidly expanding one. As technology continually advances, however, two developments occur: (1) As we learn about new technology, we project it forward into the Soviet arsenal, thereby creating new potential contingencies to be covered by our own forces; and (2) the new technology raises the possibility of designing weapons systems to guard against contingencies which it had not been possible to protect against previously.

Continually advancing technology and the risk aversion of military planners, therefore, combine to produce ever more complex and expensive weapons systems and ever more contingencies to guard against.

Let me give an example. According to Dr. John S. Foster, Jr., deputy director of defense research and engineering in testimony before the Senate Armed Services Committee last year, the Poseidon missile system was originally designed to penetrate the Soviet TALLINN system—a system originally thought to be a widespread ABM defense. When this system turned out to be an antiaircraft system, the deployment decision on the Poseidon was not revised. Rather it was continued as a hedge against a number of other possible Soviet developments, including in Dr. Foster's words the possibility that "The Minuteman force could be threatened by either rapid deployment of the current Soviet SS–9 or by MIRV'ing their existing missiles and improving accuracy."

Once the Soviets began to deploy the SS–9 in apparently larger numbers than earlier estimated, however, this gave rise to the decision to deploy a "Safeguard" ABM defense of Minutemen sites.

In short the sequence went like this: (1) The Poseidon deployment decision was made against a threat which never materialized; (2) despite the disappearance of the threat against which it was designed, the Poseidon was continued, presumably as a hedge against other potential threats, including faster-than-expected Soviet deployment of the SS–9; (3) but now a decision has been made to hedge against the SS–9 by building a "hard-point" ABM—so we are presumably building the Poseidon as hedge against a number of possible threats, including the SS–9, and then building a hedge on top of that; (4) finally, new technology has made it possible to design a hard-target killing accuracy into the Poseidon—an accuracy not needed to preserve our second-strike capability against either the SS–9 or a Soviet ABM. The technology is available—why not use it! Yet the existence of that capability may well force a major Soviet response.

Another example of hedging against remote threats is the currently planned program of improvements in our continental air-defense system. The existing SAGE system cost $18 billion to install but is apparently not very effective against low-altitude bomber attack. Although the Soviets have a sizable intercontinental bomber threat, the decision has been made to go ahead with major investments in a new air-defense system. The major reasons given for this decision are these: to deter the Soviets from deciding to reverse their long-standing policy and develop a new bomber; to guard against one-way kamikaze-type attacks by Soviet medium-range bombers; and to protect those of our missiles which would be withheld in a retaliatory strike. There is admittedly no direct threat to be covered. But a number of more remote threats are covered. And since we cannot defend our cities against Soviet missiles, it gives small comfort to have them protected against as yet nonexisting bombers or kamakaze attacks.

Another case in point is the new F–14 navy aircraft. Both the F–111B and its successor, the initial version of the F–14, were designed to stand off from the carrier fleet and, with the complex Phoenix air-to-air missile, defend the fleet from a Soviet supersonic bomber-plus-missile threat, in the context of a major Soviet attack against our carrier forces. But as the Senate Defense Preparedness Subcommittee noted last year, this threat is "either limited or does not exist." Or as Chairman Mahon of the House Appropriations Committee noted, "The bomber threat against the fleet, as you know, has been predicted by navy officials for some time. It has not, of course, developed to date."

The problem of what contingencies and risks are to be guarded against goes to the very heart of priority analysis. Primarily what we buy in the military budget is an attempt to protect the nation and its vital interests abroad from the danger and risks by hostile forces. We seek either to deter the hostile force from ever undertaking the particular action or if worst comes to worst, to ward off the action when it does occur. Similarly, in designing particular weapons systems, the degree of complexity and the performance requirements built into the systems depend in part on an evaluation of the various kinds of contingencies which the weapon is expected to face. Now there are almost an unlimited number of "threats" which can be conceived. The likelihood of their occurrence, however, ranges from a significant possibility to a very remote contingency. Moreover, the size of the forces and complexity of the weapons systems needed to guard against a particular set of threats depends upon whether the threats materialize simultaneously or not. If they do not occur simultaneously, then very often forces developed to meet one contingency can be deployed against another. But the probability of two or more remote contingencies occurring simultaneously is obviously even lower than either taken separately.

Clearly we cannot prepare against every conceivable contingency. Even with a defense budget twice the present $80 billion, we could not do that. The real question of priorities involves the balance to be struck between attempting to buy protection against the more remote contingencies and using those funds for domestic purposes. In any given case, this is not a judgment which can be assisted by drawing up dogmatic rules in advance. And, since it is a question of balancing priorities, it is not a question which can be answered solely on military grounds or with military expertise alone—although such expertise must form an essential component of the decision process.

For what it is worth, it is my own judgment that we generally have tended in the postwar period to tip the balance too strongly in favor of spending large sums in attempting to cover a wide range of remote contingencies. And, as I have pointed out, this tendency—combined with the relentless ability of modern technology to create new contingencies and new systems to combat them—threatens to produce sizable increases in the defense budget.

A third important factor which is responsible for driving up the size of defense budgets is "modern-

ization inflation."[2] The weapons systems we now buy are vastly more costly than those we bought 10 or 20 years ago. The F–111A and the F–14A, for example, will cost 10 or 20 times what a tactical aircraft cost at the time of Korea. A small part of this increase is due to general inflation. But by far the largest part is due to the growing complexity and advanced performance of the weapons. In the case of tactical aircraft, speed, range, bomb load, accuracy of fire, loiter time, ability to locate targets, and other characteristics are many times greater than models one or two decades older. The same kinds of performance comparison can be drawn between modern missile destroyers and their older counterparts, and between modern carriers and their predecessors. We pay sharply increased costs to obtain sharply increased performance. Yet seldom if ever is this advance in "quality" used to justify a reduction in the *number* of planes or carriers or destroyers or tanks. If bomb-carrying capacity and lethal effectiveness is doubled or tripled, then presumably a smaller number of new planes can do the same job as a larger number of old planes. But the numbers generally stay the same or increase. As a consequence, modernization inflation primarily causes a net increase in military budgets rather than providing—at least partially—a reasoned basis for maintaining military effectiveness while reducing the level of forces.

In some cases, of course—for example, Soviet fighter aircraft—rising enemy capabilities may reduce the possibility of substituting quality for quantity. But the same kind of argument is hard to adduce for such weapons as carriers or attack bombers.

The fourth, and perhaps most important, reason for increasing military budgets is the fact that some of the most fundamental decisions which determine the size of these budgets are seldom subjected to outside review and only occasionally discussed and debated in the public arena. This problem is most acute in the case of the budget for the nation's general-purpose forces. The fundamental assumptions and objectives of the strategic nuclear forces are more generally known and debated. But the assumptions, objectives and concepts underlying the general-purpose forces—which even in peacetime take up 60 percent of the defense budget—are scarcely known and discussed by the Congress and the public. Congress does examine and debate the wisdom and effectiveness of particular weapons systems—the TFX, the C–5A, etc. But choices of weapons systems form only a part of the complex of decisions which determine the budget for our general-purpose forces.

Those decisions can conveniently be classified into four types:

1. What are the nation's *commitments* around the world? While our strategic nuclear forces are primarily designed to deter a direct attack on the United States, our general-purpose forces have their primary justification in terms of protecting U.S. interests in other parts of the world. At the present time, we have commitments of one kind or another, to help defend some 40-odd nations around the world—19 of them on the periphery of the Soviet-Eastern European bloc and Communist China. Almost all of these commitments were made quite some time ago, but they are still in force. Unless we wish to rely solely on "massive retaliation" as a means of fulfilling our commitments, they do pose a fundamental "raison d'etre" for general-purpose forces of some size.

2. Granted the existence of these commitments, against what sort of *contingencies* or *threats* do we build our peacetime forces? A number of examples will help illustrate this aspect of decision-making:

a. Pre-Vietnam (and, barring changes in policy, presumably *post*-Vietnam), our general-purpose forces were built to fight *simultaneously* a NATO war, a Red Chinese attack in Southeast Asia, and to handle a minor problem in the Western Hemisphere, à la the Dominican Republic. Obviously the forces-in-being would not be sufficient, without further mobilization, to complete each of these tasks. But they were planned to handle simultaneously all of the three threats long enough to enable mobilization to take place if that should prove necessary.

b. The navy is designed, among other tasks, to be capable of handling an all-out, nonnuclear, protracted war at sea with the Soviet Union.

[2] This is the term used by Malcolm Hoag.

The incremental costs of maintaining in-being a force to meet the Chinese attack contingency probably amounts to about $5 billion per year. When in 1965 the nation decided to begin federal aid to elementary and secondary education—which has subsequently been budgeted at less than $2 billion a year—a major national debate took place. To the best of my knowledge, there was no public comment or debate about the "Chinese contingency" decision. Yet the decision was not classified—it was publicly stated in the unclassified version of the secretary of defense's annual posture statement several years running. This is not to say that the decision was necessarily wrong. Rather, I want to stress that it has a very major impact on the defense budget, yet was not, so far as I know, debated or discussed by the Congress. This lack of debate cannot be laid at the door of the Pentagon, since the information was made available in the defense posture statement.

3. Granted the commitments and contingencies, what *force levels* are needed to meet those contingencies, and how are they to be based and deployed?

a. The navy, for example, has 15 attack carrier task forces. The carrier forces are designed not merely to provide quick response, surge capability for air power, but to remain continually on station during a conflict. As a consequence, because of rotation, overhaul, crew-leave, and other considerations, one carrier on station generally requires two off-station as back-up. Thus for *five* carriers on station, we have *ten* back-up carriers. (The "on-station" to "back-up" ratio depends on the distance of the station from the carriers' base. The 2:1 is an average ratio.)

b. The pre-Vietnam army comprised 16⅓ active divisions with eight ready reserve divisions. The 16⅓ division force is supported by a planned 23 tactical air wing (only 21 were in-being pre-Vietnam).

c. The navy has eight antisubmarine carrier task forces.

d. Defense plans call for a fast amphibious assault capability, sufficient to land one division/air wing in the Pacific and two-thirds division/air wing in the Atlantic.

The force levels needed to meet our contingencies are, of course, significantly affected by the military decisions and capabilities of our allies. The U.S. situation in NATO, for example, is strongly affected by whether or not the divisions of our NATO allies are equipped with the combat consumables and rapid fire-power weapons enabling them to conduct a prolonged conventional war.

4. With what *weapons systems* should the forces be equipped? Such questions as nuclear versus conventional power for carrier and carrier escorts, the F–111B versus the F–14, the extent to which the F–14 replaces all the navy's F–4's, must, of course, be decided.

Let me hasten to point out that there is no *inexorable logic* tying one set of decisions in this litany to another. Do not think that once a decision has been made on commitments that the appropriate contingencies we must prepare against are obvious and need no outside review; or that once we have stipulated the contingencies that the necessary force levels are automatically determined and can be left solely to the military for decision; or that once force levels are given, decisions about appropriate weapons systems can be dismissed as self-evident. There is a great deal of slippage and room for judgment and priority debate in the connection between any two steps in the process.

Some examples might help:

There is no magic relationship between the decision to build for a "2½ war" contingency (NATO war, Red Chinese attack, and Western Hemisphere trouble) and the fact that the Navy has 15 attack carrier task forces. In the Washington Naval Disarmament Treaty of 1921, the U.S. Navy was allotted 15 capital ships. All during the nineteen twenties and thirties, the navy had 15 battleships. Since 1951 (with temporary exception of a few years during the Korean war) it has had 15 attack carriers, the "modern" capital ship.[3] Missions and "contingencies" have changed sharply over the last 45 years. But this particular force level has not.

If one assumed, for example, that the navy's car-

[3] This observation is reported by Desmond P. Wilson, *Evolution of the Attack Aircraft Carrier: A Case Study in Technology and Strategy,* Ph.D. Dissertation, M.I.T., February 1966.

rier force should provide "surge" support to achieve quick air cover and tactical bombardment during an engagement, and then turned the job over to the tactical air force, the 2:1 ratio of back-up carriers to on-station carriers would not have to be maintained and the total force level could be reduced, even with the same contingencies. The wisdom or lack of wisdom in such a change would depend both upon a host of technical factors and upon a priority decision—does the additional "continuation" capability as opposed to "surge" capability buy advantages worth the resources devoted to it, on the order of $300 to $400 million per year in operating and replacement costs per carrier task force.

Similar questions arise in other areas. Does the 16⅔ division army peacetime force need 23 tactical air wings for support, or could it operate with the marines' 1:1 ratio between air wings and divisions? Granted the 15-carrier task force, must all of their F–4s be replaced with F–14s as the navy is apparently planning.

In short there is a logical order of decisions—commitments to contingencies to force levels to weapons systems—but the links between them are by no means inflexible, and require continuing review and oversight.

As I mentioned earlier, I am impressed by the fact that the Congress tends to concentrate primarily upon debate about weapons systems to the exclusion of the other important elements of the general-purpose component of the defense budget. Many of the elements involved in military budget decision-making cannot, of course, be made subject to specific legislation—I find it hard to see how the Congress could, or should, legislate the particular contingencies against which the peacetime forces should be built. But the Congress is the nation's principal forum in which public debate can be focused on the basic priorities and choices facing the country. It can, if the proper information is available and the proper institutional framework created, critically but responsibly examine and debate *all* of the basic assumptions and concepts which underlie the military budget. And it can do so in the context of comparing priorities. The Congress can explicitly discuss whether the particular risks which a billion-dollar force level or weapons systems proposal is designed to cover are serious enough in comparison with a billion dollars worth of resources devoted to domestic needs to warrant going ahead. By so doing, the Congress as a whole can create the kind of understanding and political climate in which its own Armed Services and Appropriations Committee, the President, his Budget Bureau, and his secretary of defense can effectively review and control the military budget.

This brings me to my next point. The size and rapid increase in the defense budget is often blamed on the military-industrial complex. Sometimes it is also blamed on the fact that the Budget Bureau uses different procedures in reviewing the military budget than it does in the case of other agencies.

The uniformed armed services and large defense contractors clearly exist. Of necessity, and in fact quite rightly, they have views about and interests in military budget decisions. Yet I do not believe that the "problem" of military budgets is primarily attributable to the so-called military-industrial "complex." If defense contractors were all as disinterested in enlarging sales as local transit magnates, if retired military officers all went into selling soap and TV sets instead of missiles, if the Washington offices of defense contractors all were moved to the West Coast, if all this happened and nothing else, then I do not believe the military budget would be sharply lower than it now is. Primarily we have large military budgets because the American people, in the cold-war environment of the fifties and sixties, have pretty much been willing to buy anything carrying the label "Needed for National Security." The political climate has, until recently, been such that, on fundamental matters, it was exceedingly difficult to challenge military judgments, and still avoid the stigma of playing fast and loose with the national security.

This is not a reflection on military officers as such. As a group they are well above average in competence and dedication. But in the interests of a balanced view of national priorities we need to get ourselves into a position where political leaders can view the expert recommendations of the military with the same independent judgment, decent respect, and healthy skepticism that they view the budgetary recommendations of such other experts as the commissioner of education, surgeon general, and the Federal Manpower Administration.

In my view therefore, the issues of the military-industrial complex, and of budget review procedures are important. But they are far less important than the basic issue of public attitudes, public understanding, and the need to generate an informed discussion about the fundamentals of the military budget in the context of national priorities.

With this in mind, let me suggest a few tentative proposals for improving public understanding and putting the military budget in a priorities framework.

TENTATIVE PROPOSALS FOR IMPROVING MILITARY BUDGET DECISIONS

The proposals I have in mind are addressed primarily to the Congress. As I noted earlier, many of the basic assumptions and concepts which determine the size of the military budget do not lend themselves, in the first instance, to direct legislative actions. But the Congress has another historic function—focusing public understanding and debate on important national concerns as a means of creating the framework within which both the Congress and the President can take the necessary specific actions. It is to this second function that my proposals are addressed.

As you know, each year for the last eight years the secretary of defense has submitted to the Congress an annual *posture statement*. This statement contains a wealth of information and analysis, and lays out most of the basic assumptions and concepts on which the military budget request is based. But, as I pointed out earlier, one of the most fundamental determinants of the military budget, particularly the general purpose forces, is the set of overseas commitments in which we have undertaken to defend other nations. Yet the secretary of state submits no annual posture statement covering his area of responsibility and concern. Because of this lack of a State Department posture statement, the defense posture statement each year has devoted its lengthy opening sections to a review of the foreign policy situation.

Recommendation 1

The secretary of state should submit to the Congress each year a posture statement. This statement should, at a minimum, outline the overseas commitments of the United States, review their contribution or lack of contribution to the nation's vital interests, indicate how these commitments are being affected and are likely to be affected by developments in the international situation, and relate these commitments and interests to the military posture of the United States.

The defense posture statement itself could be much more useful to the Congress and the nation if two important sets of additional information were supplied:

Recommendation 2

The defense posture statement should incorporate a 5-year projection of the future expenditure consequences of current and proposed military force levels, weapons procurement, etc. This need not, and should not, be an attempt to forecast *future* decisions. But it should contain, in effect, the 5-year budgetary consequences of past decisions and of those proposed in the current budget request. And not only should this sum be given in total, but it should be broken into meaningful components.

One of the major problems in priority analysis is the fact that the first year's expenditures on the procurement of new weapons systems is very small. Hence it is quite possible in any one year for the Congress to authorize and appropriate, in sum, a relatively small amount for several new systems which, 2 to 5 years in the future, use up a very large amount of budgetary resources.

All sorts of technical details need to be worked out if this proposal is to be useful. What is a "decision" about a weapons system? The Defense Department plans, for example, call for three nuclear carriers to be built. Procurement funds have been requested for only two so far. Should the cost of the third be included in the projection? But with a little goodwill on both sides, these questions could be ironed out. Let me also note that I am aware that the Congress—relying on past experience with cost escalation—may want to increase the official projections of many weapons systems costs in order to get a more accurate idea of the overall total.

Recommendation 3

The defense posture statement should include more cost data on relevant components of forces and weapons systems. What is the annual cost of the forces we maintain in peacetime against the contingency of a Chinese attack in Southeast Asia? What is the systems cost of constructing and operating a naval attack-carrier task force? What is the cost of buying and maintaining one tactical air-wing? What is the annual cost of operating each of the navy's eight antisubmarine warfare carriers? These are precisely the kinds of information needed to make possible a rational and responsible debate about the military budget in the context of national priorities.

Given this information, it seems to me that the Congress could organize itself to use it effectively. To that end, very tentatively I would suggest the following recommendations:

Recommendation 4

An appropriate institution should be created within the Congress to review and analyze the two posture statements in the context of broad national priorities, and an annual report on the two statements should be issued by the Congress.

I use the peculiar terms "an appropriate institution" because I am not familiar enough with either congressional practices or congressional politics to specify its title more closely. Whether this institution should be a new joint committee, an existing joint committee, a select committee, an *ad hoc* merging of several committees, or some other form, I do not know. But I can specify what I believe should be the characteristics of such an institution:

1. It should review the basic factors on which the military budget is based, in the context of a long-term projection of budgetary resources and national priorities.
2. It should have, as one part of its membership, senators and congressmen chiefly concerned with domestic affairs, to assert the claims of domestic needs.
3. It should not concern itself primarily with the technical details of weapons systems, procurement practices and the like; while these are very important, they are the province of other committees. It is the "national priorities" of the military budget which should be the essence of the new institution's charter.
4. Above all, it should have a top-flight, highly qualified staff. The matters involved do require final solution by the judgment of political leaders, but in the complex areas with which the new institution would deal, its deliberations must be supported by outstanding, full-time, professional staff work.

The institution I have described would have no legislative responsibilities. But I do not believe that makes it any less important. After all, the Joint Economic Committee has no legislative mandate. Yet in the past 22 years, its activities have immeasurably increased the quality and sophistication of public debate and of congressional actions on matters of economic affairs and fiscal policy. Should an institution such as I have described be created, I would only hope that 22 years from now it could look back on an equally productive life.

B. THE MILITARY-INDUSTRIAL COMPLEX

THE PERVASIVE ECONOMIC IMPACT OF THE MILITARY

SEYMOUR MELMAN

In an industrial society, people depend for most of their goods and services on organized, specialized production. That is why decision-power over production affects many facets of life—by means of those things selected for, or omitted from, production, and by the design, quality, and price of those things produced. The very size of the production empire controlled by the Pentagon limits the sorts of goods that can be made available to society in general. The scope of the decision-power exercised by state-management through the Department of Defense is suggested merely by the size of its budget. For fiscal year 1970, this budget has, at this writing, been proposed at $83 billion—exceeding the Gross National Product of most of the nations of the earth. During 1968, the Pentagon bought $44 billion of goods and services, making that management the largest of its kind in the world.

The federal government takes about half of corporate profits for its use. More than half of these tax billions, in turn, are controlled by the state-management. Thereby, the state-management concentrates control over capital to a degree undreamed of by the economists of private financial and industrial capitalism. The safe-management has preempted the leading role in the control of industrial capital, once held by the chiefs of private industry and finance.

Here, I will delimit and explore several dimensions of the Department of Defense empire at home and abroad: the industrial network; manpower; control over research and development; and the worldwide sales system for military goods.

In 1950, that part of the federal budget allocated to military purposes was $12.9 billion, or 32.7 percent of the total federal budget. For the fiscal year 1969, the military budget was $81

Abridgment from Seymour Melman, *Pentagon Capitalism* (New York: McGraw-Hill, 1970), Ch. 3. Used by permission of the publisher, McGraw-Hill Book Company.

Seymour Melman is Professor of Industrial Engineering at Columbia University, New York City.

billion, or 56 percent of the federal government's total budget of $146 billion. From 1961 to 1969, United States spending for military purposes amounted to $546 billion. Over that 10-year period, approximately 10 percent of the GNP has been devoted to military purposes. This is consistent with a reported top-level policy decision, made during the 1950s, that the government of the United States ought to be spending about 10 percent of its GNP for military and related purposes.

It is likely that the total outlay for military purposes exceeded the Defense Department budget. Many activities that serve the Pentagon are formally carried out by other government agencies: the Atomic Energy Commission; the National Aeronautics and Space Administration; the Central Intelligence Agency and other intelligence organizations; nominally civilian agencies like the Department of Commerce; parts of the Executive Office; and others.

Another way to measure the resources used for military purposes in the United States is to calculate the amount on a per capita basis; $439 per capita would equal the 1969 military budget.

As of June, 1969, property owned directly by the Department of Defense amounted to $202 billion. This included land, buildings, production equipment, offices, communications facilities, airports, and the value of purchased military equipment. By 1969, the Department of Defense owned 29 million acres of land. The scope of resources controlled by the Department of Defense is further revealed in the size of the contracts awarded in a given fiscal year. Thus, for fiscal year 1967, $44.6 billion in contracts were awarded by the Department of Defense.

Finally, in assessing the economic authority exercised by the Department of Defense, it is important to examine U.S. military spending on a standardized per-capita basis, compared with such outlays in other countries. Professor Emile Benoit of Columbia University has estimated the real cost per capita (measured in dollars of equivalent purchasing power) of military budgets in the principal countries of the world. Table 1 speaks for itself.

TABLE 1. Real Cost Per Capita (1966)

United States	$322
U.S.S.R.	191
Germany (West German Federal Republic)	79
United Kingdom	105
France	94
Mainland China	9

INDUSTRY

American industry contracted for $44.6 billion of work for the Department of Defense during the 1967 fiscal year. These activities were elaborately planned by the Joint Chiefs of Staff for each of the separate services and were finally translated into industry contracts by the Defense Supply Agency and related organizations.

Pentagon control over industry is enhanced by the concentration of activity within particular firms. This is shown in the annual listing of "100 Principal Military Contractors According to the Net Value of Military Prime Contract Awards." In 1967, the 100 largest contractors accounted for some 65 percent of all military contracts awarded. The first 10 contractors on this list included: McDonnell-Douglas Corp., General Dynamics Corp., Lockheed Aircraft Corp., General Electric Company, United Aircraft Corp., Boeing Co., North American Aviation, American Telephone and Telegraph Co., General Motors, and finally, Ling-Temco-Vought. These ten firms accounted for 30 percent of total Department of Defense spending among industrial firms.

The relation of the Department of Defense to U.S. industry was strongly affected by the development of Systems Management Contracting during the 1950s and 1960s. This mode of contracting allows a particular firm to undertake overall management direction of very large military-industrial programs by means of the establishment of a subcentral office under Pentagon control. The air force inaugurated this sort of activity during the 1950s. By this means, the air force could quickly accumulate a far-flung network of industrial activities to serve its operations, in the absence of in-house research and in-house military arsenals of its own (which the army had).

The air force came out of World War II as a major organization, but without the army's sort of research and development capability. In order to inaugurate with speed many new military-industrial programs, the air force invented the device of designating private firms or newly created "nonprofit" organizations as managers over major-unit military programs. This illustrates the sustained use of negotiated contracts, as contrasted with competitive bidding. Over a period of two decades, negotiated contracts (as against advertised and competitively bid contracts) amounted to 86 percent of the Pentagon total. It is also noteworthy that from 1948 to 1966, there has been no dramatic alteration in the proportion of military-industrial work negotiated.

Who controls military industry? What part of military-serving industry is private? The 100 largest military-industry firms are almost all privately owned enterprises. But control must be differentiated from ownership. The managers of corporate industry do not own the resources of their firms, they only control them. The formally private military-industry firms operate on behalf of a monopoly customer, with no alternative customer in sight. This marketing dependency reinforces the direct managerial control system.

This market dependency is revealed by the following list of principal military contractors (Table 2), showing their sales to the Department of Defense from 1961 to 1967, and the percent of total sales from each firm to the Department of Defense.

TABLE 2. Prime Military Contracts Awards 1960–1967 to U.S. Companies, for Firms Totaling More than $1 Billion in This 7-year Period (in millions of dollars)

	7-yr. total	Percentage of total sales
1. Lockheed Aircraft	10,619	88
2. General Dynamics	8,824	67
3. McDonnell-Douglas	7,681	75
4. Boeing Co.	7,183	54
5. General Electric	7,066	19
6. No. American-Rockwell	6,265	57
7. United Aircraft	5,311	57
8. American Tel. & Tel.	4,167	9
9. Martin-Marietta	3,682	62
10. Sperry-Rand	2,923	35
11. General Motors	2,818	2
12. Grumman Aircraft	2,492	67
13. General Tire	2,347	37
14. Raytheon	2,324	55
15. AVCO	2,295	75
16. Hughes	2,200	u
17. Westinghouse Electric	2,177	13
18. Ford (Philco)	2,064	3
19. RCA	2,019	16
20. Bendix	1,915	42

u—Unavailable.

Source: Department of Defense, Directorate for Statistical Services.

At the top of the list are the Lockheed, General Dynamics, McDonnell-Douglas, and General Electric companies. The first three are overwhelmingly Pentagon subfirms. General Electric, however, averaged only 19 percent of its sales to the military. Whereas the percentage of sales to the Department of Defense has been a minor part of the total activity of the firm, that activity is characteristically concentrated in separate divisions and facilities and is managed by separately designated managements. The 19 percent of General Electric's activity for the Department of Defense was not spread among the large number of General Electric divisions. Rather, certain divisions of General Electric specialized heavily or solely in military contract work.

The idea of the privacy of military-industrial managements is a form of well-cultivated fiction which conforms with the legal privacy-in-property right but not with the reality of the prime managerial control operating out of the Pentagon. An important instrument of Pentagon control is direct ownership of the key production facilities used by major military contractors. Table 3, Pentagon-owned, industrial production equipment (located in 1,900 companies), shows that 209,000 pieces of industrial production equipment, valued at $2.5 billion, were utilized by industrial contractors, as of November 30, 1967. The state-management controlling (and owning) this basic industrial equipment is clearly one of the largest, if not the largest,

TABLE 3. Fifteen Largest Holders of Government-Owned Industrial Production Equipment, 1967

	Number of pieces	Cost
General Electric	9,011	$ 114,752,148
North American Aviation	8,924	105,636,333
AVCO	6,395	89,633,519
General Motors	6,014	83,979,781
General Dynamics	7,298	79,174,713
Lockheed	8,359	77,068,029
TRW	3,495	64,706,654
Douglas Air	4,777	57,837,398
ALCOA	457	47,505,011
Aerojet	3,666	46,119,900
Ling-Temco-Vought	2,964	42,047,137
United Air	2,141	37,115,005
Boeing	3,286	36,915,820
Curtis-Wright	2,173	36,661,534
Raytheon	4,329	32,896,692
Total for 1,900 (estimated) companies	209,598	$2,578,627,370

Source: U.S. Congress, Joint Economic Committee, *Economy in Government Procurement and Property Management,* Washington, D.C., 1968.

single management of metal-working operations in the world.

The state-management is an extensive user of automatic data-processing equipment. The U.S. government, with the Department of Defense having a lion's share of this activity, has been buying or leasing $3 billion worth of data-processing equipment each year. Studies of the aerospace industry disclose that the largest part of the heavy equipment of that industry has been financed by the federal government. Thus, the Department of Defense owns 36 percent of the large-capacity profile milling machines of the nation, and 58 percent of this class of equipment that is numerically (automatically) controlled.

By 1967, the submanagements working under the Pentagon had been supplied with $14.7 billion of government-owned property. Typically, this property is intermixed with privately owned material and gives the state-management major leverage over the submanagement.

There is no exact compilation of the number of firms involved in the industrial network controlled by the Pentagon. This is because thousands of prime contractors subcontract for work. In individual instances, it has been possible to trace out four layers and more of subcontractors. Thus, if 15 to 20 thousand firms are involved in prime contracts, then the total number of industrial and other firms engaged by the Department of Defense is a multiple of that by at least three times. For example: one version of an antiballistic missile system (Nike-X) was reckoned to cost about $5 billion (to be manufactured within five or six years). It is estimated that 15 thousand companies would produce hardware and support services for this system alone. For this project, the general system-integrator is the Bell Telephone Laboratories and the prime contractor for manufacturing the Western Electric Company. However, for the performance of this work, Western Electric would subcontract more than 60 percent of the new awards to some 3,000 companies in nearly every state of the union. Thus, major subcontracts during 1969 are scheduled to include $59 million to General Electric, $60 million to Raytheon, $55 million to McDonnell-Douglas, $35 million to Martin-Marietta, and $9 million each to RCA, Texas Instrument, and Motorola.

MANPOWER

Within the 1968 labor force in the United States of 74 million men and women, the Department of Defense controls the largest block of manpower under one management. The 10 percent of the labor force directly involved with the Department of Defense includes 1.2 million civilian employees of the Pentagon and 3.5 million men and women in uniform. In 1968, the Pentagon employed 1,384,744 civilians and 1,205,654 U.S. military personnel in foreign countries. The Pentagon had "real military property" in 2,257 "locations" in countries outside the United States. These bases cost the United States $6.05 billion in capital outlay, and they cost about $4.8 billion a year to maintain and operate. A labor force of 3 million in the United States has been estimated by the Department of Labor as being directly involved in military industry. This estimate of numbers involved in military industrial work is probably an understatement of the number so engaged, because it is difficult to account for people in the network of multiple subcontracting characteristic of military-industry operations. Also, these estimates of persons acting for the Department of Defense do not account for the men and women in federal agencies such as the AEC, the CIA, NASA, and others, who are acting primarily on behalf of the military establishment. For example, by the end of fiscal year 1968, 270,000 people in industry, universities, and government installations were working for NASA. Another way of seeing the magnitude of operations of the state-management is to note that the California Institute of Technology, whose staff administers and conducts many research and development projects for the Pentagon, has been spending more federal tax dollars per year than is required for the operation of the entire legislative branch of the federal government.

A most important aspect of the manpower engaged by the Department of Defense is its occupational mix. On the whole, people engaged in defense industries are substantially more highly skilled as a group than those engaged in civilian industry or the rest of the economy as a whole. For example, of those engaged in defense work, about 16 percent were classed as professionals, compared with 13 percent in the labor force as a whole. Also, 21 percent in the military-industry force were skilled blue-collar workers, as compared with 13.4 percent in the overall labor force. The most striking aspect of concentration of skill on behalf of the Pentagon management is seen in the employment of scientists and engineers. In the aerospace companies in 1960, 106,000 scientists and engineers were employed—12 percent of the total employed in the United States that year. This number is scheduled to amount to 194,000, or 20 percent of the total industry labor force, by 1970. A further indication of the market pressure for the employment of scientists and engineers by the military defense industry is the number of column-inches of scientist and engineer employment advertising in a recent Sunday issue of *The New York Times:* 1,900 column-inches of advertising were published for scientist and engineer employment in aerospace industry—45 percent of the total professional employment advertising space. The federal government itself has been a major employer of engineers and scientists, with a total of 149,000 in 1966. Of these, 81,000—more than half—were employed by the Department of Defense and the Atomic Energy Commission.

The state-management is involved in varied relations with trade unions. Washington offices of the AFL-CIO and affiliated unions are often petitioners to the state-management for contract assignments, thereby supplementing the efforts of local managements. The state-management is able to use national unions in its efforts to sell the Congress and the country on new military systems. Late in 1968, the Pentagon ran a set of briefings on the antiballistic missile system for the unions in the Building and Construction Trades Department and the Industrial Union Department, of the AFL-CIO. Shortly thereafter, the International Brotherhood of Electrical Workers opened the pages of *The Electric Workers Journal* (March, 1969) to give a vivid exposition of the Sentinel system—its military and construction characteristics. The IBEW members were informed: ". . . the construction phase at each site will average about 22 months [and that] at the peak of construction, the Corps of Engineers contractor will have between 900 and 1,375 construction workers on a single site, depending on which of two types of installations are involved." The January 1969, issue of *The Carpenter* conveyed the same good news to the members of the carpenters' union. In this way, the unions and their members are taught to view the state-management as the employer, apart from the identity of the submanagement (contractor) in charge at any given locality.

RESEARCH AND DEVELOPMENT

More than one-half of the research money of the nation, and as much as two-thirds of the research and development, scientific and engineering talent are at work for the state-management. By the end of 1964, after 3 years of the Kennedy-Johnson administration, a Congressional Select Committee on Government Research, chaired by Representative Carl Elliott, reported that:

> . . . in the world of our probable future, our ability as a nation to compete will depend to a great extent on the efficacy of today's research into our grave social and economic problems. . . . In the sense of mission-oriented programs, we are spending greatly on defense, space, and nuclear missions and virtually nothing on the mission of securing our probable competitive future . . . apart from strictly economic problems many of our social problems have become very costly. In comparison to the dollars spent on the space program we can well afford some additional pennies for research into these and many other areas.

The committee further stated:

> . . . it is critical that the government avoid policies or procedures which lead to inefficient deployment or stockpiling of trained personnel. Manpower cost is as important as fiscal cost in consideration of major programs. But this has not been a significant criterion in major program choices to date. The huge technical programs of NASA, DOD, and AEC have absorbed large numbers of engineers and scientists. Yet no one at the time of decision has reckoned their worth on these programs as opposed to their alternative use in teaching, private industry, or other government programs.

These judgments by a moderate congressman from Alabama reflected an analysis of government sponsorship of research after a long period during which priority was given to the military uses of engineering and scientific manpower.

Ever since his famous farewell speech the late General Eisenhower has been repeatedly quoted as calling attention to the "prospect of domination of the nation's scholars by federal employment, project allocations, and the power of money." Less attention has been given to the role he had played in initiating the "military-industrial complex" by institutionalizing control of the Department of Defense over industrial and university research and development activity in the nation. In a memorandum dated April 27, 1946, General Eisenhower outlined a general policy on scientific and technological resources as military assets and defined the desired relationship between the Department of Defense and research and development functions in the nation. The issuance of this policy memorandum was, effectively, the founding act of what the General (fifteen years later) termed the "military-industrial complex." Eisenhower announced in 1946:

> The future security of the nation demands that all those civilian resources which by conversion or redirection constitute our main support in time of emergency be associated closely with the activities of the army in time of peace. . . . In order to ensure the full use of our national resources in an emergency, the following general policies will be put into effect:
>
> 1. The army must have civilian assistance in military planning as well as for the production of weapons. Effective long-range military planning can only be done in the light of predicted developments in science, and technology. As further scientific achievements accelerate the tempo and expand the area of our operations, this interrelationship will become of even greater importance . . .
> 2. Scientists and industrialists must be given the greatest possible freedom to carry out their research . . .
> 3. The possibility of utilizing some of our industrial and technological resources as organic parts of our military structure in time of emergency should be carefully examined . . .
> 4. Within the army we must separate responsibility for research and development from the functions of procurement, purchase, storage and distribution . . .
> 5. Officers of all arms and services must become fully aware of the advantages which the army can derive from the close integration of civilian talent with military plans and developments . . .
>
> In general, the more we can achieve the objectives indicated above with respect to the cultivation, support and direct use of outside resources, the more energy will we have left to devote to strictly military problems for which there are no outside facilities or which for special security reasons can only be handled by the military. In fact it is our responsibility deliberately to examine all outside resources as to adequacy, diversity and geographical distribution and to insure their full utilization as factors of security. It is our job to take the initiative to promote the development of new resources if our national security indicates the need. It is our duty to support broad research programs in educational institutions, in industry, and in whatever field might be of importance to the army. . . .
>
> In the interest of cultivating to the utmost the integration of civilian and military resources and of securing the most effective unified direction of our research and development activities, this responsibility

is being consolidated in a separate section on the highest War Department level . . . By developing the general policies outlined above under the leadership of the director of research and development the army will demonstrate the value it places upon science and technology and further the integration of civilian and military resources.

From 1946 to 1969, the military establishment has pursued the general policy line of the Eisenhower memorandum. More than one-half of the research and development technical talent of the nation has been deployed, directly and indirectly, in the service of the Pentagon. Single firms, nominally private, have become employers of enormous technical staffs. North American Aviation could boast in August 1966: "Leonardo da Vinci advanced science in nearly every known field of his day. What would he have been able to do if he had been able to work with 16,000 scientists and engineers. . . ." That is the number of scientists and engineers engaged in diverse fields under the direction of the North American Aviation management.

During 1967, the federal government supplied $15 billion, or 63 percent, of the nation's total research and development outlays of $24 billion. Within the federal sphere, the Department of Defense and the military supporting activities of the AEC and NASA have accounted for about 80 percent of the government total.

Government financing has supported the rapid growth of research activities in industry and in nonprofit institutions. This was especially the case during the period from 1956 to 1963, when government spending for total research increased by 20 percent, or more, almost every year. After 1963, the rate of growth began to diminish. By 1965, with increased pressure on the budget from the Vietnam War, the growth of federal research outlays was sharply curtailed. Suddenly, research laboratories became highly vulnerable to federal budget decisions. Until recently, dependence on federal support for research was a central feature of the physical sciences and the engineering technologies. More recently, there have been proposals for drawing the social sciences into the orbit of government control by increasing support given to them.

In summary, the Department of Defense has built up a formidable national apparatus in research and development. This has grown to encompass the natural and the social sciences and their application to diverse technologies. The research establishments extend from those owned and operated by the state-management itself to industrial firms, to Pentagon-satellite "nonprofit" research units, to laboratories in the universities. Throughout, the trend is not only to continue the traditional lines of work related to military problems, but to expand control into spheres hitherto considered to be civilian responsibilities.

INTERNATIONAL ARMS SALES

From 1949 to 1966, the government of the United States sold $16.1 billion in arms abroad and gave away $30.2 billion in additional arms and military equipment. This $46.3 billion in arms exports by the United States was arranged by the Department of Defense, excluding private sales not arranged through the Pentagon. The value of these arms exports is about $4 billion greater than the sum of all grants and loans made under the various economic assistance programs since the middle of 1948, including the Marshall Plan. From 1962 to 1968, arms sales alone amounted to $11.1 billion, and the sales goal up to 1975 is for $2 billion of armament sales each year. The Pentagon's plans also include military grants-in-aid, amounting to about $1 billion in military hardware each year. In all, the Department of Defense plans to export $3 billion worth of arms annually until 1975. The state-management in the Pentagon has become the world's leading supplier of armaments. This export trade helps to maintain and enlarge the military-industrial production network, while extending the scope of Pentagon control over "armed forces of customers," thereafter technically dependent nations.

The role of the Pentagon managers in arranging and expanding international arms sales was confirmed by Sen. Stuart Symington in July 1967. The senator, a Missouri Democrat and former secretary of the air force, has been chairman of the Senate Foreign Relations Subcommittee for Near Eastern and South Asian Affairs. After this group held hearings on international arms sales, a report was issued in which the senator stated that ". . . There is evidence to suggest that the type and destination of American military equipment sold abroad is determined by middle-level officials in the Department of Defense, by private firms which either elude the restrictions, or are unable to get policy guidance from the administration, and by foreign governments which ignore or bypass the terms under which American weapons were provided to them." The evidence examined by this subcommittee disclosed that Pentagon managers participated in complex evasive maneuvers, by which the letter of the law was evaded, to make possible the sale of American arms to countries which had been, for political reasons, prohibited from purchasing such arms.

The sales organization, functioning under Henry Kuss in the Department of Defense, has taken on the character of a go-getting sales operation, with quotas assigned to the various regional arms salesmen.

In various public statements, Mr. Kuss has aggressively justified the international arms sales program; for example, on the grounds that $9 billion in sales during a particular period would result in nearly $1 billion in profits to American industry, with about 1.2 million man-years of employment spread through the fifty states and the District of Columbia. Thus, Mr. Kuss identified the state-management in the Pentagon as a benefactor to the American economy.

Large-scale sale of arms abroad has been facilitated by a banking operation run by the state-management. In 1957, Congress made a credit fund of $383 million available to the Department of Defense. Since the law enabling the use of this fund required that only 25 percent of the extended credit be covered by the fund, the Department of Defense was able to extend $1,532 million in credits with this sum as a base. Another source of banking support for financing overseas arms sales was the Eximbank, 25 percent of whose extended loans during the fiscal years 1966 and 1967 were for arms purchases. Altogether, the Eximbank has financed more than $2.6 billion in arms purchases since 1963. Using the Eximbank operations, the Pentagon managers have subsidized the interest which foreign buyers have been charged for the money borrowed from the Eximbank to pay for arms purchases. The Pentagon management charged the recipients of these loans a lower interest rate for the money than it, in turn, had paid to the Eximbank for borrowing the money. An analysis of loans during the years 1966 and 1967 disclosed that in a series of cases involving as many as fourteen countries, the Pentagon managers charged the purchasing governments interest rates two or more percentage points below what it cost the U.S. Treasury to borrow money for comparable lengths of time in recent years. Not only has the Pentagon been using government banking operations to facilitate the arms sales, but also using the vast funds placed at its disposal by the Congress to subsidize these overseas sales.

The international arms sale operation is a many-sided activity. From the state-management's standpoint, this activity contributes substantially to the extension of its decision-power. The extended power operates in foreign countries as a type of political control by proxy. The proxy takes several forms: officers of foreign armies trained in the United States; dependence of foreign military forces on U.S. weapons, replacement parts, and so forth; the presence of U.S. military advisors among foreign armed forces. Since the state-management reaps certain cost benefits from some of the large-scale production of weapons in U.S. industry, the Pentagon is often able to compete against other nations' arms products in cost-price terms. This advantage is used to justify further arms sales and enlargement of the allied control functions. Thus, the extension of state-management controls becomes self-powered and self-justifying.

A PROFILE OF THE MILITARY-INDUSTRIAL COMPLEX

RICHARD F. KAUFMAN

THE DEFENSE INDUSTRY

The Beneficiaries

Although a large number of contractors and subcontractors do some military business, the lion's share of procurement money is concentrated among a relative handful of giant contractors. In 1969, the 100 largest defense suppliers swallowed up $25.2 billion in contract awards, 68.2 percent of the money spent through contracts of $10,000 or more, a percentage that has been steadily growing. Firms defined by the Small Business Administration as "small businesses"—generally, independently owned with no more than a specified number of employees, usually not more than 500 or 1,000, depending upon the type of business—received less than 20 percent of contract awards compared to 57 percent a decade earlier. Table 1 lists the 10 largest military contractors and their subsidiaries according to net value of military prime-contract awards in fiscal year 1969.

(Most of the criticism of the defense industry is directed against the large contractors. Small businesses doing defense work have many legitimate gripes against the government, the most important being that they are discriminated against. For example, in any pinch they are the first to get squeezed. Whenever contract awards are reduced, small business shrinks the most. In the past two years contract awards have gone down somewhat, but on each occasion small business has been affected disproportionately. Thus in 1967 the small-business share of defense contracts was 20.3 percent, in 1968 it went down to 18.4 percent, and in 1969 it went down further, to 17.5 percent. Most small defense contractors know this; however, they are afraid to speak out about it or to criticize the special treatment given the large contractors, because of fear of reprisals. Meanwhile, the dinosaurs are eating all the fodder.)

Richard F. Kaufman is Economist-Counsel for the Joint Economic Committee of the U.S. Congress.

TABLE 1. Ten Companies and Their Subsidiaries Listed According to Net Value of Military Prime-Contract Awards for Fiscal Year 1969 (1 July 1968–30 June 1969)

Rank	Companies	Thousands of dollars
U.S.	Total	$36,888,601
	Total, 100 companies and their subsidiaries	25,175,240
1.	Lockheed Aircraft Corp.	2,004,423
	Lockheed Shipbuilding Construction	35,752
	Ventura Mfg. Co.	61
	Total	2,040,236
2.	General Electric Co.	1,619,095
	General Electric Supply Co.	1,680
	Total	1,620,775
3.	General Dynamics Corp.	1,228,903
	Dynatronics, Inc.	448
	Stromberg Carlson Corp.	10,680
	Stromberg Datagraphics, Inc.	2,879
	United Electric Coal Co.	145
	Total	1,243,055
4.	McDonnell Douglas Corp.	1,031,752
	Advanced Communications, Inc.	524
	Conductron Corp.	32,021
	Hycon Mfg. Co.	4,862
	Tridea Electronics, Inc.	584
	Total	1,069,743
5.	United Aircraft Corp.	997,380
6.	American Telephone and Telegraph Co.	152,349
	Chesapeake and Potomac Telephone Co.	13,939
	Illinois Bell Tel. Co.	217
	Mountain States Tel. and Tel. Co.	1,688
	New England Tel. and Tel. Co.	564
	New Jersey Bell Telephone Co.	578
	New York Telephone Co.	52
	Northwestern Bell Telephone Co.	236
	Ohio Bell Telephone Co.	270
	Pacific Northwest Bell Telephone	145
	Pacific Telephone and Telegraph Co.	172
	Southern Bell Telephone and Telegraph	2,325
	Southwestern Bell Telephone	1,729
	Teletype Corp.	16,926
	Western Electric Co., Inc.	723,389
	Total	914,579
7.	Ling-Temco-Vought, Inc.	26,554
	Altec Service Co.	32
	Braniff Airways, Inc.	43,327
	Computer Technology, Inc.	54
	Continental Electronics Mfg. Co.	3,895
	Jefferson Wire and Cable Corp.	138
	Jones and Laughlin Steel Corp.	2,803
	Kentron Hawaii, Ltd.	15,448
	LTV Electrosystems	182,160
	LTV Aerospace Corp.	617,706
	LTV Ling Altec, Inc.	770
	Okonite Co., The	997
	Service Technology Corp.	10,645
	Staco, Inc.	11
	Tamar Electronics Industries, Inc.	125
	Wilson and Co., Inc.	9,154
	Wilson Sporting Goods Co.	295
	Total	914,114
8.	North American Rockwell Corp.	673,840
	Morse Controls, Inc.	201
	Remmert-Werner, Inc.	134
	Total	674,175
9.	Boeing Co.	653,638
10.	General Motors Corp.	584,407
	Frigidaire Sales Corp.	32
	Total	584,439

Similarly contracts awarded by the Atomic Energy Commission and the National Aeronautics and Space Administration, both of which deal largely with the same contractors as does the Pentagon, tend to be concentrated in an élite group of corporations. Of approximately $1.6 billion awarded by the AEC in 1968 to prime industrial contractors, all but $104 million went to 36 contractors. The ten largest AEC contractors accounted for $1.2 billion. NASA spends much more of its total budget for procurement than any other federal agency. More than 90 percent of its funds are awarded in contracts to industry and educational institutions. Of its $4.1 billion worth of procurement in 1968, 92 percent of the awards to business went to NASA's largest 100 contractors.

Some firms do almost all their business with the government. Into this category fall a number of the aerospace concerns—those which specialize in advanced weapons and space vehicles—including such giants as General Dynamics, Lockheed Aircraft, and United Aircraft. For the more or less totally dependent government contractors the benefits of a large and stabilized defense budget are easily demonstrable. In 1949 more of the three firms mentioned had total annual sales of so much as $250 million per year, and one, General Dynamics, had only $45.2 million. By 1967 each was doing well in excess of $2 billion in annual sales. By any other measure they and others like them had grown like fabulous beanstalks after a steady diet of defense-contract nourishment.

For other important defense contractors, such as General Electric, AT&T and General Motors, government sales amount to only a small percentage of total business. But the tendency for such powerful companies is to enlarge their dollar value of defense work, if not their share, over the years. And whether defense contracts represent 5 percent or 50 percent or more of a corporation's annual sales, they become a solid part of the business, an advantage to maintain or improve upon. A company may even work harder to increase its military sales than it does to build commercial sales, because military work is more profitable in many ways, less competitive and more susceptible to control through lobbying in Washington. Industrial corporations of the first order, those with assets of $1 billion or more, have faithfully made their pilgrimages to the Pentagon, the Mecca of the world of contractors, with no less enthusiasm than their smaller associates.

The enormous attraction of military and military-related contracts for the upper tiers of industry has deepened since 1965 along with the sharp increase in military procurement. For example, GE's defense contract awards went up from $783 million in 1958 to $1.5 billion in 1968; General Motors went from $281 million in 1958 to $630 million in 1968. While much of this increase can be traced to the Vietnam War boom—and many contractors would suffer a loss of business if the war ended or defense spending were cut back significantly for any other reason—there was steady growth in the defense industry during the 1950s and early 1960s (in 1964 and 1965, before the Vietnam buildup, there was a decline in contract awards). In the 5 years from 1958 to 1963—5 years of peace—the value of GE's defense contracts increased by $217 million and General Motors' rose by $163 million. The same trend can be shown for many of the large corporations in the aerospace and other industries. The large sums of working capital (money), use of government-owned property, research and development financing, and freedom from competition and from other rigors of the marketplace offered as defense contract fringe benefits are just too much for many corporations to turn down.

Geographic Distribution

The geographical concentration of defense production in the industrialized, high-income states also suggests that military contracts have come less and less to be restricted to an isolated sector of the economy specializing in guns and ammunition or even warships. In 1969 the two regions receiving the highest percentage of contract awards were the Pacific and Middle Atlantic. California placed in the top five states in 18 of the 25 procurement programs, New York in the top five in 12 programs, and Ohio among the top five in nine programs. The New England region received the highest proportion of awards for weapons contracts, and the Middle Atlantic, for ships. The East North Central region received the highest number of tank and automotive awards, and the Middle Atlantic region received the most electronic- and communications-equipment contracts. California received over one-third of all military research and development awards. The South Central excelled in aircraft awards, largely because Texas is located in that region. Military business has become solidly impacted in industrial America.

Concentration and Entrenchment

Indeed, concentration and entrenchment are characteristic of the defense industry. A study by Dr. Murray Weidenbaum, former assistant secretary of the treasury for economic affairs, showed the degree of concentration of sellers in the major military product categories. Weidenbaum applied concentration ratios to air force procurement during 1966. The concentration ratio shows how dominant small groups of sellers are in any given field. According to the Weidenbaum study, four firms received 86 percent of the aircraft engine contracts; eight firms took 92 percent. Four firms took 56 percent of airframe and spare-parts contracts, and eight firms accounted for 79 percent. Eight firms obtained 56 percent of total missile and space systems contracts. Finer breakdowns within product categories show further concentration. For example, two firms, United Aircraft and General Electric, received 65 percent of the aircraft engine contracts. Two firms, General Electric and Westinghouse, dominate nuclear turbine production. One firm, Newport News Shipbuilding and Drydock Company, has a monopoly on attack-aircraft-carrier production. Defense production at its upper radius is characterized by oligopoly and monopoly.

THE INFORMAL POLITY

To see the real defense establishment in action one must look beneath the surface of formal relationships, constitutional divisions of power, organization charts, laws, regulations, contracts, budget documents, profit-and-loss statements, and pious pronouncements about national security, the public interest and free enterprise. The fact is that vested interests lobby or bargain informally to get all they can of the benefits distributed through the political and economic system. The economic pie is not divided according to an intelligent arrangement of priorities in light of the legitimate needs of all groups within society and the best use of national resources, but according to who sits at the various bargaining tables and with what strength. The only difference about the military table is that so much of the pie has been brought there under the shibboleth of "national security." Around that table sit an informal polity of military and civilian officials and private defense contractors. All meetings are held in secret, and nobody brings his organization chart or his rule book. This is not to say that military planning has no bearing on our defense posture or that many dedicated people, especially at the lower levels, are not trying to make the cockeyed procurement system work. The question is one of degree. Who decides how weapons are purchased? How much influence do the weapons salesmen exercise? How much public money is being squandered to satisfy private appetites?

Going Native

A *Look* magazine story quotes a senior Pentagon official as saying: "It happens all the time. Almost all the officers who have anything to do with procurement go into the business. Naturally, they go to the companies they've had the most contact with. If you check the history of any missile or weapon program you'll find the same story."[1] In the spring of 1969 the Proxmire committee checked one missile program, the largest one we have—Minuteman.[2]

The Minuteman program, America's first line of land-based ICBM power (the Polaris submarines also carry ICBMs), was begun in the late 1950s and is still in progress. Actually the program has proceeded in three stages. Minuteman II was announced as a new-generation missile in the early 1960s, although some experts claim that the Kennedy administration, hoist on its own nose cone after it learned that the missile gap didn't exist, merely labeled some relatively minor improvements in Minuteman I as a brand-new weapon. Having installed most of the planned Minuteman Is and IIs, the Pentagon is now planning to replace them with Minuteman III, a larger missile with about 15 warheads on each one, called "multiple independently targeted reentry vehicles" (MIRV). The same consortium of contractors, except for one or two additions, has done all the work so far: North American Rockwell, Boeing, Thiokol, Hercules, Aerojet-General, Sylvania, General Electric, and Avco. The total cost of Minuteman I and II has escalated from $3.6 billion to about $7 billion.

The committee looked into one aspect of Minuteman II, the guidance-and-control-system con-

[1] Berkeley Rice, "Generals for Hire," *Look*, August 26, 1969, p. 31.

[2] Ninety-first Congress, first session, Joint Economic Committee, Subcommittee on Economy in Government, "Hearings on the Military Budget and National Economic Priorities" Part 2 (1969), pp. 495–519, 547, 610, 751–767.

tract with the Autonetics Division of North American, and found the usual history of cost overruns, schedule slippages, and performance failures. For example, the original contract grew from $170 million in 1963 to $320 million in 1964. The problem, according to Merton Tyrrell, executive vice-president of the private consultant firm that looked into this problem on behalf of the air force, was that "there has been little intent and little action taken to control costs" on the part of either the contractor or the air force personnel responsible for the program.[3] And one major reason for the cost-careless military attitude was "the switchover of personnel between government and industry."

One general, three colonels and one major, all of whom had direct responsibilities for the Minuteman guidance-and-control system being manufactured by Autonetics, subsequently retired from the air force and went to work for North American, two of them at the Autonetics Division. Gen. W. Austin Davis was the head of the air force's Ballistics Systems Division, which had charge of the contract. General Davis became a vice-president of North American. Two colonels were the air force plant representatives at the Autonetics Division. Their job was to monitor the program for the air force. They retired and both went to work for North American, one at the Autonetics Division. The guidance-and-control project officer retired and became an assistant program manager at Autonetics. General Davis's head of missile procurement also went to work for North American.

It is no wonder that the chances of a military plant representative "going native," that is, becoming in all respects indistinguishable from the contractor, are said to be excellent. Those who make the switchover on the higher levels, general or admiral, are referred to within the defense community as "rainmakers."

The pattern repeats itself. Capt. Patrick Keegan signed the contract with Pratt and Whitney for the F–111 engines; Keegan later went to work for Pratt and Whitney as a special assistant to the executive vice-president. Gen. Nelson M. Lynde headed the Army Weapons Command, which set up the procurement of the M-16 rifle from the original sole-source contractor, Colt Industries, Inc. He personally approved the prices negotiated. A congressional investigation of the contracts with Colt found that excessive profits were taken and the rifles delivered were defective. Upon retiring General Lynde went to work for Colt as a consultant. While employed by Colt, Lynde wrote to the Army requesting copies of four classified documents relating to the M-16. The investigating committee, headed by Rep. Richard H. Ichord, concluded "that it was at least unethical for Major General Lynde to accept employment with the producer of the M-16 rifle upon his retirement from the Army."[4]

Men like these are regularly recruited from the defense industry to help make and carry out defense policy. It is not only that the Pentagon civilian hierarchy constitutes, for the most part, a business elite that is very disturbing. What is most disturbing are the unlimited and unchecked possibilities for conflicts of interests.

There is a conflict-of-interests law, but it is toothless and nearly worthless because it is vague, narrow and practically never enforced. It applies only to retired military officers, not to civilians who may have handled military procurement, and provides that a military retiree may not "sell" to the Department of Defense for three years or to his service branch during his lifetime. The word "sell" is the catch. Military retirees do not "sell"; they become technical consultants or special assistants or are given other innocuous titles. What's in a name? All that is necessary is for the rainmaker to make rain. He can beat his drum for his employer in a hundred ways, by calling old friends in the Pentagon, arranging meetings, bending an ear, leaning on a former subordinate, etc.

Jack Raymond, who covered the Pentagon for *The New York Times*, recounted the story of Adm. William M. Fechteler in a *Harvard Business*

[3] *Ibid.*, p. 501.

[4] Ninetieth Congress, first session, "Report on the Special Subcommittee on the M-16 Rifle Program of the House Committee on Armed Services," p. 5371.

Review article. The admiral retired as Chief of Naval Operations and went to work as a consultant to the Atomic Products Division of General Electric. In testimony before a congressional committee, Admiral Fechteler explained how he arranged appointments in the Pentagon for a GE vice-president: "I took him in to see Mr. Gates. I took him to see Admiral Burke. He had not met Admiral Burke before. And then I made appointments for him with the Chief of the Bureau of Ships. But I did not accompany him there, because those are matériel bureaus which make contracts, and I studiously avoid even being in the room when anybody talks about contracts."[5] Thomas L. Gates was then secretary of the navy and later became secretary of defense. As of this writing the Pentagon has moved on the conflict-of-interests law in only one case since 1962.

The danger, of course, is that procurement officials, military and civilian, will influence policies and decisions concerning the purchase of weapons while in the Pentagon, then benefit from their actions or those of their former associates when they join the defense industry. At the same time, the defense budget gets bloated by a hodgepodge of unnecessary weapons. In early 1969 Senator Proxmire compiled data showing the number of retired military officers of the rank of colonel or navy captain or above holding jobs with the 100 largest defense contractors.[6] Approximately 2,100 retired regular officers were employed by the 100 firms. Ten of the larger contractors employed almost 1,100. These figures represent a tripling of comparable data gathered 10 years ago by Sen. Paul H. Douglas. Senator Proxmire concluded that the community of interests between the military and the large contractors is growing and militates against the public interest.

An investigation by a navy team in 1969 revealed that of approximately 300 officials employed by the navy to administer its shipbuilding contracts with the Electric Boat Company, a division of General Dynamics, more than a third formerly worked for the Electric Boat Company. "The situation," according to the navy report, "is not conducive to proper and objective relationships between the Government and the shipyard." After studying the procurement and cost control practices at the shipyard, 98 percent of whose work was under navy contracts, the report concluded that there was inadequate control over the costs charged to the government and that unwarranted charges were being made, that government surveillance of contractor operations was inadequate, and that the shipyard was wasting millions of dollars.[7]

The Board of Directors

Representatives of the defense industry do a great deal of lobbying, individually through their own Washington offices and collectively through various industry associations, such as the Aerospace Industry Association. With their military counterparts—the Air Force Association, the Navy League, and the association of the U.S. Army—they make up an effective pressure group in Congress. Perhaps the most heavily financed and sustained lobby program is carried on directly by the services—army, navy and air force—which maintain direct contact with Congress through offices of congressional liaison with branches located in the House and Senate office buildings.

The informal polity works best through the semi-institutionalized organization called the "business advisory group."[8] As of December 31, 1969, there were ninety-nine of these groups that meet regularly with Pentagon officials to discuss problems of mutual interest—everything from foreign policy to proposed changes in the rules governing weapons procurement. They are the defense industry's early-warning defense system

[5] "Growing Threat of Our Military-Industrial Complex," *Harvard Business Review* (May-June 1968), p. 60

[6] The data, broken down by each of the 100 largest contractors, may be found in the *Congressional Record* (March 24, 1969), pp. S 3702–81.

[7] The report is reprinted in Ninety-first Congress, first session, Subcommittee on Government Operations of the Committee Operations, U.S. House of Representatives. "The Efficiency and Effectiveness of Renegotiation Board Operations," Part 1 (1969), pp. 44–60.

[8] They were first authorized by an Executive Order of President Kennedy in 1962.

and ministers plenipotentiary. Inside the Pentagon, members of the more powerful groups, such as the Council of Defense and Space Industry Associations (CODSIA), are known as "our board of directors." Their function clearly is to influence defense policy. They keep abreast of new developments at the Pentagon, do their best to veto unwelcome changes and exert pressure to get the government to do things industry's way. They are obsessed with two problems: profits and criticism of the defense establishment.

An important advisory group is the Industry Advisory Council (IAC), which used to call itself the Defense Industry Council (DIAC).[9] In 1969 some of its members were:

- Ruben E. Mettler, assistant president and executive vice-president, TRW
- William M. Allen, chairman, Boeing
- George R. Brown, chairman, Brown and Root
- Eugene G. Fubini, former vice-president, IBM
- Daniel J. Haughton, chairman, Lockheed
- Donald J. Holden, chairman, Newport News Shipbuilding
- Thomas J. Jones, chairman, Northrop
- James R. Kerr, president, Avco
- Roger Lewis, chairman, General Dynamics
- Thomas S. Nichols, chairman, Olin Mathieson

Of those, three formerly held high positions in the Pentagon. Eugene Fubini was assistant secretary of defense and deputy director of defense research and engineering (1961–1965). Roger Lewis was an assistant secretary of the air force (1953–1955). Ruben Mettler was aide to the assistant secretary of defense for research and engineering (1954–1955). Also members of IAC were the Deputy Secretary of Defense, David Packard, and the Assistant Secretary of Defense for Procurement, Barry J. Shillito. Both were with the defense industry before coming to the Pentagon.

A typical IAC meeting was held in October 1968. The meeting was attended by the usual crowd of giant-contractor representatives and about thirty of the highest-ranking officials of the Defense Department, military and civilian. One of the first orders of business was the presentation by the then Assistant Secretary of Defense for procurement, Thomas Morris (later a vice-president of Litton), and Ruben Mettler, of TRW, of what they called a "blueprint" for the 1969 activities of the council. It was agreed that this blueprint would be circulated among members of the council so that it might be approved as the next year's agenda for action.

Following the meeting this blueprint was distributed to the members and throughout the Pentagon on the assistant-secretary level, attached to a memorandum from Morris. It was entitled, "Fundamental Problem Areas: key areas worthy of joint exploration by DOD and industry in calendar year 1969." It is an intriguing document for the insight it offers into the defense establishment. From all the pressing issues before the highest, mightiest chieftains at their annual powwow, what had they selected as "fundamental key areas"? The impact of defense spending on the national economy? The relative strength of the United States and the Soviet Union? The need for better coordination of force levels among the service branches? Ways to eliminate cost overruns? One could think of a score of topics this group could usefully occupy themselves with. Instead, the blueprint combines an outline of their fears and anxieties with a Dale Carnegie list of how to win public funds and influence politicians.

The number one major problem area was labeled "Achieving Higher Public and Congressional Confidence in Integrity and Effectiveness of the Defense Procurement Process." Listed beneath this key issue were a number of "Detailed Problems." Some of these were:

- Government property management hearings
- Excess profits hearings
- Renegotiation Act expansion
- Truth-in-negotiations
- Lack of competition hearings
- Specific program investigation (e.g., TFX, M-14, LOH, etc.)
- Economy in government procurement

[9] See Ninetieth Congress, second session, Subcommittee on Economy in Government, "Economics of Military Procurement," Part I, pp. 127–134; Donald May, "Washington Pressures/Industry Advisory Council," *National Journal* (March, 1970), pp. 682–684.

○ Property management report, statutory profit limitations

All of these "problems" describe congressional hearings, reports, and efforts either critical of defense contracting or aimed at trying to regulate it. In other words, what worried this business advisory group was the possibility that Congress might try to tighten up contracting and gain better control over the defense establishment.

THE MILITARIZED UNIVERSITY

The spread of weapons-development production throughout industry, itself a form of militarization, has brought about a similar infiltration of important civilian institutions. The university is a prime example. The military alliance with the university can be traced back to World War II, when the academic world enlisted in what was considered a just war. Efforts such as the Manhattan Project, which began at Columbia University and later involved the University of Chicago, the University of California, and other schools, proved to be of inestimable value to the military, although the army had to be dragged into the project 3 years after it was begun. The lesson was plain: The university was a gold mine of scientific and technical talent that needed only to be tapped to enrich the field of weapons research and development. Ever since, the payoff has gone both ways: to the military, which benefits by picking the brains of the academic world, and to university administrators and faculty members, who take in hundreds of millions of dollars annually in defense and defense-related contracts.

In the process the academic world and the rest of civilian society have become poorer. The Manhattan Project was started by scientists who were also humanitarians, such as Niels Bohr and Albert Einstein, many of whom were political refugees from Europe and who feared world conquest by Germany. Since World War II it has been the prospect of profit, not the prospect of a totalitarian takeover, that has spurred the universities into the arms of the military. For example, the largest of the university military contractors, the Massachusetts Institute of Technology (MIT), was awarded $119 million for weapons research in fiscal year 1968 and a similar amount in 1969, representing about half of MIT's total budget and several times the amounts of the operating budgets of many smaller colleges and universities. When student and faculty protests against the diversion of university talent and resources into weapons research, much of it classified, flared up in the late 1960s, MIT was thrown into a financial as well as philosophical crisis. The possibility of losing such a large source of funding was something no school could look forward to without fear for survival. A university placed in such a position of dependence upon the Pentagon has lost its most important asset, its ability to function as an independent force for learning, scientific investigation and social criticism, including criticism of the military, and all of society pays the price.

MIT, of course, is not alone. In fiscal year 1968 its fellow university military contractors included Johns Hopkins University ($57.6 million), the University of California ($17.4 million), Stanford University ($16.4 million), the University of Rochester ($13.1 million), Pennsylvania State University ($10.5 million), Columbia University ($9.9 million), Michigan State University ($9.5 million) and the University of Illinois ($8.6 million), to name a few. The navy alone awards about 1,100 contracts each year to colleges and universities. In 1968, 143 colleges and universities were occupied, if not preoccupied, with air force research projects.

Fed by the same rich supply of defense contracts, the milk of human unkindness, a variety of hybrid educational institutions has grown up to serve the needs of weapons and other military research. These are the research institutes, think tanks, laboratories and other centers that owe their existence to the defense budget. Some operate in loose association with the universities out of which they sprang, such as the Stanford Research Institute–Stanford University and Cornell Aeronautical Laboratory–Cornell University relationships. Others, such as Rand and the Logistics Management Institute, were created by the Pentagon. One of the largest, the Institute for Defense Analysis (IDA), got its start from a consortium of universities put together by James R. Killian, Jr., MIT's chairman of the board. All maintain ties with universities because they are sources of trained manpower and respectability.

But the university tradition, whatever is left of it in America, of independent scholarship hardly persists beyond that point, with the exception of a few dissident researchers who are attempting to reclaim their academic birthright. The primary function of "nonprofit" institutions such as IDA, as James Ridgeway has pointed out, is to serve as an adjunct to the Pentagon where bright university scientists can be enticed into its service without the tedium and low pay of civil service government work.[10] The same point can be made about the university-based military projects. There, too, defense work is a lucrative source of income to scientists who would be paid on a lower scale for doing the same research in a government laboratory. The contract system thus operates in part as a scheme for the Pentagon and its workers to evade civil service salary limitations.

In 1968 over $665 million in military prime contracts were awarded by the Pentagon to colleges, universities, think tanks, and other nonprofit institutions (see Table 1). In addition, NASA awards to this class of contractors amounted to over $165 million, and AEC awards were another $163 million, making a total of close to a billion dollars in defense and defense-related contracts to universities and other nonprofits.

Much ado has been made by all sides over the classified projects on campuses, as if their elimination would remove the chief source of friction between the military and the universities. This, in my opinion, is a shortsighted view of the problem. Classified research represents a relatively small percentage of university projects, a percentage that could be easily reduced further if the Pentagon wanted to declassify those projects which ought not be classified in the first place. For example, in 1968 the air force had 1,090 contracts with university scientists. Of those only 88 were classified, 22 of which were classified only because the principal investigator had access to classified information, not because the work itself was of a classified nature. An air force regulation permits declassification in such instances. Although the secrecy involved in classified work militates against the intellectual environment that ought to exist in schools of higher learning, the corrosive effects of military influence would persist through the bulk of the nonclassified projects.

The problem is the loss of independence, and the difficulty lies as much in the attitudes of university administrators and faculty contractors as it does in the Defense Department. Universities that have gotten used to steady flows of money from the military have learned to bathe comfortably in them. They like being dependent upon the Pentagon, although they may delude themselves with notions of their essential independence, just as industrial contractors delude themselves about being free enterprises while enjoying their dependence upon military contracts. Nor have the universities, now addicted to the habit-forming doses of money, been shy about coming to the Pentagon to ask for more. Senator Stennis observed in 1969 that "at some of our Appropriations Committee hearings, we see where these universities come down here fighting tooth and nail to get that money."[11]

A scholar working on a defense contract must apply his scholarship within the narrow bounds of his contract; for most practical purposes he is no longer a scholar, he is a military-contract employee. His allegiance has now been diverted away from the university and society at large. A billion dollars buys a lot of scientific talent, talent that becomes obligated to the purposes of its military and military-related benefactors, the effects of which are to deny its use for other purposes.

A scientist on a government contract, whether

[10] James Ridgeway, *The Closed Corporation: American Universities in Crisis.* (New York: Random House, 1968), p. 132.

[11] Ninety-first Congress, first session, "Hearings on Authorization for Military Procurement, Research and Development, Fiscal Year 1970," p. 1553.

in a university or a think tank, has moved within the Pentagon's sphere of influence and is subject to military control. He is no more free to be openly critical of military programs or military policies than he would be were he employed in a government laboratory or for a defense contractor, which is to say not at all. The fear of falling out of favor with the Pentagon, of having a contract terminated, of being blacklisted from obtaining future contracts or from receiving a high-level appointment to the Defense Department is always present.

C. WEAPONS PROCUREMENT

THE ECONOMICS OF MILITARY PROCUREMENT

U.S. CONGRESS
JOINT ECONOMIC COMMITTEE
SUBCOMMITTEE ON ECONOMY IN GOVERNMENT

1. MILITARY PROCUREMENT POLICY: A PROBLEM OF UNCONTROLLED COSTS

A. There exists in the Department of Defense a set of practices and circumstances which lead to:

1. Economic Inefficiency and Waste

The extensive and pervasive economic inefficiency and waste that occurs in the military procurement program has been well documented by the investigations of this subcommittee, by other committees of the House and Senate, and by the General Accounting Office. The absence of effective inventory controls and effective management practices over government-owned property is well known. In the past, literally billions of dollars have been wasted on weapons systems that have had to be canceled because they did not work. Other systems have performed far below contract specifications. For example, one study[1] referred to in the hearings shows that of a sample of 13 major air force and navy aircraft and missile programs initiated since 1955 at a total cost of $40 billion, less than 40 percent produced systems with acceptable electronic performance. Two of the programs were canceled after total program costs of $2 billion were paid. Two programs costing $10 billion were phased out after 3 years for low reliability. Five programs costing $13 billion give poor performance; that is, their electronics reliability is less than 75 percent of initial specifications.

Actual costs of expensive programs frequently overrun estimated costs by several hundred percent. Assistant Secretary of the Air Force Robert

Excerpted and reprinted from *The Economics of Military Procurement,* U.S. Congress, Joint Economic Committee, May 1969.

[1] Stubbing, Richard A., "Improving the Acquisition Process For High Risk Military Electronics Systems," *Congressional Record,* Feb. 7, 1969, p. 1450.

H. Charles testified that "The procurement of our major weapons systems has in the past been characterized by enormous cost overruns—several hundred percent—and by technical performance that did not come up to promise." The greatest amount of cost overruns occur in negotiated, as opposed to competitive, contracts. Even where overruns do not occur, there is evidence that prices are being negotiated at too high a level from the beginning. Most procurement dollars are spent in the environment of negotiation. It is precisely in this area that the DOD [Department of Defense] has the heaviest responsibility for obtaining the best military equipment and supplies at the least possible price. In the judgment of the subcommittee, the DOD has not adequately fulfilled this responsibility.

2. A Subsidy to Contractors

The major portion of procurement costs are in the costs of research and development, material, labor, and overhead for which contractors are reimbursed. In theory, competition requires contractors to be efficient in order to minimize costs and maximize profits, and inefficient contractors should not be able to underbid their more efficient competitors. Competition is a method of cost control. However, as we have said, most defense contracts are awarded through negotiation, not competition. A number of mechanisms, such as the cost and other price data submissions required by the Truth in Negotiations Act, and incentive contracting, have been designed to act as cost controls for negotiated contracts, in lieu of competition. In the judgment of the subcommittee, these mechanisms have not constituted an effective system of controls over the costs of procurement.

The result of the absence of effective cost controls, coupled with a number of policies and practices discussed in this report, has resulted in a vast subsidy for the defense industry, particularly the larger contractors. These practices include loose handling of government-owned property, interest-free financing of contractors, absence of comprehensive profits reports and studies, lack of uniform accounting standards, reverse incentives, and a special patent policy lucrative to the contractor. All of these things tend to benefit the contractor at the public's expense.

3. An Inflated Defense Budget

The total effect of unnecessary cost overruns, of hidden profits in "fat" contracts, of inefficiency and waste, and of the absence of cost controls is to create a bloated defense budget. Admiral Rickover testified that $2 billion of excessive costs results from the absence of uniform accounting standards alone. There is evidence that literally billions of dollars are being wasted in defense spending each year.

It is the judgment of the subcommittee that the defense budget has been bloated and inflated far beyond what an economy-minded and efficient Department of Defense could and should attain.

B. These practices include:

1. Low Competition

Defense-buying practices are reducing competition for government contracts and increasing economic concentration within the defense industry. Formally advertised competitive military contract dollar awards dropped from 13.4 percent in fiscal year 1967 to 11.5 percent in fiscal year 1968. Single-source procurement increased to 57.9 percent. These figures constitute a record low for competition and a record high for single-source procurement over the past 5 years. Negotiated procurement in which more than one source was solicited comprised 30.6 percent of total contract awards, also a record low over the past 5 years.

The DOD maintains that there is a substantial degree of competition in negotiated procurement where more than one source of supply was solicited. However, too often in these cases technical performance rather than price has been the basis for contract awards. Competition must involve dollar cost as well as nonprice elements such as technical performance and date of delivery. Activity involving only one nonprice element usually cannot be considered competition, nor does it contribute beneficially to the public interest in defense procurement.

It is widely acknowledged that *true* competition significantly reduces the costs of procurement. Some experts believe that in the absence of effective competition, procurement costs are 25 percent to 50 percent higher than what they would be under competitive conditions. However, instead of competition, it is becoming increasingly clear that the "buy-in, get well later" method is commonly employed by contract rivals. Under this approach, a contractor may bid a lower price, higher performance, and earlier delivery than his rivals, knowing Pentagon officials will accept increased costs, less than promised performance, and late delivery. Inadequate management controls at the highest levels of government have contributed to the development of these practices. The prevalence of these practices goes far in explaining why the estimated costs of individual contracts almost always increased and the performance of the weapon procured was often less than promised. Weapons procured in this manner, in the absence of true competition, have been characterized by high costs, poor performance, and late delivery of the end product.

2. Government-Owned Property

In addition to the lack of competition for defense contracts, the Defense Department's policy of providing government-owned property and working capital to defense contractors constitutes a government subsidy and contributes to concentration within this industry. The cost of government-owned equipment supplied to contractors sometimes exceeds the value of property owned by the company. While the total value of government-owned property in the hands of contractors declined from $14.6 billion in fiscal year 1967 to $13.3 billion in fiscal year 1968, reflecting primarily a drop in the amount of materials, in the important category of industrial plant equipment costing over $1,000, there was an increase from $2.6 to $2.7 billion. A disproportionate amount of this equipment was held by the larger contractors. Defense Department assurances that it is aware of the problems surrounding the use and control of the enormous amount of Government-owned property have so far yielded little tangible results in the form of improved performance in this area.

Last year this subcommittee found loose and flagrantly negligent management practices in defense procurement largely on the basis of facts surrounding government-owned property furnished to contractors.[2] The subcommittee has no reason to alter this judgment.

3. Progress Payments

The Pentagon makes so-called "progress payments" to reimburse contractors for up to 90 percent of incurred cost, on a pay-as-you-go basis. These payments are not necessarily related to progress in the sense of work completed. Costs are often incurred greatly in excess of original estimates. It is possible, for example, for a contractor to incur costs equal to 75 percent of the original contract price while completing only 50 percent, or less, of the job. A more accurate term would be "incurred-cost reimbursement payments."

The important point is that the payments are made interest-free, prior to completion or delivery of the end-product. The contractor could operate largely without his own working capital, on capital supplied by the federal government, particularly in expensive, long-leadtime procurement. For example, in the C-5A case, Lockheed received "progress" payments of $1.207 billion on reported incurred costs of $1.278 billion, as of December 27, 1968. In addition, the contract is being performed in a government-owned plant. The plant and the government-owned facilities employed at the plant have an original acquisition cost of $113.8 million.

In effect, considering the extensive use of government-owned property and government-supplied working capital—"progress payments"—the Defense Department provides negative incentives for the use of private capital, and tends to develop

[2] Economy in Government Procurement and Property Management, Report of the Subcommittee on Economy in Government, Joint Economic Committee, April 1968.

a financial stake in its contractors, especially those larger contractors which it favors with great amounts of government-owned property and interest-free working capital. Contractors so favored have a sizable competitive advantage over others in the defense and civilian industries, and are actually highly subsidized.

Money advanced to contractors in the form of progress payments are really no-interest government loans which inflate contractors' profits. Armed with free working capital a contractor may be able to bid low for more government work, "finance" commercial work, or otherwise compete unfairly in the commercial market.

4. Patent Policy

The government's patent policy similarly tends to reduce competition and increase the concentration of economic power. Briefly, the government permits contractors to obtain exclusive patent rights, free of charge, on inventions produced in the performance of government contracts. The Defense Department normally retains only a non-exclusive royalty-free license for itself. The contractor, in other words, obtains a monopoly which he can exploit for his own private gain in the commercial market for inventions paid for by public moneys. This "fringe benefit" of doing business under government contracts does not get reported as part of the contractor's profits. In effect, the public pays twice. Once through the government contract; again in the marketing of the private monopoly.

It should be noted that the contractor's own patent policy differs from that of the Department of Defense. When contractors award contracts to independent research institutes, the contractors, not the research institutes, retain the patent rights. Further, the employees of contractors generally must agree that the contractor gets the patent rights to any inventions developed during their employment.

Admiral Rickover and Professor Weidenbaum agreed that permitting contractors to obtain patent rights from government contracts reduces competition in defense industries because the "ins" get a competitive advantage over the "outs." Rickover stated that one-half of the patents acquired by contractors as a result of Government-financed research and development work are owned by 20 large corporations, ". . . the very same companies that receive the lion's share of contracts."

In contrast to general government policy, the Atomic Energy Commission and the National Aeronautics and Space Administration are required by law to take government title to inventions developed under government contracts, subject to waiver of rights by the government. The government's policy amounts to a special privilege to contractors at the expense of taxpayers.

5. Subcontracting and Profit Pyramiding

The study of subcontracting in defense procurement is important for at least two reasons. First, subcontracting can provide an opportunity for small business to participate in government work. Most small businesses cannot obtain prime contract awards. But they can supply prime contractors with a variety of goods and services. Second, profits in subcontracts turn up as part of the costs of the prime contract. Information about the amount and type of subcontracting and of subcontract profitability could be a valuable guide to current procurement costs and future policy. Unfortunately, the Defense Department has not been able to supply good information on these subjects.

DOD's collection of subcontracting data is inadequate. The only data which has been collected is the percentage of subcontracts that go to small business, on the basis of sampling. In fiscal year 1968, 886 large prime contractors awarded subcontracts worth $15.2 billion. Of this sum, $6.5 billion went to small businesses, according to DOD. DOD also *estimates* that approximately 50 percent of the total amount of prime contract awards is subcontracted. This estimate seems to be based on data gathered by DOD during 1957–1963 when prime contractors were required to report such information. Data on the total amount of subcontracting has not been collected since

1963. DOD cannot state with certainty whether subcontracting has increased or diminished since 1963, or whether prime contractors are tending to keep more or less of their work in-house.

Because DOD no longer collects complete data on subcontracting, we cannot know whether subcontracting is being awarded competitively or through sole sources, what kinds of work are being subcontracted, or whether subcontractors are required to submit cost data in compliance with the Truth in Negotiations Act. Admiral Rickover testified that there is a lack of effective price competition both at the prime contract and subcontract levels in shipbuilding procurement and that some major subcontractors have never provided the cost data required by the Truth in Negotiations Act.

Another serious omission has been the failure to collect information on subcontractor profits. The DOD profit review system compiles profit data for a sample of prime contract awards. These figures do not reflect profits taken by subcontractors which could involve several tiers. For example, a prime contractor might purchase a piece of machinery from a subcontractor. The subcontractor might purchase a component for the machinery from another subcontractor, and so on. Each of the subcontractors will earn a profit on the item supplied. The same final item, therefore, is likely to include a profit as part of its cost for each time it changed hands. In this manner, subcontractor profits are pyramided, layer upon layer, into the final cost.

When the prime contractor obtains the item, he, too, will add his profit to its cost. The government pays for it on the basis of the prime contractor's cost plus the prime contractor's profit. Included in the prime contractor's cost are the pyramided profits of several subcontractors. However, profits are often considered to be only the amount realized by the prime contractor. Profit studies normally do not consider the hidden, pyramided layers of subcontractors' profits buried in the prime contractor's costs. Whether subcontractor profits are reasonable is entirely unknown to DOD or any other government group. For this reason alone, defense profits may be seriously underestimated because the studies include only prime contractors' profits. The present policy of not gathering adequate information on subcontracting could be calculated to minimize the total amount of defense profits that are reported and to frustrate the thorough study of this important subject.

It is well recognized that subcontractors doing government or nongovernment business should be allowed to earn reasonable profits for their work. The issue here is that the DOD does not collect sufficient information to know whether subcontractors' profits on defense contracts are reasonable or excessive. The available data is also inadequate to reveal the level of competition among subcontractors, and the precise interrelationships between the prime contractors and the subcontractors. Further, it is presently not possible to determine whether prime contractors are charging the government unreasonably for work done by subcontractors. In the subcommittee's judgment, the thorough study and full disclosure of all the facts with respect to subcontractors' costs and profits, and their effects on the final costs to the government, is frustrated by the DOD's present policy and practice.

6. Noncompliance and Waiver of the Truth in Negotiations Act

The Truth in Negotiations Act was passed in 1962. Its purpose was to give the government better access to contractors' cost data so as to place government on a more equal footing with industry in negotiating the prices of contracts. The act is supposed to protect the taxpayer against overpricing where there is no true competition.

Investigations by this subcommittee and others over the past 2 years have demonstrated widespread noncompliance and other shortcomings with truth in negotiations. The government's failure to fully implement it seems to be one of the major reasons. Lack of implementation occurs in two ways. First, the government contracting officer can make a determination that competition is adequate, or that the price is based on a standard catalog price, and therefore that the act should not apply. Such determination can be made with respect to a negotiated procurement even though there is, in fact, little or no actual competition for the contract. Once there is a determination that adequate competition exists, the government does not obtain or evaluate cost and pricing data, or require the contractor to reveal the basis for his cost estimates, or to certify the completeness or accuracy of his cost information. Nor does the government subsequently review the contractor's books or records. In effect, the price is set on the basis of uncertified, unevaluated data supplied by the contractor.

Second, the government can waive the requirements under the act for cost data. There is evidence that waivers are granted to many large contractors. In one recent case, the navy waived the requirement for cost data in a $10 million procurement of propulsion turbines. According to Admiral Rickover, the price of the equipment was substantially higher than for similar equipment on a prior order. In addition, the price included a profit of 25 percent of costs. The contractor was one of the only two available sources capable of building the machinery. In response to requests for cost data, the contractor declined on the grounds that the proposed price was established "in competitive market conditions" and that "to supply any cost estimating data could only lead to misunderstanding." The waiver was granted over Admiral Rickover's objections.

The subcommittee also received evidence that the manufacturers of large computers are simply refusing to supply information specified in the Truth in Negotiations Act on orders for new design computers. In the face of contractor refusals to supply cost or pricing data for computers costing millions of dollars each, the government has waived the provisions of the act. According to the testimony of the General Services Administration, the government is faced with a take-it-or-leave-it situation. The contractor will simply refuse to sell if the government insists on the cost data. Moreover, there is evidence that few basic material suppliers such as steel mills, nickel producers, and forging suppliers comply with the cost data provisions of the act. Again, the tactic is (1) to persuade the government contracting officer that competition is adequate, or that the price is based on a standard catalog price, and that the act should not apply; or (2) to obtain a waiver of the cost data provisions.

The Truth in Negotiations Act permits the government to make preaward audits of contractors' books to determine the adequacy of cost data in cases where the act is applied. Investigations by GAO (General Accounting Office, an audit agency which reports to Congress) have revealed substantial overcharges to the government as a result of the failure of the Department of Defense to obtain adequate cost and pricing data. Because preaward audits were not always effective in disclosing inadequate cost estimates, Congress amended the act to give the government postaward audit rights, Public Law 90–512. The effectiveness of the postaward audit provision has not yet been determined. However, it should be kept in mind that the postaward audit provision cannot solve the problem of the failure to apply the act, or the granting of waivers. Furthermore, the comptroller general testified to this subcommittee in 1967 that a GAO review showed there had been full compliance with the act in only about 10 percent of the transactions tested. We are not aware that the record of compliance has improved.

7. Absence of Uniform Accounting Standards

In addition, the Truth in Negotiations Act often cannot place the government on a more equal footing with industry in negotiating the prices of contracts, even when there is compliance, because of the inherent difficulties of determining costs and profits under present accounting practices.

For example, it may not be possible for the government to determine whether direct and indirect costs on government and commercial work have been properly allocated by the contractor. In one case, reported by Admiral Rickover, the navy allowed a shipbuilder to charge salaries and other pay directly on government contracts, while similar costs on commercial contracts were charged as overhead and allocated to both government and commercial work. The government was thus paying directly for work done on government contracts and indirectly for work done on commercial contracts. The navy had accepted these costing methods because the contractor's system conformed to "generally accepted accounting principles." In this particular case the GAO eventually found that the government had been overcharged by over $5 million.

The fact is that there is wide disagreement on how particular costs should be handled and profits calculated under "generally accepted accounting principles." For this reason, experts may come to completely different conclusions about costs or profits in an individual case. In a case still pending, where the government entered into several multimillion-dollar contracts with the Westinghouse Co. for nuclear propulsion components, the contractor indicated his price included a 10-percent profit based on costs. GAO found that the contractor made actual profits of 45 to 65 percent of costs, and that he knew or should have known at the time he submitted cost breakdowns that the higher profits would be realized. Later the Defense Contract Audit Agency decided the contractor should have expected to realize 20- to 27-percent profits. Thus, two different government auditing agencies are in sharp disagreement over the amount of profits in these contracts. The vagueness of "generally accepted accounting principles" is generally acknowledged. In a recent case, the Armed Services Board of Contract Appeals stated in its opinion: "Except insofar as the ASPR (Armed Services Procurement Regulation) cost principles themselves reflect generally accepted accounting principles, it is difficult for the Board or the parties to cost contracts to govern their determinations by such an elusive and vague body of principles."

Under the Armed Services Procurement Regulations, cost principles are set forth for cost-reimbursement-type contracts for the purpose of denying certain costs, such as bad debts. These principles are not mandatory in fixed-price contracting. Yet fixed-price contracts constitute more than 75 percent of defense procurement. Thus there are no mandatory cost principles in the regulations for 75 percent of defense procurement. The cost principles that do exist have the effect of only disallowing certain items. They do not constitute uniform standards.

Finally, contractors are not required to maintain books and records on firm-fixed contracts, constituting 53 percent of defense procurement. Where contractors are required to maintain records, they must conform only to "generally accepted accounting principles," and may not show the cost of government work. Admiral Rickover testified that a sole-source supplier of nuclear propulsion units refuses to keep accounting records showing the cost of manufacturing the components. Thus, although he complies with the Truth in Negotiations Act, the absence of accounting records prevents a determination on whether his prices are reasonable. For example, a contractor may submit cost data at the time the price of the contract is being negotiated, but afterward, during performance of the contract, not keep adequate books and records. Colonel Buesking testified, "I have yet to see a contractor's accounting system in major programs that can adequately determine the unit cost of hardware."

Uniform accounting standards for all defense contracts have been advocated to facilitate the measurement of costs and profits. The GAO is now undertaking a feasibility study of such standards at the direction of Congress. Regardless of the outcome of the study, it is clear that the government often cannot determine the reasonableness of costs or profits on defense contracts under present cost-accounting methods.

8. Voluminous Change Orders and Contractors' Claims

It is often necessary to make changes in the design or production of an item after the contract is awarded. This is especially true for the more complex weapons and equipment such as missiles, fighter planes, bombers, and their electronic components. There may be thousands of changes on such procurements. The production of the B-47 bomber in the 1950s involved about 8,000 changes. The Minuteman program has involved at least that number. Change orders generally increase the cost of a contract.

The government pays the price if it originated the change or was in any way responsible for it. Because of the great number of changes, and the fact that the total cost of the changes may exceed the original price of a given contract, it would be reasonable to assume that records are maintained of the cost of each individual change and of their origin as to the government's liability. Again, DOD has failed to keep adequate records or to even require that contractors keep adequate records.

Contractors are not required to account for change notices separately. As a result, it is usually not possible to determine the cost of individual changes. Typically, the government is forced to negotiate a lump-sum settlement to pay for numerous changes since most changes are not priced in advance of the work, and the government has not checked to see what the cost of the change should have been. Admiral Rickover testified. "Thus, contractors can use change orders as a basis for repricing these contracts. They have almost unlimited freedom in pricing change orders because their accounting system will never show the cost of the work. The Government can never really evaluate the amounts claimed or check up to see if it paid too much."

Under the present system of nonaccountability, it is possible for contractors to inflate costs by pricing changes, and to attribute cost overruns to contract changes. In the vernacular of the world of defense contracts, change notices are sometimes referred to as control nourishment.

Many claims against the government result from formal contract changes. Others are produced by constructive change notices, which may occur in a telephone conversation between a DOD official and an officer of the contracting company. The contractor might obtain relief orally from meeting a contract specification, or claim that an act of God or a strike prevented him from meeting the contract schedule.

Regardless of the origin of a claim, the government is often at a disadvantage in meeting it. A contractor may have a large staff begin preparing and documenting a claim the day work begins on the contract. Although fully documented, however, accounting records seldom support the costs claimed. Nevertheless, the claim may be pursued over a period of years until it is finally disposed of. DOD does not keep records of unfounded or exorbitant claims, nor does it consider such information in awarding subsequent contracts.

9. The Failure of Incentive Contracting

Another attempt to find a substitute for competition has been the use of incentive contracts. The Defense Department began using incentive contracts extensively in 1962. The shift in emphasis reflected the widely held belief within the Defense Department that the cost-plus-fixed-fee (CPFF) contracts commonly used up to that time for major weapons systems procurement did not result in adequate control over costs. Since 1962 the decline of CPFF contracts and the increase of incentive contracts has been substantial.

The goal of the incentive contract is to motivate the contractor to be efficient and control his costs. The mechanism is a provision in the contract entitling the contractor to retain a portion of any cost underrun as additional profits. That is, the government and the contractor agree on a target cost as part of the contract price. They also agree on a profit as part of the price. If the actual costs turn out to be less than the target cost, the contractor retains part of the underrun as an increased profit. If the actual cost exceeds the target costs, the contractor must bear a portion of the overrun and his profit is reduced. The profit-sharing provision is the hoped-for incentive which will cause the contractor to increase the underrun so as to increase his profit.

The Defense Department has maintained that incentive contracting is an improvement over CPFF contracts. Beyond question, the problem of cost control during the period when CPFF contracts predominated was very great. Assistant Secretary of the Air Force Robert H. Charles referred in his testimony to the "enormous cost overruns of several hundred percent" for major weapons systems procurement in the past. He attributed a substantial portion of the cost overruns to the use of cost-reimbursement-type contracts and the absence of price competition.

The question, however, is, first of all, whether incentive contracting is, in principle, an effective means of controlling the costs of procurement, and secondly, whether it has succeeded in practice. The Defense Department claims success on both counts, although conceding the difficulty of demonstrating the effectiveness of incentive contracts as opposed to CPFF contracts, since they cannot both be utilized on the same project at the same time. On the other hand, much evidence was received which casts doubt on the proposition that incentive contracts result in cost savings, at least in practice.

Indeed, the experience of incentive contracting shows that it can increase both profits *and costs.* For while a contractor may increase his profit by performing efficiently to produce an underrun, another way of producing an underrun is to inflate the original target cost as much as possible. As Irving Fisher of the RAND Corp. pointed out in the hearings November 13, 1968, the problem of overstated target costs is significant because most weapon system procurement is negotiated without price competition, and many of the development contracts awarded competitively are awarded on the basis of technical or nonprice rivalry. In situations where target costs are negotiated, the opportunity for contractors to increase them is great.

The evidence suggests that incentive contracts have not accomplished their intended goal of increased efficiency or reduced costs, and that they may actually be contributing to a general upward shift in target costs. Whether this is inherent in the incentive-contracting approach, or the result of poorly applied but valid concepts, we are not prepared to say. However, we feel that burden of proof that the concept is indeed valid rests squarely on the Department of Defense. We are so far unconvinced that this approach is the best that can be designed to effectively control procurement contract costs.

10. The Conceptual Problems in Using Historical Cost Analysis and the Failure to Use "Should Costing"

The analysis of cost and pricing data is a crucial factor in determining the amount the government spends on weapons programs. Without good cost analysis and cost estimation, the government is unable to control the cost of procurement, much of which is based on original estimates. That is, the price of a contract is negotiated on the basis of cost estimates submitted by the contractor. An inflated estimate can result in an inflated price unless DOD can properly evaluate estimated cost data. Yet, as indicated above, the Defense Department's ability to adequately analyze cost data is severely limited by the lack of information on profitability, the absence of data on subcontracting, the shortcomings of the Truth in Negotiations Act, and the nonexistence of uniform accounting standards.

Another obstacle to adequate analysis is the fact that cost estimation presently relies extensively on past experience; that is, historical costs are used to provide estimates of the future costs of proposed weapons systems. Historical costs refer to the actual costs of performing earlier contracts. They are often insufficient and misleading guides to estimating the costs of new contracts for several reasons. For example, it is possible for the cost of performing a contract to be inflated intentionally or through contractor inefficiency, and for the cost of that contract to influence the estimation of costs on subsequent contracts.

As the testimony showed, historical costs are no better than the underlying data on which they are based. If the costs of previous procurements were obtained without competition, estimates based on them probably would not be comparable to costs determined competitively. As we know, most procurements in the DOD data bank were not awarded competitively. In fact, many of the earlier contracts were the CPFF type in which some of the most extreme cases of cost overruns occurred.

The use of historical costs may give the contractor a premium to inflate his cost base. The inflated costs of previous contracts may then become the new cost base figure for subsequent production runs and subsequent contracts. If profit is calculated by DOD as a percentage of costs, the contractor may be given a profit motive to increase costs. The only party hurt in this scheme is the American taxpayer.

Implicit in the criticism of historical cost is the

point that the cost of a particular contract may have been excessive because of contractor inefficiency. The possibility that contractor inefficiency may be a significant problem was brought out in the testimony of Colonel Buesking (U.S. Air Force, retired) and A. E. Fitzgerald, deputy for management systems, Office of the Assistant Secretary of the Air Force. Both witnesses compared the probable cost approach, which employs historical costs, and the should-cost approach to government estimates.

The should-cost approach attempts to determine the amount that weapons systems or products *ought* to cost given attainable efficiency and economy of operation. The method of determining the should-cost figure is based on a combination of industrial engineering and financial management principles. Briefly, a study is made at a contractor's plant of each of the cost elements of the contractor's operation to ascertain what the product should cost the government, assuming reasonable efficiency and economy on the part of the contractor. Obviously, this approach differs sharply from the traditional one in which costs are estimated in advance on the basis of earlier costs, and in which the government thereafter reimburses the contractor for incurred and allocable costs without finding out whether the costs were reasonable.

According to the testimony, when the should-cost approach was employed by the navy in connection with the TF-30 engine contract for the F-111 program, substantial inefficiencies were detected in the contractor's plant. As a result of the study, the contract price was later reduced by more than $100 million.

It is difficult to see how the government can be assured that incurred costs will be reasonable on negotiated contracts without the benefit of a should-cost type in-depth study and evaluation. Col. A. W. Buesking testified that selected evaluations of resource planning and control systems conducted to assess contractors' capability to meet standards of efficiency revealed that control systems essential to prevent excessive costs were absent. He estimated that costs in such plants are 30 to 50 percent in excess of what they might be under competitive conditions. When Admiral Rickover was asked to comment on Colonel Buesking's statement, he said, "His estimate is a conservative one." Establishing objective costs performance standards would be an important step toward cost control.

11. Absence of Ongoing Cost Reports to Congress

Equally important is the need for devising a method to periodically report actual costs to Congress as they are incurred on large negotiated contracts. Presently, it is difficult for the members of Congress and the public to know whether a program is staying within or exceeding original cost estimates and the negotiated price, during the period of contract performance. Reports of actual costs should be correlated with planned cost of work segments satisfactorily completed. In this way, cost estimates could be compared with incurred costs.

It may also be desirable to relate progress payments to real progress, in the sense of work segments satisfactorily completed, rather than simply incurred costs, and to report the volume and cost of contract change notices. Finally, a full cost-report system would include the profit rate negotiated and realized, and estimated and realized profits as a return on investment. If this were done, Congress would at least have available to it indicators of contract objectives and contract costs which would make it possible to detect serious overruns and delays, and to determine on an ongoing basis the cost status of the contract.

C. *The manifestation of these practices are:*

1. High Defense Profits

Perhaps the most glaring fact about defense profits is that not enough is known about them. The DOD cannot accurately state what profits are in defense procurement. First, it defines profits as a percentage of costs, and does not report profits as a return on investment. Second, DOD does not obtain complete information about profits on firm fixed-price contracts. During fiscal year 1968, firm fixed-price contracts made up about 53 percent of total expenditures for defense procurement. Third, without uniform accounting standards, it is difficult, if not impossible, to discover the costs and profits in defense production unless months are spent to reconstruct contractors' books. The reason for this is that contractors are not required to maintain books and records on most defense contracts. Thus, while the profit *rate* is designated at the time a contract is negotiated, the profit actually realized in the performance of the contract cannot be known and verified without an expensive, time-consuming audit.

The DOD collects data on less than half of annual contract awards, and the data it collects is inadequate. Studies conducted independently of the Pentagon are admittedly sketchy. Among other problems, (1) the trend toward conglomerate mergers among large defense suppliers obscures the opportunity for determining defense profits as their data is published in the aggregate without separating sales and profits by division, and (2) neither the DOD nor its contractors will readily furnish profit data to congressional or academic investigators.

No complete and comprehensive study of this subject has ever been made by any agency of the executive branch or by the GAO. Contractors are not required to report their profits on most government contracts. The DOD does not keep adequate records of contractors' profits. In view of the tens of billions of dollars of taxpayers' money spent on defense contracts each year, the government's lack of knowledge about defense profits is inexcusable.

One difficulty is in defining what is meant by profits. GAO and Defense Department surveys deal with profits as a percentage of costs. On this basis a 10-percent profit rate on a contract for a weapon that cost $1 million to produce would result in a profit of $100,000. But profits as a percentage of costs or sales is often an inaccurate indicator of true profits. For example, if a contractor is able to use government-owned equipment or operate in a government-owned plant, he may have a relatively small investment in a given contract. In such a case, his profit may be more accurately measured as a percentage or return on investment. Thus, on a $1 million contract, performed in a given year, where the contractor had an investment of $500,000 worth of plant and equipment, a $100,000 profit would be equal to a 20-percent return on investment.

An example of how a low profit as a percentage of costs can be misleading is found in a case decided by the tax court involving air force contracts (*North American Aviation Inc.* v. *Renegotiation Board, 1962*). In that case, while the contract provided for 8-percent profits as a percentage of costs, the tax court found the contracts returned 612 percent and 802 percent profit on the contractor's investment in 2 succeeding years, according to Admiral Rickover. In that case 99 percent of the contractor's sales was to the government. Indeed, profit as a return on investment is the preferred method of measuring profitability. Stockholders are concerned with the return on their investment, not with profits as a percentage of costs or sales. Return on investment is also a better indicator of the profit in relation to the contractor's input.

It is interesting to note that defense companies operate on smaller profit margins, based on percentage of costs, than do typical industrial corporations. Basically, this is because they often operate with large amounts of government-supplied capital. Professor Murray Weidenbaum studied a sample of large defense contractors doing three-fourths or more of their business with the government compared with similar-sized industrial companies doing most of their business in the commercial market. Net profits as a percentage of stockholders' investment was 17.5 percent for the defense contractors and 10.6 percent for the industrial firms, for the period 1962–1965.

The first question asked in this investigation was whether defense contractors' profits are too high. Much criticism of defense profits has been made in recent years. Critics maintain there is a serious problem of excessive profits. Others assert the opposite, that defense profits may be too low.

Although our present knowledge is incomplete, there is evidence that profits on defense contracts are higher than in related nondefense activities, and higher for the defense industry than for the manufacturing industry as a whole. There is also evidence that this differential has been increasing. The arguments of the Department of Defense to the contrary are unconvincing. The Pentagon's own figures show a 22-percent increase in profit rates on negotiated contracts under the weighted guidelines method of profit computation. The GAO found a 26-percent increase in a study comparing the 5-year period from 1959 through 1963 with the average profit rate negotiated during the last 6 months of 1966. DOD claims the increases relate only to "going in" profits negotiated, and that actual "coming out" or realized profits are less. But the DOD in-house profit review survey shows that contractors are coming out with profits that are substantially the same as the going in rates. In addition, when Admiral Rickover made a comparison of profits reported and actual profits as determined by government audit for five contractors, actual profits were found to be much higher than profits reported. Admiral Rickover also testified that suppliers of propulsion turbines are insisting on 20- to 25-percent profit on costs as compared with 10 percent a few years ago, that several nuclear equipment suppliers are requesting 15- to 20-percent profit, that profit percentages on shipbuilding contracts doubled in the past 2 years, and that a large company recently priced equipment to a navy shipbuilder at a 33-percent profit.

Col. A. W. Buesking testified that profits based on return on investment in the Minuteman program, from 1958 to 1966, were 43 percent. Profits for the large companies seem to be relatively higher than the smaller and medium-sized ones, according to the studies already completed.

Officials of the Department of Defense have attempted to answer the criticism of high profits in defense contracting by citing Renegotiation Board figures. Yet, in the annual reports, the Renegotiation Board warns against using its figures for generalizing about defense profits. One of the reasons for not using these figures is the fact that a large amount of contract awards are exempt from renegotiation and therefore do not show up in the totals for renegotiable sales. In addition, the board does not publish figures for profits as a return on investment, nor does it disclose the names of contractors who have been ordered to return excessive profits to the government and the amounts involved. Unless such disclosures are made so that profits on renegotiable sales can be fully analyzed, we agree that Renegotiation Board figures should not be used to generalize about profitability in defense contracting.

Officials of the Department of Defense have also attempted to answer its critics with the results of a study performed by the Logistics Management Institute (LMI). LMI was created by the DOD and in the past has worked almost exclusively for DOD. The LMI profits study was financed by DOD.

The LMI study used unverified, unaudited data which was obtained through the voluntary cooperation of a sample of defense contractors. Those who did not wish to do so did not participate in the study. Forty-two percent of those contacted provided no data. As Admiral Rickover pointed out, one of the faults with such a study is that the contractors making high profits would naturally be reluctant to supply information and could simply choose not to participate. In addition, the study fails to distinguish between profits of the larger contractors and the medium-sized and smaller ones.

These facts are cited to underline the continued need by Congress for an objective, independent, and comprehensive study of defense profits. This need cannot be satisfied by a DOD in-house study, or by an organization dependent upon the DOD for its funds.

2. Cost Overruns: The Case of the C-5A Cargo Plane

The contract with the Lockheed Aircraft Corporation for the C-5A airframe is a negotiated, fixed-price incentive fee contract. It is also the first contract utilizing the total package procurement concept (TPPC). Two major objectives of the concept, according to the Defense Department, are to discourage contractors from buying in on a design and development contract with the intention of recovering on a subsequent production contract, and to motivate contractors to design for economical production and support of operational hardware. Thus, TPPC is supposed to act as a deterrent against cost overruns and less-than-promised performances. To accomplish this, all development, production, and as much support as is feasible of a system throughout its anticipated life, is to be procured in a single contract, as one total package. The contract includes price and performance commitments to motivate the contractor to control costs, perform to specifications, and produce on time. As the C-5A is an incentive contract (TPPC does not necessarily result in incentive contracting) it contains the usual financial rewards and penalties associated with incentive contracting.

The C-5A contract for the airframe provides for five research, development, test and evaluation aircraft plus an initial production run of 53 airplanes (the total of 58 planes is called run A), and a government option for additional airplanes. The present approved program for the C-5A is 120 airplanes comprised of run A (58 airplanes) plus run B (57 airplanes) plus five airplanes from run C.

The testimony received during the November 1968 hearings indicated a cost overrun in the C-5A program totaling as much as $2 billion. A "cost overrun" is the amount in excess of the original target cost. According to the testimony, the program originally called for 120 C-5A airplanes to cost the government $3.4 billion, but because of cost overruns mainly being experienced in the performance of the Lockheed contract actual costs would total $5.3 billion.

Following the November hearings, Senator Proxmire asked GAO to investigate into the causes and amount of the C-5A overruns and other matters relating to the contract. Follow-up hearings confirmed the existence of the approximately $2 billion overrun in the C-5A program, the reverse incentives container in the repricing formula, and large overruns in other air force programs.

According to the air force, the cost growth in the C-5A program has resulted from normal development problems associated with complex weapons and inflation. However, the subcommittee notes that the C-5A was chosen for the first application of the TPPC partly for the reason that it was not considered a highly complex weapon system requiring technological advances beyond the state of the art. The inflation argument, which is supposed to account for $500 million of the cost growth, appears questionable. The contract contains an inflation provision to protect the contractor from unforeseeable price changes in the economy, to go into effect 3 years after the issuance of the initial contract, that is, October 1, 1968. The initial 3-year period was supposed to be considered a normal business risk. The air force official explanation of this provision states: "The contract thus included in the price an amount which reflected a projection of the mounting cost trend in the economy of labor, materials, equipment, and subcontract prices." If future inflation for at least 3 years was included *in the price,* it is hard to see why inflation should be a major factor in later increasing the price. Without a more thorough investigation of the C-5A program, the technical problems encountered, the failure to anticipate them at the time of the negotiations, and operations of the inflation provision, the subcommittee cannot form any firm conclusions about the reasons for the enormous overrun.

A repricing formula built into the contract was also revealed in the November testimony. The repricing formula is one of the most blatant reverse incentives ever encountered by this subcommittee. It should be recalled that the C-5A contract is supposed to represent an important step toward cost control. An air force manual on the TPPC dated May 10, 1966, states that "It should produce not only lower costs on the first production units, but, in turn, a lower take-off point on the production learning curve, thus benefiting every unit in the production run." The facts about the C-5A are just the reverse. Costs for the first production units are greatly exceeding original estimates, resulting in a higher take-off point on the production learning curve, thus inflating every unit in the production run. In addition, the contract is supposed to provide the Government with binding commitments on price and performance. Obviously, there is in fact no binding commitment on price if the price can be modified upward, as is being done in the C-5A, because actual costs are exceeding estimates. Whether the actual performance of the C-5A lives up to its promise remains to be seen. On the matter of delivery, it is interesting to note that the air force announced on February 25, 1969, a 6-month delay in the first operational C-5A aircraft, from June 1969 to December 1969.

Not only were the price increases made possible by the repricing formula, but the cost overruns which are resulting in the higher prices may very well have been encouraged by the existence of the formula and by the nature of the formula. For the mere fact that a repricing provision existed in the contract constituted a built-in get-well remedy for almost any kind of cost growth. According to this provision, the price of the second increment (run B) could be increased on the basis of excessive actual costs on the first increment (run A). The motivation, if any, of the incentive feature of the contract is thereby largely nullified, provided the contractor is confident that the government will exercise the option. Why bother to keep costs down if their increase forms the basis for a higher price? Additionally, because of the nature of the formula, the higher the percentage of overrun over the original contract ceiling price on the first increment, the higher the percentage by which the second increment is repriced.

THE PROBLEM OF COST OVERRUNS

FREDERIC M. SCHERER

In this paper, I will focus on just one symptom of the current national concern over the role of the military-industrial complex. While it is not the most important symptom of our current malaise, it is one on which an economist has some special competence. I refer to the enormous cost of weapons system research, development, and production programs and to the large cost overruns which appear to pervade those programs.

PAST OVERRUN EXPERIENCE

The problem is not a new one, nor is it partisan in nature. It has been with us through both republican and democratic administrations. Some years back I participated in a research project at Harvard University which compiled detailed case studies of 12 major weapons development programs conducted largely during the 1950s. Among other things, my colleagues and I found that on the average, actual development costs in the 12 programs turned out to exceed original predictions by 3.2 times, or 220 percent.[1]

When he took office as secretary of defense in 1961, Mr. McNamara was conscious of this record. He exerted strenuous efforts to bring costs and cost estimates under control. The results are now becoming apparent.

Two of the most widely acclaimed showpieces in his cost-control campaign were the F-111 and C-5A programs. The cost of developing the F-111 was originally estimated at $700 million by General Dynamics and $900 million by military analysts. By 1968, actual development costs had soared to $2 billion. The Phoenix air-to-air missile for the navy version of the F-111 was to be developed for $175 million. Actual costs were

Excerpted and reprinted from statement of Frederic M. Scherer in *The Military Budget and National Economic Priorities*, Part 1, Hearings of the Joint Economic Committee, U.S. Congress, June 1969.

Frederic M. Scherer is Professor of Economics at the University of Michigan, Ann Arbor, Michigan.

[1] M. J. Peck and F. M. Scherer, *The Weapons Acquisition Process: An Economic Analysis* (Boston: Harvard Business School Division of Research, 1962), pp. 19–22.

nearing $420 million when the program was terminated. The cost of the TF-30 jet engine for the F-111 rose from an estimated $273,000 per unit in early 1967 to $700,000 just a year later when contract negotiations began. After what must have been some of the toughest negotiating by a government team on record, the actual price was reduced to $620,000 per unit.

No one seems to know what the true overrun in the C-5A program is, but as nearly as one can tell, the cost of the first 58 airframes will exceed Lockheed's contract cost estimate by about $900 million, or 64 percent. Compared to the F-111 experience this is not at all bad. But transport programs have traditionally attempted less ambitious technical advances than combat weapon systems, and their cost overruns have been correspondingly lower. A RAND Corporation study showed the average unadjusted cost increase in four transport programs of the 1950s to have been 30 percent.[2] By this yardstick, the C-5A is hardly an improvement.

Many similar experiences of recent years can be cited—i.e., the AH-56 Cheyenne helicopter program; the army's Main Battle Tank development program; the Boeing short-range attack missile (SRAM) program; the NR-1, Dolphin, and Narwhal submarine programs; and (in another agency using kindred contractors) the Apollo program. Clearly, we have not yet mastered the overrun problem.

SOME CAUSES

There are a number of reasons why overruns persist. When ambitious research and development goals are set, technological uncertainty inevitably makes precise cost estimation impossible. The methods by which contractors are selected to carry out major new weapons and space program assignments encourage the submission of optimistic promises—"bidding and lying competitions," they are called in the trade. Despite numerous reforms, the contractual environment within which defense producers operate has not been able to root out inherent biases toward inefficient operation. Economy-wide inflation has also been a contributing factor in the last few years, although it is a little hard to take seriously claims that much of the C-5A's 64-percent overrun is attributable to this cause when the wholesale price index for metals and metal products rose by only 11 percent between 1960 and 1968. Any one of these influences could warrant an extended analysis. However, I should like to concentrate on another cause which is more troubling, and about which Congress might be able to do something.

Getting a major new weapons development program going is not easy. Risks and uncertainties are always substantial, and realistic cost estimates have a sobering effect. Recognizing this, industrialists and military officers are inclined to view a program's future prospects through rose-tinted glasses. There is a common belief at the intermediate levels of the military decision-making hierarchy that one should not rock the boat too vigorously through criticism at the start of a program. Troubles can be pinpointed and corrected later, when the program has its own momentum. This attitude contributes significantly to the subsequent appearance of cost overruns, and it can lead to seriously defective decisions.

That such things happen is well known, but the point is so important that I should like to illustrate it with two case studies. Neither is particularly unusual in the kinds of pressures experienced and the way decisions were reached. One, the Skybolt program, is singled out here because its ultimate consequences were so momentous. The other, Nike Hercules, is chosen because it bears on one of the great decisions before Congress at the present time.

Illustration: The Skybolt Program

Prime contractor for the Skybolt guided missile program was the Douglas Aircraft Company. How it came to that role is an important part of the story.

[2] A. W. Marshall and W. H. Meckling, "Predictability of the Costs, Time and Success of Development," in the National Bureau of Economic Research conference report, *The Rate and Direction of Inventive Activity* (Princeton, N.J.: Princeton University Press, 1962), pp. 465–469.

In the spring of 1959, when 14 firms were competing for the Skybolt job, Douglas was in trouble. It had been one of the first aircraft manufacturers to enter the guided missile field, and it had done extraordinarily well. Its responsibilities in the Nike Ajax, Nike Hercules, and Thor missile programs were discharged with admirable dispatch and efficiency, but the flow of orders from those programs was ebbing. To fill the gap, Douglas competed vigorously for the Minuteman ICBM prime contractor's job in 1958, but the award went instead to Boeing, which had experience in only one prior missile program—the Bomarc antiaircraft effort, generally acknowledged to have been a dismal failure. After this defeat, Douglas found its backlog situation desperate.

Skybolt, a proposed medium-range missile to be launched from B-52 bombers, appeared to be its best new opportunity, and it went all out in the design competition. It abandoned its traditionally conservative engineering philosophy, accepting extreme technical risks in order to promise maximum technical performance to the air force contractor selection board. It underestimated the difficulty of the Skybolt development tasks, submitting optimistic cost and delivery date estimates in the expectation that it would be "bailed out" a year or so later when final contract provisions were negotiated. That Douglas's estimates were unduly optimistic was well known in aerospace industry circles at the time. Whether this knowledge pervaded the air force general staff is not clear. That it did seem probable, however, for Air Force Chief of Staff Thomas White nearly let the cat out of the bag in 1960 by announcing that the Skybolt development program would require eight years. This "accidental mistake" was quickly corrected by a Pentagon spokesman, who set the "correct" estimate at four or five years.[3]

Full understanding of Douglas's optimism evidently did not reach the very top of the government decision-making structure, for in April and May of 1960 the United States negotiated with Great Britain an agreement to supply Skybolt missiles to extend the operational life of England's deterrent force mainstay, the Vulcan bomber. Doubts soon arose, however. George Brown of the opposition Labour Party asserted in September 1960 that the Skybolt development had already slipped behind schedule by 10 months, but the air force vehemently denied delay of any "significant event" in the program.[4] When he took office as secretary of defense, Mr. McNamara also had doubts about the program, but he apparently elected twice not to press for more accurate information in order to avoid a fight with air force generals, whom he had angered with his ICBM and B-70 bomber decisions.[5] Thus the program and the agreement with Great Britain continued through 1961 and into 1962.

By late 1962 the truth had become too compelling to deny. The cost of the program, originally estimated at $890 million, had risen to $3 billion and was still climbing. The delivery schedule was slipping steadily. Rumors of cancellation leaked out in early December, drawing heated protests from the British, who would have to spend large sums to maintain an independent strategic deterrent if Skybolt missiles were not available for their Vulcan bombers. Nevertheless, on December 13 Pentagon officials announced that the program would be continued only if the British agreed to pay the remaining development costs, estimated to be at least $500 million, plus the steadily rising costs of producing the operational missiles they needed. To resolve the dispute, President Kennedy and Prime Minister Macmillan agreed at their pre-Christmas meeting in Nassau cooperatively to build up in place of Skybolt a "multilateral force" of submarines armed with Polaris missiles. France was invited to join in the MLF effort. But President de Gaulle was infuriated that England and the United States had made this critical decision on NATO policy without the simultaneous participation and consent of his country. It is probable that the Skybolt-MLF affair cemented his determination to block British entry into the European

[3] U.S.-British Deal on Missiles Is Set," *The New York Times,* June 2, 1960, p. 3.

[4] "Delay on Skybolt Seen," *The New York Times,* September 2, 1960, p. 2.

[5] Arthur M. Schlesinger, Jr., *A Thousand Days* (Boston: Houghton Mifflin, 1965), pp. 857–862.

Common Market, and in the years thereafter the MLF issue contributed importantly to a deterioration of relations among NATO allies. Thus, the repercussions of the deceit in early Skybolt decisions plus inept handling of the diplomatic dilemmas into which those decisions carried the nation are with us even today.

Illustration: The Nike Hercules Program

A second, less dramatic illustration can be drawn from the history of the Nike Hercules surface-to-air guided missile program, executed under army prime contracts by Western Electric and its affiliate, Bell Telephone Laboratories. Formal development of Nike Hercules began in 1953. At the time, the research and development team presented estimates of the cost of converting existing Nike Ajax ground guidance and control equipment to handle the more powerful, longer-range Hercules missile. It was projected that the conversion could be effected by using a field modification kit at a cost of $210,000 per battery. This estimate was increased slightly in a further presentation during February of 1954. However, when negotiations for the first production contracts began in the early months of 1955, Western Electric announced a new approach, arguing and convincing army officials that the conversion could be done more economically by producing complete new guidance and control units in the factory, instead of making field modifications. This turned out to cost $1.7 million per battery—eight times the original cost estimate. The chief reason for this change in plans was that Western Electric had included in its original conversion cost estimates only the cost of parts and equipment, excluding the much larger outlays on field modification labor. When the full cost picture was considered, field modification no longer looked like the originally promised bargain. In interviews, Western Electric representatives acknowledged that their production-engineering staff members knew early in the game that a field modification program would prove to be impractical, but that they had presented the highly optimistic field modification cost estimates because they were more "sellable" to the army and Congress.

What is unsettling about this fragment of ancient history is its possible implications for the current ABM debate. Western Electric is the leading prime contractor in the ABM program; indeed, the Nike Hercules project sired the ABM effort. Western is undeniably a public-spirited corporation. It has been one of our most capable and successful defense and space contractors. Yet when the pressure to "sell" its program was great, it knowingly submitted misleading cost estimates. Now it is confronted with similar pressures. I have absolutely no evidence that the present ABM program cost estimates are in fact optimistic. But there is also little assurance that the ABM contractors will not yield once again—no doubt in a more subtle way—to the temptations of optimism.

THE NATURE OF THE DECISION-MAKING PROCESS

From these case histories and many like them two immediate morals can be drawn. One is mundane: that the competitive forces playing upon weapons and space contractors induce them to make optimistic predictions which eventually result in large cost overruns and faulty decisions. The second is more vital: that the weapons program decision-making process by its very nature tends to generate faulty choices based upon inaccurate and misleading projections.

Some elaboration on this second point may be useful. Decisions are not likely to be much better than the information and analyses on which they are grounded. In weapons development program decisions, most of the information on costs, schedules, and detailed technical performance expectations originates with the contractors. Obviously, contractors have an incentive to present their prospective programs in a favorable light, and so they tend to be optimistic. On its way to the apex of the defense decision-making hierarchy, this information passes through what organization theorists call "filters"—the program management offices of the military services and higher-level military staff units. Organizational filters could conceivably serve to correct initially inaccurate information inputs, but in the present context the military officers involved are themselves advocates, so they often fail to make such corrections. Sometimes they even add their own distortions by screening out information which reflects adversely on a program they favor.

The task falls then upon the Office of the Secretary of Defense to bring back some semblance of realism before major program decisions are approved. This has always been recognized, although there have been differences over time in the vigor with which an independent corrective role has been pursued. Secretary McNamara went further than any previous secretary in trying to develop his own independent bases for decision-making. As the evidence accumulates, we see that he was less spectacularly successful. Why this was so is a difficult question, but permit me to offer a few observations in partial explanation.

For one, the lines of communication between the Office of the Secretary of Defense and the actual laboratories and production shops where weapons program work is done are quite long. They are also not easily bypassed. Much of the information with which members of the secretary's staff work comes either through the filtering process I have described or from formal briefings which can be channeled and controlled, no matter how astutely and penetratingly the persons being briefed raise questions. There are also formidable barriers to having a member of the secretary's staff visit a contractor facility and simply wander around unguided, talking confidentially with many people, though this is the best way to find out what is really going on. The mantle of authority erects walls around its bearer. Consequently, members of the OSD staff have had to make their own seat-of-the-pants estimates on such matters as costs and technical feasibility. These have been remarkably good sometimes, but only sometimes. When a person becomes a "desk engineer," his feel for the technologies and (equally important) organizations with which he is dealing can deteriorate rapidly. Because he lacks first-hand contact with the technical problems faced, it is possible for him to go seriously astray in his independent cost and performance estimates.

To compensate for these problems and to supplement the limited internal staff resources at its disposal, OSD has turned to such organizations as the Institute for Defense Analyses and the RAND Corporation for independent counsel. They have helped, but they are no panacea. Their staff members are also far removed organizationally from the locus of actual weapons research and development work. Their access to work sites is limited. For instance, when a RAND Corporation cost analysis group estimated that true RS-70 program costs were likely to exceed original contractor estimates by nine times, they were barred from the grounds of North American Aviation plants for many months. There are also many pressures impinging upon the independence of organizations providing advice to government decision-makers. At the time when groups in the RAND Corporation began raising embarrassing questions about the RS-70 program, RAND suddenly found itself having difficulty getting its contract with the air force renewed. However courageous an organization's leaders may be, a certain amount of prudent restraint is almost certain to be exercised under such circumstances. And to note one further problem, there is reason to believe that the quality of the personnel staffing such organizations as RAND and IDA has deteriorated over time as the novelty of working for a military think tank wore off and senescence set in.

Another limitation of analytic staff groups in the Pentagon has even more disturbing ramifications. I suspect that a subtle kind of natural selection process makes it difficult for the secretary of defense to get no-holds-barred, broad-ranging counsel from his technical staffs on new program proposals and options. One of the striking phenomena of the past 8 years has been the invasion of the Pentagon by economists. It has been interesting to observe which members of my profession accepted Pentagon jobs and which were successful there. By and large, those who have agreed to do Pentagon staff work accept with only modest reservations the orthodoxy of the cold war: to oversimplify, that we can solve problems of international conflict by achieving military superiority, and by using force or threatening to use it. I happen to think that such a chauvinistic view is unsound and even dangerous in a world of reciprocal suspicions, misunderstandings, and arms races. I would give odds that a sizeable majority of economists presenting papers at this year's annual meeting of the American Economic Association and the Econometric Society would share my apprehension. So the Pentagon economics staff is probably not a random sample of the economics profession's mainstream. There have, to be sure, been some notable exceptions to this cold-warrior staffing bias. But except for the few who arrived on the early McNamara-Hitch bandwagon in 1961, OSD staff economists who have seen fit to contest the hoary shibboleths of the cold war have not been very successful in the Pentagon. The persons who get elevated to top jobs tend to be those who either embrace orthodoxy or at least keep their doubts below the surface. Those who voice fundamental objections are passed over, become frustrated from being ignored, and/or develop an uneasy sense of being out of place. They resign to accept more satisfying assignments elsewhere. And so the natural selection process biases the composition of the secretary's staff and prevents him from getting a multisided analysis. To give an illustration, I have been told by a former staff member that for nearly 18 months the Office of the Assistant Secretary of Defense for Systems Analysis worked under guidelines specifying that Soviet and Chinese reactions were to be excluded from consideration in analyses of the Sentinel ABM program. Yet this was the very essence of the problem, and to ignore it was to guarantee an ill-conceived decision. I have no first-hand knowledge as to whether this selection bias extends to the defense secretary's scientific and engineering staff. It would be quite surprising, however, if it did not.

Lest this criticism be misunderstood, I hasten to add my opinion that the OSD system analysis staff has done a good job in many respects. The nation would be worse off if it were eliminated or emasculated. Subject to the information limitations I have noted earlier, it has worked hard and with some success to ensure that programs patently more costly or in other ways inferior to available alternatives were eliminated. It has also helped hold the line against certain new programs—e.g., the RS-70—which would have shaped U.S. military capabilities in directions inconsistent with approved strategic doctrines. For a while too—but not consistently—it called attention to the potentially destabilizing character of certain ballistic missile defense deployment strategies. However, because of built-in organizational and staffing biases, it has been much less effective in challenging the basic strategic assumptions underlying many program decisions, i.e., whether the Soviet Union in fact posed the qualitative and quantitative threat taken for granted in many decisions. Thus, it has worked to see that the best weapon systems were chosen for specific missions, but it has not questioned deeply whether the missions themselves were justified. It has also failed to take into account with any degree of consistency how our force structure and strategy choices influence the reciprocal force structure decisions of the Soviet Union and other nations systems analysts so blithely call "the enemy." As a result of these shortcomings, the United States has continued to place its emphasis in international relations upon military solutions which in the long run are both self-defeatng and enormously costly due to the inexorable dynamics of the arms race.

Furthermore, once decisions have been taken by the secretary of defense, members of the systems analysis staff tend, like all good organization men, to fall into line and cease whatever criticism and opposition they exhibited. Vigorous critical give-and-take ceases for the sake of a uniform position; doubts are transformed into certainties. And so hundreds of millions of dollars or perhaps even billions are expended in approved programs until some series of events demonstrates dramatically and unmistakably that the original assumptions were faulty.

Unless these observations miss the mark completely, it follows that the program recommendations and decisions emanating from the Office of the Secretary of Defense are based with alarming frequency upon distorted data and poorly-framed myopic analyses. As such, they deserve to be received with considerable skepticism. To accept them at face value is to insure a continuation of high cost overruns and programs which consume billions of dollars, but whose effectiveness is quickly nullified by Soviet Union countermeasures.

"REFORM" OF PENTAGON PROCUREMENT OR GILBERT FITZHUGH'S GOLDEN FLEECE

A. ERNEST FITZGERALD

On July 27, 1970, the secretary of defense released the, till-then secret, Fitzhugh Report. He indicated that it would recommend changes in Pentagon procurement designed to prevent massive losses to taxpayers because of cost overruns on weapons programs. The Pentagon was to be brought under control.

The Fitzhugh Report itself covered a broad range of Pentagon management problems, but the best-publicized items dealt with big weapons procurement and civilian control. The costly, overrun-producing procurement practices of the McNamara era were to be replaced by a careful, conservative, step-by-step procurement approach, popularly called "fly before you buy." Civilian control would be strengthened, with the Joint Chiefs of Staff put in their place through reorganization.

All this was handled masterfully, with the appearance of great toughness on the part of the administration and Fitzhugh, the chairman of the board of the Metropolitan Life Insurance Company. Fitzhugh held a press conference in which he expressed wonder that the Pentagon works at all, which gained him the reputation for having smitten the Pentagon. *The New York Times* and other leading journals hailed the "new critic of the Pentagon." The press, TV, and radio consensus was that the Fitzhugh Report was not a whitewash after all and that those who had said it would be should take it all back and be ashamed of themselves.

Reprinted from A. Ernest Fitzgerald, "Gilbert Fitzhugh's Golden Fleece," *The Washington Monthly* (November 1970), pp. 44–55. By permission of *The Washington Monthly*.

A. Ernest Fitzgerald is Director, Performance Technology Inc., formerly Deputy for Management Systems, U.S. Air Force.

A BOUNTIFUL GRACE

The Fitzhugh Panel grew out of controversies in the spring of 1969, when the Department of Defense was beset by trouble from all sides—

including embarrassing probes into the Pentagon's sordid procurement mess and the enormous waste of military-spending programs. Secretary Laird was hopping mad about the bad press which the big procurement programs were receiving. On March 27, he wrote a letter to his assistants: "I am increasingly concerned about allusions in the press and elsewhere to runaway costs on such key or major programs as the C-5A." He then went on to ask for suggestions: "What sorts of actions on DOD's [Department of Defense] part can be taken to thwart or ameliorate the continuing adverse commentary on program costs and suspect technical effectiveness?"

Soon the decision was made to employ the hoariest trick in the bureaucratic book. A panel would be appointed to study the problem, and all the trimmings of the study commission syndrome were used. The establishment of the group was announced with flourish by the president himself. The panel was to have a year to complete its work, which would buy valuable time to mend fences and dim the public memory of the then-fresh horror stories (the current White House staff is generally believed to be dedicated to the proposition that the public memory is about three weeks long). The scope of the panel's study was broadened to include the structure of the entire defense establishment, which helped dilute the attention given to the spending-control issue. Finally, the panel was composed of individuals who either knew nothing about military procurement or were beneficiaries of current practices.

In the year of grace bought by the Fitzhugh study, the Pentagon's big spenders have done a remarkable job of strengthening their coalition of supporters. Until last year, most of the burden of selling the big military programs had been borne by Pentagon officials and their larger suppliers, the classic military-industrial complex. However, since then all the principal beneficiaries of the process have been organized into a spending lobby of awesome power.

True, the Congress has cut the Pentagon's spending requests in each of the last two years. Last year Rep. George Mahon's House Appropriations Committee cut the Pentagon's requests by more than $5 billion and has cut about $2 billion more this year. In the first critical debates and serious floor challenges in my memory, the Pentagon has been in logically and morally vulnerable positions on most issues subjected to questioning. Yet, they have won almost every open fight and have avoided outright terminations of their most militarily suspect and most expensive programs. Most of the cuts have been "stretch-outs," or reductions of funds and planned quantities on still-active programs.

Despite public statements deploring excessive military spending, the biggest banks in the country lobbied vigorously and effectively for specific programs, particularly for congressional action to finance Lockheed's C-5A overruns. With jobs scarce, big political labor has joined the gaggle, lobbying to protect big military-spending programs. AFL-CIO bigwigs have been particularly candid in their pitch. They want jobs, period. They lobbied especially hard for ABM expansion and C-5A overrun financing. With a few notable exceptions, the business community is now either pumping for more military spending or is silent.

All in all, the Pentagon has done a remarkable job of organizing a broader new military-spending coalition. This is one product of the Fitzhugh Panel grace period, and another is the report itself. Let's consider what we obtained by waiting for the report's recommendations, beginning with those on the organization of the Pentagon.

SMOOTHING THE WRINKLES

This section of the report was highly advertised as strengthening civilian control of our military establishment. Its salient feature was the recommendation to remove the Joint Chiefs of Staff from immediate control of military operations. Presumably, this responsibility was to be assigned to an individual "drawn from civilian life." Political and press reaction to this feature was overwhelmingly favorable. Many liberals were ecstatic, forgetting for the moment that we already have civilian control in the persons of Sen. John Stennis and Rep. L. Mendel Rivers. They will be disillusioned to learn that the new post of chief of the Pentagon's military operations section has been filled by the chairman of the Joint Chiefs of Staff. This possibility was suggested by Fitzhugh himself.

So the most widely heralded organizational recommendation has amounted to exactly nothing. Admiral Rickover, among others, has been predicting this for months. Speaking of the Pentagon's civilian and military bureaucrats' propensity to fake corrective actions by reorganization, he said, "Every time they have trouble, they change the organization. Generally, they change the telephone numbers." The admiral, a long-time bureaucrat-watcher, recognized early on that the Pentagonists would not even alter the historic pattern or sequence of bureaucratic protective reactions. He knew that nothing would really change.

However, in the present instance, this is not quite the case. Things are not the same, for the Fitzhugh Report contains many other organizational recommendations, some of which actually make things worse.

One example affects the principles of internal control in procurement. Sizeable businesses usually keep separate the functions of generating requirements for purchases, placing purchase orders, certifying satisfactory delivery, approving invoices for payment, and issuing checks. This is done to minimize the possibility of collusion and defalcation. These functions have tended to be drawn together in the Pentagon's big weapons development programs, supposedly for speed in handling contractual matters. In those few instances in which reductions in weapons costs have been made, the government contracting officers, or purchasing agents, have been independent of the government program offices. Program offices, the government's focal points for day-to-day management of military systems, generally view the government-industry relationship as a partnership rather than an arms-length, buyer-seller situation. In several cases these contracting officers have used their independence and their considerable legal powers to very good effect.

In any event, it has long been an article of faith among the larger military contractors that government contracting officers should be placed under the direction of the program offices, where they would be more "responsive" and would be more "understanding of industry problems." Key industry associations, especially the AIA (Aerospace Industry Association) and the CODSIA (Council of Defense and Space Industry Associations) have long favored this arrangement.

With knowedge of this background, I was not surprised that the Fitzhugh Report recommended giving the government program manager directive authority over the contracting officer. Still, it was an incredible recommendation for a businessman to endorse.

A second example of a poorly considered organizational recommendation comes from the data-processing section. In 1966, when I first became alarmed at the C-5A's state of health, I was assisted by an extremely able air force officer, Col. Joe Warren. Colonel Warren had a fine war record and an outstanding record as a manager. He was perceptive and fearless enough to write and sign the first report which stated bluntly that the C-5A, then called "a miracle of procurement," was a disaster. Within days after he submitted this report, Joe Warren was found to have absolutely unique qualifications to be air attaché in Addis Ababa.

The purpose of this move was outrageously apparent, of course, and friends of Warren fought back. Robert Anthony, then comptroller of the Defense Department, came to the rescue with a higher-priority job in his office, and Colonel Warren's Ethiopian assignment was canceled. The Defense computer operations were a shambles, and Joe Warren was assigned to do something to improve them.

He found computer utilization to be under 50 percent (the Fitzhugh Report acknowledges 50 to 60 percent now), with much of the work being done of doubtful value. The Pentagon clearly had far more computers than needed, and more were being bought. Justification procedures for buying more computers were a sham, and symptoms of political shenanigans abounded. After many adventures, Joe Warren succeeded in putting some teeth into justification procedures. Moreover, he used the procedures in several instances to block poorly justified proposed acquisitions altogether and to send applicants back to the drawing boards.

The computer industry, which needed new business, was collectively furious. Their analysis of their problem was excellent. The problem was Joe Warren, and the solution was reorganization, using the Fitzhugh Report as a vehicle. And the report did recommend reassigning responsibility for Joe Warren's function to a civilian assistant secretary, citing procurement delays as a major problem. Interestingly, even though the report acknowledged low equipment utilization, the possibility of overbuying was not even discussed.

DISCOVERING THE OLD NONPOLICY

Most of the Fitzhugh Report's favorable publicity was focused on the recommendations for acquiring big new weapons systems. "Fly before you buy" was the keynote recommendation. This breakthrough was trumpeted around the world.

Now, as far as this goes, it is hard to argue with. It is particularly attractive if coupled with a further objective of retaining competitive options as long as possible. It's neither a new idea nor an untested one, but it's a good suggestion nonetheless. If this had been the report's only recommendation, and if the Pentagon had followed it in good faith, the taxpayers would have gotten their money's worth from the Fitzhugh Panel.

Sen. William Proxmire tested the Pentagon's sincerity when he introduced an amendment calling on the Pentagon to report its loudly announced policy, just to report after the fact on whether the policy had been followed.

Laird, Packard, Stennis, and Company opposed Proxmire fiercely. They said that his proposal was "premature," despite the fact it supposedly had been their de facto policy for more than a year, and formal policy for almost three months. Laird said that "it would eliminate flexibility in acquisition strategy," notwithstanding the fact that Proxmire's amendment required only an after-the-fact report. In short, the Pentagon had no intention of really following the practice if it could be avoided.

This was not news to Proxmire, of course. For one thing, he had the hard evidence of the Pentagon's recent past and future commitments to buy before flying in almost every big program. Furthermore, his subcommittee for economy in government had heard testimony on the subject from the three assistant secretaries of installations and logistics (procurement) in May, 1970. Two of the three dismissed fly-before-you-buy (FBYB) as impractical. Why? Because it did not provide adequate contractor employment during the interval between completion of the prototype and beginning of production. As most of us know by now, providing employment is a major objective in most cases. In some cases, it is the name of the game.

It is strange that the Fitzhugh Panel did not address this question except in their vague endorsement of the old industry chestnut of "maintaining a viable industrial mobilization base," whatever that is. Since the procurement chief's objections to FBYB were well known long before the panel's report was issued, it seems the panel should have dealt with the objection if it really anticipated adoption of FBYB.

THROW THE BABIES OUT

It is also strange that the panel, while giving lip service to improving the engineering definition of new weapons with FBYB, summarily dumped the Pentagon's established procedures for contract definition. These procedures call for thorough studies of proposed new weapons systems aimed at ensuring that big, expensive systems do not involve undue technical uncertainties. Most students of the process would agree that contract definition as carried out under existing procedures is too laborious and too dependent on paper studies. However, these procedures contain good features, too, and the chief problem has been a lack of enforcement. Fitzhugh has thrown out the baby with the bathwater. With existing contract definition procedures abandoned and with FBYB revealed as a public relations ploy, the Pentagon is left bankrupt with regard to advance definition of contract baselines.

But then, the Pentagon has long advocated what used to be called "the rubber baseline." This permits plans to be progressively modified to approximate actual performance, a comfortable operating mode.

A look at the Pentagon's recent history and future plans for FBYB should have tipped off a prudent man not to place heavy dependence on such documents as Packard's policy memo, as Fitzhugh apparently did. Last year, Congress and Secretary Laird vied for credit for "killing" the production program for the navy's new F-14 fighter until the plane could be flown long enough to work out the bugs. Yet during the year, in closed hearings and before the plane had flown, Laird requested and received approval to begin spending production money. Similarly, the air force's new fighter, the F-15, is not following FBYB, nor is the ABM or any of the big new ship programs, such as Representative Stennis' Mississippi-built DD963 destroyer, or the larger tank programs such as the Sheridan.

In seemingly contradictory recommendations, Fitzhugh endorses "flexibility in selecting [the] type of contract most appropriate," but then unequivocally endorses "a prohibition of total package procurement" (TPP). In the latter case, I believe he is again abandoning a lot of good but unenforced features to get rid of a few bad ones. There have been three basic problems with TPP in the past. One, the initial contract definitions have been inadequate and vague. Two, the government has repeatedly demonstrated its unwillingness to enforce the contracts. The contractors know this and behave accordingly. Three, the TPP fixed-price incentive contracts have been effectively converted to cost-plus contracts, with full application of the repricing formulas, or "golden handshake" clauses. All the principal air force TPP contracts were flawed by the repricing formulas. Commenting on Lockheed's C-5A package, Bernard Nossiter wrote in *The Washington Post:* "If Edward Lear and Salvador Dali had collaborated on an economic text, they might have come up with the contract that the Air Force has made with Lockheed for the big C-5A jet transport."

As things developed, the C-5A contract really was grotesque. Lockheed found that their actual costs on the first order of C-5As would probably exceed the ceiling price of their contract, which would result in their losing money on the first order alone. But overruns over the ceiling price of the first order triggered repricing of the second order, and Lockheed could use the repricing formula to reduce overall losses by overrunning even further.

Rather than plugging the loopholes in TPP, Fitzhugh would throw it out altogether. Again, this looks bad, until you read what he *does* recommend.

HOW TO BORE A LOOPHOLE

The report endorses level-of-effort contracting, which is another way of saying that the contractor's product is man-hours expended. Under this plan, the contractor has no real commitment to deliver anything, much less a necessity to excel. The same holds true for the present yearly $700 to $800 million of independent research and development grants for larger contractors. I can't think of any weapons system invented under these grants. Apparently, neither can Senator Stennis's committee, which, along with Senator Proxmire, has questioned the size and wisdom of the grants. The Fitzhugh Report is vague on the handling of the independent research and development grants subsidy, but it is critical of congressional questioning and appears to endorse the present no-strings-attached grants.

Fitzhugh also endorses parametric cost estimates for procurement. This approach builds in, and indeed amplifies, mistakes and inefficiencies of the past in establishing prices for new procurements. While the parametric, or "will-cost," approach to estimating has some application in projecting funding requirements, the "should-cost" approach is infinitely better in procurement if one is interested in saving money. (A distinction should be drawn between saving money and eliminating overruns as such. In theory, at least, overruns could be eliminated by making initial estimates fat enough to accommodate shoddy engineering and bad management. This would not save money. On the other hand, demanding but attainable estimates are a first step in the series of management actions needed to cut costs.)

The should-cost approach, which seeks to identify and eliminate "fat" in cost estimates, has had considerable publicity of late. In a good move, the Army rediscovered this old-fashioned, hard-nosed approach. According to testimony before a Joint Economics Committee subcommittee in May of this year, its first should-cost study identified about 34 percent of the contractor's proposed cost as "fat," or potential savings. Based on my own experience, this is about what should be expected on small-weapons programs such as the army's pilot program, the Hawk missile. Large-weapons programs are usually much fatter. Naturally, the large contractors and industry associations oppose should-cost and endorse will-cost pricing. The latter approach is, of course, a comfortable, congenial, and gentlemanly approach. It is also ruinously expensive. Under the will-cost approach, ever-increasing prices are mathematically justified and everybody wins except the taxpayers, who are generally ignorant of the process and consequently do not complain. Fitzhugh's endorsement of will-cost or parametric pricing delighted the military-spending coalition.

Despite acknowledgments of "poor management" in weapons contracts in public statements by Packard, Fitzhugh does not mention this unpleasantness. He says nothing about overhead increases, decline in labor efficiencies, or the like. He ignores the fact that the Pentagon does not knew whether its giant contractors are overrun or underrun on work done through a point in time, nor does it know the specifics of any deviation from plan. That is, it doesn't know whether overruns are traceable to increases in labor, material cost, or overhead expenses. Most hot-dog stand owners would know, but the Pentagon and its large contractors have barely a clue.

These omissions are apparently the result of the panel's assumption of a trend toward fixed-price contracts in which the contractors would have more responsibility and in which the government's need for monitoring would be reduced. The report states the assumption boldly: "During the past decade, the trend in government contracts for developments has shifted markedly from cost-plus-fixed-fee toward fixed-price contracts, many of which have embodied incentive features." They are simply dead wrong here. The C-5A airplane and Cheyenne helicopter contracts are to be converted to cost reimbursement. The new programs such as the F-14 navy fighter, the F-15 air force fighter, and the B-1 bomber are starting out as cost reimbursement (cost-plus) contracts. The trend is in the opposite direction from fixed-price contracts.

Even if the administration were serious about its FBYB policy, the effect of other new policies could dissipate any possible savings. Starting with a cost-plus development contract, then negotiating the follow-on production contract without competition and with pricing based on past actual cost rather than should-cost, prices of weapons will be even more bloated than at present. True, the *appearance* of overruns will be avoided by having contract prices adapt to actual costs, but the taxpayer will have to pony up additional money just the same. He'll feel better about it, though, because he won't realize what's happening to him.

Another of Fitzhugh's recommendations is to abandon the Selected Acquisition Reports (SAR), the quarterly reports on status of weapons systems programs. The Fitzhugh Panel comments that the SARs "measure subsequent events in the development against the standard of the original estimate." Deviations from the plan require explanations and, according to the panel, this produces further ill effects: "These explanations in turn generate further detailed examination of deviations by the Department [of Defense] and especially by the Congress. All this has led to an understandable but nonetheless undesirable rigidity on the part of the project manager to stay as close as possible to the cost and schedule as originally estimated." Clearly, this will never do. If this kind of factual exposure is allowed to continue, the taxpaying natives may get restless.

THE MISSING HUSTLE FACTOR

The most serious omission, perhaps the most serious shortcoming of the entire report, is the failure to deal with the problem of the motives involved in arms procurement—motives which often lead to lucrative but dishonest collusion. Maybe Fitzhugh and other nice men like him just can't believe the people in the Pentagon really have poor intentions. Maybe they don't understand that Pentagon managers are not motivated by the profit and loss goad which is so effective in the competitive business world. It must really be hard for them to believe that Pentagon managers work hard at devising ways to take a dive, to throw the game, in contract negotiations with giant firms. Anyone who has any doubts about this should go over the air force's plan for making Lockheed well again, which was outlined in a set of 25 "Official Use Only" briefing charts dated August 31, 1970. After hiding the C-5A overruns, admitting they falsified government reports to protect Lockheed stock prices, and juggling figures to "avoid the appearance of excess profits on run B" (the second order of C-5As), the air force came up with a masterpiece. In summary, here's what they proposed to do:

1. Lockheed would agree to accept a "fixed loss" (an indefinite amount but a fraction of their loss otherwise), which would be lent back to them with repayment to begin in 1974 *if* the Pentagon should choose to ask for repayment, and *if* the Pentagon wouldn't choose simply to give Lockheed more money.
2. The Pentagon would remove contractual ceilings on Lockheed's expenditures.
3. Lockheed would be absolved of guaranteeing the performance of the airplanes and of managing the program.
4. Penalties for substandard performance and late delivery would be removed.
5. Lockheed and the Pentagon would agree to circumvent the normal legal procedures designed to protect the taxpayers.
6. The air force would get whatever number of C-5As Lockheed chose to produce.

To me, the air force's bail-out plan is evidence of the Pentagon's collapse of will in dealing with its giant contractors. If the Lockheed bail-out precedent is established, how can the Pentagon *ever* hold a large contractor to his commitments? What is the significance of any procedural or organizational reform if the overall intent problem is not solved? If the government's policy is to accept whatever the giant contractors produce and give them whatever money they need, why should managers of these big firms concern themselves with making quality products, with meeting specifications, and with holding costs down?

In justice to Lockheed and the C-5A project, I should acknowledge that other large recipients of contract funds generally get the same kid-glove treatment in dealings with the Pentagon. The F-111 airplane, the Mark II avionics system for the same machine, the Minuteman II missile, the SRAM, the MBT-70 tank, the Mark 48 torpedo, and numerous other projects failed about as badly as Lockheed's C-5A program. None met their original specifications, and all were vastly overrun. Nevertheless, none of the large prime contractors has suffered unduly as a result of their failures.

Lockheed is just unlucky. Usually the bail-out is accomplished routinely, though somewhat clandestinely, through the simple mechanism of contract changes, known in the trade as "contract nourishment." Publicity, along with the enormous sums of money involved, is making the Lockheed bail-out more difficult.

A JURY OF DEFENDANTS

I am at a loss to explain the Fitzhugh Panel's failure to deal with the problem of intent. It is completely beyond me how any reasonably intelligent group of experienced businessmen could spend a year studying the Pentagon's Augean contracting mess without even speculating about the possibilities inherent in enforcing contracts with large firms. One popular theory is that the panel missed the major causes of the Pentagon's procurement mess because the study was planned that way and was staffed to guide the report to its bland outcome.

The business connections of the panel's members do not inspire confidence in their objectivity, to say the least. Shortly after the panel was formed, Senator Proxmire let loose a blast at the panel, charging that there were apparent conflicts of interest on the part of panel members. The specifics are worth reviewing.

The chairman, Gilbert W. Fitzhugh, was not only chairman of the board of the Metropolitan Life Insurance Company but also a director of the Singer Company. Metropolitan Life held over $35 million in common stock of 24 of the 100 largest Pentagon contractors, and had outstanding loans of $1,325,000,000 to 24 of the top 100 military contractors. The Singer Company also held military contracts. Fitzhugh resigned his positions with these companies, temporarily at least. He is now back in the harness at Metropolitan.

Next on the list was Robert C. Jackson, chairman of the board of Ryan Aeronautical Company. At the time of Jackson's appointment, Ryan held military contracts worth $293,158,000. Jackson also held memberships in the Air Force Association, the Navy League, the Army Aviation Association, and the Defense Orientation Conference Association, all of which are self-interested and outspoken supporters of Pentagon activities.

Following Jackson was Lewis Franklin Powell, Jr., whose Richmond law firm, Hunton, Williams, Gay, Powell, and Gibson, represented Newport News Shipbuilding and Dry Dock Company, then the 34th largest military contractor with $181,309,000 in contracts. Powell did merger work for the company and represented it before the Virginia General Assembly. He was also a director of the Chesapeake and Potomac Telephone Company, which holds $13,018,000 in military contracts. Powell was an air force intelligence officer at one time and was a reserve colonel when appointed to the panel.

Ruben Mettler was executive vice president, assistant president, and a director of TRW, Inc., which held $127,467,000 in military contracts. Mettler was also industry vice chairman of the Industry Advisory Council, a joint Pentagon-contractor group which functions as the board of directors of the military procurement community. Mettler was with Hughes Aircraft, another top contractor and then became a special consultant in the Defense Department. He went to TRW in 1955.

Wilfred McNeil was a Pentagon employee from 1941 to 1959, during which time he was released from active duty from the navy with the rank of rear admiral. As a civilian, he reached the position of assistant secretary of defense and comptroller. He was a director and adviser of Fairchild-Hiller Corporation when appointed to the panel. Fairchild-Hiller had $121,259,000 in contracts. He was also a member of the Lower Manhattan Advisory Board of the Chemical Bank, which had extensive loans outstanding to Pentagon contractors. McNeil was then a member of the Navy League and past president of the New York state division of that organization.

William Blackie was the board chairman of Caterpillar Tractor Company, which held $42,753,000 in defense contracts. He was also a director of Shell Oil Company, which held $32,754,000 in defense contracts.

Following Blackie was John Maurice Fluke, president of John Fluke Manufacturing Company. His company held $1,472,000 worth of defense contracts.

George Champion followed Fluke on the contractors' list. Champion was a director of the International Paper Company, which held defense contracts totaling $665,000. He was also a director of American Smelting and Refining Company, which held $448,000 worth of military contracts. Champion's major position was his board chairmanship of the Chase Manhattan Bank, also a big lender to the military contractor community.

Next was William Clements, Jr. Clements was chairman of SEDCO, Inc., which held $93,000 in military contracts. Additionally, Clements was chairman of the board of governors of Southern Methodist University, which held $735,000 worth of military contracts.

These eight panel members, representing a

majority on the 15-member panel, had official positions with 12 different companies which held a combined total of at least $1,021,902,963 in military contracts.

Further objectivity was lent to the panel by such members as Joseph Kirkland, secretary-treasurer of the AFL-CIO when appointed, and Hobart Lewis, president of Reader's Digest.

J. Fred Buzhardt was the administrative officer of the staff. He is a graduate of the United States Military Academy. He spent 8 years as a staff member with Sen. Strom Thurmond. During that time, his biography stated, he was "assigned largely to work with staff of Senate Armed Services Committee and Military Preparedness Sub-Committee." At the time of his appointment he was on the Pentagon payroll as a special assistant, and is now general counsel to the Pentagon.

The apparent domination of the panel by individuals with Pentagon contractor viewpoints makes the suspicion of bias unavoidable. This suspicion is heightened by the fact that most of the actual work of the panel's review was done by Pentagon employees or by Stanford Research Institute and other Pentagon contractors. So far as can be determined, the Pentagon paid all the bills.

WHO WILL RINSE THE WHITEWASH?

When Senator Proxmire revealed the business connections of the panel members last year, he predicted a whitewash in the report of weapons acquisition activities. According to *The Washington Post,* Fitzhugh responded with the hope that the panel's report "would be judged on its own merits" and not on the make-up of the panel.

They have flunked the course on both counts, at least in the procurement area. The report is a whitewash written by whitewashees. Defenders and beneficiaries of the mess are still trying to cure it by pouring money on it, then scratching dirt over it. Once the slogans are disposed of (fly-before-you-buy and civilian control), the Fitzhugh Panel's report amounts to such a nonsolution.

With all this, it is tempting to write off the whole Fitzhugh Panel effort as just another of the endless series of bureaucratic anesthetics for the taxpayers. From my point of view, there is only one reason to reserve judgment on the final outcome of the whole episode. That reason is the man himself, Gilbert Fitzhugh. He seems sincere. He has a fine reputation to protect. It is possible that he was used by the self-serving authors of the incredibly bad weapons acquisition recommendations. After all, he did state early in his review that he knew little or nothing about the process. He has now been educated by some of the country's most successful participants in the Pentagon's on-going procurement swindle.

If I were in Fitzhugh's position and had not been a knowing party to the whitewash, I would be extremely annoyed to learn that I had been used as a patsy. I would take a hard second look —and consider things like the hustle factor and the problem of honest contract enforcement with large corporations.

It would be most refreshing to see a businessman make some businesslike recommendations for a change: like objective evaluations of true need for the weapons in the first place; like writing sound, well-defined, binding contracts, with improved definitions resulting from competitive prototypes where possible; like enforcing the contracts, even if some of the lodge brothers lose money occasionally; like finding ways to get more competition, both in initial awards and continuing programs; like negotiating tough prices, based on what the work should cost with the fat squeezed out; like keeping track of program status, and insisting that problems be fixed before they become national disasters; like controlling spurious get-well contract changes; like setting difficult, specifically quantified cost reduction goals for Pentagon managers; like fixing the Pentagon's rewards system so that those who underrun are promoted and those who overrun are disciplined (has *anyone* ever been fired for overrunning?).

The report wouldn't be hard to write. Let's hope Gilbert Fitzhugh writes it.

V. FEDERAL CIVILIAN SPENDING

INTRODUCTION

That policy decisions on the military budget are heavily influenced by powerful vested interests is now widely accepted. It is less recognized that the same sort of dominance pervades decisions on civilian programs. No matter where one turns in the federal budget, one finds the existence of subsidy accruing to corporations and individuals at which a program is targeted. In turn, having detected a subsidy, it is an exorable law that an organized and powerful vested-interest group will be found. The purpose of such organizations is to protect the program which is the source of the subsidy, to influence decision-makers associated with the program, and to provide "advice" on how the program can be improved—often meaning how the program can be altered to increase the flow of the subsidy.

The efforts of such powerful interests have a remarkable "track record." It is the rare case in which a concerted effort by such interests is rebuffed by either the executive branch or the Congress. Given the current organization of the Congress and the executive branch and the structure of incentives implicit in the political system, this result is not surprising. The following quotations summarize some of the most significant organizational and structural characteristics of the system—characteristics which foster this inordinate power of subsidized vested interests.

To achieve their own personal objectives, national policymakers—elected or appointed—must avoid the alienation of "clients."

It would not miss the mark by far to claim that the public policymaker is a rational, calculating, pain-pleasure machine. He lines up all of his alternatives, weighs the advantages and costs (to him) of each, and then chooses that option which leaves him better off than any other. While, obviously, a multitude of things may give him satisfaction—including material gain, favorable peer-group response, security, doing his job well, helping other people, getting reelected—the decision-maker implicitly calculates gain and losses of each alternative so as to maximize his own, personal satisfaction.

Because each person involved in a public decision has different objectives and different values, the outcome is the result of a *bargaining process*. Each participant haggles, using his influence and power, to reach a final outcome that is the most congenial to his personal interests. Indeed, influence and power become the "currency" with which the parties to a decision "buy" or "sell" in order to achieve the most personally congenial outcome. For these people, the favorable reaction or support of followers, constituents, customers, employees, employers, and colleagues is an important (if not primary) component of those things which bestow satisfaction or utility rewards. To lose this favorable reaction or support is a satisfaction or utility penalty.[1]

The congressional appropriation process vests program control in a limited number of powerful and "tenured" members of Congress.

Since all appropriation bills have their beginnings in the House, the importance of the House Appropriations Committee is great because it begins the "beginnings." Yet, despite its importance, or perhaps because of it, the Appropriations Committee operates under rules which are as archaic as they are undemocratic. . . . The House Appropriations Committee is divided into 13 subcommittees, each of which has jurisdiction over a particular prescribed area of governmental activity.

. . . The decisions of the subcommittees are rarely overruled by the full committee, the meetings of which are merely cursory rituals of ratification. Assignment to subcommittees is within the sole discretion of the committee chairman after consultation with the ranking minority members as to minority assignments. In this power of assignment by the chairman is embedded his ability to color all the deliberations of the committee and to shape its decisions in his own image and in conformity with his own political philosophy. . . . Thus, it is understandable that [the current chairman] has constituted himself as chairman of the Defense Subcommittee and has backstopped himself on that subcommittee with members having a similar point of view. For instance, the next ranking member after the chairman is a congressman who is a major general in the army reserves.

On the other hand, if the chairman believes that the funds for a particular program should be curtailed, he need merely assign to the subcommittee in charge a majority of House Members known to be unfriendly to that program. . . .

The chairmen of the various subcommittees pretty much run the shows of their panels. They are all very knowledgeable, although not always sympathetic, concerning the agencies and programs under their jurisdiction. They schedule the witnesses . . . After each witness concludes his statement, it is customary for the subcommittee chairman to question him at length. When he is done not only is the subject usually exhausted, but also so are all participants. If other congressional subcommittee members do any questioning, it usually is very brief.[2]

The process of congressional committee appointments biases decisions toward organized vested-interest groups and insulates the budget subsidizing such groups.

I happen to be on the steering committee of the Democratic Party. It is this committee which assigns the Democratic membership to the available committee vacancies.

[1] Robert Haveman, *The Economics of the Public Sector* (New York: Wiley, 1970), pp. 142–143.

[2] Congressman Charles S. Joelson of New Jersey, *Congressional Record* (January 29, 1968), pp. H432–H433.

In the deliberations of this committee, there are enormous pressures to place those senators whose states benefit from, say, public works appropriations on either the Senate Interior Committee or the Public Works Subcommittee of the Appropriations Committee. In fact, a senator who is from a state which benefits substantially from these programs is, at least in the short term, rather clearly serving his own best interests and those of at least some of his constituents if he attains a seat on one of these committees. The net result of all of this, however, is that the committee structure develops a built-in bias toward higher budgets. Because the people who serve on each committee have an interest in seeing the budget for which they are responsible increase, they often fail to encourage careful evaluation and analysis of expenditures.

An example of the bias which results from this process is clearly seen by observing the state membership of the Senate Committee on Interior and Insular Affairs. The Democratic members on that committee are from Washington, New Mexico, Nevada, Idaho, Utah, North Dakota, South Dakota, Wisconsin, Montana, and Alaska. The Republican membership is from Colorado, Idaho, Arizona, Wyoming, Oregon, Alaska, and Oklahoma. With the exception of my able colleague, Gaylord Nelson, there is no senator on this committee representing a state east of the Mississippi River.

Largely as an outgrowth of this built-in committee bias, the relationships between the staffs of the committees and snbcommittees and their counterparts in the agencies is hardly one of arms-length dealings. The degree of mutuality of interest between the executive staff and those on legislative branch committees is substantial.[3]

The lack of information on government subsidy programs seriously reduces the chances for effective challenges to them. The federal budget, for example, is a chief offender on this score.

Several billion dollars of annual direct federal expenditures provide subsidy to special groups or individuals. While some of these subsidy programs are designed to give incentive to individuals and businesses to pursue social objectives, others represent outright gifts or grants with no implied private response. While some of these programs grant subsidy by directly transferring income to the selected individuals, other subsidy programs aid the beneficiary groups by giving them valuable goods and services either free of charge or at a price which is below cost. Still other government subsidies are awarded through special allowances in the tax system—"tax expenditure"—or loans provided at preferential terms.

Often as a side effect of their primary purpose, these programs provide implicit subsidy to particular groups at the expense of taxpayers in general. For this reason, they should come under particularly close scrutiny by the Congress and the administration.

Although considerations of efficiency in government demand that particularly careful and regular scrutiny be given these subsidy programs, the budget document provides no assistance whatsoever. There is no special analysis of these subsidy programs and their budgetary costs, nor is there any analysis of their future budgetary requirements, the characteristics of the people being subsidized, and the amount of subsidy which they are receiving. In fact, there are no regular reports from the Budget Bureau or any other executive agency on the economic and equity impacts of subsidy and subsidy-like programs. The executive branch and especially the Bureau of the Budget should, in the course of the budgetary process, recognize their responsibility to provide the Congress with the data and analysis necessary for informed decisions on these public subsidy

[3] Sen. William Proxmire, "PPB, The Agencies and The Congress," in U.S. Congress, Joint Economic Committee, *The Analysis and Evaluation of Public Expenditures: The PPB System* (1969), pp. vii–viii.

programs. Improved public policy in these areas requires the clearest possible exposition of their purpose and economic effects.[4]

The financial resources available to vested interest groups can "buy" insulation of individual subsidy programs.

WASHINGTON—One morning last March Secretary of Agriculture Clifford Hardin announced a sudden change of mind that's still paying off both for the nation's dairy farmers and for President Nixon's political financiers.

Mr. Hardin revealed that he was raising government price supports for "manufacturing" milk, a basic grade used to make butter and cheese. Just 2 weeks earlier, he had declared there would be no change in support levels. His reversal of policy came 48 hours after a dozen disgruntled dairymen visited President Nixon in the Cabinet Room of the White House.

To dairy farmers, the increase in supports means higher prices for their products; the government is committed to purchase, if necessary, enough dairy products to keep the prices up at the new levels. To Mr. Nixon's political money men, the policy reversal means an outpouring of perhaps $1 million in campaign gifts for the President's 1972 reelection campaign from the grateful milk lobby. Of this expected total, $250,000 has already arrived, mostly through secret channels.

On March 11, "after careful review of the situation and the provisions of law," Secretary Hardin pegged price supports for manufacturing milk in the marketing year beginning April 1 at $4.66 a hundred pounds, the same as for 1970; when market prices fall below the support level, the government begins buying butter, cheese and nonfat dry milk, assuring the farmer a place to sell at guaranteed prices.

The secretary said raising supports might prompt overproduction, glutting the market and piling surpluses into government warehouses. "We must avoid this," he declared.

The President's Council of Economic Advisers approved the Hardin refusal to push props higher, according to Hendrik S. Houthakker, who was a member of the council at the time though he later resigned. Mr. Hardin's refusal also was cleared through the Office of Budget and Management.

Then on March 22, one day before the dozen dairy spokesmen visited with the President in the Cabinet Room, TAPE (Trust for Agricultural Political Education) donated $10,000 in chunks of $2,000 and $3,000 to four regularly operating Republican committees.

At the White House next day the dairymen gave Mr. Nixon a strong pitch for higher supports. But no assurances were given and no participant mentioned political contributions, according to John Butterbrodt, president of the Associated Milk Producers, who has 40 registered Holsteins at his farm in South-central Wisconsin.

"Those things aren't discussed at meetings like this," Mr. Butterbrodt says.

Next day, however, the SPACE (Special Political Agricultural Community Education) fund gave $25,000 in five $5,000 donations to regular Republican committees (Democrats got nothing), and on March 25 Mr. Hardin changed his mind, announcing a 27-cent increase in price supports to $4.93 a hundred pounds. This sudden switch surprised Mr. Houthakker. "I'd say it could cost consumers hundreds of millions of dollars because retail prices depend indirectly on support prices," he reasons.[5]

The result of these characteristics and others like them is to bias the operation of government in the direction of the organized and the powerful interests in the

[4] U.S. Congress, Joint Economic Committee, *Economic Analysis and the Efficiency of Government,* Report of the Subcommittee on Economy in Government (1970), pp. 21–22.

[5] *Wall Street Journal,* September 28, 1971, p. 38:1.

country. More seriously, the effect is to seriously erode the ability of government to perform efficiently and equitably. The following is the conclusion of the Congressional Subcommittee on Economy in Government after receiving the testimony of economists on a wide range of public programs.

1. In planning and implementing programs, the federal government has often ignored the existence of powerful incentive, penalty, and reward systems. Neglect of these structures has fostered serious inefficiencies and performance shortfalls.
2. The common practice of giving the benefits of public programs to particular individuals and groups free of charge has fostered serious overspending on some programs and has generated undue pressure for increased support by those subsidized.
3. Many federal programs commonly depicted as providing public services to a wide cross section of citizens in fact channel most of their benefits to the rich and well-to-do at the expense of lower income groups. Other federal programs impose enormous costs on low-income citizens which are neither compensated nor taken into account in program planning decisions.[6]

[6] U.S. Congress, Joint Economic Committee, *Economic Analysis and the Efficiency of Government*, op. cit., pp. 30–31.

A. AGRICULTURAL POLICY

U.S. FARM POLICY: WHO GETS THE BENEFITS

CHARLES L. SCHULTZE

INTRODUCTION

Between 1956 and 1970, federal budget outlays for farm price support programs and related direct payments to farmers averaged $3.1 billion per year. In the last 3 years of this period, 1968 through 1970, annual budget outlays averaged $5 billion. These costs of supporting farm prices and incomes were paid by the taxpayer. But consumers also pay, through higher prices, part of the costs of farm price support programs. Federal farm programs are designed—recently through output restrictions, in earlier years through loans and purchases of farm products—to raise the price of farm products above what a free market would have yielded. While estimates vary, actual farm prices in recent years would have been perhaps 15 percent lower had federal price support programs not been in effect. At supported prices the value of farm marketings in 1969 amounted to over $47 billion. With prices 15 percent lower, the same volume of farm output could have been purchased for about $7 billion less. Some $1.5 billion of this reduction would represent lower prices paid by farmers themselves in buying feed, seed, and livestock. Lower prices for exports would represent another $1 billion. Nonfarm consumers, therefore, paid in recent years about $4.5 billion more for the farm products they purchased than they would have had there been no federal price support programs.[1]

Farm price support and related programs thus cost the taxpayer some $5 billion per year in budgetary outlays, and consumers of food and fiber some $4.5 billion in higher food prices—although the latter figure may overstate somewhat

Adapted from *The Distribution of Farm Subsidies: Who Gets the Benefits?* by Charles L. Schultze (Copyright © 1971 by the Brookings Institution, Washington, D.C.); reprinted with permission of the author and publisher.

Charles L. Schultze is Senior Fellow at the Brookings Institution, Washington, D.C., and Professor of Economics at the University of Maryland, College Park, Maryland.

[1] With output restrictions removed and prices lower, more food and fiber would be produced and consumed. As a consequence farmers' cash receipts from marketing would not fall by the same percentage as prices.

the long-term price-raising effects of farm support programs. The total transfer from consumers and taxpayers, in the range of $9 to $10 billion, compares with a total federal, state, and local cost of various public assistance (welfare) programs, including medicaid, of slightly over $10 billion in 1969. Procurement, operation, and maintenance of the nation's strategic nuclear forces cost about $9 billion in fiscal 1969.

In terms of their cost, farm subsidies clearly rank among the more important public programs. They have a noticeable effect on many vital factors in the national economy—the allocation of resources, the location of population and industry, the balance of payments, and so on. One of the major impacts of farm subsidies is upon income distribution, which raises the question "Who gets the subsidies?" Specifically, to what extent do farm programs represent a transfer of income from a relatively affluent urban population to a relatively depressed and low-income farm community? While such a transfer would not necessarily in itself justify the programs, it would at least indicate an effort to distribute income in a way that most people would consider equitable.

In 1969 the median family income of the nonfarm population was $9,600, that of farm families $6,400, or some 33-percent lower. The transfer of substantial sums from the nonfarm to the farm population would thus seem likely to distribute income more evenly. This is not the case, however. Farm subsidies are not distributed in accordance with income levels—poor families receiving the most assistance and rich families the least. Rather they tend, at least roughly, to be distributed in proportion to the volume of production on each farm. The more a farm produces, the greater the value of price supports. Moreover, most of the cash payments a farmer receives from the government depend on the size of his acreage allotment or his production, both of which vary directly with the size of his farm.

A relatively small number of large farmers produce the bulk of agricultural goods sold in the United States. Three-fourths of the sales of farm products are made from 568,000 farms with annual sales of $20,000 or more. Those farms comprise only 19 percent of all farms. The average income of their operators, from farm and nonfarm sources, was $19,900 in 1968 and $20,900 in 1969. Since farm subsidies accrue roughly in proportion to sales, it follows that the bulk of subsidies go to that fifth of farmers with the highest average income. At the other end of the scale are 1.5 million small farmers with annual sales of less than $5,000 and annual incomes, from farm and nonfarm sources, averaging about $7,900.[2] They account for only 5 percent of farm sales and a correspondingly small fraction of farm subsidy benefits.

Most farm subsidy programs are vested not in the farmer as an individual but in the land on his farm. The farmer's benefits are based on his acreage allotment or acreage history. This determines how many acres he must refrain from planting, as a condition for participation in the program. Should the farmer leave the farm, he cannot directly take his subsidy with him. The subsidy privileges remain with the land. As a general rule, the land retains its acreage allotment and its acreage history, whoever owns it. Naturally, therefore, the value of the annual subsidy tends to get reflected, at least partially, in the price of the farmland.[3] In combination with a number of other factors, this capitalization process has tended to drive the price of farmland up. As a consequence, the chief benefits of farm subsidies have accrued to those who purchased land before subsidies became prevalent. Farmers buying land in later years, however—younger farmers and those expanding their acreage to take advantage of technological advances—have received less advantage from the farm programs. The benefits of higher prices and direct subsidies have at least partly been offset by the added costs incurred because of higher land prices. And farmers who have rented land have found many of the benefits disappearing in higher rental payments to landlords.

Indeed, at the limit, a subsidy attached to land

[2] A large number of parttime farmers are included in this total. The average net income of this group from farming is only $1,300.

[3] Cotton and tobacco allotments may be sold. Thus the capitalized value of the subsidy program may be separated from the land, and the farmer can realize that value without selling the land itself.

eventually ends up granting no benefits to farmers. To the extent that the value of the subsidy is capitalized into land prices, the higher carrying costs soak up the annual subsidy, as land gradually changes hands over the years. But since subsidy values are frozen into the price of land, any attempt to reduce or remove them would leave recent purchasers of land with incomes below what they would have been before the subsidy program started and confront them with a capital loss. Paradoxically, therefore, after a number of years have passed, such programs end up transferring little net income to the second generation of recipients, but at the same time become so frozen into asset values that their removal would bring substantial hardship.

Whatever the advantages or disadvantages of the farm subsidy program, it is not a welfare program in the sense of transferring income to low-income farm families. The bulk of the subsidies accrue to that small group of farmers with net incomes averaging $20,000. And because the value of the subsidy tends to get reflected in farmland prices, the subsidies are gradually translated into capital gains for long-term holders of land, while recent purchasers and renters receive a much smaller benefit, losing at least part of the subsidy in higher carrying costs or rents.

FEDERAL FARM PROGRAMS

From hindsight it seems clear that long-term problems of excess agricultural capacity began for the United States in the 1920s. These problems were recognized in the McNary-Haugen bills of 1927 and 1928 (vetoed twice by President Coolidge) and in the creation of the Federal Farm Board in 1929 with a $500 million revolving fund to engage in price stabilization operations. The depression of the 1930s saw the introduction of price support loan techniques and various supply management programs. But the special character of the farm problem was obscured by the pervasiveness of the depression. The subsequent sharp increase in demands on U.S. farms during World War II and the immediate postwar reconstruction period postponed the problem for almost a decade. Supplies were not excessive; farm incomes were rising. During this period, however, the concept of mandatory price supports was accepted with the enactment of programs for a number of major commodities.

The outbreak of the Korean War, with its inflationary consequences and worldwide anticipatory buying of commodities, further postponed the long-term consequences of rapidly rising farm productivity and low elasticities of demand. The buildup in Commodity Credit Corporation (CCC) stocks, which had begun in 1948 and 1949 as postwar inflationary demands tapered off, was reversed. Farm income rose sharply. It was not until the end of the Korean War that the problem of excess capacity began to make itself felt in a serious way.

The price support and supply management programs now in effect emerged from a long period of controversy and experimentation that began in the mid-1950s. As agricultural supplies rapidly outpaced demand, the maintenance of price supports at high levels forced the CCC to acquire a mounting inventory of agricultural products. Despite some reduction in price support levels after a politically charged congressional debate in 1954, CCC inventories and loan portfolios continued to rise sharply. The CCC investment in commodity inventories and price support loans, which had totaled $1.3 billion in June 1952, had by June 1955 reached $6.7 billion, and by June 1959, $7.7 billion. Although legislation had been enacted to create the soil bank, through which the government paid farmers to retire land from production, the volume of acreage retired was not sufficient to prevent a continuing production excess at supported prices and a consequent buildup in CCC stocks.

The incoming Kennedy administration, as one of several major steps in implementing its farm policy, raised support levels sharply on most basic crops. Farm income was increased, from an average of $2,832 per farm in 1956-1960 to $3,749 in 1961-1965. It also placed substantially greater emphasis on supply management programs, in order to raise farm income through output restrictions rather than continuing CCC acquisition of commodities. After experimenting with mandatory controls on output, the administration gradually came to rely on direct federal payments as a means of buying output restrictions from farmers. Direct payments currently provide a technique for keeping support levels high while reducing market prices to world levels—the payments make up the difference. Payments are also made on feed grains and wheat to purchase acreage restrictions, without which market prices would fall even lower. As a result of the acreage restrictions, farm output has been reduced sufficiently below sales that the CCC has been able to sell off a large part of the excessive inventories it had acquired under the high price supports of earlier years.

The farm programs that had gradually taken shape by 1965 were extended in that year's legislation for a 5-year period. In November 1970 President Nixon signed a new 3-year farm bill that continued, with certain changes, these basic farm price support programs. The new legislation places a limit of $55,000 per year on the amount an individual farm may receive on its wheat, feed grain, or cotton crop. This limitation, which will fall primarily on very large cotton farmers, will reduce direct government subsidies by an estimated $58 million per year. Other changes in the legislation provide somewhat more flexibility for farmers in deciding how they would use their land under voluntary acreage control programs. While it has been impossible to carry out a detailed analysis of the new law, there is little reason to believe its provisions would substantially affect the conclusions of this study. Because of the payment limitation, some 1,100 of the nation's 3 million farms will experience reductions in direct federal subsidies. But the distribution of subsidies by broad economic classes will probably not be sharply different from the estimates presented here.

Wheat, Feed Grains, and Cotton

For the three major crops—wheat, feed grains, and cotton—domestic market prices are now supported at or near world levels, rather than at the much higher prices initially set by the Kennedy administration. Producers who agree to restrict their acreage within, or in some cases below, their acreage allotments receive cash payments from the government, related directly or indirectly to their volume of production (payments may not exceed $55,000 on any one crop under the 1970 legislation). The cash the farmer receives for his crop is therefore a blend of market prices and government payments. Part of the direct payments for wheat are financed by processors, who must purchase marketing certificates proportional to the amount of wheat they process, at a 1969 price for certificates of 75 cents per bushel of wheat. Thus, some of the direct payments are borne by the consumer rather than the federal budget.

Direct payments for feed grains are the necessary price of getting producers to cooperate in reducing acreage by a sufficient amount to hold market prices at the support level. The same is true for wheat, but the level of payments is probably larger than needed simply to buy output restrictions. In other words, part of the wheat payments are pure income supplements, and part the price of purchasing supply controls. Direct payments are not needed to purchase output restrictions on cotton.[4] Traditionally, cotton producers have been willing to accept, by referendum vote, mandatory marketing quotas. Hence the current payments are primarily a means of maintaining cotton farmers' income while keeping prices near world levels.[5]

Tobacco, Rice, Peanuts, and Soybeans

Prices of tobacco, rice, peanuts, and soybeans are supported by CCC loans and purchases. Direct payments are not made. Acreage allotments and marketing quotas are used for the first three commodities to keep output at a level consistent with

[4] The 1966 and 1967 cotton programs did provide for substantial cuts in planted acreage, and special payments were made to secure this diversion. For these two years, crop production was held below consumption and exports in order to reduce the very substantial carryover that had been built up earlier. The reduction has now been accomplished.

[5] Similar views on the relationship of direct payments to supply control objectives in the three major crop programs can be found in John A. Schnittker (former Undersecretary of Agriculture), "The Distribution of Benefits from Existing and Prospective Farm Programs" (paper presented at the Symposium on Public Problems and Policies, Center for Agricultural and Economic Development, Iowa State University, May 27, 1969; processed).

price support objectives, minimizing the need for direct CCC outlays. Acreage controls are not used in the soybean program.

Dairy Products

Dairy prices are supported by CCC purchases of manufactured milk products (butter, cheese, and dry milk) and through federal milk marketing orders that specify minimum prices of fluid milk in various dairy markets.

Sugar

Sugar prices are supported by the imposition of import quotas on foreign sugar and through acreage allotments to U.S. producers. As a consequence of this program, domestic raw sugar prices are maintained in the range of 6 to 8 cents per pound, while world sugar prices, in most years, range between 2 and 4 cents per pound.[6] In addition, sugar producers receive direct federal subsidies on their production, on the condition that they agree to maintain certain minimum wage levels for hired farm labor.

Wool

Domestic wool producers receive a direct subsidy per pound of wool produced (27.2 cents per pound in 1969). No production controls are imposed.

Land Retirement

At the end of 1967, some 9 million acres were still retired from crop production under the old soil bank contracts. By January 1, 1970, almost all of these contracts had expired. Since 1967, about 4.5 million acres have been retired each year under the cropland adjustment and conversion programs. Such land retirement programs reduce potential farm output and help maintain prices above free market levels.

Agricultural Conservation Program (ACP)

The federal government makes direct payments under ACP to farmers for undertaking certain conservation practices—constructing water storage reservoirs, terracing, establishing vegetative cover, and the like. While the purpose of the program is the conservation of land, in practical terms it provides a subsidy to farmers, principally realized through an enhanced value and sales price of farmland.[7] This program's outlays are included among the direct farm subsidies examined in this study.

Program Costs

The transfer costs of the farm programs may be divided into two parts: a federal budgetary cost represented by the direct payments, and a cost to food and fiber consumers represented by the excess of supported farm prices over the level that would prevail in a free market.[8] During the past decade some of the costs shifted from the consumer to the budget as the direct payment programs for wheat, cotton, and feed grains were introduced—that is, market prices were reduced and the difference was made up through direct payments. But even in these three cases the resulting market prices are still above free market levels. Also during the past decade the total cost of the programs has increased, reflecting the higher support levels and income objectives adopted in the early 1960s.

The benefits of farm price support programs are

[6] This difference may overstate the subsidy, since the level of world market prices for sugar is artificially depressed by the fact that many major consuming nations have special arrangements with particular supplier nations.

[7] For many years the administration in power has consistently attempted to reduce the size of this program. Among President Nixon's earliest budget recommendations was a proposal to abolish this program. But each year the Congress continues to appropriate some $200 million for ACP.

[8] Farm subsidy programs involve economic costs as well as transfer costs. The economic, or welfare, costs represent the net loss of output to the economy as a whole that results from the reallocation of resources involved in the farm program.

TABLE 1. Direct Payments under Various Farm Programs, 1955 through 1969 (in millions of dollars)

	Farm program								
Year	Conser-vation[a]	Soil bank	Sugar	Wool	Feed grain	Wheat	Cotton	Cropland adjust-ment	Total
1955	188	—	41	—	—	—	—	—	229
1956	220	243	37	54	—	—	—	—	554
1957	230	700	32	53	—	—	—	—	1,016
1958	215	815	44	14	—	—	—	—	1,089
1959	233	323	44	82	—	—	—	—	682
1960	223	370	59	51	—	—	—	—	702
1961	236	334	53	56	772	42	—	—	1,493
1962	230	304	64	54	841	253	—	—	1,747
1963	231	304	67	37	843	215	—	—	1,696
1964	236	199	79	25	1,163	438	39	—	2,181
1965	224	160	75	18	1,139	525	70	—	2,463
1966	231	145	71	34	1,293	679	773	51	3,277
1967	237	129	70	29	865	731	932	85	3,079
1968	227	114	75	66	1,366	747	787	81	3,462
1969	201	46	78	61	1,643	858	828	78	3,794

[a] Includes payments under the agricultural conservation program (ACP) and the Great Plains conservation program.

Source: USDA, Economic Research Service (ERS), *Farm Income Situation*, FIS-216 (July 1970), p. 64.

measured in this study principally in terms of the income farmers receive beyond what they would have received in the absence of the programs. This additional income is composed of both direct payments and price support benefits resulting from the support of farm market prices at levels above what a free market would yield.[9]

DISTRIBUTION OF BENEFITS BY INCOME GROUPS

Determining how the benefits from U.S. farm programs are distributed among farmers of different income levels presents three major problems: measuring the magnitude of the benefits; estimating the distribution of benefits to farms grouped according to economic class; and relating the economic class grouping to a net income grouping.

[9] The use of the term "price supports" can sometimes be confusing. In the case of corn, for example, farmers receive a market price for their crop, plus a direct government payment per bushel produced. These direct payments are called "price support payments," and the sum of the two (market price plus price support payments per bushel) is called "the support price." For purposes of clarity, price supports in this study refer to actions taken to hold actual market prices above free market levels. Payments received from the government (including the value of wheat certificates) are called "direct payments."

Measuring the Magnitude of the Benefits

Data are readily available on the magnitude of direct payment benefits. Table 1 summarizes those payments annually from 1955 to 1969. Except for income and price support objectives adopted in the early 1960s. Beginning in 1961, direct payments were made to feed grain producers as a means of purchasing acreage restrictions. In 1963, direct payments were partially substituted for high market price supports and mandatory controls in the feed grains program, in 1964 in the wheat program, and in 1965 in the cotton program. Continued large increases in yields raised the cost of achieving supply controls for feed grains and to a lesser extent wheat. At any given support price level, increases in yields raise the potential return on planted acres and, therefore, the cost of inducing farmers to forego planting.

Farm income exclusive of direct payments has remained remarkably constant since the late 1950s. The continuing rise in total farm income is therefore due to the steady increase in direct payments (Table 2).[10] Total income per farm has risen even more sharply.

TABLE 2. Net Farm Income, with and without Direct Payments, 1955 through 1969

Period	Realized net income, excluding payments	Direct payments[a]	Realized net income, including payments
	Average annual total income (millions of dollars)		
1956–60	11,666	10	11,676
1961–65	11,755	1,230	12,985
1966–69	12,774	2,660	15,434
1967–69[b]	12,430	2,704	15,134
	Average annual income per farm (dollars)		
1956–60	2,761	2	2,763
1961–65	3,307	345	3,652
1966–69	4,123	857	4,980
1967–69[b]	4,074	885	4,959

[a] Direct payments for wheat (including value of certificates paid by processors), feed grains, cotton, sugar, and wool; excludes portion going to nonfarm landlords.

[b] These figures show the final period excluding 1966, a year of exceptionally short crops and high income.

Source: *Farm Income Situation,* July 1970, pp. 44, 46, 57, 64.

Price support benefits are, of course, much more difficult to estimate than direct payment benefits, since they represent the difference between income actually earned by farmers in the sale of farm products and the income they would have earned under free market conditions. Without supply controls, production of most, if not all, price-supported crops would increase. Prices would fall, and with low price elasticities of demand, cash receipts of farmers would be reduced. The prices, output, and incomes that would prevail under these conditions must be estimated in order to measure price support benefits.

In the short run the major impact of the removal of price supports would fall directly on the price-supported crops. After some period of time, livestock prices and cash receipts would drop as lower grain prices stimulated additional meat production. Also, the lower returns from planting the previously price-supported crops would induce larger production and lower prices for other crops. Even those relatively efficient farmers who today produce the bulk of farm output and earn returns on their investment and labor equivalent to what they would realize in nonfarm employment would, for some time at least, earn subnormal returns.

Over a longer period of time the reduced returns from producing farm commodities should lead to some restrictions of supply and to a partial recovery of prices. While the larger farmers who produce most of agricultural output might not cut back their production, many marginal farmers would in the long run be forced out of farming altogether. The exodus from farming would be accelerated (unless unemployment rates outside of farming were high). Prices would rise more nearly to cover costs, including a reasonable return on investment and family labor for those who produced the bulk of farm output. Whether farming would eventually become as economically attractive as other sectors of the economy, and how long it would take for subnormal farm returns to be eliminated, is a matter about which there is much controversy and little knowledge. In any event, current farm programs are primarily designed precisely to avoid this long period of subnormal returns to large farmers.

The estimates of free market prices and incomes used in calculating price support benefits do not take into account the long-term adjustment. They cover a period long enough to allow the impact on livestock production and non-price-supported crops to occur, but not long enough to allow for an accelerated exodus of farmers to other occupations. As a consequence the measure of price support benefits used here—however accurately it may portray the short- and intermediate-run effects of current farm programs—does overstate the long-run supplement to farmers' income these programs provide.

[10] This is not to say that income per farm, exclusive of direct payments, would have remained constant had farm programs been abolished and direct payments been eliminated. Because they were used in part to purchase reductions in farm output, direct payments helped keep farm prices and cash receipts from marketings at higher levels than would otherwise have prevailed.

Free Market Estimates of Farm Prices and Incomes

In the early 1960s a number of pioneering efforts were undertaken to construct models of the farm economy that could be used to predict farm prices, output, and income under varying conditions. Some of these models were designed in response to congressional requests for estimates of the consequences of various alternative farm programs, including one without price supports or supply controls.

Despite the potential differences, the results of these models are not markedly different. The ERS model assumes that price supports were removed after the 1960 crop season, so that by the 1965–1967 period the prices of livestock and non-price supported crops would have been affected. Farm income was estimated to be $6 billion lower under free market conditions. According to the Senate and JEC models, which assumed the removal of price supports after the 1959 crop season, farm income would have dropped $7 billion. The actual figures used in the ERS model show that the larger part of the income decline was due to the cessation of direct payments and the smaller part to price support actions.

Table 3 presents the information on direct payments and combines it with the distribution of price support benefits to reach a distribution of total benefits from farm programs in 1964. The total benefits per farm are then compared to the average net income of farmers in each economic class.

In 1969 Class I farms accounted for 7.1 percent of all farms. But they received 40.3 percent of the benefits from farm commodity programs. Average net income of these farm operators (from both farm and nonfarm sources) was $33,000, of which 42 percent, or $14,000 per farm, could be attributed to farm commodity programs. Class I and II farms taken together represented only 19.1 percent of all farms but received 62.8 percent of total benefits. Farm commodity programs contributed $8,000 of their $21,000 average net income.

At the other end of the scale Class V and VI farms accounted for 50.8 percent of total farms,

TABLE 3. Distribution of Farm Program Benefits and Income by Economic Class, 1969

	Economic class							
Item	I	II	III	IV	V	VI	I & II	V & VI
Aggregate benefits				(Billions of dollars)				
Price supports	1.90	0.76	0.55	0.22	0.08	0.09	2.66	0.17
Direct payments	1.08	0.09	0.88	0.43	0.20	0.30	1.98	0.50
Total	2.98	1.66	1.43	0.65	0.28	0.39	4.64	0.67
Distribution of benefits				(Percentage of total)				
Price supports	52.9	21.0	15.4	6.1	2.2	2.4	73.9	4.6
Direct payments	28.5	23.7	23.2	11.3	5.3	7.9	53.6	13.2
Total	40.3	22.5	19.4	8.8	3.8	5.3	62.8	9.1
Income and benefits per farm				(Thousands of dollars)				
Farmer's net income	33.0	13.7	9.6	8.1	7.0	8.1	20.9	7.9
Net income from farming	27.5	10.5	6.5	3.6	2.1	1.1	16.8	1.3
Price supports	9.0	2.1	1.1	0.6	0.3	0.1	4.7	0.1
Direct payments	5.1	2.5	1.7	1.1	0.7	0.2	3.6	0.3
Total	14.1	4.6	2.8	1.7	1.0	0.3	8.3	0.4
Net income from farming under free marketing conditions	13.4	5.9	3.7	1.9	1.1	0.8	8.5	0.9

Source: Appendix B, Table B-1 of Charles L. Schultze, *The Distribution of Farm Subsidies: Who Gets the Benefits?* (Washington, D.C.: The Brookings Institution, 1971), and *Farm Income Situation*, July 1970.

but received only 9.1 percent of the subsidy benefits. The average net benefit per farm was only $400, about 5 percent of their average net income from farm and nonfarm sources.

The proportion of benefits received by large-scale farms rose between 1964 and 1969. This change reflects in part the steady trend toward larger farms; the proportion of total production and cash receipts accounted for by Class I and Class II farms continued to rise. The concentration of direct payments also increased because the benefits of the cotton price support program enacted in 1965 were heavily concentrated among large producers.

By their very nature, current farm programs tend to provide benefits—paid for by both consumers and taxpayers—primarily to those larger farmers who produce the bulk of agricultural output. Conversely, the very large number of small farmers, who in the aggregate produce only a modest fraction of total farm output, are helped relatively little by these programs.

B. NATURAL RESOURCES AND ENVIRONMENTAL POLICY

THE WATER GIVEAWAY: A CRITIQUE OF FEDERAL WATER POLICY

MASON GAFFNEY

The many wasteful policies and procedures in federal water resources programs have been much analyzed by economists and other scholars. Agency benefit-cost practices have been found wanting. Benefit estimates have been biased upward and cost estimates downward. Environmental effects of projects, often adverse, are not weighted enough. I generally endorse the thrust of these criticisms and will not repeat them here. Rather, I will discuss a few equally significant questions which have been neglected.

WASTEFUL PRACTICES AND THEIR CONSEQUENCES

Giving Away Public Resources

Public water policy has been dominated by a giveaway psychology. Damsites, water rights, and *de facto* licenses to pollute water have gone free of any but occasional nominal charges of individuals, corporations, and municipalities. It is as though the Interior Department gave Texaco the rights to offshore oil *gratis*—and then paid for their drilling rigs to help develop the country.

Economists have rightly condemned the use of submarket interest rates in appraising federal works. The use of zero-interest for all costs that ingenuity can allocate to "irrigation" benefits of a project is an outstanding outrage. The use of zero rent on public sites and waters is equally outstanding.

The resulting damages are several:

1. The pressure to put resources to their best use is abated. When valuable land and water inputs are entered at zero value, any of several projects can show super-unitary benefit-cost ra-

Excerpted and reprinted from statement of Mason Gaffney in U.S. Congress, Joint Economic Committee, *Economic Analysis and the Efficiency of Government,* Part 2, Hearings of the Subcommittee on Economy in Government, September 1969.

Mason Gaffney is a Research Associate at Resources for the Future, Inc., Washington, D.C.

tios and appear economical. When these resources are appraised at their highest and best use, and their value entered as a cost, only one use plan for a given resource is economical: the best. It has a ratio of one: all others fall below. (It is not, incidentally, the same project whose ratio is highest when no rent is charged. Rather, it is the project yielding the greatest excess of benefits over costs, i.e., net benefits or surplus.)

That is just elementary economics, one of the first things we teach freshmen. But analysts of public projects often overlook it, perhaps trying to accommodate themselves to the giveaway tradition. The result is often to fail to scan all alternatives for a site or stream. For example, a recreational use might be highest for Canyon X, but if a power company gets it before the Park Service does and can show a ratio of 1.01, it's gone.

2. The pressure to develop water prematurely, preemptively, is paramount. The prospect of future rents has a present value long before there are any present rents. Enjoyment of those future rents goes to him who establishes his claim, usually by first possession and use. It takes little imagination to foresee the results, which one observes everywhere. Scores of state and federal agencies, municipalities, corporations, and individuals race for one resource after another, not because they need it now, but to keep those greedy other fellows from hogging it.

Congressmen will recognize the same uneconomic motivation at work in the scrambles for broadcast licenses, air routes, quotas, trucking routes, pipeline routes, bank charters, and other valuable resources and monopolies it gives away without competitive bidding.

At least four congressional policies reinforce the overwhelming pressure toward premature capture and development of water.

One is an income tax matter. The premature developer of a resource may lose money for years while it is submarginal. These losses are currently expensible, i.e., shared by the Treasury each year. Actually they should not be, for they are a long-term investment designed to capture the resource while it rises in value. Now if Congress had accepted the advice of eminent public finance economists such as Joseph Pechman, William Vickrey, and Richard Musgrave, and moved to a "comprehensive income tax base" (often called a "Haig-Simons" definition of income) as Canada's Carter Commission has recommended there, and subjected the capital gains accrual of resource value to the same effective tax rates as ordinary income, it would be all right to expense those early losses. But Congress has not done so. So the taxpayer can expense early operating losses which he invests to capture a resource, while he pays no tax on the resource appreciation which he captures.

Looking at this in terms of "tax expenditures," the United States is not only giving away water resources, it is advancing some half of the private investment required to capture the resource with little hope of ever getting its principal back. The best it could do through future taxes is recover its own principal with interest. The private investor's interest is tax-free.

A second reinforcing policy is racing for farm production quotas. During the Korean War, for example, cotton quotas were eased. The availability of water let California expand cotton acreage and establish histories of production. After the war when quotas were reimposed, California was "in"—more accurately, those landowners were "in" who had access to uncommitted land and water at the crucial time.

A third reinforcing policy is that old devil, "logrolling." Whenever there is a giveaway, naturally eveyone wants some. Since a Congress cannot very well commit its successor to honor cloakroom bargains, everyone wants some right now. A concrete start is the most convincing commitment Congress can give. And so we have chronically too many starts and too few completions. The economist would say, rank your projects and give priority to those that generate the most surplus of benefits over costs (present-value basis). The exigencies of vote-marshaling interfere with such priorities, and say, start something everywhere at once.

A fourth reinforcing policy is in the public regulation of utilities. Rates are reckoned so as to allow a specified return on the "rate base," or invested capital less depreciation. Every utility seeks to magnify its rate base. One way is to invest in submarginal waters. Regulatory policy lets utilities recoup the losses by charging higher rates in their rich, surplus-yielding territory.

Of course Congress has only limited influence on state regulation, but it has greater influence on federal commissions, and potentially could dominate most power utility regulation because of interstate ties and the use of federal property.

3. A third damage from giveaways is distributional. The successful early preemptors of submarginal waters are those with the greatest waiting power. That is, they are the wealthy. But regardless of who they were before, they become wealthy and powerful once they have nailed down the resource, and it rises in value. They become a privileged class.

4. Water is misallocated. Some submarginal projects remain submarginal, but they do not lose control of their water. Some allocations, that once were economical, become obsolescent and stop yielding surpluses; but they keep their water. Water is very hard to transfer, once allocated, because the beneficiaries generally have no clear title they can convey—after all, they never bought one. The federal owner is not charging them any rent, so they hang on without cost to themselves.

5. Water is underpriced and wasted. Underpricing results not merely from the water giveaway, of course, but from that plus other subsidies like zero interest.

The wastes that ensue are more than meet the eye. It is often assumed that cheap water encourages intensive farming, but the reverse is true. If California farmers had to pay $20 an acre-foot for water they would feed the world. It takes intensive farming to pay such prices, and this may be observed in areas of dear water. As one moves from south to north in California, for example, the humidity rises and the agriculture declines. Cheap water favors sloppy, extensive farming, with water being substituted for labor and farm capital.

This in turn affects project costs. To achieve a given output, when water is cheap, more water must be delivered per acre, and more acres served. Distribution being the costliest element of water supply systems, this magnifies costs.

Dear water from federal projects would encourage economy not just of water but of land. The Bureau of Reclamation does not sell direct to individuals, but wholesales water to irrigation districts. These pass on the cost to their land-owners, but not entirely as user charges. They also levy land taxes, and these encourage early, compact, and intensive use of land under the ditch.

Imbalance, Deferred Impact, and the Unknown

Considering the several subsidies involved, capital obviously flows more easily into water projects than into ordinary private investments like barns, fences, or machines. Thus public investment tends to get ahead of matching private land development. This adds to the waiting period during which the public investment is sterile.

The balance is partly redressed, but on the whole probably worsened, by the impact of federal taxes on land developers.

The favored treatment of capital gains makes it very attractive simply to hold land while federally financed flood control or water supply enhance its value. The result is "irrigation sprawl," or simply agricultural sprawl, in flood-protected areas. Land speculation jeopardized land development long before income tax accounting became a major factor; now the holdout motives are redoubled. Federal subsidies also mean that local property taxes are minimized, and those that do come are deductible, i.e., shared by the Treasury.

On the one hand, capital investments in "water conservation" are expensible. Expensing of capital investments is tantamount to complete tax exemption or more, because the most the Treasury can recover is interest on its own investment. This, coupled with SCS [Soil Conservation Service] subsidies, has certainly caused enormous capital to be invested on private land.

Some of this capital must complement public works and help redress the balance. On the other hand, some of it no doubt is completely substitutional. Indeed, the assessments paid to irrigation districts, through which public water must be distributed, are *not* deductible, so tax shelter is denied to the most complementary of all local water investments.

Regardless of the balance between public and private works, there is clearly a bias toward water-related capital. Here we are flying blind. No one seems to know how much capital has been invested in farm water systems. There is a remarkable gap between $13 billion of net farm income estimated by the Commerce Department and U.S.D.A. and $2.5 billion dollars reported to the Internal Revenue Service, which no one can explain, except that the discrepancies are on the cost side. Expensing of capital investments is certainly involved. Big capital items that may be expensed are breeding stock, soil conservation, and water conservation. The enhanced land value that results from the last two is virtually tax-exempt income for anyone with a good lawyer.

So Congress is continuing to subsidize a particular kind of capital outlay without much knowledge of how much has been sunk already. It is reasonable to infer that water-related capital has now gotten far ahead of its complements, and further subsidy is undesirable.

Slow Payout

Premature investments, and submarket interest rates, and logrolling, and waiting for capital gains, all imply a long wait between investment and payout.

From a certain narrow political view this has attractions. Many constituents are enriched by unrealized, untaxed capital gains. And since production increase is at a minimum, prices are sustained, letting more and more land be enhanced elsewhere.

When we look at some other burning issues, the picture changes. One is inflation. Investments whose output is small or deferred are inflationary, creating demand without supply.

Another is poverty. Investments which lie on the land passively for decades before turning over are complementary to land but not to labor. Just as water which is recycled rapidly can do more work and complement more inputs than water which is recycled slowly, so capital turning over fast employs more men, and relieves more poverty, than the same capital turning over slowly. Every time capital turns over and is reinvested it employs men, and feeds their families. Federal policy tends to freeze capital in massive monuments from which it is seldom recovered fast. Federal works are capital-intensive; they create a minimum of jobs per thousand (or in this case million) dollars sunk.

When the Bureau of Reclamation began business in 1902 it had something called a "revolving fund." It was to recover this each 10 years and reinvest it, so the same capital would by now have been used several times. It was a splendid idea, but that the fund has yet to complete the first revolution. This, I am afraid, symbolizes the whole dreary tale of dragging, lagging results and payouts from federal water enterprises.

Regressive Distribution

The prime beneficiaries of federal water and flood control projects are landowners. The holdings are often very large, the benefits narrowly focused on a small number. No one at all familiar with the Tulare Basin, the West Side of the San Joaquin Valley, or the Mississippi Delta will question this for a moment. These are extreme cases, where some ownerships exceed 100,000 (sic) acres receiving benefits, and more elsewhere. Obviously in other service areas ownerships may be smaller but still represent large fortunes.

The costs are borne by the federal taxpayer. Until recently, "everyone knew" that the federal income tax was highly progressive. This year, thank goodness, the truth has dawned and everyone knows that the federal income tax has devolved into a payroll tax, with high exemptions on property income.

The income of the wealthy beneficiaries of water service may be very lightly taxed. A recent U.S.D.A. study shows that of the largest 66,000 farms in the United States two-thirds reported net losses from farming! These, incidentally, are those large farms which "everyone knows" are more efficient. As to their accrual of land value, that is virtually exempt from income tax in practice. I ask leave to submit an appendix on the many routes by which land income escapes taxation.

IS REFORM POSSIBLE?

Water institutions have proven peculiarly refractory to reformers. Ten years ago I had a go at them, and soon felt like the melodious Paul Simon whose "words like silent raindrops fell, and echoed in a well of silence." Lest this seem like a personal Cassandra complex, I and others have found a warm welcome in tax reform; but, other critics of water policy have been equally unavailing. Few policies, indeed, have been so exposed and pilloried by so many economists, and so little defended, with so little result.

Nothing improves. On the contrary, wilder and wilder plans are seriously discussed in these very halls. That "great land-locked" Tulsa is soon by your hand to become an ocean port, and I do not doubt the Corps of Engineers would carry the channel to the summit of Pike's Peak should you authorize it.

The line-up of vested interests opposing reform is formidable. Water law is a WPA for lawyers. Every project is a WPA for civil engineers, who have been defined by Boulding as men who can tell you the best way to do something that should not be done at all. Many projects are WPAs for marginal mountain counties who sell their votes for local dams. Every project is a consumer of cement. Every project extends the job security of bureaucrats, whose motto might be "pour cement or perish." And above all the beneficiary landowners are constantly lobbying, and playing on the hysteria so easily aroused in matters regarding water. It may not be irrelevant that water and land are symbols of motherhood.

Who, then, will speak for mankind? Is there any hope of a breakthrough? I believe I see several counter-forces developing.

One is the universities. For years, their influence was thrown the other way under the sway of Keynesian doctrines that endorsed all public spending. Today they are dropping that and analyzing choices among alternatives. Since one major alternative is the university itself . . . need I go on? Governor Reagan dramatized the point recently by offering to trade a university for a new water source.

Another is the acute capital shortage of our times. High interest rates are the market's way of signaling the shortage of housing, inventories, gymanisums, equipment, urban sewers, and a hundred other capital items we have failed to replace and expanded while freezing our treasure into cement yielding 3 percent or nothing, and quite irrecoverable for years (wouldn't it be nice to have it back now at 10 percent?). Fun is fun, but many of these shortages are reaching crisis proportions and cannot be ignored.

A third is the youth rebellion, with all it implies. The effective rebels of course are not the louts, but the working leaders like Nader and Yannaconne who have learned how to mobilize idealism and move mountains.

Fourth is the wilderness conservation movement, spearheaded by the redoubtable Sierra Club and its new, taxable lobbying incarnation. They may be True Believers. But if we must choose—and we must—between them and the excesses they fight, they are clearly the better choice. And so I think there is some hope of reform.

POLICY RECOMMENDATIONS

Congress obviously suffers from certain problems of internal organization. I will not presume to comment on these before men who know them better than I. Rather I will tell you what if I were king I should try to accomplish.

Congress needs a superior substitute for logrolling. Trading votes is essentially the way one region pays another for a share of the common wealth—basically a reasonable concept. A problem is that often the only coin in which payment can be made is another water project, when a hospital is needed more; or a project of any kind, when reduced taxes are needed more. Another problem is that all jurisdictions have equal bargaining strength, while capital is much more productive in some than others.

So how else may the beneficiaries of public works compensate other Americans? *By paying more taxes.* It's surprisingly simple. The whole wretched, corrupting business of lobbying for and horse-trading federal largesse, which seems so intractable that many observers and citizens lose hope in Congress and lean more and more towards a strong executive—this whole business has a solution. Lincoln Steffens observed that the troublemaker in Eden was not Eve, nor yet the Serpent. It was the Apple! Taxing the beneficiaries of federal works should serve wonderously to dehydrate the apples of discord on Capitol Hill.

The beneficiaries of public water works are surprisingly easy to identify. The works service certain defined lands. The landowners gain. Other local beneficiaries are subject to competition from immigrants. Land cannot immigrate; it appreciates instead.

But federal income taxation virtually exempts land appreciation. If you work for a living you pay the full tax rate on ordinary income. If you improve land under federal works and match the federal enterprise with private enterprise, your land income is mostly "ordinary" and taxed at full rates. But if you can influence public officials to improve your land while you do nothing, your income is almost all your own.

And so it pays landowners to commit great effort to drumming for federal aid. This has always been a problem, but has worsened in our times because of the cumulative perversion of the federal income tax into a payroll tax. Another problem is the declining role of the property tax, which used to socialize a good share of land value increments. The latter long decline is in a short-run reversal. The former is in the hand of Congress. As you labor in the vineyard of tax reform, you have an opportunity to prune the apple tree of discord with the same strokes.

Congress should charge market prices or rents for federal property. It should encourage the states to do likewise with state property, as a condition of federal aid. No state should get away with giving away its valuable resources to local influentials and then pleading poverty in Washington. Congress should assert federal property rights aggressively when they are paramount, and convey them unequivocally and explicitly when it releases them, not to the end of grabbing everything in sight but of creating a certain and workable tenure system.

It should certainly not do this in one stroke, without detailed analysis. Hydrology and water law are complicated. It should immediately commission a group to return recommendations for clarifying federal water rights. The difference between this and previous and ongoing efforts would be the posture of the United States as a great landlord seeking to maximize income from its domain. Economic analysis will show this is also the way to maximize general welfare.

The benefits are the converse of the problems cited under the section entitled "Giving Away Public Resources." There is more pressure to put resources to the highest use. Premature preemptive appropriation is stopped. Distribution is better. Allocation is better. Waste is reduced.

An important added gain from asserting public property rights is to solve the "pollution conundrum" of who should pay whom for doing or not doing what. To some people it is self-evident that polluters are no better than louts who would nuisance on the public streets, and should control themselves at their own cost and be grateful if they are not jailed for past obscenities. To others it is equally clear that people who want a clean environment should pay polluters not to pollute. The latter school is waxing mighty in the learned journals. Although I have never understood how they would limit the number of those who must be paid not to pollute, they have managed to lend respectability to those who would love to be paid a good price to relinquish the waste-removing capacity of the common water which they have appropriated in the past.

Assertion of public ownership resolves the conundrum. Neither beneficiary of water pays the other. Rather, both pay the government: the ones an effluent charge for unavoidable waste disposal; the others a variety of user or standby charges, depending on their terms of access to the water.

As part of this effort, Congress should assume great responsibility to use its unique powers in resolving interstate water conflicts. It should abandon such economic monstrosities as the Colorado River Compact, which rigidly divides water among political states regardless of demand, and find a formula that recognizes productivity and requires repayment.

Another function uniquely tractable to federal powers is that of pooling and integrating local projects. Power pooling is a fact over wide areas. Pooling of water supply, storage, power generation and flood control are much more limited. Conjunctive use of surface and ground storage is barely begun. The obstacles of law, institutions, and local-vested interests are formidable. The federal might is often the most potent available engine of reform.

Congress should move toward full-funding of a few projects at once, and away from yearly appropriations for more projects than available funds can complete in a reasonable time. A "reasonable time" depends on the interest rate. Money doubles in a number of years equal to 72 divided by the interest rate. At 7.2 percent, for example, money doubles every 10 years, and quadruples every 20. If a construction job is stretched out to 20 years the early costs are quadrupled by the delay. Obviously, the delays we learned to accept at low interest rates are no longer reasonable.

Once the logrolling logjams are broken by tax reform and beneficiary charges, endless possibilities open up for rationalizing the timing of works, and ranking projects by priority. This requires use of a reawakening subdiscipline of economics known as "capital theory." Congress should commission expert studies on this topic to develop criteria for priorities.

Now, some development is postmature. Probably more is premature. In general, priority should go to projects yielding the greatest surplus per dollar of cost, as of now, on a present-value basis. But this needs to be tempered by holding off on sites that are ripening very fast to still higher uses. Capital theory needs to teach us how to make this trade-off.

Congress should scratch "regional development" as a benefit from any project. All projects are regional. The concept is either meaningless, or else a thin cover for vote-swapping, maintenance of obsolete congressional districts, and sinking the nation's dwindling treasure into submarginal projects.

Congressmen who are tempted to go on piling concrete into every narrow gorge with a strident lobby could do worse than to review the history of a previous boom in water works, the canal boom that busted in 1836. They went wild, simply wild over regional development. Some states have outlawed state bond issues ever since.

Another pressure to resist is that of designating the Corps of Engineers and the S.C.S. as "anti-poverty" agencies. A dollar invested in any hamburger stand does more to fight poverty than ten spent by the corps, which has demonstrated beyond misunderstanding its eagerness to serve the very, very, very rich by servicing their lands, free. It is an "arrangement" of long standing, a scarlet affair beside which the novel of the same name pales into dull gray.

Not only does the hamburger stand employ more people per dollar of capital, it feeds them as well, and it does both things many times a year as each dollar turns over and over. If we aim to deploy our capital to fight poverty we need channel more of it into small, labor-using businesses that produce useful goods. The Corps of Engineers does not recover its capital outlays for decades, if ever, either directly or from increased tax collections. Each new project requires new capital, so that over the years the sum of capital invested for every job created is greater than in any private industry except tombstones. Monumental engineering works are the tombstones of civilizations. Pharoah had his pyramids; Caesar had his aqueducts; and Uncle Sam . . . may profit by their example.

CLEAN RHETORIC AND DIRTY WATER: THE FAILURE OF FEDERAL WATER POLLUTION CONTROL POLICY

A. MYRICK FREEMAN, III
ROBERT H. HAVEMAN

For nearly two decades now, the United States has been passing new legislation to improve the quality of the environment. Numerous laws with environmental implications have been passed, and rivers of rhetoric have flowed from members of Congress and executive agencies. We have seen the Water Pollution Control Act of 1956, the Water Quality Act of 1965, the Clean Water Restoration Act of 1966, and the Environmental Quality Improvement Act of 1970, among others. In 1965, we heard President Johnson say, as he signed the Water Quality Act, "Today, we begin to be master of our environment"; and in 1971, President Nixon stated, "The battle for a better environment can be won and we are winning it."

Unfortunately, the facts of environmental quality do not jibe with the rhetoric. Indices of environmental quality show that the waste loads imposed on environmental resources have been growing continuously, and rising waste loads mean deteriorating environmental quality. The recent report of the Council on Environmental Quality, for example, indicates that emissions of all the major air pollutants have increased at an overall rate of over three percent per year and that, in recent years, "the overall quality of the nation's waters probably has deteriorated because of accelerated eutrophication, increased discharges of toxic materials, greater loads of sediment, and other factors." The legislation of the past decades has, in fact, failed to deliver on its promises.

Existing legislation is based essentially on a regulatory strategy, with an added carrot of federal subsidy enabling the budget to reflect "environ-

Reprinted from A. Myrick Freeman, III and Robert H. Haveman, "Clean Rhetoric and Dirty Water," *The Public Interest*, No. 28 (Summer 1972) pp. 51–65. By permission of National Affairs, Inc.

A. Myrick Freeman, III is Associate Professor of Economics, Bowdoin College, Brunswick, Maine. Robert H. Haveman is Professor of Economics, University of Wisconsin, Madison, Wisconsin.

mental priorities." This rule-making enforcement strategy pits the power of public agencies against polluters in a context in which the rules of the struggle and the information available to each party are biased against the government. Not surprisingly, this effort at regulation has failed to induce private sector behavior leading to achievement of the objectives of the legislation. Even more serious, this strategy fails to recognize the basic economic nature of the problem. Use of the services of scarce environmental resources continues to be free, and as a result there is no cost to a person who overuses, misuses, or abuses them. Moreover, no effective institutional mechanisms, with clearly spelled out functions and operating procedures, have been established to manage the utilization of environmental resources or to guide them into their most productive uses.

EXISTING LEGISLATION

Present federal water pollution control policy has two main elements. The first is a program of federal subsidies to cities for the construction of waste treatment plants. The second is a procedure for establishing regulations to limit discharge and for enforcing these rules through the police power of the state and, ultimately, the courts.

The Water Pollution Control Act of 1956 established the first federal subsidy for treatment plant construction. This subsidy takes the form of federal grants to municipalities which cover up to 55 percent of the cost of plant construction. As an added incentive, some states have augmented the grants to the point where cities are responsible for only 15 percent of total construction costs. Since 1956, this program has grown rapidly, and today nearly $1 billion per year is being spent by the federal government for such construction. This money is allocated among states on the basis of a formula which assigns the first $100 million according to population and inversely according to per capita income, and the rest according to population alone. To be eligible for such grants, a state must have adopted a plan for achieving water quality standards acceptable to the Environmental Protection Agency (EPA). Present regulations stipulate that such plans must require a minimum of secondary treatment (85 percent removal of organic wastes) or its equivalent.

This program encourages cities to provide at least secondary treatment to the wastes of all dischargers who use municipal sewer systems. These dischargers include the bulk of the nation's households and commercial enterprises, but the majority of the nation's *industrial* wastes are discharged directly into rivers and streams. To encourage waste treatment activities by these dischargers, the Tax Reform Act of 1969 allows accelerated depreciation of waste treatment plant investments for tax purposes. The objective of this $120 million annual "tax expenditure" is to stimulate more spending on pollution control by reducing the after-tax cost of such investments.

In addition to these subsidy programs, federal policy provides for regulations governing the disposal of wastes into rivers and mechanisms to enforce these rules. The first provision for federal enforcement actions against water polluters was contained in the 1956 Water Pollution Control Act, which relied primarily on voluntary compliance stemming from abatement conferences attended by polluters and government officials. Under this provision it usually proved impossible to get beyond the conference stage, and only one case ever got to court.

The Water Quality Act of 1965 assigns primary responsibility for implementing pollution control plans to the states. It requires states to establish water quality standards and to develop a program for attaining them. This program was envisioned as a bench mark for judging the progress of a state in attaining its water quality standards and for assisting federal officials in determining when and where to undertake federal enforcement actions. In implementing this program, state agencies must first determine the maximum amount of discharges consistent with their water quality standards. Then they issue licenses limiting dischargers in aggregate to this maximum. To enforce these license provisions, states must monitor dischargers and initiate judicial or quasi-judicial proceedings when violations occur.

The 1965 law also authorizes federal enforcement actions whenever it is found that state water quality standards are being violated. (A governor or state agency can also request EPA to initiate enforcement efforts to deal with an interstate pollution problem.) EPA can initiate court actions 180 days after notifying violators. This provision of federal law was not used at all until August 1969, and as of the end of 1971, EPA had issued only 27 notices.

The decision to proceed to litigation ultimately rests with the administrator of EPA. Because of the lack of guidelines for deciding when a pollution problem is sufficiently serious to warrant legal action, this decision becomes a political matter. Thus enforcement at the federal level is, in practice, far from comprehensive or uniform. While the large municipality or firm may confront a probability of ultimate legal action, the small polluter is virtually immune.

In practice, federal and state pollution control efforts have been limited in scope and coverage in two respects. First, they have been aimed primarily at organic pollutants and have given relatively little attention to nonorganic pollutants such as plant nutrients, heavy metals (e.g., mercury), toxic materials, and heat. This is less the result of any limitations in either federal or state law than of the fact that organic pollution is the most noticeable in its effects and is relatively easy to deal with, given present technology. In the second place, pollution control efforts to date have been limited to discharges from point sources (i.e., factories and sewer pipes) and have ignored pollution arising from erosion and siltation, agricultural fertilizer, irrigation water, pesticide run-offs, and other nonpoint sources. This is an area where neither technology nor policy is well developed. Yet as point sources are brought under better control, pollution from nonpoint sources will loom as a larger problem—both relatively and absolutely.

THE RECORD OF FAILURE

If its objective is the improvement of the quality of the nation's rivers, as it surely must be, then existing federal water pollution policy has been a dismal failure. In 1969, a General Accounting Office (GAO) study of several rivers concluded that even though $5.4 billion had been spent at all levels of government for waste treatment plant construction during the previous 12 years, the nation's rivers were in worse shape than ever before.

This record of failure is attributable to both the subsidy and the enforcement aspects of current policy. Consider, for example, the waste treatment grant program. Because of the structure and administration of that program, much was spent but little achieved. Five of the chief reasons for this result are:

1. By subsidizing only conventional "end-of-the-pipe" treatment systems, the grant program induces planners to overlook what in some cases may be less costly or more effective alternatives, such as the storage (ponding) of wastes during critical periods of lowstream flow and the augmentation of the assimilative capacity of the stream through instream aeration and other devices.

2. Current regulations require secondary waste treatment for *all* municipalities along a watercourse. An optimal basin-wide plan would relate the degree of desired municipal treatment to streamflow conditions and downstream uses (among other variables). In this optimal plan, some municipalities may require tertiary treatment while others may require only primary treatment. The drive for uniform secondary treatment results in excessive treatment costs at some outfalls and insufficient treatment costs at others.

3. States have failed to target federal funds on the municipalities with the most harmful discharges. More than one town situated downstream from major industrial locations has used federal funds to build treatment plants with the result that *its treated effluent is of higher quality than the river into which it is discharged.* Also, federal funds have been concentrated on smaller, largely suburban communities rather than the larger cities with the most pollution. For example, nearly 40 percent of the federal grant money has gone to towns with populations of less than 10,000, which contain less than 16 percent of the U.S. urban

population. The largest cities, containing 25 percent of the total urban population, have received only 6 percent of the total federal grant money.

4. *Construction* of treatment facilities does not guarantee their effective *operation.* In fact, the structure of the recent program creates incentives which work in the opposite direction. A second study by the GAO has confirmed the widely held belief that municipal plants are often operated inefficiently. Over one-half of the plants surveyed were providing inadequate treatment, due to overzealous efforts to reduce plant operating costs, the difficulty and expense of hiring trained personnel to operate the plants, and the failure of cities to maintain and repair equipment. By subsidizing only one part of the cost of effective waste treatment—plant construction costs—the federal government has induced resources into construction activity but has provided no similar inducement for efficient plant operation.

5. Federal grants for municipal waste treatment plant construction provide an indirect subsidy to industrial and commercial waste dischargers. By subsidizing the capital costs of municipal treatment facilities, the existing policy tends to reduce the sewer charges imposed on industrial, commercial, and domestic waste dischargers connected to the sewerage system. Because approximately 50 percent of the wastes handled by municipal treatment plants are from industrial sources, the size of the subsidy to business is substantial. The effect of this subsidy is to weaken the incentives for waste dischargers to seek such alternatives to the public treatment of their waste flows as production process changes, recycling, and materials recovery. There are many such alternatives, and these are often less costly. Yet because they do not receive federal subsidies, firms overlook them. The tax subsidies have a similar distorting effect on the decisions made by firms as to the techniques they choose to reduce their discharges.

Thus, through federal grants for municipal waste treatment facilities, as well as through tax subsidies for industrial pollution-control equipment, current policy is, in effect, allowing polluters to generate and dispose large quantities of wastes without bearing the full cost of their discharges—and then using taxpayers' money to clean up after them. With little effective constraint on the generation of industrial wastes and with rapid economic growth, the burden on the environment will skyrocket in the coming decades. One recent study showed that the *annual* costs of applying secondary treatment to an unconstrained flow of wastes would be $18 billion in 1973, $27 billion in 1980, and $55 billion by the year 2000. The continued spending of taxpayers' money to clean up after polluters—along the lines of the current strategy—is going to be an enormously expensive and relatively fruitless venture.

WHY "ENFORCEMENT" DOESN'T WORK

In regard to the regulatory/enforcement aspects of present policy, it is widely agreed that enforcement has not been effective so far, both at the federal level and at the state level, where the primary responsibility now lies. The question is whether the regulatory/enforcement strategy can be made to work by tightening the laws and increasing our efforts, or whether failure is inherent in the enforcement process. We incline to the latter view and believe that both history and a clear understanding of the nature of the regulatory process support our position.

It is in the American tradition to create regulatory agencies to deal with problems caused by malfunctions in the economic system. The existence of agencies such as the Interstate Commerce Commission, the Federal Power Commission, and the Federal Drug Administration is sufficient to convince most people that the problems for which these agencies were created are being dealt with successfully. But a careful analysis of the evidence shows that this is rarely the case.

The naive view of the regulatory process is that the agency establishes rules and regulations to govern the behavior of the regulated and to further the public interest. The threat of sanctions is thought to be sufficient to deter violations; but if any occur, it is assumed that violators are quickly brought to justice. The reality is quite different.

Regulatory agencies have substantial discretionary power concerning the interpretation and application of their rule-making and enforcement powers. As a consequence, regulation/enforcement becomes essentially a political process entailing bargaining between parties of unequal power. In this process the real issues are camouflaged in technical jargon, and the regulators are largely isolated from political accountability for their actions. The regulatory agency and the interests they regulate bargain over the regulations to be set. They bargain over whether violations have occurred and, if so, who was responsible. They bargain over what steps shall be taken to correct infractions. And in the rare instances where the bargaining process breaks down and the conflict moves to the courts for resolution, the judicial system seeks an "acceptable solution" or a "reasonable compromise." Only rarely is it forced by the flow of events into making either/or choices. At every stage of this multi-level bargaining process those being regulated have a lot at stake, while the public interest is diffuse, poorly organized, and poorly represented. Predictably, the bargains struck favor those being regulated.

The regulatory/enforcement strategy pits the power of pollution-control authorities against the power of the polluter in an unending sequence of skirmishes and battles over licensing and the enforcement of regulations. As a consequence, the enforcement process is long and drawn out and often inconclusive. Industrial polluters get higher returns from hiring lawyers to fight enforcement than from money spent on pollution control.

The inherent difficulties with the regulation/enforcement process are nowhere more apparent than in the recent attempts to make the 1899 Refuse Act work. This law prohibits the discharge of "any refuse matter of any kind or description whatever" into any waters unless the discharger has obtained a permit from the U.S. Army Corps of Engineers. Virtually none of the present estimated 40,000 industrial dischargers holds a valid permit. This all-but-forgotten law made headlines beginning in 1969 when charges were brought against several firms as a consequence of individuals' initiatives. Some convictions were obtained, fines levied, and rewards paid to vigilant citizens, as the law provides. But in June 1970, as the number of cases began to increase, the Justice Department issued guidelines to its attorneys instructing them not to bring charges against firms for which residuals discharge was a part of normal plant operations, or against firms holding a permit issued by a state or local government. With this action, the Justice Department, in effect, established a policy of selective nonenforcement of one of the nation's laws. This policy was reinforced in December 1970, when the Administration announced that, while permits were required of all dischargers (including those "exempted" by the earlier Justice Department policy), no prosecutions would take place so long as an application had been filed by July 1, 1971 and not subsequently rejected by the government. The effect of this is to grant firms an immunity from prosecution which is likely to last for several years while the government works its way through the backlog of unprocessed permit applications. And since all permit applications are forwarded to the relevant state for certification that the discharge is consistent with the state's pollution control plan, the new policy has contributed nothing to the establishment of a more effective pollution control effort. It has, however, generated a flood of new permit applications to burden the work load of federal and state officials while, in effect, repealing the one potentially effective federal law against pollution.

THE MUSKIE BILL

Although there is growing disenchantment with federal water pollution control policies, the recent legislative response has been more of the same. Both the Senate and the House have passed bills in 1971–1972 which are based on a legislative finding that past efforts have failed. Quantum jumps in regulatory controls and subsidies are contained in both bills. But if past experience is any guide, these efforts will at best be patch jobs on an already sieve-like structure.

The clearest example of the "let's hitch our belts one notch tighter and forge ahead" philosophy implicit in these efforts is the so-called "Muskie bill," which passed the Senate by an 86-0 vote late in 1971. That bill essentially ends the use of water quality standards as the measuring rod for performance and substitutes standards or regulations regarding effluent control and treatment. The bill requires that industry apply the "best practicable" waste treatment technology available by 1976 and completely eliminate discharges of pollutants by 1981 if it can be done at "reasonable cost." If zero discharge cannot be attained at reasonable cost, industry must install the "best available treatment" facilities, "taking into account the cost." A date of 1985 is set as a target for zero discharge.

The basic weakness of the bill is its reliance on precisely that sort of discretion which has vitiated numerous other rule enforcement efforts. Who is going to define "reasonable," "best available," and "best practicable," and who is going to "take into account the cost"? All of these terms are open to widely divergent interpretations, and none has a precise legal meaning. Perhaps more important, this bill implicitly requires federal surveillance and enforcement action on a case-by-case basis on each of 40,000 industrial pollution sources to police the ill-defined discharge standards.

Aside from these enormous administrative difficulties, there is the further consideration that, should the rules actually be enforced, the cost would be enormous. Given existing technology and its foreseeable developments, attainment of either the best available technology or the zero-discharge goals will be prohibitively expensive. Because costs rise swiftly at very high treatment levels, the total cost of meeting these objectives could be several times that required to meet current quality standards and far in excess of any benefits resulting from elimination of the last few units of residual discharge. As the Report of a Panel of Experts to the Director of the Office of Science and Technology stated:

> The . . . costs in achieving or even approaching such a goal would be very great and would almost certainly in every instance constitute a misallocation of the nation's resources. Removing the last few per cent of the common pollutants from water is usually extremely costly, yet the added benefits due to the extra treatment in that regard are extremely questionable in all cases.

The subsidy component of the present strategy is also reaffirmed and extended in this bill. Appropriations of $20 billion are authorized through fiscal year 1975, and a minimum of secondary waste treatment is required for all municipalities by 1976. The share of municipal waste treatment construction costs to be covered by federal grants is also enlarged.

PAYING BY THE POUND

If our appraisal of the effectiveness of both the current strategy and recent legislation is correct, a major restructuring of water pollution control policy is required if we are to improve water quality. This restructuring, to be successful, must recognize the basic economic nature of the pollution problem and the economic incentives governing the behavior of polluters. It must force waste dischargers to bear the costs which their actions generate. If these costs can be imposed on dischargers, incentives will be present to constrain the waste generation proclivities of industrial and municipal polluters and to keep valuable environmental resources from being diverted to low-valued uses. The necessary incentives can be created by imposing user or effluent charges on waste dischargers such that the size of the charge is related to the volume of harmful substances which is released into the environment. In effect, waste dischargers should be required to "pay by the pound."

Numerous arguments can be offered in support of this user-charge strategy. The most cogent argument is that it will succeed in reducing waste discharges—not just retarding their growth. The recorded response of waste dischargers to the imposition of municipal sewerage charges provides strong evidence. For example, after putting a relatively small user charge into effect, the city of Cincinnati reported that industrial waste was reduced nearly 40 percent in one year. Another city found discharges cut to one-third of the former level.

That user charges have induced such dramatic reductions in waste discharges is not surprising. When a price is placed on wastes discharged into watercourses, a number of actions that previously looked unattractive to dischargers become appealing alternatives. These include changes in production procedures within the plant to reduce waste generation, as well as the installation of waste treatment facilities at the plant site. Moreover, such charges would stimulate research and development efforts aimed at developing new technologies for reducing waste generation or recycling wastes. Finally, if environmental services are priced, those commodities whose production imposes large environmental damages will experience price increases relative to commodities whose production imposes minor environmental costs. Because higher prices mean smaller demand, production and consumption would tend to be shifted away from those commodities with the most damaging environmental effects.

In addition to providing incentives for reductions in waste generation, a comprehensive national effluent-charge policy would have a second important effect. It would end the system of bargaining and negotiating between agencies and individual producers—a system which rewards delaying tactics—and replace it with a system which rewards compliance and effective and continuing controls on waste discharges.

Finally, while the current strategy has placed substantial demands on a tight federal budget, a user-charge strategy would actually *generate* revenues. These revenues could be used to finance environmental measures that municipalities and firms cannot be expected to undertake, such as basic research and development, establishment of regional or river basin authorities to manage the use of regional environmental resources, and construction of installations to artificially reaerate streams or to increase stream flows during low-flow periods.

In evaluating the merits of an economic—i.e., user-charge—approach to environmental policy, it must be emphasized that an effluent charge will, by itself, be inadequate to insure the efficient use of environmental resources. For one thing, it cannot cope with nonpoint sources of pollution such as agricultural fertilizer and pesticide runoff. But this is also true of the subsidy/enforcement strategy. Comprehensive environmental management requires the establishment of regional authorities whose responsibilities would include planning for the optimal use and augmentation of environmental resources; undertaking collective investments; setting water and air quality standards and charge levels designed to meet these standards; monitoring discharge levels into both water and air resources; and regulating patterns of regional land use. To be effective in managing the environment consistently with regional preferences, these authorities should be governed by directly elected rather than appointed officials. The sad history of the appointive regulatory commissions and their capture by those interests which they were supposed to regulate should be a powerful lesson.

THE CONVENTIONAL OBJECTIONS

Proposals for an economic-incentives approach to pollution control have not been enthusiastically received by waste dischargers—especially industrial polluters. Indeed, powerful corporate interests have objected strenuously to the effluent-charge strategy. Industry, it is claimed, is already spending as much as possible on pollution-control efforts. As H. C. Lumb, vice-president of Republic Steel Corporation, stated before a congressional committee, "Taking money away from industrial companies in the name of a tax on pollution . . . would harm the cause of pollution control." The vacuousness of this position should be apparent. By implication, it denies that economic incentives —prices and costs—influence business decisions and behavior, a contention that is contradicted by daily observation. For example, when firms purchase labor-saving capital equipment in response to rising wages, they are demonstrating not only their responsiveness to economic incentives but their ability to finance cost-saving investment. The purpose of an effluent-charge policy is to provide a similar economic incentive. The financial resources for responding can be found. Industry expects to spend $4.9 billion on pollution control in 1972. But this figure is only 5.3 percent of all planned capital expenditures. A doubling in the level of spending for pollution control could be accommodated with only a 5.6 percent reduction in other capital spending. It is not financial resources that are lacking but the incentive is to use more of these resources for pollution control.

A second objection which has been raised to an effluent-charge policy is that it will be too complex to administer and that, as a consequence, its effectiveness will be eroded by powerful interests. This objection, we would argue, sees the real situation in reverse. In our view, the effluent-charge strategy will be more straightforward to administer and far more effective than the current regulatory strategy.

Once environmental quality standards have been set, a single charge would be levied on each unit of the prominent harmful substances found in effluents or emissions. Each discharger would be responsible for monitoring his discharge, reporting its composition and quantity to the public authority, and making the appropriate payments. There is an obvious comparison with the system of reporting and paying income taxes. As in the case of the income tax, rules and standards of accuracy for measurement would have to be specified, and audits for compliance would have to be undertaken. Dischargers would be required to install and maintain the required monitoring equipment, subject to audit and calibration for accuracy by the authorities. Information on discharges and payments would be recorded and made available for public scrutiny.

With such a system there is little room for administrative discretion and bargaining. The primary decision is the level of the charge to be imposed, and this decision is a significant and highly visible one. There is also a clear performance criterion by which to judge the correctness of the decision on the level of the charge. If water quality standards are being met, the rate is high enough—if not, the rate should be raised. Moreover, while the zeal and effectiveness of regulatory agencies diminish over time, the effect of an effluent charge is durable. It remains in place unless there is an explicit political decision to remove it.

It is clear, then, that an effluent-charge system poses no unique or particularly difficult administrative problems. In fact, it is an administratively simple strategy which avoids many of the pitfalls of the regulatory/enforcement approach, and which leaves little room for powerful interests to gain special advantages through low-visibility negotiations with the regulatory agency.

A PROBLEM OF PLURALISM

When one compares the failure of existing policy with the widely acknowledged potency of an economic-incentives strategy, a natural question arises: If improved water quality is a national objective, then why the reluctance to modify policy and incorporate the advantages of a promising alternative strategy? The answer is to be found in the nature and dynamics of a pluralistic representative democracy.

The political system is in large part a mechanism for reconciling conflicting interests. With respect to the pollution issue, the conflict is over how much cleaning up of pollution is actually going to be done and who is going to pay for it.

Now, policymakers, like other decision-makers, act in their own self-interest. Elected officials behave so as to assure their own reelection; bureaucrats behave so as to be promoted, not to alienate the legislature, or to assure themselves of a lucrative position in private industry at a later date. If a policymaker supports a policy which takes something away from a part of his constituency, he alienates that group. As a consequence, he would tend to support any policy only if the losers were small in number or without influence and if the beneficiaries were large in number or influential. Thus, policymakers search for policies whose costs are hidden or can be shifted to less influential or less organized elements of their constituencies. Policymakers also try to postpone decisions (since every decision has a cost) and to avoid the costs of a decision by shifting the responsibility for making it to another place in the political system.

In a system with full information on the part of both policymakers and voters and with no basic structural imperfections, a decision-maker would be accountable to all groups affected by his decisions, and all of these groups would have access to him.

Such perfection, however, does not characterize our political system. Certain institutional arrangements, such as the congressional seniority system and loose campaign-finance regulations (which enable economic power to be readily transformed into political power), undermine both accountability and accessibility. And when such structural imperfections persist, policymakers gain the leeway which they desire to avoid those decisions likely to alienate major sources of their support. They have the latitude to choose those strategies which shift costs to unwary sectors of their constituencies, which shift responsibility for unpopular decisions to other parts of the political system, and which postpone those decisions likely to generate adverse political repercussions.

These few rough propositions about pluralistic democracies provide some insight into why the type of pollution-control policy that has emerged from our political process is not surprising. Let us review some of the characteristics of existing policy:

- Through existing and pending legislation, federal legislators have consistently shifted the burden for making difficult decisions to the states (e.g., the setting of standards) or to decision-makers within the federal bureaucracy. Federal legislation typically passes the Congress with large majorities, sometimes—as with the Muskie bill—unanimously. One can only conclude that if all legislators are for the policy, they must have found some way to duck the real issues.
- Policymakers have been willing to subsidize industrial dischargers wherever this could be hidden in tax depreciation formulas or municipal cost-sharing programs.
- Federal law fails to require states to hold public hearings on the setting of water quality standards. Obviously, there can be considerable public controversy surrounding the choice of standards. The failure to stipulate public hearings serves the interests of dischargers at the expense of the public, whose accessibility to the decision-making process is greatly diminished.
- Setting environmental quality standards is a meaningless exercise unless effective mechanisms are developed for achieving the standards. Without exception, states have placed primary reliance on some form of licensing of discharges (including discharge limits) accompanied by judicial enforcement of the license terms. As we have seen, this leads to multi-stage bargaining with minimal accessibility and accountability, and the consequence is delay or nonenforcement of the standard.

In short, the political response to the water pollution problem has been to shift the real decisions from the federal to the state level and from the legislature to the bureaucracy; to make decisions in arenas where there is less accountability and accessibility; and to avoid once-and-for-all resolutions of the political conflicts in favor of the piecemeal, fragmented decisions characterizing the enforcement process. These tendencies work against the public interest in pollution control and in favor of polluters.

The economic-incentives approach which we (along with many other economists) have suggested has therefore had little political appeal. This is in part because it runs directly counter to the tendencies cited above. Establishment of a pollution-charge system in conjunction with environmental quality standards would resolve most of the political conflict over the environment. And it would do so in a highly visible way, so that those who would be hurt by such a policy could see what was happening. It is the openness and explicitness of such choices that policymakers seek to avoid.

It is not entirely facetious to suggest that the reason an economic-incentives approach has not been tried in this country is that it would work. In the absence of effective pollution-control policies, polluters are able to expropriate the environment for their own use by the act of discharging wastes. A system of pollution charges, on the other hand, would establish the principle that the environment is owned by the people as a whole and that the polluters must pay for the privilege of using part of the environmental for waste disposal. Such massive transfers of "property rights" and the wealth they represent seldom occur without political upheaval. Viewed in this light, the most formidable barrier to controlling pollution is probably not technology, population, or public attitudes, but rather the politics of power in our pluralistic democracy.

THE SYSTEM OF GOVERNMENT SUBSIDIES TO THE OIL INDUSTRY

WALTER J. MEAD

It seems entirely appropriate for the Senate Subcommittee on Antitrust and Monopoly to conduct hearings on governmental intervention into the market mechanism of the petroleum industry. There is in fact a system of tax subsidies to stimulate petroleum resource discovery and production, together with production and marketing controls designed to restrict supply and thereby maintain oil prices substantially above competitive levels. Import quotas have been instituted in order to insulate the domestic oil market from the challenge of foreign competition. Given this barrier to free entry into the U.S. market, the price of crude oil in the United States is approximately double the free-market world price. In the first half of 1968 the Japanese government purchased approximately 2.3 million barrels per day of largely Middle Eastern crude at prices averaging $1.42 per barrel. This oil had an average API Gravity rating of 32.3 degrees. In contrast crude oil prices in the United States for similar gravity ratings have been about $3.00 per barrel.

The largest Japanese purchases were of Iranian heavy crude oil at a price of $1.35 per barrel. Table 1 shows that this oil might be transported to

TABLE 1. Comparison of U.S. and World Prices of Crude Oil

Middle East crude oil	
Price of Iranian heavy crude 31.0° average gravity FOB	$1.35
Transportation cost to U.S. East Coast port	.75
Total delivered price before tariff	$2.10
U.S. tariff 10½¢ per barrel	.10
Total delivered price after tariff	$2.20
U.S. Crude Oil	
Price of Texas crude 31–31.9° gravity, Refugio, Texas	$3.12
Transportation cost to East Coast port	.30
	$3.42

Reprinted from Walter J. Mead, "The System of Government Subsidies to the Oil Industry," *Natural Resources Journal,* vol. 113 (January 1970) pp. 113–125. By permission of the *Natural Resources Journal,* published by the University of New Mexico School of Law, Albuquerque, New Mexico.

Walter J. Mead is Professor of Economics at the University of California, Santa Barbara, California.

the East Coast markets of the United States and would have a delivered price of about $2.10 per barrel before payment of tariffs. U.S. crude oil, having the same gravity rating, can be purchased at a Texas Gulf port for $3.12 per barrel and delivered to the East Coast at a delivered price of about $3.42 per barrel. This delivered price difference of $1.32 per barrel could not exist except for the protection afforded by the tariff and import quota.[1]

Further evidence supporting the price differential shown in Table 1 is provided by the fact that import "tickets" have in recent years had a market value of about $1.25 per barrel. The value of a ticket to import one barrel of crude oil into PAD districts I-IV (east of the Rocky Mountains) has recently, and probably temporarily, fallen from $1.25 per barrel to about 75 cents per barrel.[2] This is the result of substantially higher freight rates due in turn to the Suez Canal closure and to a shortage of large oil tankers.

A recent U.S. Department of Interior study conservatively estimated that if import quotas were removed the impact of world competition would cause the American price of crude oil east of the Rocky Mountains to decline approximately 95¢ per barrel.[3]

The relatively high U.S. price of crude oil is the result of a complex system of tax subsidies and production restrictions imposed on behalf of the domestic oil industry. Import quotas are simply a capstone which the system requires in order to be insulated from foreign competition. The purpose of this paper is to review the system of oil industry subsidies in total.

[1] All should be warned that oil price and cost data are extremely complicated. Free market prices are scarce and may involve tax conditions, side payments, trades, as well as quality and geographical differences that are not clear.

[2] Oil and Gas J., December 2, 1968, at 25.

[3] Office and Assistant Secretary of the Interior, Cost of the Oil Import Program to the American Economy 1 (January 16, 1969). Since this study was authorized and issued by the department administering the oil import program, any bias would be expected to minimize the cost to the economy by minimizing the spread between U.S. and world crude prices.

PERCENTAGE DEPLETION ALLOWANCE

Percentage depletion must be distinguished from the conventional right to a tax-free recovery of a previous investment. Rather, it is historically based on a tax-free flow of income equal to the *estimated value of the oil property at the point of discovery*. The Revenue Act of 1918 granted a 100-percent tax-free income equal to the discovery value of the oil property, independent of discovery costs. The Revenue Act of 1924 reduced the tax-free income flow to a maximum of 50 percent of the property's net income. In 1926, the present rule of thumb was established permitting 27.5 percent of the gross income (not net) from an oil property to be free of tax, up to a limit of 50 percent of the net income from that property. Thus, where the full value of the depletion allowance is used, the effect is to reduce the federal income tax rate on oil income by half.

While percentage depletion allowance is based historically on discovery value rather than a tax-free return of an initial investment, the latter is also permitted for important items of exploration and development cost. The present law permits *depreciation* of all tangible equipment costs for producing wells. In addition, lease rentals and all intangible drilling costs may be *expensed* as incurred including expenditures for labor, fuel, power, materials, supplies, tool rental, and repairs of drilling equipment in connection with drilling and equipping wells. Therefore, a taxpayer electing to take percentage depletion instead of cost depletion not only receives up to 50 percent of the property's net income free of tax, but receives a tax-free return of all his initial investment except his lease acquisition costs and his exploration expenses. For productive wells, he may recover these costs only by electing to take cost depletion in lieu of percentage depletion. For nonproductive wells, even these may be expensed when the property is abandonded.

Various devices are also available and are used to minimize the effect of the 50-percent limitation. For example, an integrated oil company may be able to increase its reported income per property by either or both shifting some expenditures from charges against the property to charges against other corporate income, and by inflating the accounting value of its oil at well head. Both devices will increase the reported net income of the oil property and thereby weaken the 50-percent limitation. Further, the "ABC deal" involving production payments may be utilized to increase net income for an oil property in a year in which the *50-percent limit* would otherwise restrict depletion allowance benefits.[4]

Percentage depletion allowance benefits were introduced during and following World War I as a tax subsidy to encourage oil exploration and development. Since investors make investment decisions on the basis of their anticipated after-tax rates of return, and since the depletion allowance permits a sizable reduction in corporate or personal income taxes, we should expect an increased flow of capital into oil exploration and production at the expense of other investment alternatives. This should be followed in time by expanded output.[5] As a further consequence, the price of oil would be reduced below levels which would otherwise prevail.

MARKET-DEMAND PRORATIONING

Price-depressing effects of the percentage depletion allowance tax subsidy were accentuated, probably fortuitously, by the discovery of the East Texas oil field in 1930. This discovery substantially increased the supply of oil at a time when demand was declining. Consequent sharp declines in the price of oil, together with unrestricted drilling and production from jointly owned oil properties, culminated in the passage of prorationing laws in the leading oil-producing states.[6]

Prorationing may be defined as "the rules and procedures by which a regulatory agency determines the total crude oil production from a state and allocates the total among the various reservoirs and to the producers in each reservoir."[7] Prorationing consists of two parts: (1) MER (maximum efficient rate) prorationing, and (2) market-demand prorationing.

MER prorationing attempts to calculate the maximum efficient rate of production, presumably on the basis of physical characteristics of the reservoir, and production quotas are then prorated (rationed) among the producers involved. These permitted levels of production are called "allowables." The need for MER-type prorationing follows from the fact of common reservoir ownership. In the absence of unitization and MER-type prorationing, each owner of the common property, oil, in a given reservoir would compete to recover at least his full share before it was drained away by other owners. The result would be vast overinvestment and inefficient utilization of the oil reservoir. While the need for MER-type prorationing is granted, the only justification for market-demand prorationing is from the resource owner's point of view, who presumably would prefer high prices for his crude rather than low prices.[8]

[4] For a discussion of the ABC Deal see Wilkinson, *ABC—From A to Z,* 38 Tex. L. Rev. 673 (1960), and Galvin, *The "Ought" and "Is" of Oil and Gas Taxation,* 73 Harv.L.Rev. 1499 (1960).

[5] The assumption is made that the supply of uncommitted oil leases is not perfectly inelastic. We have no information on the extent of the current increase in production due to this tax subsidy. It is obvious that the tax subsidy does not increase oil in the ground, but presumably causes it to be produced earlier rather than later. For a discussion of the resource misallocation effects of the percentage depletion allowance provision, see A. Harberger, *The Taxation of Mineral Industries* in Federal Tax Policy for Economic Growth and Stability (A Compendium of Papers presented to the Joint Committee on the Economic Report), 84th Cong., 1st Sess. (1955); S. McDonald, Federal Tax Treatment of Income From Oil and Gas (1963) (especially ch. 3); Kahn, A. *The Depletion Allowance in the Context of Cartelization,* Am. Econ. Rev. 54:295, 1964.

[6] The first state to undertake prorationing was Oklahoma. The Oklahoma Corporation Commission instituted prorationing in September 1928. Texas followed with its first attempt at statewide prorationing in 1930. On August 27, 1935, Congress approved the Interstate Compact to Conserve Oil and Gas and the Interstate Oil Compact Commission was created on September 12, 1935. The purpose of the compact was "To conserve oil and gas by prevention of physical waste thereof from any cause." Interstate Compact to Conserve Oil and Gas, ch. 780, 49 Stat. 939 (Aug. 27, 1935).

[7] W. Lovejoy and P. Homan, Economic Aspects of Oil Conservation Regulation 127 (1967).

[8] While granting the need for MER-type prorationing, the manner in which it is currently administered has been subject to widespread criticism. The calculation itself has

Under market-demand prorationing the state regulatory agency determines and restricts production to the level calculated to equal the quantity demanded at the prevailing price. This determination is made on a monthly basis. Market-demand prorationing normally further restricts production below the maximum efficient rate of production. For example, the Texas Railroad Commission has determined that for the month of February 1969, nonexempt operators in Texas may produce at only 42.8 percent of their allowable production. Thus while the MER allowable is theoretically related to production efficiency for a given reservoir, market-demand prorationing is related to the quantity that the market will absorb at a "desired price" of crude oil. The desired price is maintained by restricting the level of production. Article V of the Interstate Oil Compact specifically denies any price fixing intent. Article V states, "It is not the purpose of this Compact to authorize the states joining herein to limit the production of oil and gas for the purpose of stabilizing or fixing the price thereof, or to create or perpetuate monopoly. . . ." However, unless the law of demand has been repealed for oil, larger quantities will be demanded at lower prices, and production restrictions will generate higher prices.

The price effect of market-demand prorationing can be clearly seen in Figure 1. At P_1, the quantity demanded equals the quantity supplied at Q_1. This is the normal situation in a free price market. Where a higher price is desired, for example, P_2, the quantity demanded is only Q_3. But at this more attractive price, from the seller's point of view, Q_2 will be supplied. The excess of quantity supplied over quantity demanded (the distance

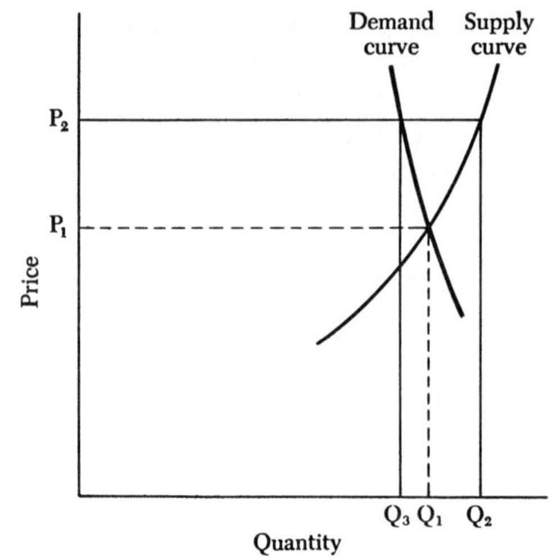

FIGURE 1. Schematic Drawing of "Excess Capacity."

Q_3 to Q_2) would force the price downward toward P_1 in a free market system. In order to obtain the desired higher price (P_2) producers must submit to production controls. Specifically, production must be limited to Q_3 since this is the quantity which the market will demand at P_2 the desired price. The function of market-demand prorationing is to restrict output to some level such as Q_3 since this is the quantity which the market will absorb at the desired price. Market-demand prorationing at less than 100 percent of the maximum efficient rate of production creates a situation of excess capacity with its consequent social cost of overinvestment.[9]

Administrators of state prorationing systems have maintained the judicious fiction that the objective of prorationing is the prevention of waste. One official, when questioned about the price effect of prorationing, replied "We have nothing to do with price. We are forbidden to consider eco-

been shown to be faulty from the economic analysis point of view. Further the most inefficient wells are frequently exempt from prorationing (particularly market-demand prorationing in Texas) while the most productive wells are forced to curtail output and thereby to operate inefficiently. Hardwicke has estimated that the economic waste due to unneeded wells in Texas alone amounts to more than $1 million a year. *See* Hardwicke, *Oil Well Spacing Regulation and Protection of Property Rights in Texas,* 31 Tex, L. Rev. 99 (1952). For an extensive analysis of economic inefficiency see Lovejoy and Homan, *supra* note 7, at chs. 4–7.

[9] While one may dispute the exact degree of supply and demand elasticity (the slope of the supply and demand curves) and the deviation of P_2 (the present price of American crude) from P_1 (the price which would prevail in a free market), Figure 1 describes the essence of the market-demand prorationing problem. The demand curve illustrated in Figure 1 is shown to be relatively inelastic as is generally assumed. (*See* Interstate Oil Compact Commission, A Study of Conservation of Oil and Gas in the United States 122, 1964.)

nomics; purely physical waste. I know nothing about price."[10]

As indicated in Section I above, percentage depletion allowance, as a significant tax subsidy, has the effect of shifting the supply curve for oil to the right and, in the long-run, depressing oil prices. The 27.5-percent depletion allowance rate has now been in effect for 43 years and presumably would have brought about an expansion of oil production and depressed prices to the point where the after-tax rate of return on oil exploration and development investments would be only normal. The price-depressing effect, however, has been prevented by market-demand prorationing. In effect, one interference with the market mechanism (depletion allowance) has stimulated production and brought forth a second interference with the market mechanism (prorationing) introducing production controls.

Market-demand prorationing, however, rests on a precarious foundation. The leading oil-producing states, excepting California and Wyoming, have market-demand prorationing controls. Lovejoy and Homan found that the states having market-demand prorationing account for 75 percent of U.S. crude production.[11] These states bear the burden of price fixing. Their dilemma is that of a dominant firm (or group of firms) that chooses to behave as a monopolist in an oligopolistic industry. They must restrict output in order to maintain the desired price while producers in non-market-demand states are free to maximize their own profit given the artificially maintained high price. As recently as mid-1966, Oklahoma, the fourth largest oil-producing state, restricted production to 38 percent of the maximum efficient rate. For February 1969 the permitted rate was raised to 90 percent. Effective for March 1969 the Oklahoma Corporation Commission announced that production at 100 percent of the maximum efficient rate would be permitted. Thus, if we may assume that Oklahoma's MER-type prorationing involves no price fixing features, then Oklahoma has in effect passed the burden of price stabilization to other market-demand states.

[10] Testimony of Ernest O. Thompson, Member of Texas Railroad Commission, at the Hearings of the Committee on Interstate and Foreign Commerce, House of Representatives, 85th Cong., 1st Sess. (1957) in W. Lovejoy and P. Homan, Economic Aspects of Oil Conservation Regulation 240 (1967).

[11] *Supra* note 10, at 129.

OIL IMPORT QUOTAS

Under conditions of free trade, the ability of an oil price conspiracy to raise domestic prices above the competitive equilibrium level is limited by the prevailing world price plus freight charges to the United States. If the domestic producers desire a price in excess of this premium then they must obtain import barriers usually in the form of tariffs or import quotas. The American oil industry has obtained both. The current tariff on crude oil is 10.5 cents per barrel. This rate has been in effect since 1943.

On July 29, 1957, President Eisenhower asked oil importers operating east of the Rocky Mountains to voluntarily reduce their crude oil imports to 0 percent below their average for 1954–1956; that is, to about one million barrels per day. Under strong pressure from the Independent Petroleum Association of America, supported in turn by the National Coal Association, President Eisenhower on March 10, 1959 ordered mandatory quotas on imports of crude oil, gasoline, and other finished petroleum products. On April 30 the order was amended to exempt from the mandatory limits oil shipped by overland transportation from Canada and Mexico. Imports into Districts I-IV (the area east of the Rocky Mountains) are limited to 12.2 percent of estimated domestic production in these districts, less the exempted production from Canada and Mexico. Imports into District V (the area west of the Rocky Mountains) were limited to the difference between (1) the sum of District V domestic supply and exempt imports from Canada and Mexico and (2) total demand (at the desired price) in that district as estimated by the Bureau of Mines.

Given the relatively high U.S. price for crude oil, resulting in part from market-demand prorationing, U.S. oil exports declined and imports into the United States increased sharply. The trends from 1939 through 1958 are shown in Figure 2. Figure 3 shows the ratio of crude oil imports to the domestic demand for all oil products from 1939 through 1968. We find that imports increased from 2.7 percent of total demand in 1939, to 11.6 percent in 1957 when voluntary import restrictions were imposed. From 1957 to date the ratio of imports to domestic demand has declined under the impact of import quotas. Figure 2 shows, however, that the absolute level of imports increased after the imposition of controls, but at a lower growth rate.

Import restrictions have had the effect of producing a gap between American and world crude prices amounting to approximately $1.32 per barrel in excess of transportation charges. Thus import quotas and the tariff are part of the system of subsidies received by the oil industry. Market-demand prorationing, as a price-fixing device, would have limited effectiveness in the absence of import restrictions.

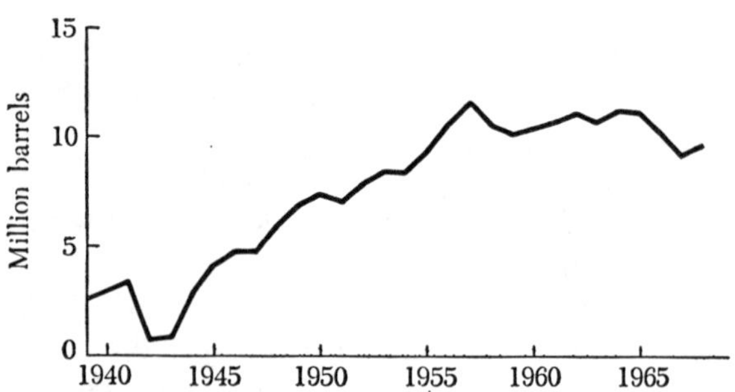

FIGURE 2. Graph Shows Ratio of Crude Oil Imports to Domestic Demand for All Oils.

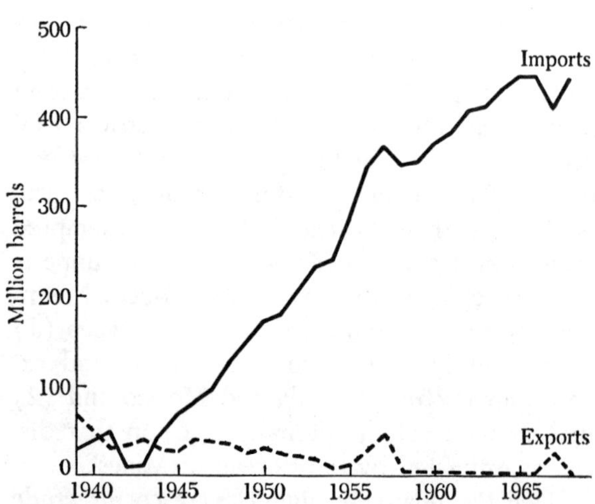

FIGURE 3. Crude Oil Exports and Imports

U.S. FEDERAL INCOME TAX CREDIT FOR FOREIGN ROYALTIES PAID

Another major subsidy is available only to the international oil companies. In the United States when oil companies pay royalties to landowners, whether government or private, such royalty costs are treated as normal expenses of doing business. But when certain legal formalities are observed, royalties paid to foreign governments may be classified as foreign taxes and are treated in lieu of U.S. corporate income taxes. This tax treatment means that such foreign royalty expenses involve a zero after-tax cost to the American oil firm. In effect, the U.S. government pays about 100 percent of the foreign royalty charges. The consequences are at least twofold. First, foreign oil development is stimulated at the expense of development in the United States. It should be noted here that this subsidy runs counter to the stated intent of depletion allowance—to stimulate domestic oil exploration and development. Second, U.S. income taxes paid by American oil companies with international operations already reduced by the percentage depletion allowance and other tax favors, are further drastically reduced. The record shows that Standard Oil Company of New Jersey, the largest U.S. oil company, had an effective federal income tax rate of only 3.8 percent over the 5-year period 1962–1966. The 22 largest U.S. oil companies had an effective federal income tax rate averaging slightly more than 6 percent.[12]

[12] Congressional Record, vol. 113 (1967), 24310 (Remarks of Senator Proxmire).

RESOURCE MISALLOCATION

The net effect of the entire subsidy system available to the oil industry is over-investment in oil exploration and production and consequent misallocation of the nation's resources. We are developing resources at social costs of about $3.42 per barrel, that have a social value of about $2.10 per barrel. Resource misallocation in turn results in a lower standard of living than is otherwise available to the nation. To the extent that we do not wisely use our limited natural resources, our long-run ability to defend ourselves is weakened.

The social cost of the system of subsidies for the oil industry is extremely high relative to subsidies paid to other sectors of the American economy. Professor Adelman has estimated that "the annual charge of this whole system of organized waste, including the import controls needed to insulate it from foreign competition . . . in my opinion is just over $4 billion."[13]

The effect of market-demand prorationing and import quotas is to substantially raise the domestic price of crude oil and oil products. The effect of favored tax treatment is to reduce tax costs for oil companies relative to firms in other industries. These measures taken together substantially raise the expected after-tax profit rates on oil industry exploration and development investments in what would otherwise be submarginal uses of scarce capital. Investment in petroleum exploration and development is indeed expanded to the point where the after-tax rate of return is approximately equal to that which may be obtained on alternative uses of capital. Professor Kahn has summarized the misallocation effect as follows: "The fact that net returns on investment after taxes in the oil industry may not be unusually high thus constitutes not a defense of the (percentage depletion) allowance but the clearest possible proof of the misallocation it causes."[14]

Oil industry spokesmen have defended their various subsidies with the question, "If we receive all the subsidies which our critics allege, why is our rate of return on invested capital not substantially higher than other nonsubsidized industries?" The answer to this question is that a subsidy will raise the profit rate at the point in time at which it is conferred. Its effects, however, are eroded away with time as producers react to their more profitable situation by expanding into otherwise submarginal areas. This expansion leads to a decline in the rate of return toward a normal yield and to resource misallocation as well.

The oil spillage case in the Santa Barbara Channel is directly related to the subsidy system. Leases were purchased and drilling occurred in the California offshore area because such operations were made profitable by the subsidy legislation. Under free market conditions, oil prices would be substantially lower, tax costs substantially higher in the oil industry, and the profit inducement to buy leases in the channel would probably be lacking. To develop oil from such sources is to use up more economic value than is produced. In addition to this probable waste of resources, we have the external cost (aptly called "spillover costs" even before this oil spillage case) of environmental pollution.

Data are not available to test the proposition that removal of oil subsidies would remove the economic incentive to buy oil leases in the Santa Barbara Channel. Production records are not yet available on the federal leases, and may never be. Further, oil companies do not disclose their estimates of probable production, revenue, and costs of exploring for and developing the channel oil resources.

However, we do have 14 years of data for the 1954 and 1955 federal leases on the outer continental shelf offshore from Louisiana. From the record of oil and gas production on these leases, a projection of future revenue may be made. We know that bonus payments totalling $216 million dollars were paid for these federal leases. These bonuses in total represent the bidders' best estimates of the discounted present value (in 1954 and 1955) of expected future net income after

[13] M. Adelman, *Efficiency in Resource Use in Crude Petroleum*, S. Econ.J.31:105, 1964.

[14] A. Kahn, *The Depletion Allowance in the Context of Cartelization*, Am. Econ. Rev., 54:295, 1964.

taxes for these leases. We have precise information on all physical production of oil and gas by years from the leases, annual rental payments, royalty payments, and well-head value for oil and gas. Reliable estimates may be made for presale exploration cost, well drilling and equipping cost, and operating cost.

Revenue from oil production, actual through 1967 and projected thereafter to the year 2,000, may be adjusted downward to the point where the U.S. crude price is equal to the world price (on a delivered basis to East Coast ports). A price decline amounting to $1.32 per barrel is assumed.[15]

This adjustment would follow from the removal of the existing quotas and tariff, making prorationing unworkable. Further, tax costs may be adjusted upward from the 6-percent average rate actually paid by the 22 largest oil companies, to the 48-percent statutory rate. These adjustments to compensate for the removal of the major subsidies not only eliminate the entire $216 million of discounted present value (the bonus payments), but in addition result in an internal rate of return on the 1954–1955 leases amounting to only 4.5 percent after taxes. This assumes zero bonus payment. These findings indicate that if oil companies expect to earn more than 4.5 percent after taxes on their oil development investment, they should have regarded the 1954–1955 leases in total as having no present value.[16] This evidence lends support to the assertion that oil leasing in the Santa Barbara Channel would not have taken place in the absence of the subsidy system.[17]

Congress is now considering bills to prohibit further drilling and production of oil from the channel area. If the system of subsidies is retained, such legislation may be necessary. However, the root of the problem lies elsewhere and it seems futile to prohibit, in new legislation, what is made very profitable by existing legislation.

I would recommend that steps be taken to internalize the external costs that society bears in the form of environmental pollution (that is, to make oil companies fully liable for all public and private damage).

I would further recommend that the system of subsidies described here be phased out over a period of about five years.

When the important external costs (and benefits) are internalized, and when subsidies are removed, private and social benefits from oil production will more nearly correspond. Only when these two steps are taken will the massive burden of resource misallocation in this industry be removed as a drag on this nation's strength.

[15] World prices are assumed to be unaffected by the removal of U.S. subsidies. Further, the increased efficiency in domestic production that would result from removal of MER prorationing in the Louisiana outer continental shelf area has not been considered.

[16] Since some tracts were regarded as more promising than others, bids might have been submitted on some of the tracts, even under a no-subsidy system.

[17] We know that some physical conditions in the channel differ substantially from those in the Gulf of Mexico. In the California OCS area, water depths are greater, drilling costs are higher, and production is more hazardous due to the geological structure of the area. On the other hand, the U.S. Department of Interior study of import quotas estimated that in Region V the price decline due to the removal of quotas would be 20 cents per barrel less than for the Gulf of Mexico.

C. TRANSPORTATION POLICY

U.S. MARITIME POLICY: SUBSIDIZING WASTE AND INEFFICIENCY

LEONARD A. RAPPING

Sophomores in economics have little difficulty in identifying the fallacies in most arguments given in support of existing merchant shipping subsidy policy. They also find it easy to spot the form of the many subsidies for what they are—invitations to economic inefficiency in ship operation and ship construction and a guarantee that the United States will continuously be faced with a continuing merchant marine "crisis." It is considerably more difficult to explain to them why the federal government persists in a program which violates the basic canons of sound economic policy. In this paper, I will present a brief description of current policy and an explanation of why it must be totally abandoned. In particular, it is my view that all forms of government cargo preference should be discontinued, all operating and construction differential subsidies should be discontinued, all forms of special tax advantage and credit aids should be discontinued, the prohibition on foreign-flag participation in the U.S. domestic trades should be discontinued, military cargo preference should be greatly relaxed, and unrestricted commercial ship purchase in low-cost foreign yards should be permitted. This is drastic surgery but nothing short of fundamental reform will permit the United States to develop a sensible maritime policy.

A Government subsidy program may be judged a failure either because its goals are incorrectly specified or because the means for achieving the specified goals are economically inefficient. On both counts United States shipping policy must be judged economically wasteful. The objectives of U.S. shipping policy as stated in the 1936 Merchant Marine Act and restated in the 1954 Cargo Preference Acts are more appropriate for seventeenth-century mercantilist England than for twentieth-century America. The program is protectionist and the usual arguments against pro-

Excerpted and reprinted from statement of Leonard A. Rapping in U.S. Congress, Joint Economic Committee, *Economic Analysis and the Efficiency of Government,* Part 2, Hearings of the Subcommittee on Economy in Government, September 1969.

Leonard A. Rapping is Professor of Economics at Carnegie-Mellon University, Pittsburgh, Pennsylvania.

tectionism apply with equal force in this case as in most others. It is difficult to argue for the maintenance of an expensive U.S.-flag merchant marine on commercial grounds. Any economic activity which requires subsidization is, by definition, an activity in which the market value of the industry's services is less than the cost of providing the services. Unless there are nonmarketable commercial benefits (i.e., positive externalities) the subsidy prevents the intelligent use of limited social resources.

Except for the argument that the U.S.-flag fleet could *in principle* be used to temper the rate-setting policies of existing international shipping cartels, euphemistically known as conferences, it is difficult to give much credence to the list of nonmarketable benefits often cited by the subsidy proponents. Arguments that the fleet earns foreign exchange, provides jobs, generates national prestige, aids in the development of new trades, or prevents collusive foreign-flag exploitation against American exports and imports are either specious or in practice irrelevant. For example, the often-cited argument that U.S.-flag ships aid in the conservation of foreign exchange is qualitatively correct but in practice the government must pay well over one dollar in subsidy for each dollar of foreign exchange conserved, a rather expensive way to conserve on foreign exchange. In summarizing my skepticism with regard to the usual commercial justification for a U.S.-flag merchant marine, I would like to cite the conclusion of the Northwestern Transportation Center Study (1961), a study financed, but needless to say not endorsed, by the Committee on American Steamship Lines:

> A finding that a program which has been in effect in one form or another for over 40 years and an industry of the magnitude of the subsidized liner industry make little net economic contribution is a serious conclusion. The finding is based upon the best analysis it has been possible to make; the available empirical information, both statistical data and testimony, has been used to check and extend the analysis. The authors are convinced that the findings are sound.

What remains is the argument that the merchant marine is a useful military auxiliary. With this argument remaining, we must conclude that U.S. maritime policy has resulted in an excessive number of vessels in the post-World War II period. This excess of ships results from the natural tendency for the military to overestimate its shipping requirements. In part this overestimation is because the budgetary costs of maintaining these vessels are not borne by the Defense Department. Moreover, the Congress does not generally view maritime appropriations as defense appropriations.

Not only are the objectives of U.S. maritime policy ill-conceived but the choice of subsidy and subsidy-like programs stimulates inefficiency in both ship operation and ship construction. Moreover, the unnecessary complexity of the program precludes intelligent congressional control over the total maritime subsidy budget which is in the appropriations to many different agencies.

The total maritime subsidy in fiscal year 1965 was at least $550 million. Of this total $190 million was paid to subsidized lines operating about 300 dry-cargo and passenger vessels. About $125 million was paid to American shipyards through the subsidized operators in the form of construction differential subsidies and approximately $200 million was paid to the subsidized and so-called "nonsubsidized" operators of foreign trade vessels in the form of premium rates on protected government-generated cargoes. These protected cargoes result from the 1904 act which requires that all military cargoes move in U.S.-flag vessels and from the 1954 Cargo Preference Acts requiring that 50 percent of Department of Agriculture, Agency for International Development, as well as other government-generated cargoes move in U.S.-flag vessels. The $550 million figure excludes various other indirect subsidies which are important but difficult to estimate. In particular, the subsidized operators receive additional subsidy in the form of preferential tax treatment and government mortgage guarantees on new ship purchases. Further, merchant seamen receive free medical care and they benefit from government-subsidized officer training programs. These aids might run as high as $30 to $40 million per year.

The above-mentioned figures do not include the large costs imposed on the economy by the

Cabotage Laws which prohibit foreign-flag participation in U.S. coastal, intercoastal, and noncontiguous trades. These restrictions protect U.S. flag domestic trade tankers and dry-cargo vessels from foreign-flag competition which of course imposes costs on the U.S. economy. These costs are roughly $150 to $200 million per year, but they are not borne directly by taxpayers. Rather they are paid by domestic shippers in the form of higher-than-necessary transportation costs. Adding the costs resulting from Cabotage Laws to the direct and indirect charges on government budgetary accounts provides a convenient approximation of the burden which the U.S. maritime program imposes on the economy. Thus, in fiscal year 1965 the merchant shipping subsidy program probably cost the economy (in terms of foregone product) between $700 and $750 million per year to support a fleet of about 950 U.S.-flag merchant vessels.

The direct and indirect operating subsidy costs to the U.S. taxpayer are excessive because the current method of paying subsidies is economically inefficient. Recipients of operating differential subsidies can pass any increase in subsidizable costs (mainly wages) on to the government because the subsidy is designed to equalize foreign operating costs and U.S. operating costs. Increases in U.S. manning scales and/or wage rates are imposed on the taxpayers. Similarly, other "nonsubsidized" foreign trade operators eligible for government-guaranteed cargo can pass on wage increases to the government with comparative ease. Under these circumstances, operators do not resist union demand for wage increases and the form of the subsidies has contributed to the phenomenal secular growth in seamen's wages, particularly since 1950.

Another kind of inefficiency arises because the present operating differential subsidy distorts the American operators view of the true cost of his factors of production—labor, capital and fuel. In particular, they have little incentive to seek more capital-intensive means of production, to automate their vessels, to build faster vessels and to seek more efficient technologies for producing shipping services.

Finally, inefficiency arises because the Cargo Preference Laws, the Cabotage Laws, as well as complicated tax and credit aids are implicit rather than explicit subsidies, making it virtually impossible for a busy Congress to know the amount of subsidy actually being paid by the government. Not only are many of the subsidies hidden, but the subsidy or subsidy-like programs are administered by a diverse set of uncoordinated government agencies including the Department of Defense, the Agency for International Development, the Maritime Administration, the Department of Agriculture, the Post Office, the Export-Import Bank and the State Department. Moreover, there are many other government agencies and departments interested in or participating in the regulation of maritime rates and services. This incredible complex web of bureaucratic control makes intelligent congressional policy control virtually impossible.

Not only are these numerous government departments often working at cross purposes, but even within the Maritime Administration itself considerable confusion arises in the administration of the program. For example, the Maritime Subsidy Board has arbitrary and irrelevant criteria for determining when they should award subsidy status to new applicants ("section 605(c) cases"). Among other things the applicant must demonstrate the "inadequacy" of existing service. The concept of inadequate service is meaningless so long as freight rates are positive and can still be driven lower by additional tonnage. Therefore it is not surprising that the board in the final analysis simply protects existing subsidy recipients from competitive pressures. Of course, the problem of vague and uninterpretable guidelines is not peculiar to the maritime regulatory process; it is an endemic disease of the American regulatory process.

The farmers of the 1936 act did not envisage the development of large Department of Defense and other protected cargo movements which would divert subsidized operators from commercial to government-generated cargoes. Yet in the pre-Vietnam year of 1964 the subsidized operators received about 38 percent of their reveune from government-generated protected cargoes. During the peak of the Vietnam-generated cargo movement this figure, which is difficult to estimate, was probably in excess of 45 percent. The original purpose of operating differential subsidies was to equalize the costs of American and foreign operators, the presumption being that these two groups were competing in the same market. However, the subsidized operator's principal competitor for guaranteed cargoes is the "nonsubsidized" American carrier. Both carriers receive similar freight rates on guaranteed cargoes. The subsidized operator is in fact receiving double subsidy, once in the form of direct-operating differential subsidies and again in the form of premium rates. While the excess subsidy is difficult to estimate, I would judge that it was about $75 million in 1964. This dearly violates the spirit of the 1936 act which provides for subsidy recapture on the pro rata share of revenue earned by foreign trade-subsidized operators on the protected noncontiguous (e.g., Hawaiian) portion of their business. It is difficult to understand why this situation is permitted to continue.

Assuming that we must subsidize our merchant marine, a far from obvious assumption, the current subsidies should be restructured. On the grounds that explicit subsidies are preferable to implicit subsidies and that subsidy payments should be designed to stimulate rather than discourage cost reduction, the present operating differential subsidies, all nonmilitary cargo preference subsidies, as well as all noncritical Department of Defense cargo preference subsidies should be discontinued. A new operating subsidy formula should be adopted. In this regard the formula recommended by the Interagency Maritime Task Force (1965) is particularly attractive. They recommend a subsidy paid on a per dollar of revenue earned from the carriage of all commercial and nonpreference government cargoes. Under this plan revenues earned from the carriage of reserved military cargoes would *not* be eligible for revenue subsidy. This subsidy formula has the major advantage that any cost reduction achieved by operators would generate greater profits, providing an incentive to control costs. It is also proposed under the reformed subsidy program to abandon the "essential" trade route concept which more than anything else appears to aid in the monopolization of those markets in which Department of Defense, AID, and other government-reserved cargoes move.

For all practical purposes, eligibility for various privileges under U.S.-flag operation requires that both domestic and foreign trade operators construct their new vessels in high-cost U.S. shipbuilding yards. Shipbuilding in the United States is highly inefficient by world standards and the industry's competitive position has deteriorated steadily in the post-World War II period, despite massive injections of federal funds. At present, U.S. shipbuilding costs are over twice those in many foreign yards. This cost disadvantage is not a result of high American wage rates. Other high-wage American industries like the airframe industry are immensely successful at competing in world markets. And, even a high-wage country such as Sweden is a viable competitor in the world market for ships.

The excessive costs of building vessels in U.S. yards has discouraged most "nonsubsidized" foreign trade operators as well as domestic trade dry-cargo, dry-bulk carrier, and tanker operators from modernizing their fleets. Witness for example the steady deterioration of our Great Lakes shipping fleet. On the other hand, those operators receiving differential subsidies have been replacing their vessels but only because they are eligible for construction differential subsidies which are designed to cover the difference between U.S. and foreign construction costs. They are also subsidized in the form of deferred taxes and credit aids. These subsidies, coupled with the requirements that "nonsubsidized" operators purchase their vessels in U.S. yards, have guaranteed a market for U.S. commercial shipbuilders. But the form of the current subsidy as well as the administration of the subsidy contains important self-defeating elements.

The American shipbuilding industry is technologically obsolete as compared to the industry in northern Europe and Japan. The "reverse technology gap" is ironic since foreign shipbuilders have borrowed many American production techniques used during World War II. Yet after World War II the U.S. industry reverted to the handcrafting of ships mostly at government expense. In part the undercapitalization of most individual U.S. shipyards (but not the industry as a whole) has resulted from procurement policies by the navy and by the maritime administration. In brief, there has been very little effort to standardize vessel design and to concentrate procurement in a few yards, a policy which if followed would result in capital improvements and other efficiencies associated with series production. But one should not be too sanguine about the possibility of reducing taxpayer costs by more rational procurement devices like "block buys." A reduction in shipbuilding production costs need not reflect itself in reduced ship prices. A vigorous attempt by MARAD to concentrate merchant ship construction in one or perhaps two yards would still leave open the question of whether sufficient competitive pressures were present to force a reduction in ship prices. Such pressures can only be exerted by subjecting the domestic shipbuilding industry to foreign competition.

More important than the question of how to efficiently subsidize the construction of merchant vessels in U.S. shipbuilding yards is the question of why subsidize them at all. The shipbuilding industry has no more claim on public funds than any other industry and it should not be subsidized for its own sake. Many of the arguments given for U.S.-flag operating subsidies are also given in defense of merchant shipbuilding subsidies. They are equally unconvincing in both cases.

Direct shipbuilding subsidies as well as indirect subsidies in the form of "Buy American" requirements have not revitalized the American shipbuilding industry. At the same time they have discouraged many U.S.-flag operators from improving their fleets. We have paid a high price for our protectionist shipbuilding policy. Both from the point of view of stimulating the modernization of our active fleet of merchant vessels as well as subjecting our shipbuilding industry to the salutary effects of foreign competition, the U.S. government should adopt a policy to permit unrestricted ship purchase abroad. Such a policy would obviate the need for construction subsidies and all of the associated aid like government mortgage guarantees and tax deferred reserve funds.

The Navy's expenditures on ship procurement and repairs generates a prodigious shipbuilding and repair program and alone they make the U.S. shipbuilding industry the largest in the world. Indeed, total industry employment on navy construction and repairs now exceeds the 120,000-man industry employment level in 1939, a year in which an incredibly successful mobilization began (by 1943 total shipbuilding employment was 14 times the 1939 level). At present large merchant ship construction and repair contracts make up at most 10 to 20 percent of the entire dollar volume generated by the U.S. shipbuilding industry. Under these circumstances a policy designed to permit *all* U.S.-flag vessels, including those in the domestic trades, to be built abroad with full U.S. privileges would not by any means eliminate the nation's capability to produce ships. In any event, if the navy wishes shipbuilding reserve capability in addition to that generated by its own procurement program they can achieve this out of their own budget. Indeed, at a time when Congress is attempting to reassert control over total military appropriations it is essential that militarily oriented expenditures appear in the military budget and not in that of some other department.

WHITE ELEPHANTS, WATERWAYS, AND THE TRANSPORTATION ACT OF 1966

ROBERT H. HAVEMAN
PAULA STEPHAN

Over $1 billion is annually appropriated by the Congress to the U.S. Army Corps of Engineers for the planning and construction of hundreds of navigation, flood control, and other water resource projects. Incredible as it may appear to those who believe that the Corps must "pour concrete or perish," during the 1960s the agency made substantial efforts to improve the benefit-cost criterion used to estimate the economic worth of waterway projects. This criterion requires the calculation of the social benefits and costs of waterway projects and forces each proposed project to demonstrate that the benefits to be generated exceed the costs. These new procedures eliminate some of the most spurious "benefits" which have crept into Corps evaluations. Application of them would deny funding to many of the most wasteful of the proposed waterway projects, and produce enormous savings for taxpayers.

The commendable development of these procedural improvements by the Corps was viciously opposed by the organized waterway interests. Because of the power and influence of these interests, the Congress in 1966 rejected the improved evaluation procedures and wrote into law a set of standards which will permit nearly every stream requiring a bridge to qualify for large federal appropriations. As one discouraged Corps' official put it in referring to the congressional action: "With these standards we can justify the construction of ocean liner facilities at Ogden."

Because the legislated version of these new and toothless standards was neatly disguised in complicated economic language, few realized the extent to which their implementation would lead to waste and inefficiency through the construction of uneconomic and only partially used waterway facilities. The following relates how vested inter-

Robert H. Haveman is Professor of Economics, University of Wisconsin, Madison, Wisconsin. Paula Stephan is Assistant Professor of Economics, Georgia State University, Atlanta, Georgia.

ests, operating through powerful members of Congress, were able to scuttle the improved policy-planning procedures and hence, the public interest.

Since early in the nineteenth century, the Corps of Engineers has had primary responsibility for the construction of navigation and other water resource investments funded by the federal government. Appropriations for the construction of these facilities are made by Congress only after it has the Corps' statement that the economic benefits of a project are expected to be at least equal to project costs. Clearly, the procedures used in estimating these benefits and costs are crucial in the process of evaluating projects and choosing those which are economically worthwhile.

To understand how these procedures aid in determining which public projects should be built, a few simple economic notions must be mentioned. The construction of a waterway generally permits raw materials and manufactured goods to be transported more cheaply than they could be shipped by railroad or truck. These transportation cost savings are of benefit to the nation. However, in order to secure these benefits, the nation must expend labor, capital, and other resources to construct and maintain the waterway. On balance, the nation benefits by constructing a waterway only if the costs of the waterway are less than the benefits (in the form of reduced transportation costs) attributable to the waterway.

Clearly, to calculate these benefits from a waterway, one must multiply the costs saved on *each ton* of cargo shipped via the waterway by the number of tons of cargo expected to travel on the waterway. For example, if it costs $20 to ship a ton of steel by railroad and only $12 to move it on the waterway, $8 of costs are saved on each ton of steel shipped on the waterway. If there are one million tons of steel which must be moved, the nation will save $8 million if the waterway is built.

In addition to these real transportation cost savings or benefits the construction of a waterway will provide subsidy gains to those who transport commodities on the waterway—often at the expense of offsetting losses suffered by other groups. Because of the heavy and bulky nature of the commodities which most frequently travel by barge, these subsidy gains often accrue to some of the nation's largest corporations, i.e., Peabody Coal, U.S. Steel, Standard Oil, etc. However, to the extent that the subsidy gains received by these special groups are matched by losses to other groups in the society, the nation as a whole gains nothing. Money is simply shifted from some people's pockets to other people's pockets. For example, when the opening of a new waterway permits, say, steel manufacturers to gain through lower transportation charges, these shipper gains have an equal and offsetting effect in the lowered income of the railroad. While shippers gain, the railroad and its stockholders lose. These pairs of offsetting effects represent only income transfers. The analyst evaluating the worth of the waterway must be careful to keep them out of his estimates, since to the nation as a whole, there is no net gain. Clearly, if these income transfers are added on to the national savings in transportation costs, the total will exaggerate the waterway's true worth.

In the practice of evaluating the real worth of a proposed waterway, there are a number of subtle ways in which these subsidy or transfer benefits can be included in the evaluation thereby overstating the real social benefits of the waterway. One way is to measure the savings from moving a ton of cargo on the waterway as the difference between railroad *rates* and waterway *rates* instead of using the appropriate method of measuring the differences in national transportation *costs*. The use of rates overestimates savings because ineffective railroad regulation by the Interstate Commerce Commission has permitted rail rates to exceed rail costs by more than waterway rates exceed waterway costs. For example, assume that it costs only $20 to move a ton of steel by railroad, but that rail rates are $30 per ton. Assume also that it costs $12 to transport a ton of steel on the waterway, while barge rates are $14 per ton. Finally, assume that one million tons of steel are to be moved on the waterway. The appropriate comparison of transportation *costs* would yield a benefit estimate of $8 million ($20 × 1,000,000

− $12 × 1,000,000). However, by comparing rates instead of costs, the benefit estimate can be artificially blown up to $16 million ($30 × 1,000,000 −$14 × 1,000,000). The difference is the subsidy gain to shippers which is just offset by losses to other people.

A second means of exaggerating the real worth of the waterway is to overestimate the volume of commodities which will be shipped on the waterway. This can be done by ignoring some of the effects which construction of the waterway will have. For example, one of the effects of the waterway will be to force down railroad rates by providing new competition. If the analyst ignores this effect, he will predict that substantially more traffic will shift to the waterway than will occur in reality. Again, the estimate of waterway benefits will be greater than is warranted.

Through both of these procedures, then, waterway evaluations can be given a rosy glow that has no real basis. While waterway benefits which are estimated by either of these procedures may include real social benefits, they also include income transfers and other inappropriate values and lead to substantially exaggerated estimates of the national saving from the waterway.

Until 1960, the procedures employed by the Corps for calculating waterway benefits incorporated both of these kinds of errors. First of all, they defined the benefits on a ton of cargo as the difference between current waterway rates and the "lowest *present charges* [rates] actually paid or available to the shipping public," in most cases current railroad rates. Secondly, the Corps estimated the traffic which would move over the waterway by assuming that present railroad *rates* would neither be bid down by the competition of the waterway nor fall naturally because of technological improvements in the railroad industry. By employing these procedures, the navigation benefits estimated by the Corps included substantial amounts of income transfers and just plain air, neither of which represent true national benefits. By utilizing benefit estimates which included gains to some people but which neglected the offsetting losses to other people, the Corps was justifying projects which, while they were in the interest of certain groups, were not in the interest of the entire nation.

In 1960 the Corps undertook a major revision of its procedures so as to correct the errors by which benefit estimates were artificially bloated. Instead of the savings in transportation costs being computed on the basis of current rates, savings were to be appropriately determined by anticipated reductions in the *cost* (in terms of national resources saved) of moving cargo on the proposed waterway. The values which were to be used in making the benefit estimates were appropriately the costs of waterway transportation and the costs of the next cheapest way of shipping the cargo. The 1960 change also recognized that the amount of traffic which would move on the waterway depended on the rates which the railroads would charge after the waterway was built. In the language of the Corps *Manual*, traffic estimates should "recognize the possible impact of varying [railroad] rate levels and include an analysis of the effect upon projected use of the waterway of significant deviations in rates from cost levels." As a guide for the efficient development of transportation facilities, these changes were most important. Indeed, by eliminating mythical gains from benefit estimates the revised procedure comes very close to measuring only those benefits which accrue to the nation as a whole.

While in concept the change represented a marked improvement, in practice it became largely nullified. The Corps, under pressure from barge lines, shippers, and the Congress for the approval of more projects, was unable on short notice to develop a rigorous method of measuring rail costs to implement its new procedures. Moreover, the Corps *Manual* containing instructions to field office contained a loophole. If railway cost estimates were not obtainable, rates *could* be used instead of costs when, "in the opinion of the reporting officers, the rates fairly represent the costs." Not surprisingly, rates were used instead of costs in nearly all cases.

In hopes of making the procedure viable, the Corps formulated an "interim procedure" to be used "until acceptable data for consistent application of the cost basis in the evaluation of waterway transportation benefits" could be developed. Without question, this interim procedure, which first appeared in the fall of 1964, was a political compromise. The Corps came to realize that until an accurate and consistent method of estimating rail costs was devised, the 1960 change could not survive the attacks of vested interests, speaking through powerful voices on Capitol Hill. To the credit of the Corps, the compromise does recognize the concept of national resource savings through the use of railway rates which reflect the competition of the waterway to estimate future traffic. This, at least, assures that the traffic estimates will not be arbitrarily bloated. Moreover, the compromise did not regress to the use of current rates in estimating per ton transportation savings. Rather, the more appropriate notion of expected future railroad rates without the waterway was employed. Because these rates may reflect lower costs due to improved technology, they are superior to current rates, though clearly less preferable than costs themselves.

The interim procedure, however, had a very short life. In August of 1966 it was rescinded and the Corps, under severe pressure from interest groups subsidized by waterway construction, reverted to the arbitrary, pre-1960 evaluation procedures. Because of the massive lobbying effort generated by these forces, the interim procedure, to say nothing of the optimum procedure the Corps was attempting to perfect, came under severe criticism on the Hill. Ed Edmondson (Oklahoma) did not speak alone when he referred to the interim procedure and its rigorous standards as a "danger" to which "every American who is interested in the continual development and improvement of our rivers and inland waterways should be alerted at once. . . ."

The vested interests and their congressional spokesmen, desiring a revision to pre-1960 procedures, defended the inappropriate use of current railway rates for benefit estimation by noting that easily measurable data, even if wrong, are to be preferred to data more difficult to secure, even if correct. The argument went like this: Current railroad rates are definite; crystal balls are needed to estimate future rates in the face of waterway competition. Therefore, current rates are to be preferred. This position was buttressed by the claim, expressed to congressmen by lobbyists for the waterway interests, that the pre-1960 Corps traffic estimates based on current rates had proved "fully justified by experience." These groups failed to mention that this "experience" was in no wise universal and that when the Corps traffic estimates were realized, it was because of unanticipated developments.

A second argument mounted by the interest groups against the use of future competitive rates was that the use of these rates would permit the railroads to veto a waterway project. As one congressman stated, "All the railroads need do under the [interim procedure] . . . is contend that they are going to lower their rates, kill a navigation project, and when the water project funeral is over, raise their rates back up or curtail their so-called 'improved service.'" No one stopped to ask how the temporary lowering of current rates would affect the benefit estimate which was based on a forecast of rates expected to prevail in the future under competition.

Congressional spokesmen for the waterway interests also expressed concern that it was unfair to change rules in the middle of the game—why should some projects have been justified by the use of lenient criteria, while future proposals must face a more stringent test. Rep. Kenneth Gray (Illinois), carrying the concept of fairness to the extreme, stated that he was "appalled that any agency of our government would propose to use such stringent criteria in figuring justification for water transportation when other methods of transportation are not required to meet such tests." Apparently, it is unfair to apprehend some criminals when so many others are left to go free.

Finally, it was argued that an objective of waterway construction was to regulate railroad rates by providing more competition and that the use of current rates would help to attain this objective by justifying the construction of more projects. As Sen. George Aiken (Vermont) put it: ". . . It is perfectly sound to take the existing rail rates in estimating whether a waterway is feasible. I think we can be sure that no railroad is going to reduce voluntarily its present rates unless forced to do so by competition or law." Again, no one bothered to ask if there might not be a cheaper way of regulating the railroads than by the construction of billions of dollars worth of half-used waterways. No one questioned the failure of the Interstate Commerce Commission to fulfill its function as the regulator of railroad rates.[1] No one spoke for the public interest.

Although the congressional advocates of less rigorous standards never admitted that they desired some combination of income transfers to the special interest they favor, an unmolested barrel of waterway pork, and the regulation of railroad rates at the expense of creating monstrous white elephants, this is all that can be inferred from their words and their deeds. On the floor of the Senate, only Sen. William Proxmire (Wisconsin) spoke on behalf of the improved Corps procedures. By excluding income transfers to special groups which were offset by losses to others, he noted, the revised Corps procedures encouraged project evaluation which was in the interest of all of the people.

> Now that the Corps has implemented a system which more accurately measures future benefits, it is only natural that it should come under fire from legislators who are threatened with the loss of multimillion dollar projects. . . . I believe it is high time someone spoke out in support of the Corps efforts to spend our tax dollars wisely. . . . The very purpose of benefit-cost analysis is to eliminate those projects which imply a waste of the society's resources. To plead for a return to an erroneous measurement technique because it yields a greater public works program is, quite frankly, to plead for an increase in uneconomic and wasteful government expenditures.

Senator Proxmire's detailed analysis in defense of improved agency practices, however, had little impact. On October 13, 1966, Congress passed the Transportation Act which created the Department of Transportation. Buried in Section 7 of that Act was a provision which forced the Corps to revert to the arbitrary pre-1960 evaluation procedures. In Sen. Karl Mundt's (South Dakota) opinion, this section was "one of the most important changes which we [the Senate] made." By specifying that benefit estimates must be based on *current* rates, the Congress assured that a steady stream of public waterway projects bearing nominal benefit-cost ratios high enough to "justify" sizable appropriations would be forthcoming. Indeed, in going out of his way to state the intent of Congress on this matter, Sen. Henry Jackson (Washington) stated: ". . . It is our intent that . . . the resulting calculation of navigation benefits will be essentially those historically employed by the Corps of Engineers prior to the development of new procedures adopted in 1960. . . ." To this Sen. John McClellan (Arkansas) added: "I especially want to pay tribute to . . . [Senator Jackson] and to our fellow conferees in being able to retain my amendment to section 7 of this bill relating to water resource projects. It is high time that Congress recapture the initiative in developing the natural waterways of this nation, and it will be able to do so through the language incorporated in section 7 of this bill."

A tracing through the legislative process of the original administration version of the Transportation Bill, and especially section 7 of that bill, reveals clearly the forces operative in this unfortunate action. As introduced by the Johnson administration, the bill included a sound section 7 which would have required the secretary of the new department to "develop [binding] standards and criteria consistent with national transportation policies, for the formulation and evaluation of all proposals for the investment of federal funds in transportation facilities. . . ." In the judgment of one student of domestic transportation policy, the nation would "benefit greatly" by this provision. It would "cause all transportation investment of a public nature to be considered in an overall context from the standpoint of national good."

Following the introduction of the bill, hearings were held by the Senate Committee on Government Operations under the chairmanship of Senator McClellan. From the very outset of the

[1] As one student of the regulatory commissions has stated: "The ICC has become an integral part of the railroad industry, and its record reflects its commitment to the welfare of that industry."

hearings, the senator mounted an attack on section 7. He badgered the acting chief of the Corps of Engineers who testified in support of the administration version; he mustered a formidable array of waterway lobbyists to decry the evils of the new secretary's anticipated support of the improved Corps procedures; he spoke often and at length of his "very satisfactory . . . experience with the Corps of Engineers" in securing the Arkansas River project and of his desire not to "disrupt" the continued construction of waterways; he ignored the recommendations of the Corps, the Council of Economic Advisors, the Bureau of the Budget, the comptroller general, and independent transportation authorities in support of the original section 7.

The result of these hearings was the amended section 7. This amendment emasculated the original version by taking all control of economic criteria for navigational projects out of the executive agencies. It legislated the procedures that the Corps was to use in evaluating navigation projects. Not surprisingly, these procedures were the erroneous, pre-1960 procedures, replete with the opportunity to bloat benefit estimates to any level necessary to justify project construction. This amendment (referred to by Senator McClellan as "my amendment") became incorporated into the final form of the bill and with its passage became written into law.

Given Senator McClellan's close ties with the vested interest groups and his own personal interest in the maintenance of a steady stream of navigation projects, his support for and sponsorship of such an amendment was not unexpected. What was surprising, however, was the senator's word-for-word and letter-for-letter adoption of a suggested amendment written and introduced into the hearings by the long line of waterway lobbies and bargeline interest groups. This group was led by the National Rivers and Harbors Congress (of which Senator McClellan was at one time president and Representative Edmundson is a director) and included the Mississippi Valley Association, the Ohio Valley Improvement Association, the Arkansas Basin Development Association, Inc., the Coosa-Alabama River Improvement Association, Inc., the Florida Waterways Association, the Trinity Improvement Association, the American Waterway Operators, Inc., and an assortment of other bargeline interests and dredging companies.

The Corps clearly realized that the procedures written into the Transportation Act would entail the construction of numerous inefficient though nominally justified waterways. In response, the agency, in 1967, decided to perform a supplementary analysis of all proposed projects in order to display both the benefits to the nation as a whole and the benefits bloated by income transfers accruing to the waterway interests. One such project then under consideration was the $1 billion Trinity River, Texas, project. In submitting its budget for the study of the project, the Corps included a request for the funding of such an analysis. Congress, not unexpectedly, showed no interest and the request was denied. Surely, it is easier to swallow a wrong answer if one is not confronted by the right answer.

In short, through the Transportation Act, Congress, in response to the wishes of organized and powerful vested interests, has opened the gate for a procession of monumental white elephants. If they have no other purpose, these unjustifiable public works projects will at least remind the nation of its apparent inability to otherwise regulate the railroads and other industries with market power. They also stand as monuments to the power of organized vested interest groups to dominate the legislative process and to turn tax revenues into subsidies for themselves. Only if one believes that such undertakings are the only way of effectively regulating railroad rates of that shareholders in Federal Barge Lines, Peabody Coal, Bethlehem Steel, and Standard Oil are particularly worthy of special favor in the form of income transfers, can one consider the revision by the final form of the act to be an improvement in policy planning.

THE FEDERAL HIGHWAY PROGRAM

LOUIS M. KOHLMEIER

From the point of view of an automobile-happy America, highways are an unmitigated private blessing. From Washington's point of view, highways always have come under the heading of public works, with all the political meanings that attach to those words. Federal highway construction projects, like river and harbor improvement projects, mean local benefits and construction contracts that can be distributed with political patronage in mind. Throughout history federal highway funds have had larger political meanings. Early in the nineteenth century, before the government began to promote railroad construction with land grants, Congress helped to finance the building of a national pike and other roads as a means of hastening economic development and westward expansion. That spurt of federal road building lasted only briefly, and when Congress again appropriated funds for highways it was not motivated so much by desires to improve the nation's transportation facilities as by the need, or desire, to assist agriculture by improving mobility, and, during the depression of the 1930s, to make work for jobless thousands. Road building required for transportation was left largely to the states. It was not until the end of World War II that Washington once more began building highways for the sake of highways.

The Army Corps of Engineers has so much waterways money nowadays that it no longer misses its loss of highway jurisdiction. Under the 1824 law that established its water domain, the Corps of Engineers also was the federal highway builder. But that small measure of transportation coordination began to disappear in 1894, when the secretary of agriculture set up an Office of Road Inquiry that blossomed into what today is the Bureau of Public Roads.

The feeding and growth of the Bureau of Public Roads demonstrates very well why the federal

Reprinted from Louis M. Kohlmeier, Jr., "Highways" in *The Regulators* (New York: Harper & Row, 1969), pp. 152–159. By permission of Harper & Row Publishers, Inc.

Louis M. Kohlmeier is a correspondent for the *Wall Street Journal.*

transportation bureaucracy today is uncoordinated and chaotic. The Federal-Aid Act of 1916, which marked the humble beginning of modern federal highway planning, was primarily aimed at "getting the farmer out of the mud." Consequently, the 1916 law and the $5 million that Congress appropriated were administered by the Office of Road Inquiry that had been set up in the Agriculture Department in 1894. In the 1930s when federal road building became principally a public works measure to get the country out of the Depression, the highway planners, by then called the Bureau of Public Roads, were shifted to the New Deal's Public Works Administration.

The Depression over, PWA was abolished and the bureau was moved to the General Services Administration, the government's humdrum housekeeper. And after World War II, when highways once more became important to the federal government, Harry Truman reorganized the Bureau of Public Roads and put it into the Commerce Department. Lyndon Johnson reorganized some more, and in 1967 the bureau was placed in the new Department of Transportation.

Federal highway spending never stopped growing after 1916, but still Washington didn't become the nation's chief road planner until after World War II. Before the war, federal money could be spent only on rural highways, and Washington limited its contribution to 50 percent of the cost of these roads. In 1944 Congress said the federal planners could enter the nation's urban areas. Gradually Washington lifted its share to 60 percent, and then, in 1956, came the 90-percent federal: 10-percent state ratio on which the 41,000-mile National System of Interstate and Defense Highways is being built.

The road show that Congress began with a $5 million authorization in 1916 has grown since 1956 into the largest single federal transportation spending program, with annual outlays running about $4 billion.

The grand total of federal funds authorized in all the years between 1916 and 1956 was about $8 billion (not including make-work highway funds spent directly by PWA in the 1930s). Bureau of Public Roads annual spending didn't cross the $1 billion-per-year mark until 1957. Since then, the grand total has topped $30 billion, of which about $20 billion was earmarked for the Interstate System and $10 billion for other primary and secondary roads and their urban extensions. The 41,000-mile Interstate System will require a total federal outlay of $50.6 billion by the time it is finished in 1972. Total cost of the Interstate System is expected to be greater than $55 billion including the states' 10-percent share.

Washington is now paying for almost half the grand total of $8.5 billion that all levels of government in the United States spend annually on new construction of streets and highways. According to the Bureau of Public Roads, about half the nation's total motor traffic now moves on roads, highways, and expressways that federal money helped to build. The states nominally remain in charge; the federal spending takes the form of grants to the states which build, own, and operate the highways.

In truth, the states have been relegated to the role of a construction straw boss. What Washington pays for, Washington controls. The states build roads that are master-planned in Washington, they lay concrete according to "guidelines" set down in Washington, and step by step their progress is reviewed by Washington. The federal government has used the threat of curtailment or withdrawal of highway aid to persuade the states to adopt federal standards for the control of advertising billboards and auto junkyards along roads. Now Washington worries about the annual death toll on the nation's streets and highways and the states apparently are unable to halt the rising tide of casualties. The "solution" may very well be federal drivers' licenses and federal policing of the nation's major traffic arteries, in addition to the federal safety specifications for automobiles that Congress has legislated in the past several years.

Federal road building, the biggest public works project in peacetime history, is a program arrived at in the political arena with precious little concern for what had gone before in transportation and with no regard for what might come after. There is no evidence that the presidentially-appointed National Inter-regional Highway Committee, whose 1944 survey of national highways needs was the basic foundation of the Interstate System which Congress subsequently voted, gave any serious consideration to the relative efficiency or need of rail, water and air, as well as highway, transportation.

To the contrary, the federal highway program is as muddled a product of congressional politics and administrative bureaucracies as the federal waterways program. And, like the Corps of Engineers, the Bureau of Public Roads has powerful special interests on its side. Bureau workers fondly call them "our industries."

The American Road Builders' Association is the major such industry. Its 5,400 members are a grass-roots network of highway promoters located in every congressional district in the land. The road builders think exactly like the bureau. The association's executive director (a retired Army Corps of Engineers major general) has told Congress, "Our objective is the long-range highway program . . . adequate for the growing demands of highway traffic, the needs of an expanding economy and the requirements of the national defense."

The rest of "our industries" don't always see eye to eye with the Bureau of Public Roads but they too help promote the Interstate System. They include the American Trucking Associations, the American Automobile Association and the American Petroleum Institute. Last but certainly not least on one bureau insider's list is the Automobile Manufacturers Association, which gave the Interstate System that final necessary push in Congress in 1956 after it had been defeated in 1955, despite the best efforts mustered by the bureau and "our industries."

Like the waterways, the federal highway program has been adorned with an economic justification ratio that indicates the nation could hardly afford not to build the Interstate System. It purports to show the system will produce "benefits" of $11.4 billion annually after 1972, but the Bureau of Public Roads' concoction is even more nebulous than the cost-benefits ratio of the Army Engineers. The bureau's calculation of benefits is derived from estimated reductions in car- and truck-operating costs; an estimated dollar value of time saved; an estimate of the worth of fewer accidents and highway deaths and the value of reductions in the "strains and discomforts of driving."

The highway program is adorned with several more such baubles. One is called the Highway Trust Fund. It looks a little like an industry profit and loss statement: federal excise taxes on gasoline, tires and other highway-use items go into the fund, construction money goes out and income and outgo are to balance off on September 30, 1972, when the Interstate System is scheduled for completion.

The fund might look like a means of transportation coordination and highway justification; if income failed to cover costs, the highway planners presumably would quit or cut back. But it doesn't work that way. The 41,000 miles of Interstate System roads are fixed by statute and when income looks as if it won't cover anticipated costs the government simply jacks up excise taxes. The trust fund and its "user charges" make more fiscal sense than the way the army engineers build waterways, but its real significance is as a highway-financing device; with it, highway promoters can be a lot more certain of having 41,000 miles of Interstate System roads under their belts by 1972 than if the program had to go through the traditional annual appropriations mill on Capitol Hill.

Another gem was pinned on the highway program rather after the fact. Congress in 1962 amended the highway statutes to deny federal aid to urban expressway construction in metropolitan areas of more than fifty thousand population, where local planners by July 1, 1965, had not launched "a continuing comprehensive transportation planning process." The congressional intent, which sounded rather like the 1940 preamble to the ICC Act, was to promote "the development of long-range highway plans . . . properly coordinated with plans for improvements in other affected forms of transportation." It's not very meaningful either. The Bureau of Public Roads did not insist on a plan, only on evidence of the beginnings of a "planning process." No matter anyway: the planned 41,000 miles of interstate highways will be built whether or not cities try to coordinate their highway planning with local rail, subway, and bus transportation. Cities and states will build more superhighways simply because the federal funds are available to them for highways. If they do not build highways they will lose the funds. There are no comparable federal billions available to the cities and states for rail, subway, or bus transportation. Washington, quite simply, has left the cities and states with no practical alternative to building more highways.

In any event, the Bureau of Public Roads is hardly the place in Washington to begin to establish a federal responsibility for coordinated transportation. The highway planners believe in highways no less sincerely than the Army Corps of Engineers believes in waterways. The bureau's chief planner once put it this way: Highways are so obviously popular and essential that "the highway planner is in the unique and favorable position of being able to plan almost without regard to other modes of travel."

Still, as if to embarrass the highway planners where they live, the Federal City is gripped by local controversy over freeway construction. Plans for building $182 million of additional superhighways in and near Washington are fought by residents who place a lower social value on concrete than on the city's great variety of flowering trees that line stately avenues with their traffic circles—circles, with small parks in their center's, that are relics of an age of nonrush. Citizens' associations in the city's handsome and largely white northwest sector battle the highway planners. Blacks in the city's less handsome sectors also oppose the planners and their allies, who include the Washington Metropolitan Highway Users Conference, the chairman of which is the chief Washington representative of Firestone Tire and Rubber Company.

The controversy in Washington is beginning to be repeated with appropriate variations in cities and communities across the nation. But the citizens fight a losing battle, for the controversy in truth is not between citizens and highway special-interest groups but between citizens and citizens. The issue is not whether highways will be built but where they will be built. Federal law providing for the 41,000-mile Interstate System has required the states to hold public hearings on where the highways will go, not on whether they'll be built. The Bureau of Public Roads, at the direction of the secretary of transportation who was responding to the growing volume of citizen complaints, in 1968 proposed rules providing for larger state hearings on highway routes. The proposal was vigorously opposed by the American Road Builders Association and the American Association of State Highway Officials. Little matter, for the highways will be built somewhere. Citizens who want no highways at all in preference to ribbons of concrete through their suburbs or ghettos have no recourse except to the courts. The federal courts have found no legal basis for a claimed right of freedom from highways and have left the choice of routes to the expertise of the federal and state planners.

Fears grow in the cities that more highways will not relieve traffic congestion but will increase it more. No matter how rapidly the highway planners build, they seem unable to keep up with a still more rapidly growing population of automobiles and trucks. Lyndon B. Johnson, on addressing himself to the transportation problem, noted that the mileage of paved roads and streets in the United States had doubled since World War II, rising from 1.5 million miles in 1946 to 3 million miles in 1966. That is nearly a mile of concrete and asphalt roadway for every square mile of land, and still, President Johnson observed, there is "no relief from time-consuming, frustrating and wasteful congestion."

The automobile and the truck have never been economical means of transportation. The motor vehicle is a relatively expensive method of going from one place to another. But ever since Henry Ford rolled out his first Model T, the motor vehicle has offered transportation convenience and flexibility in greater measure than are available from so-called "common-carrier" types of transportation such as the railroad, the bus, and the subway. Today, the motor vehicle undeniably offers less convenience and flexibility than once it did because there are so many motor vehicles relative to the available streets, highways, and parking spaces. There were about 9 million motor vehicles in the nation in 1920, about 32 million in 1940 and today there are more than 90 million autos and trucks on the streets and highways.

Perhaps the federal highway planners did not singlehandedly create the motor chaos that today faces the nation. The cities and states that now are most bogged down in traffic are those in the Northeast that began massive road-building programs of their own before Washington took almost full charge of highway planning. On the other hand, it is to be doubted that highway construction would have gone so far so fast without federal planning and federal money. Federal law creates a uniformity across the land that does not bend to the varying needs and desires of the states and cities. If Washington had not in 1956 adopted the largest public works program in peacetime history, each city and state predictably would have adjusted highway construction to local needs and would have coordinated highways with other forms of transportation. Washington surely could have been a more modest or less dogmatic highway promoter. The federal government could, for instance, have paid for 90 percent of intercity highway construction and allowed each state and city to decide for itself whether federal aid to be expended inside city limits would be spent for highways or for some locally determined combination of highways, subways, railways, and buses. An even larger choice might have been left with the states to decide whether federal transportation grants for intercity transportation would be spent for highways or for a mix of highways, railroads, and airport facilities.

But federal transportation planning is not coordinated, nor do the splintered transportation bureaucracies in Washington permit much coordination by the states or the cities. With the $50.6 billion federal Interstate Highway System still some years from completion, the nation already is beginning to feel the effects of an uncoordinated overbuild of urban and intercity superhighways at the expense of other forms of transportation. Just as the federal highway program is unprecedented in size, so too will be the public costs of resuscitating other forms of transportation.

D. URBAN AND SOCIAL POLICY

EVALUATING EFFICIENCY AND EQUITY IN FEDERAL URBAN PROGRAMS

ANTHONY DOWNS

BASIC PROBLEMS THAT CAUSE MISLEADING ECONOMIC ANALYSIS REGARDING FEDERAL URBAN PROGRAMS

In theory, an economic analysis of any proposed federal program should identify all the significant costs and benefits thereof, estimate their size, and weigh them impartially in order to determine whether the benefits exceed the costs. But in reality this is impossible. Even to roughly approximate this desired outcome is extremely difficult because of certain characteristics of both urban life and federal programs.

The most fundamental difficulties arise from the complex interdependencies inherent in modern urban life. Consequently:

1. No one knows—or can know—what all the likely impacts of any given program upon an urban area will really be.
2. It is impossible, or at best extremely difficult, to measure the magnitude of many impacts that are known. In some cases, they are inherently immeasurable. This is especially true of psychological impacts. In other cases, the effects of an intended program cannot be separated from those of other actions or forces occurring simultaneously. In still other cases, known impacts could be measured, but only at tremendous cost in complicated and lengthy studies.
3. Since many effects cannot be measured, it is impossible to know which ones are large enough to be significant, and which ones can be ignored because they are relatively trivial.

For the above reasons, it is inescapable that both the identification of impacts, and the selection of those regarded as important enough to analyze, are arbitrary acts of judgment which cannot be made on a "purely scientific" basis. Thus, what one analyst regards as an impact worth taking into

Reprinted from statement of Anthony Downs in U.S. Congress, Joint Economic Committee, *Economic Analysis and the Efficiency of Government*, Part 1, Hearings of the Subcommittee on Economy in Government, September 1969.

Anthony Downs is vice president of Real Estate Research Corporation, Chicago, Illinois.

account may differ from what the next one so regards, and each may be capable of defending his choice quite well. Nevertheless, undoubtedly most qualified analysts would at least be able to agree on a significant proportion of the effects worth taking into account if they would consider each case carefully.

A second fundamental problem in economic cost-benefit analysis involves the distribution of costs and benefits among different persons or groups. If all the benefits go to one group, and all the costs are borne by another, the program concerned may be regarded as quite undesirable even when total benefits greatly outweigh total costs. On the other hand, it might be regarded as quite desirable even when total costs outweigh total benefits. The relative weights assigned to the welfare of one group versus that of another is actually a political judgment that cannot be done without noneconomic value judgments. All that economists can be expected to do is identify who receives or pays what, and to what degree, as guidance to political decision-makers. Yet many cost-benefits studies fail to distinguish which specific groups get the benefits and which pay the costs. Rather they assume that benefits received by anyone can logically offset costs paid by anyone. Hence, whenever benefits outweigh costs in the aggregate, a project is desirable; or if the reverse is true, it is undesirable. In my opinion, this is a gross error in almost all cases, even though it makes every economic analysis much easier.

The two fundamental problems described above mean that it is impossible to carry out really complete, accurate, and comprehensive economic analyses of all the major costs and benefits of most federal urban programs. (I believe this is also true of nonurban programs.) We must therefore resort to a significant amount of what has been called "disjointed incrementalism" in the design and execution of urban policies. That is, we must necessarily assume that any preliminary analysis of program impact will have left out something significant which can only be discovered after the program has come into being. This procedure is equivalent to the saying, "Let's run it up on the flagpole and see whether anyone salutes." A lot of salutes will encourage expansion of the program; whereas a great many boos or cries of anguish will encourage its contraction or modification. However undesirable this procedure may seem, we cannot avoid it.

The necessity of leaving an important part of program assessment to experience has one crucial implication: new programs should be tried out on a pilot basis before they are expanded to nationwide or massive scale. I realize that Congress has in the past been extremely reluctant to include any initial "experimental" phase in major federal programs. Most congressmen believe—probably correctly—that their constituents do not like to be regarded as "experimental guinea pigs." Also, many problems are regarded as so urgent that, by the time Congress acts upon them, the need for nationwide action seems quite pressing. Finally, concentration of pilot programs in a small number of areas as part of an experiment is contrary to what I call the "Iron Law of Political Dispersion." According to that "law," the benefits of any program must be sufficiently scattered among congressional districts—or among voters within one district for local programs—to generate wide political support for the program, regardless of the economic benefits of concentration. In spite of these factors, I believe the inherent uncertainties of program effects should lead us to do experiments in many cases.

Merely because economic analysis of federal urban programs will necessarily be imperfect and influenced by arbitrary judgments does not mean that such analysis cannot be improved, or that no principles can be designed to guide it. In fact, my experience indicates that certain biases in economic analysis which could be eliminated tend to appear over and over again. This paper is directed at identifying those biases in general, providing specific examples of the misdirections of policy they have created, and suggesting ways they can be avoided in the future. The principal biases I am referring to are as follows:

1. *Federal agencies sponsoring programs often define their effects too narrowly in order to strengthen the case for adoption of those programs, and to reduce the costs associated with them.* If they

broadened the scope of their analysis to include more effects, they would uncover significant additional costs generated by the programs concerned. These costs, if identified and measured, might convince Congress not to adopt the program at all. Or at least they would convince the persons who must pay the costs involved to demand compensation—thereby increasing the appropriations necessary to accomplish a given objective.

2. *When a specific federal agency is made up primarily of technicians from one discipline, they tend to confine their analysis of cost and benefits to those normally considered in the province of that discipline.* The most outstanding example has been the excessively narrow focus of highway engineers upon mobility effects in assessing the benefits and costs of expressways.

3. *Analysts often assume relatively effective free-market conditions exist, and ignore certain institutional rigidities that weaken the accuracy of the purely economic methods of reasoning.* The most commonly-ignored rigidities include:

(a) Lengthy administrative delays in carrying out programs. These delays can have tremendous effects upon the total costs and benefits of a program, and may even generate specific costs and benefits in themselves.

(b) Relative immobility and ignorance among consumers, including the intended program beneficiaries.

(c) Rigidities on the supply side of a market which prevent increases in output in response to rising expenditures. A striking example is in slum housing, where increases in welfare rent allowances are reflected in higher rents rather than in more units being made available.

4. *Economists often ignore widely diffused impacts because it is not practical to compensate individuals for them (or to collect special assessments from individuals when the impacts are benefits).* For example, when a federally financed highway destroys many houses occupied by low-income households, one effect may be to cause an upward pressure on rents for *all* low-income households in the vicinity, including those who were not displaced at all. But this effect cannot be measured, since it is impossible to separate it from the results of other forces in the environment simultaneously affecting rents. However, I believe we should introduce the concept of *compensating the entire market* by requiring actions that offset this diffused impact. An example would be requiring highway agencies to build one new housing unit accessible to low-income households for each unit they destroy.

SPECIFIC EXAMPLES

The following examples of undesirable results from faulty economic analysis connected with federal urban policies illustrate the general principles set forth above:

1. *In Baltimore, demolition of housing occupied by low-income Negroes to make way for a variety of government projects (mostly federally financed) from 1951 to 1964 destroyed the equivalent of 21 percent of the entire housing inventory occupied by such families in 1960. This undoubtedly worsened the already acute shortage of housing among poor Negroes in Baltimore, since they are denied access to most housing by both low incomes and racial discrimination.* Most of the families affected were renters—including both those displaced and those in nearby housing where rents went up as a result of the increased shortage. Hence they received no compensation whatever for these losses. About 89 percent of all households displaced by government projects in Baltimore during this period were Negroes, although Negroes form less than half of Baltimore's total population.

Insofar as economic analysis was used to justify this process, it failed to take into account the following factors:

(a) *The impact of housing demolition is not spread evenly over the entire population of an area, but concentrated upon the local market where the demolition occurs.* Thus, the number of units destroyed (890 per year on the average) seems small in comparison to the total housing inventory in Baltimore. But is much larger in comparison to the inventory of units actually available to the people displaced.

(b) *The effects of one project may seem small, but the effects of all government programs taken together can be very large, especially when considered over several years.* But economic studies generally look at only one project at a time, rather than the cumulative effect of many projects over a long period. Hence the really significant impact of government projects in creating worse housing conditions for Baltimore low-income Negroes was ignored because the projects were viewed one-at-a-time.

(c) *The effects of destroying an existing amenity are felt not only by those compelled to move out of it, but by others who now have more competition for their own amenities.* Thus, households living *near* a government project, but not displaced by it, suddenly had more competition for their quarters, and so had to pay higher rents.

(d) *Seemingly offsetting effects may impose costs on a group with little capacity to pay, while awarding benefits to another group with much more capacity to pay.* Insofar as higher rents increased property values in the areas near government projects, the owners gained windfall benefits which might seem to offset the windfall losses caused by renters paying higher rents. But many units were owned by absentee landlords with incomes much higher than those of their tenants. Thus, these costs and benefits redistributed wealth from the relatively poor to the relatively wealthier, rather than truly offsetting each other.

(e) *Analysis requirements concerning relocation of persons displaced by a proposed project often confuse the ability to relocate specific individuals or households displaced with the net effects of the displacement upon the market as a whole.* Since about 20 percent of all U.S. households move each year, a large number of units are always being made available for occupancy through turnover. It may be quite possible to find housing for those displaced by taking advantage of this fact (especially since most displaced households relocate themselves without assistance, so only a few need to be officially rehoused). Yet even if all the particular households displaced have been relocated, the net effect can still be negative because some units have been removed from the supply once-and-for-all. It is like a giant game of musical chairs. The fact that a single player may get up and yet find another chair when the music stops does not alter the impact upon the game as a whole of removing one or more chairs. The same number of households are now competing for fewer units —although this fact may be hidden by a public agency's successful relocation of the particular families displaced by a public project. Thus, insofar as economic analysis connected with displacement by public projects focuses mainly upon actual ease of relocating specific households rather than upon the net total impact on supply and demand, it may lead to erroneous conclusions.

2. *In many federally financed urban projects long administrative delays both unjustly impose uncompensated benefits upon some property holders, and unjustly create windfall gains for others. If these costs and benefits were taken into account in the analyses of the projects' net effects, they might significantly alter the results of those analyses.* Specifically:

(a) Public announcement that a particular area is under consideration for an urban renewal project creates great uncertainty about the future of the area—at least until it is decided whether or not the project will be adopted. This makes people reluctant to buy property in the area, or invest large sums in improvements needed to up-grade existing property there, or even to maintain it properly. Consequently, a "maintenance gap" usually follows such an announcement, and the area begins to deteriorate. This may cause property values to fall—a result further aggravated by the reluctance of investors to buy there. Hence owners of existing property in the area find it difficult to sell when they need to do so. They may be compelled to accept much lower prices than would have prevailed in the absence of this announcement. This establishes a low level of values which is used to set government acquisition prices when the project finally becomes adopted—if it does. *Thus, by announcing a possible project in an area and then delaying action for several years, the government can actually cause the area to deteriorate and decline in value,* so that it needs to pay less for acquisition than it would have if no announcement had been made.

This process imposes unjust capital losses on owners of property in the area, who are injured by government action (or inaction) but not compensated for that injury. An example of this effect was in the contemplated path of the interstate highway in Baltimore. It was under consideration for almost 10 years before final decisions were made to acquire land.

(b) *Another type of cost imposed by delay is the loss of property taxes on land acquired under urban renewal powers and then left standing vacant for long periods—often years.* Normally, potential increases in property taxes collectable from a given site are used as an important justification for public action to "renew" the site. But if project development includes a long period when no taxes at all are collected because the land is held vacant after acquisition by public authorities, a huge loss of potential revenue may occur. It may be large enough to more than offset the planned gains in tax revenues for many years. In this connection, it should be remembered that the average urban renewal project takes from 6 to 9 years to complete—and "slow" ones take much longer.

(c) *The "time-gap" between initial public consideration of a project and its official legal adoption may also cause property values in the area concerned to rise rapidly through speculation.* We studied alternative locations for a possible new airport serving a major U.S. city. In estimating the price the government would have to pay for the land, we had to make an allowance for the amount land values would rise through speculation from the time that site was announced as a *possible* location, until the time it was officially adopted—when values could be legally "frozen" for public acquisition. We estimated that this land would more *than double in value* during this waiting period. This would provide a windfall gain of many millions to landowners in the area—and a windfall loss to taxpayers. Yet not all economic analyses of future projects take this cost into account.

(d) Another source of frequent error in estimating costs for public projects is *not allowing sufficient margin for future increases in construction costs.* The longer the delay in constructing the project, the larger this error becomes. The Bay Area Rapid Transit District got into serious trouble because it underestimated the delays in building it would encounter, and the rate of inflation in costs that would occur. No one can perfectly foresee future delays and cost changes. But project estimates should be made to more accurately reflect past experience in delays than they often do and should even include a time allowance for unforeseeable delays.

3. *Code enforcement programs have sometimes erroneously confused what is legally required with what is economically feasible, and thereby stimulated undesirable consequences. In particular, compelling owners of deteriorated buildings in low-income neighborhoods to bring buildings up to code may cause them to abandon the buildings rather than comply, because it does not pay to rehabilitate them.* Many low-income households simply cannot afford to pay sufficient rent to pay for adequate property maintenance of old buildings—especially in areas with high rates of vandalism. The owners can obtain a return on their investment only by failing to maintain the property—which is illegal. This behavior may be highly undesirable and exploitative. Yet it is naïve for analysts trying to correct poor housing to sup-

pose that owners will ignore their own economic interests completely, to the extent of causing ownership to result in drastic losses rather than profits. Many would rather give up their ownership first. So about 800 to 900 buildings per year are being abandoned by their owners in New York City alone, and more in other cities. This saddles local governments with the choice of either continuing to violate their own laws, or paying large sums to rehabilitate slum buildings. Such sums cannot be recovered in subsequent sales, because the rent-collection ability of the buildings does not rise commensurately.

4. *Federal programs often fail to take into account varying degrees of institutional rigidity and consumer immobility in the environments and lives of their intended beneficiaries. Economists are too prone to assume that free-market conditions exist, when in fact market imperfections are the chief causes of many problems at which programs are directed.* Specifically:

(a) *The same dollar income from federally financed transfer payments provides very different purchasing power, not only among different regions, but even within different parts of a single metropolitan area.* In particular, many urban Negro families with no cars and low incomes normally pay much more for a given quality of food, housing, and consumer durables than do similar white families in the same city, or higher-income white families there. These Negro families pay more for food because they have to buy from small local stores which charge higher prices than big supermarkets. They pay more for rent because there is a more acute housing shortage at low-income levels, and because of racial discrimination. They pay more for consumer durables because of exorbitant interest rates charged by merchants in their areas. The failure of economic analysts to take these factors into account means that federally-financed programs which are ostensibly impartial in distributing benefits (such as Social Security and welfare programs) actually provide higher real incomes to some people than to others.

(b) *Services dispensed at inconveniently located facilities often fail to reach those who need them most.* They are ignorant of them, rarely leave their neighborhoods, and do not know how to travel to procure this assistance. This is especially true of medical aid. Recently, federal program analysts have begun to take more account of this fact, and to decentralize service delivery facilities. But strong pressures on the supply side still keep many facilities centralized (such as Cook County Hospital in Chicago).

5. *In federal housing programs, treating indirect public assistance to middle-income and upper-income groups as fundamentally different from direct assistance to lower-income groups creates an artificial division of interest between these groups. Consequently, the amount of direct aid to low-income groups—who need it most—is restricted because it is not seen as related to the much larger amount of indirect aid that goes to higher-income groups.* And many members of the latter are led to look down upon the former, even though both have a common interest in gaining housing aid from the federal government. Most home owners in the United States benefit from three tax advantages they receive: they can deduct mortgage interest payments from federally taxable income, they can deduct local property taxes from federally taxable income; and they do not have to report as income the "imputed rent" which they are implicitly (as owners) charging themselves (as occupants). These advantages are essentially housing subsidies, but are not regarded as such—even by the Department of Housing and Urban Development. The savings in federal taxes thus received by middle-income and upper-income groups are much larger than direct housing subsidies paid to, or for the benefit of, lower-income groups—both in total, and per household in these different groups. By not recognizing the common subsidy element in these different forms of assistance, federal analysts tend to isolate aid programs for low-income groups as somehow a form of

"relief" not received by more affluent citizens. They do not say this, but it is an inference widely drawn by Americans who do not realize they are receiving housing subsidies too. Hence, instead of regarding themselves as cobeneficiaries of housing assistance, many Americans attack or refuse to support direct housing assistance for the poor as an undesirable form of interference in free-market income distribution, even though they are drawing even larger benefits from a similar interference.

6. *Narrow restriction of benefits and costs considered to those connected with transportation has caused many federally financed highways to impose very substantial but uncompensated costs upon persons affected by nontransportation impacts of such highways.* Specifically:

(a) Disruption of traffic flows and accessibility of specific commercial or residential areas, or noise and vibrations, during periods of construction impose serious costs on local merchants and industrial firms, but they receive no compensation.

(b) Moving costs are grossly undercompensated, especially for large establishments in states where compensation limits exist.

(c) Many small businesses are forced to liquidate because they are cut off from their markets, or compelled to move away from their established clientele, or forced to leave low-rent quarters and move to high-rent quarters they cannot afford.

7. *The total noncompensated cost of these and other injustices resulting from both federally financed highways and federally financed urban renewal projects will amount to somewhere between $156 and $230 million per year in the next few years, according to my admittedly crude estimates.*

About 237,000 displaced persons and another 237,000 nondisplaced persons per year will be affected. This amounts to a potential noncompensated loss of from $812 to $1,194 per household affected—or from 20 to 30 percent of the average household income of those concerned. If the government paid the full costs involved, this would add 14 to 21 percent to the total costs of acquiring all the real property concerned. *Hence the magnitude of the injustices arising from such narrowness of viewpoint—is hardly trivial. Rather it is huge.* I believe the figures from this one form of injustice alone are persuasive evidence that more comprehensive economic analysis is necessary for proper assessment—and execution—of proposed federal urban projects.

INCENTIVES FOR INEFFICIENCY IN MEDICARE AND MEDICAID

VINCENT D. TAYLOR

This paper will discuss the Medicare-Medicaid programs and their relations to medical costs. In this regard, I wish to make just a few simple points:

First, the federal government is now a major factor in the medical marketplace. The Medicare and Medicaid programs alone now finance nearly one-fifth of all of medical care expenditures. The share of the health budget represented by federally controlled programs is growing.

Second, the influence of the federal government on medical costs is far greater than its share in the National Health Budget. As the operator of the largest medical insurance program in the country, it acts as the example and pacesetter for private insurance organizations with respect to the extent of coverage and terms of purchase. Because of its size, it must also accept a significant share of the responsibility for the very rapid rise of medical prices in recent years.

Third, the federal government should use its purchases to encourage greater economy and efficiency in the provision of medical services. Medicare and Medicaid do not presently do this.

The last point is the really important one. The first two points emphasize the importance of Medicare and Medicaid in the health services sector. The substantial role of the federal government in financing purchases of medical care and its influences on other purchasers of care are matters of fact. In themselves, they do not suggest any change in government policy. It is the third point that suggests a change in government policy.

I will concentrate my remarks upon the third point—the need to introduce incentives for efficiency and economy into the Medicare and Medicaid programs. To provide a context for this discussion, I will present a concrete example of an instance where rewards for economy appear appropriate and desirable. The example involves the Kaiser Health Plan, a prepaid health plan pro-

Reprinted from statement of Vincent Taylor in U.S. Congress, Joint Economic Committee, *Economic Analysis and the Efficiency of Government,* Part 1, Hearings of the Subcommittee on Economy in Government, September 1969.

Vincent Taylor is an economic consultant.

viding comprehensive care to almost two million persons, the majority of whom live in California.

THE GROWING FEDERAL ROLE IN HEALTH

The rapid growth of federal influence in the health services sector is apparent in the data presented in Table 1.

TABLE 1. Selected Health Data[1] (Fiscal Years) (dollar amounts in billions)

	1965	1966	1967	1968	1969 (estimate)
Total U.S. health care expenditures	$35.7	$38.8	$44.3	$49.1	[2] $54.4
Federal health care expenditures	3.1	3.7	8.0	10.9	[3] 12.6
Federal share of health care expenditures (percent)	9	10	18	22	23
Medicare expenditures			3.4	5.3	6.2
Medicaid expenditures			3.1	3.7	4.6
Federal			(1.2)	(1.8)	(2.0)
State and local			(1.9)	(2.8)	(2.4)
Total, Medicare-Medicaid			6.5	9.0	10.8
Medical care price index	122	127	136	144	155
Annual increase (percent)	2.4	4.1	7.1	5.9	7.6

[1] Unless otherwise noted, all figures are from "The Budget of the United States Government," 1968, 1969, 1970; Barbara S. Cooper, "Public and Private Expenditures for Health, Fiscal Years 1965–1968 and Calendar Years 1965–1967," research and statistics note, Social Security Administration, note No. 22–1968, Nov. 11, 1968.

[2] Author's personal estimate.

[3] Bureau of Labor Statistics, Consumer Price Index, medical care component for June of each year.

Fiscal 1967 was the first year in which both Medicare and Medicaid were in full force. In that year, the federal share of health care expenditures jumped to 18 percent from the 10-percent share of the previous year. Federal health care expenditures are estimated to be $12.6 billion in fiscal 1969, or 20 percent of total U.S. expenditures. State and local expenditures made under the Medicaid program, and thus subject to the federal regulations governing Medicaid, are estimated at $2.4 billion; thus total expenditures under federally sponsored health programs in fiscal 1969 totaled $15 billion, or 28 percent of total U.S. expenditures. The great bulk of these expenditures were under the Medicare and Medicaid programs.

The obvious point of all these numbers is that Medicare and Medicaid have made the federal government a major factor in the market for medical care.

THE WIDESPREAD INFLUENCE OF MEDICARE-MEDICAID

Achieving economy in the Medicare-Medicaid programs is an important objective not only because these programs represent major items in the federal budget, but also because they exert substantial influence on overall medical costs. The Medicare program, in particular, has served as a model for others to follow. For example, the military services prior to Medicare had a fixed schedule of fees for physician services purchased outside of the military medical system. After the implementation of Medicare, the military switched over to using the "usual and customary fee" reimbursement procedure of Medicare. Many Blue Cross agencies that formerly paid hospitals on the basis of negotiated rates are now using cost-based reimbursement similar to that used by Medicare. Private insurance plans are under increasing pressure to provide coverage of medical services unrelated to hospitalization, as do Medicare and Medicaid. Medicare is so large and has been so widely endorsed that it inevitably serves as a model and a benchmark for judging other insurance programs.

Medicare and Medicaid have also influenced general medical costs by means of their substantial impact on the demand for medical care. It is more than mere coincidence that the rise in medical prices accelerated sharply in 1967, the first full year of Medicare and Medicaid. Even before these programs came into existence, there was an evident shortage of skilled health personnel, particularly physicians and nurses. Medicare and

Medicaid added billions of dollars to the demand for medical care, thereby worsening the manpower shortage and contributing to the upward pressures on medical prices. As Table 1 shows, medical prices, which had been rising at about 2.5 percent per year during the first half of this decade, rose 4 percent in 1966, and then by about 7 percent in each of the three years following the implementation of Medicare and Medicaid. During these same three years, hospital charges per day rose a total of nearly 50 percent, a rate of increase far more rapid than that of prior years. Although the general price level also rose during this period of time, its rapid rise began well after that of medical prices, and its rise was also far smaller than that of medical care prices. Thus, is seems fair to conclude that Medicare and Medicaid must accept a significant share of the responsibility for the sharp rise in medical prices that has been experienced in recent years.

THE IMPORTANCE OF INCENTIVES FOR ECONOMY

Medicare and Medicaid reduce the financial burden of illness by lowering the price their beneficiaries must pay for most medical services to zero or close to it. Although making medical care essentially free does have the desired result of eliminating financial barriers to adequate care, it has a considerably less desirable implication for economy and efficiency in the medical care sector.

Since insured individuals pay little or nothing for the care they receive, they are little concerned over the amount or the cost of care they consume. Since consumers are unconcerned about costs, providers need not be concerned either. Hospitals need not worry about consumer resistance to higher prices resulting from inattention to costs or additions of sophisticated services that duplicate, perhaps unnecessarily, services of neighboring hospitals. The government will pay the bill. An important restraining influence also has been removed from the physician. When the patient was paying the bill, physicians generally gave careful consideration to the costs of alternative courses of treatment for a patient's illness and attempted to choose the least costly acceptable one. A physician also had to be concerned about whether the fees that he charged would be acceptable to the patient or would cause the patient to seek care elsewhere. Neither of these factors are of importance when the government is paying the bill.

Medicare and Medicaid (and I might note, many other private insurance plans) effectively eliminate the powerful force for economy that consumers normally exert in the marketplace. It is impossible to estimate exactly how costly this loss has been, but the acceleration in the prices of medical services as insurance coverage spread provides no ground for complacency.

PRESENT INCENTIVES IN MEDICARE AND MEDICAID

What can be done about this situation? An important beneficial step would be for insurance organizations to substitute for the consumer in exerting pressures for economy. The government now makes some effort to control costs through utilization review in hospitals, recertification of hospital patients after specified lengths of stay, and review of physician charges for reasonableness and to detect possible fraud. Although such measures may prevent blatant abuses, they fall far short of providing a forceful spur toward economy. The consumer is an effective force in the marketplace because he spends his dollars where he gets the most value for his money. If the federal government is to be effective in improving efficiency and economy in the health sector, it must bring its power of the purse to bear on the providers of medical services. Insurance payments must reward those who produce acceptable care at below-average costs and should penalize those who fall short of meeting acceptable standards of quality of care or efficiency.

Medicare- and Medicaid-reimbursement procedures presently provide no rewards or incentives for improved economy. Physicians are paid for all of the services that they prescribe, so long as their fees are considered acceptable. Physicians or groups which are able to provide good care at lower total cost do not gain anything thereby. If they cut expenses by 20 percent, the amount that they are paid drops by 20 percent. Given this situation, they have no reason to attempt to conserve on expenses. Until recently, hospitals were reimbursed on the basis of costs plus 2 percent, a method that actually rewarded inefficiency. The higher the costs of a hospital, the larger was the dollar amount of the 2-percent bonus. The 2-percent bonus was recently dropped eliminating the perverse incentive, but there still is no positive incentive or reward for better performance.

We thus have a situation in Medicare and Medicaid where neither the consumers nor the producers of care have any powerful motives to economize on the amount of care consumed or to be concerned with the efficiency of the services being provided. Given this situation, it is little wonder that the costs of these programs and the prices of medical services have been expanding rapidly. The expansion promises to continue unless and until positive incentives for economy are introduced into the system.

ECONOMIES IN THE KAISER HEALTH PLAN

There are a number of possible ways of structuring insurance payments so that they provide producers of care with positive incentives for economy. Rather than going into the details of these alternatives, I would like to stress the basic principle that should be followed: Providers who can demonstrate that they are supplying acceptable care to federal beneficiaries at below average cost should be given a share of the savings they achieve. Perhaps the best way of illustrating this principle is by providing a concrete example of a situation where it should be appropriately and beneficially applied. The example concerns the Kaiser Health Plan experience under Medicare.

The Kaiser Foundation Medical Care Program provides comprehensive health care services to 1.9 million subscribers on a prepaid basis. It has traditionally operated in four distinct geographic regions on the West Coast and in Hawaii, but has recently opened regions in Colorado and Ohio. The Kaiser Health Plan operates its own hospitals and is provided with physician services by independent groups of physicians in each region. Although the Kaiser Foundation Hospitals, the Kaiser medical groups, and the Kaiser Foundation Health Plan (which collects insurance premiums from subscribers and contracts with the hospitals and physicians for services) are formally separate entities, management of all three is closely interrelated.

The Kaiser Foundation Medical Care Program has many unique features and, for an extensive discussion of this program, I would like to refer you to the 1967 Report of the National Advisory Commission on Health Manpower. Of particular importance for this discussion are the economic incentives that operate in the Kaiser Health Plan. Since Kaiser agrees to provide comprehensive medical care for a given population during a given time at a fixed fee, it must perform within its estimate to avoid losing money. Conversely, lower than anticipated costs result in excess funds (which are distributed as additional compensation to the medical group physicians and also used to finance new hospital facilities). Because of this way of doing business, all of those involved in the management of Kaiser are strongly motivated to keep costs down, to avoid waste, and to provide appropriate care in the most economical manner. Thus, the incentives facing Kaiser physicians and hospitals are exactly of the kind that it would be desirable for Medicare and Medicaid to give to all providers of care.

Kaiser not only has a desirable internal incentive structure, but also an extremely competent management and the advantages of large-scale operation. All of these factors contribute to good performance. A staff study of the National Advisory Commission on Health Manpower concluded that the average Kaiser member obtains high quality medical care for 20 to 30 percent less than the average cost in California of comparable care obtained outside the plan. Given the better cost performance of Kaiser, it would seem very much in the interest of Medicare to encourage Kaiser to actively expand the number of Medicare persons that it covers. Far from encouraging such action, present payment terms actually discourage it. The cost-based reimbursement provisions of Medicare mean that every dollar Kaiser saves goes to the government. Further, Medicare does not do business with Kaiser on the same terms as its other subscribers. As a result, there are many reasons why Kaiser might prefer to expand by acquiring more non-Medicare rather than more Medicare subscribers. And, Kaiser is in a position to choose, since demands for membership far exceed the ability to meet them.

MEDICARE AND MEDICAID REIMBURSEMENT EXPERIMENTS

The legislation governing Medicare and Medicaid payment procedures does not presently permit the sharing of savings with the providers of care; thus it is not possible under normal regulations to give Kaiser or other efficient providers rewards and incentives to expand. An amendment, however, to the Medicare-Medicaid legislation permits the Secretary of Health, Education and Welfare to waive normal reimbursement regulations in order to experiment with payments to provide positive incentives for efficiency. This provides an opportunity to apply the principle of sharing the savings with any provider who can demonstrate that he is supplying acceptable care to federal beneficiaries at below-average cost. In the case of Kaiser, this would mean negotiating payment terms that were based on Kaiser's costs relative to the average cost of Medicare for covering a comparable population outside of Kaiser. In return, the government might hope to obtain agreement from Kaiser to expand its enrollment of Medicare subscribers. Such an arrangement could result both in saving money for Medicare and increasing the funds available to Kaiser for expansion of its activities.

Unfortunately, although HEW was given the mandate in 1967 to experiment with cost-saving incentives on a large scale, there have been only a few, relatively small experiments approved. There has been an apparent reluctance to approve an experiment that *might* fail to show savings to the government—but the possibility of failure is inherent in any true experiment. If we had all the answers we would not need to experiment.

A more important shortcoming of the approach taken by HEW so far has been a complete unwillingness to agree to payment terms that would result in higher payments than are now being made to a provider—no matter how much more economical than average is the care he provides. To make this point clear, let me give a hypothetical example. Suppose a provider can demonstrate that he is caring for Medicare patients at \$100 per year, compared with an average of \$200 per year for other providers in his service area. If he proposes an experiment that would involve raising his payment per person to \$110 per year and doubling the number of beneficiaries covered, my understanding is that HEW would not accept the proposal—even though it would stand to save \$90 on each new beneficiary coming under his care, while spending only \$10 more on each of the beneficiaries now covered by him.

There is a general reluctance in the medical area to pay any organization an amount that significantly exceeds its costs of providing care. Although understandable, this attitude contributes to preserving inefficiency in the health sector. If efficient organizations were permitted to share the savings they achieve (that is, were paid more than their costs but less than the average of costs prevailing in the community), they would be provided with the funds needed to underwrite expansion. Over time, efficient organizations would expand more rapidly, taking away the customers of the less efficient, and the average level economy in the health sector would improve significantly. Present payment methods help to preserve inefficiency by paying both high- and low-cost producers the same amount in relation to their costs.

As a final point, I would like to stress that although I have used as an example a prepaid, group-practice health plan, my remarks about the desirability of incentive payments apply equally to all providers of care. The basic principle should be to provide financial rewards to *any provider* who can demonstrate that he is supplying acceptable care at below-average costs.

FEDERAL HOUSING POLICY AND THE HUD BUREAUCRACY

HOWARD E. SHUMAN

In late 1968, the Douglas Commission completed a 2-year study of urban problems which has since been called "the most exhaustive of its kind ever undertaken for the federal government." By almost any standard—but certainly by that of weight and volume—the description was apt. In mimeographed form, the commission's final report, *Building the American City,* was so mammoth that the commission furnished reporters with shopping bags in which to lug it away. Even in published form, it would put James Michener to shame: the report runs to 502 large, double-column pages. More important, the presidentially appointed group, formally called the National Commission on Urban Problems, delved deeply into its work and came up with revelations that could be extremely useful in fashioning America's urban destiny.

Reprinted from Howard E. Shuman, "Behind the Scenes and Under the Rug," *The Washington Monthly,* (July 1969) pp. 14–22. By permission of *The Washington Monthly.*

Howard E. Shuman is Administrative Assistant to Sen. William Proxmire.

While the hearings, studies and final report are now public, little has thus far been revealed concerning the commission's formation or the misleading promises, defensive reactions, and hostility within the Johnson Administration that characterized its 2-year charter.

GENESIS

One day in late November 1966, Special Assistant to the President Joseph Califano called at the Old Senate Office Building to talk with Sen. Paul H. Douglas. The senator was licking his wounds at the time. Earlier in the month he had lost his race for a fourth term when a coalition of negative events and a young and glamorous opponent, Charles H. Percy (R-Ill.), combined to defeat him.

Califano urged Douglas to head a Presidential Commission that President Johnson had proposed in both his 1965 message on the cities and in his 1966 Syracuse speech. The commission, Califano said, would examine urban problems, with emphasis on housing and community life as well as such mundane topics as building codes, zoning, and taxation.

Although the catastrophic 1967 riots were yet to come, this was a time when the sickness of cities was nonetheless approaching the top of the nation's domestic agenda. The Johnson administration seemed to feel that it would be a considerable coup to get a man of Paul Douglas's knowledge and stature to head a Commission on Urban Problems. The senator had managed the landmark 1949 Housing Act in the Senate; he had been the second-ranking member of the Senate Banking Committee, which handled housing legislation; he had introduced the original Model Cities bill; and he had been involved in every major piece of housing legislation for over 18 years.

A few days later, in my role as the senator's administrative assistant, I looked up the legislative authority for the commission. To my surprise, I found that the 1965 Housing Act authorized a "committee" under the Secretary of Housing and Urban Development—not a "commission" reporting directly to the President. The sum of $1.5 million had been appropriated to carry out its work.

I relayed my findings to Senator Douglas and urged him to turn down Califano's proposal unless: (1) the senator were to head a commission, rather than a "committee"; (2) the commission would be independent of HUD and report directly to the President; and (3) the commission's charter clearly included housing and urban affairs, as well as the narrower topics of codes, zoning, and taxation. The senator agreed. He dispatched me to the White House to negotiate the points.

Both Larry Levinson, Califano's agent, and Undersecretary of HUD Robert C. Wood greeted the conditions with favor and even enthusiasm. This was not surprising. Wood himself had chaired a 1964 task force which had proposed a new Hoover Commission to look at ways to redesign the government to meet problems brought on by the "urban dynamic." And the President had said publicly, only a few months earlier, that he would appoint a "commission" of distinguished citizens to study urban affairs. For these and other reasons, the White House accepted the senator's conditions with alacrity.

Although we did not know it at the time, this was not the case with Secretary Robert C. Weaver and the HUD bureaucracy. In fact, HUD had gone to great and devious lengths to avoid just such a commission as the President had originally proposed. When the President issued his 1965 housing message calling for a commission, the HUD legal experts quietly downgraded it by writing legislation that would establish nothing more than a "committee" under the thumb of the secretary. This had been done with the secretary's approval.

After the White House staff agreed with our proposal, Levinson, some other White House staff assistants, and I jointly drafted a press release announcing the commission and its broad objectives. Then we worked it over again into what was to be the final version of the release. In the meantime, Senator Douglas sought direct confirmation of the understanding from the President. In a phone conversation between the senator and the President, Mr. Johnson offered no objection to Douglas's conditions.

The White House agreed to the senator's request that a woman, a Negro, and some academic types—then the neglected minorities—be represented on the commission. All parties also agreed that the formation of "The Commission on the Problems of the American City" as a valuable "new addition" to a government-wide effort to ". . . not only avert the growing deterioration of our central cities, but to bring about an urban renaissance" would be announced before the Christmas holidays so that Senator Douglas could get the commission underway before leaving on a short vacation after a crowded and tumultuous year.

Time passed from late November, to early December, and on through the Christmas holidays. No announcement. Finally, the senator left Washington for his much-needed vacation.

In early January, I visited Secretary Weaver to discuss the commission's organization. With a frantic wave of his hand, he urged me to work on the arrangements at home and to stay out of sight. If I occupied a spot either at HUD or at the Executive Office Building, he said, word of the still-unannnounced commission might leak out. He was insistant and highly nervous about this. I thought at the time that the Secretary was the most insecure public figure that I had ever met. (It was only later that I learned of the reasons for his agitated state: he had recently undergone a Presidential tongue-lashing over his inept showing before the Ribicoff committee, and the White House had just killed his embryonic Comsat housing proposal because word about it leaked out prematurely.)

Late in the afternoon on January 12, Levinson called me—not, as I expected, to say that the announcement was imminent, but to say that it had been made. I scurried over and picked up a copy of the release, which the White House had unobtrusively issued at five o'clock on a Friday afternoon, along with a handful of minor appointments. As any reporter knows, this is the least favorable time and day for news to be announced.

But even worse, I found that the language in the release was a far cry from what all parties had agreed to. It assigned the commission only a twofold charter:

> First: to work with the Department of Housing and Urban Development and conduct a penetrating review of zoning, housing, and building codes, taxation, and development standards. . . .
>
> Second: to recommend the solutions, particularly those ways in which the effort of the federal government, private industry, and local communities can be marshalled to increase the supply of low-cost decent housing.

What should we do? Should we go along with the announcement or withdraw from the whole affair? The agreement had been violated, but the release did include the important issue of how to provide an abundance of housing for low-income families. Both White House assistant Levinson and Undersecretary Wood claimed that the change was a formality; its sole intention was to keep the commission's functions technically in harmony with the legislation. They explained that the President had, in fact, established a commission which was to work *with* but not *under*, the secretary of HUD, but which was to report to Mr. Johnson.

The senator was in the Caribbean at the time and not immediately available. After consulting briefly with trusted friends, I decided against making a public objection to our revised charter. (I had been appointed executive director of the commission.) Our independence seemed secure enough so that, given continuing White House support, I felt we could function as independently as a commission should.

Thus, the commission's birth was not a happy event, or even a very public one. There was no Oval Room pageantry, no dispensing of Presidential ballpoints, and only minor mention in the few newspapers which carried the announcement at all. For months afterward, old friends asked what had become of us. At times we felt like former Russian political figures, references to whom had been expunged from all public records.

HELMSMANSHIP

Larry Levinson's parting shot as I left the White House that evening in January, 1967, had been, "If you have any trouble with those HUD bureaucrats, just let us know."

Trouble was not long in coming. Secretary Weaver, who it was now clear had spent the time from early December until January 12 trying to retrieve for himself what the White House had given us, sent Douglas an insulting memo stating that the commission ". . . will develop . . . an agreed-upon [with HUD] budget" for the commission's operation. We knew that control of the purse strings was vital to our independence. We politely, but firmly, told him "no."

Weaver decreed that at least one HUD employee must attend all of our meetings. We declined to honor this as a "right," but we did agree—I now think wrongly—to "invite" a HUD representative to each of the formal commission meetings. This was a mistake because every criticism of HUD during both our private sessions and our public hearings went to the secretary from his inside agent.

The secretary's memo even outlined what our general study areas were to be and specified that we should set up five study panels—one each on building codes, housing codes, zoning, taxation, and development standards. He did not even mention the real meat: housing programs and broader urban problems. In sum, his "directive" was generally unacceptable if we were to function as an independent body.

The memo died but the ensuing struggle over staff, funds, and operations continued. When the secretary learned that Douglas was determined (with the commission's concurrence) to embark on a series of hearings in the ghettos of 22 major cities of the country, the fur flew again. He claimed that we were exceeding our authority and purpose. But the real fact was that he feared such hearings would embarrass HUD. We went ahead with our plans. As it turned out, those sessions provided a common and unifying experience for the entire commission; without them a unanimous and hard-hitting final report would have eluded us. In the end it was the very best thing we could have done.

The hearings infuriated Secretary Weaver and HUD. In New Haven, HUD's showcase for urban renewal, we sensed great local hostility to the program. Over $800 per capita had been spent —the highest rate in the country—but the community was seething and later erupted in a riot. Unknown to us until the end of our day of hearings there, the New Haven police had been stationed inside and outside the hall in case our hearings got out of hand. We prevented that by welcoming the views of unscheduled as well as scheduled witnesses. In fact, the "walk-in" witnesses talked with a fire and an eloquence which the others did not match.

Everywhere we went—Baltimore, Boston, Detroit, San Francisco, New York, Philadelphia, among other places—witnesses scathingly criticized the HUD and FHA bureaucracy and told of unbelievable delays in processing housing programs.

As Commissioners Richard O'Neill and Jeh Johnson wrote in the summary of the commission's final report:

> The civil disorders of the hot summer of 1967 followed us and preceded us. We saw the ugly burned-out urban streets that were still smoldering in some places, and we sensed the tension and anxiety in communities that would erupt not too long after our being there.
>
> We could have stayed in Washington and gathered statistics, but statistics do not tell enough about a slum. One has to see and touch and smell a slum before one fully appreciates the real urgency of the problem.

As the disturbing facts emerged, the secretary repeatedly denounced our activities to the White House and claimed that we had exceeded our scope (if not our grasp). In private conversations with commission members, his lieutenants spoke of our efforts with a rage and fury which had to be heard to be believed. They were especially sensitive to our report on HUD's neglect of the housing needs of the large poor family.

What we found included:

1. While the 1949 Housing Act authorized 800,000 units of public housing to be built in six years, only two-thirds of that six-year total had been built in almost 20 years.
2. In 1967, only 30,000 public-housing units a year were being built. Of these, more than half were efficiency and one-bedroom apartments for the elderly. Much of the remainder was built in the smaller cities. In other words, virtually no housing was being built in the ghettos of the United States for the poor families—particularly poor Negro families—who needed it most.
3. The moderate-income housing program (known in the trade as the 221 (d) (3) program) authorized 45,000 units a year since its beginning in 1961. Yet it took six years to build the number of units authorized for a single year.
4. Urban renewal had destroyed 400,000 units of housing for poor people. But on the sites it had bulldozed, the program had planned to build only 20,000 public housing units, or one-twentieth the number of units destroyed.
5. When HUD claimed that the major reason for the low production of all forms of subsidized housing was the lack of sites, we established that over half the land in the urban renewal areas of the central cities had not yet been "committed" to

any building whatsoever. There were sites in abundance.

In Detroit and Cleveland, for example, vast acreages were lying idle when those two cities blew up. In Detroit, hundreds of sites had been bulldozed. As a result, excessive overcrowding existed in the riot areas while the urban renewal land lay idle. Future plans provided no remedy; they called for a medical center, luxury housing, an industrial park, and athletic facilities for Wayne State University.

6. All in all, government action had destroyed far more housing units for the poor than it had built. While about two million units of housing had been destroyed by urban renewal, highway programs, demolitions for public housing, code enforcement, and other actions, only a million units of subsidized housing had been created. Our projections—based on the present pace of construction—showed that this pattern would continue.

7. Processing time for all major programs was so slow that it strained the commission's credulity. One-third of the completed urban-renewal projects had taken longer than nine years. Public housing routinely took three to four years to complete. The same was generally true for the moderate-income program.

8. Up until the 1967 riots, the FHA had refused to guarantee housing loans in what were called "red-lined areas" in the central cities. These areas were so named for the mythical red lines drawn on city maps by the banks, savings and loan institutions, and the FHA. The red lines embraced ghetto areas where the banks automatically refused to grant loans and the FHA automatically refused to guarantee them. Thus, the official policy of the United States was against insuring housing where it was needed most.

9. The value of government housing subsidies for the upper 20 percent of income groups in the 1960s—through the deduction of property taxes and interest paid on mortgages by homeowners—was twice that of housing subsidies for the bottom 20 percent of income groups, as measured by direct housing subsidies and welfare payments. While ignoring the poor, and especially the Negro poor, HUD and FHA had helped to provide vast opportunities for the white middle and upper classes. Here, they were a big success.

We thought the facts enumerated above were important in evolving public policies. HUD wanted them swept under the rug. But the cities were blowing up and lack of housing was a major cause.

HOME STRETCH

In spite of HUD's opposition, the commission pushed ahead. By the fall of 1968, it had published five volumes of hearings, as well as individual studies on housing programs, zoning exclusions, land use, property taxes and their regressive impact, and building and housing codes. The 16 members, all private citizens, had met for more than 70 days. Attendance at meetings and hearings had been phenomenal. The final report went through four major revisions in which the commission or its subcommittees examined it line by line. Huge portions were written by individual members as well as by key members of the staff.

During the first week of November 1968, we sent one copy of the final draft to Secretary Weaver and one copy to the White House. Chairman Douglas then wrote Califano, requesting a time for the commission to present its report to the President. There was no reply. Phone calls to Califano went unreturned. When called at the White House, he was "at home." When called at home, he was "in the shower." He was at home or in the shower for almost a month.

Finally, Califano agreed to meet with Douglas on December 3rd at 12 noon at the White House. Douglas cooled his heels there for more than an hour. When Califano arrived, he asked whether the report was unanimous. It was. This news apparently came as a surprise to him, since one of Secretary Weaver's themes to the White House had been that the commission was wracked with dissension.

Douglas again requested an opportunity for the members to present the report to the President and to be thanked by him for their diligence and devotion. Califano replied that Mr. Johnson was angry about press reports of the critical studies issued previously by the commission. According to Califano, the President became incensed every time the commission issued one.

The Senator told Califano that the study reports were truthful. He also argued that the final report was honest and comprehensive; it was, he said, the kind of report that the President likes. Douglas was aware of the President's populist streak and visceral reaction for the poor; indeed, it was one thing they had shared in common in the 18 years since they entered the Senate together.

In what was clearly an intended slight, Califano then insisted that the report be submitted to President-elect Nixon, rather than to President Johnson. Douglas firmly told him "no." The law prescribed that it be submitted by December 31, and he had promised his former colleagues in the House and Senate that it would be released as soon as possible. Besides, he had no intention of sending it to anyone but the President of the United States. It would break the law to withhold the report until Mr. Nixon was sworn in. Douglas flatly refused to report to a non-President, as Califano insisted.

In fact, he told Califano, he intended to release it for Sunday, December 15.

"I can't tell the President that," Califano said.

"I don't care what you tell the President," Douglas replied. "But I am telling you. We are releasing the report."

That ended the conference.

As a hedge against any attempt at suppression, we Xeroxed a dozen copies and got them into the hands of *The Washington Post, The New York Times,* and the wire services. We also bought 2,000 mimeographed copies for immediate distribution. It was these copies—each almost a foot thick—that reporters carried away in shopping bags.

The White House made two final attempts to upstage the report's December 15 release date. The President was scheduled to dedicate some low-cost housing units in Texas on Saturday, December 14—coverage of which could have competed with release of the commission's report in the Sunday papers. The plan called for the President to take attention away from news of the report by dedicating the units. But the President upset the applecart. Speaking extemporaneously at the dedication ceremonies, Mr. Johnson said that one of his biggest disappointments had been the government's failure to provide a decent home for all American families. His unexpected but deeply felt statement—which squared with the thrust of our findings—complemented the story of the commission's report.

In a second attempt to upstage the commission report, some White House staff members dusted off an unknown internal HUD report on city and suburban problems and leaked it to *The New York Times* for use on Sunday, December 15. If our report had not been in the hands of the wire services, the *Times,* and other newspapers several days in advance, this action by the White House might have knocked the story of our report off the front page and relegated it to the dustbins of history. This White House-HUD effort failed, and the Douglas Report made the front page of almost every major paper in the country. The leaked "suburban" report, which the *Times* used on page 1 along with the story of the Douglas Report, is still buried in the HUD files. It has never been publicly released.

UNDER THE KNIFE

The crowning blow came on December 31. Under Section 301 of the Housing Act of 1965, the Secretary of HUD was required to submit our report to Congress. By this time Secretary Weaver had left the government and Robert Wood, the commission's early supporter, was in charge of HUD. In carrying out his legal obligations, he transmitted to Congress and the President less than half of the commission's final report.

Wood refused to send those sections which criticized public housing (or lack of it), urban renewal, and other HUD programs. All criticisms of FHA's red-lining, the paucity of housing for the poor and the Negro poor, the lengthy delays in processing time, and the excessive demolitions ended up on the cutting-room floor. So did the 50 detailed recommendations on how to speed up and improve the programs and to build more housing for the poor. Sections on population, poverty, and race went out, as did those on the need for larger urban government units, on city neighborhood organization, and on the design and improvement of the urban environment.

Among the most glaring omissions was a detailed chapter on revenue-sharing. This chapter, written by Allen Manvel of the commission's staff, proposed that federal funds by-pass the states and go directly to the larger cities. It provided a formula for channeling rewards to states and cities which made an extra fiscal effort. This chapter and its detailed recommendations were left out because the White House opposed revenue-sharing.

When I told Secretary Wood that I felt his failure to transmit the complete version of our report was a needless and hostile act that only served to demean him, he claimed that he had left out only those sections which, in his view, had gone beyond the scope of our charter. That seemed odd, coming from the man who was the first to welcome a broad authority for the commission.

The basic problem, of course, was that the commission worked hard and wrote an honest, full report. In massive detail, it provided the facts about the past and suggested, in equal detail, a program for the future.

Commissions are generally established to buy time on an immediate and politically tender issue —or, as someone else has said, to treat the politics of a situation rather than the situation itself. They are expected to go into seclusion and not rock the boat. They usually report many months later —after public clamor has died down—and their work gets filed with the great unread literature of the world.

But commissions are worthwhile only if they tell the truth, act independently, and detail past mistakes in such a way that the chances of future improvement are enhanced. This goal, even when sought by an individual commission, is almost never shared by the federal agencies whose work comes under its scrutiny. In the case of the Douglas commission—even during the legislative drafting period—HUD tried to turn the President's proposal for a commission reporting to him into a committee dominated by the secretary.

These plans backfired on the secretary and the permanent bureaucracy when Douglas insisted on an independent role. In hindsight it is clear that the secretary saw the commission idea as a threat. He worked from the beginning to control and thwart the commission's inquiry and conclusions. The White House staff, originally enthusiastic, was caught between the commission's public criticisms of HUD and Secretary Weaver's contention that those criticisms put the administration in a bad light. Eventually, they caved in to the secretary's importunings.

But what if they had used the commission ". . . to add significantly to the momentum of our existing urban programs" and to help bring about an "urban renaissance," as those agreed-upon drafts of its charter had proposed? Instead of acting defensively about HUD's miserable track record, suppose the secretary and the White House had welcomed the commission's activities as a lever to jolt the FHA, to light fires under the bureaucracy, and to help transform HUD from an agency hostile to the housing needs of the poor into one which seeks to meet their legitimate housing needs?

That was perhaps too large an order for either HUD or the White House staff to accept.

But the voluminous commission work is there. As the hearings, studies, and final report are read and acted upon, the country may yet benefit from the fierce independence of a working commission and its energetic, intellectually honest members. Such would not have been the case if it had abjectedly succumbed to HUD's pressures and accepted a role as HUD's handmaiden and apologist. That would merely have helped to perpetrate what unkind persons call the Department of No Housing (for the poor) and Urban Development.

VI. FEDERAL REGULATORY AND INFORMATION POLICY

INTRODUCTION

In addition to raising revenue through a variety of taxation measures and spending it on numerous military and civilian programs, the federal government engages in a wide variety of other activities. Some of them involve the management of Research and Development and other property owned by the government; others involve the collection and dissemination of data and statistics; still others involve the government in the making and enforcement of rules within which private-sector transactions must operate.

Although most of these activities—especially the rule-making and enforcing activities—are performed by special agencies, they are in no way restricted to such agencies. For example, the Department of Transportation, not usually considered a regulatory agency, makes rules regarding the safety devices which must be built into automobile design. Similarly, the Environmental Protection Agency has the power to establish and enforce air quality standards in certain air pollution regions and the U.S. Army Corps of Engineers has responsibility under an 1899 act to regulate the disposal of wastes into rivers and streams through the issuing of permits.

While not the sole possessors of rule-making responsibilities, the regulatory agencies are the primary loci of such activities. In most cases, these agencies have jurisdiction over one or another private-sector industry which for some reason Congress judged to be in need of federal regulation. Hence, the Interstate Commerce Commission has jurisdiction over the transportation industry, the Federal Power Commission over the electrical generation and marketing industry, the Federal Communications Commission over the broadcasting industry, etc. In most cases, the primary mandate of these commissions is to establish the rates and prices at which the commodities of the regulated industries sell. Less well recognized, but equally important, the commissions regulate the organization of these industries, establish and enforce rules guiding the provision of their services, and certify or license certain investments or developments.

The regulatory agencies are unique in that they are not faced with difficult decisions involving the expenditure of billions of federal tax dollars. However, their functions are economic functions. Regulatory decisions cause significant reallocations of the nation's resources and redistribution of its income. As FCC Commissioner Nicholas Johnson has emphasized: "The impact of this sector of governmental activities on the functioning of the economy and the efficiency of government is almost impossible to overestimate." If these decisions are made without consideration or knowledge of efficiency or equity impacts or without explicit consideration of the range of alternatives for attaining a specific objective, the public interest will not be served. Similarly, if the decision process is biased toward specific interests, the result will be both inefficiency and inequity, and again the public interest will not be served.

In this section, a few aspects of the performance of the regulatory agencies are described and evaluated. Of central concern is the decision-making process of these agencies, i.e., the quality of the information on which they base their decisions and, in particular, the extent to which regulatory decisions are dominated by the very industries and interests who are supposed to be regulated in the public interest. The papers included in this section describe the process by which the regulated come to control the regulators and indicate a serious shortfall in the efficiency with which these agencies function.

A few of the causes of this inadequate performance were recently summarized by a congressional committee in the following terms:[1]

1. The practice of making decisions only in response to a petition from outside and the lack of statutory authority constrains the regulatory agencies from considering a range of alternatives or adopting a comprehensive, economy-wide perspective.
2. Regulatory agencies fail to undertake sufficient economic analysis of either the decisions which they make or the industries they regulate.
3. No agency outside of the regulatory bodies, including the Bureau of the Budget, scrutinizes the effectiveness of regulatory decisions or subjects them to explicit economic and equity analysis.
4. The rule-making process lacks a formal advocacy of the public-interest position in the cases and issues on which it must make decisions.
5. The regulatory agencies fail to recognize the substantial economic value of the common property resources which they are allocating and forego the benefits from applying user or beneficiary charges both to recover this value for the public and to efficiently regulate the use of these resources.

[1] U.S. Congress, Joint Economic Committee, *Economic Analysis and the Efficiency of Government,* Report of the Subcommittee on Economy in Government, 1969.

6. Federal agencies responsible for assuring compliance with laws and regulations are understaffed and, more significantly, lack interest in determining and revealing the serious extent of noncompliance with federal laws and rules.

The final two papers in Part VI deal with an issue which pervades all of the policy areas which have been discussed in the volume, namely, the right of the people to information about what their government does and how it is done. As the Mueller paper emphasizes, this right to know applies to both governmental decisions and those of large corporate conglomerates which are, in a real sense, private governments. Progress in increasing the responsiveness of public and private governments to the people requires substantial improvement in the access of citizens to information about the structure and behavior of these institutions. This issue, brought home so clearly in the Pentagon and Anderson Papers incidents, may be the most important issue discussed in the volume.

THE REGULATORS AND THE REGULATED

LOUIS M. KOHLMEIER

The men and women who regulate industry in the public interest deal occasionally with the White House, frequently with select members of Congress, and constantly with executives of regulated industries. All manner of procedural formalities have been borrowed from the courts to ensure fairness when the regulators and the regulated meet in open public hearings. But no equally meaningful procedures or incontrovertible guidelines have been developed for the far more frequent meetings of the regulators and the regulated that do not take place in public hearing rooms. Clearly, regulators are not judges and it would be wholly inappropriate to ban all informal contact and communication between them, who are supposed to be technical experts in industry affairs, and the industries they regulate. Equally absurd would be the isolation of agencies, such as the Civil Aeronautics Board, that by law are charged with promoting as well as regulating, from their industries. The as yet unanswered question is how and where regulators may meet with private industry without compromising, or appearing to compromise, the public interest.

According to the mores of regulation, there are two types of dealings between the regulators and the regulated that take place outside of formal public hearings. The first consists of nonpublic meetings concerning specific cases or policy issues pending before an agency. These usually are small meetings, called for the purpose of disposing of small cases, and they take place constantly in almost all the agencies. The process is known as "informal adjudication." From a public point of view, it leaves something to be desired, yet the agencies could not possibly dispose of their more than 100,000 items of business annually if each case had to be decided in a formal hearing. Sometimes, closed and informal meetings involve more people and large public policy issues; when

Reprinted from Louis M. Kohlmeier, Jr., "The Regulators and the Regulated," in *The Regulators* (New York: Harper & Row, 1969), pp. 69–82. By permission of Harper & Row, Publishers, Inc.

Louis M. Kohlmeier is a correspondent for the *Wall Street Journal.*

the regulators are thinking of adopting a new policy with industry-wide application, they habitually discuss the matter with corporate and trade-association executives prior to public announcement. The Securities and Exchange Commission, for example, has called in stock exchange officials before proceeding with the public adoption of new exchange rules. The Federal Trade Commission has met with automobile manufacturers before acting publicly to correct misleading new-car warranty practices. All of these nonpublic dealings, on matters small or large, are not wholly consistent with the spirit of consumer protection, but all take place within the context of defined cases or issues, and the agencies' ultimate dispositions of course are publicly announced.

The second and distinctively different type of dealing among the regulators and the regulated consists of the infinite variety of informal contacts that are, or are supposed to be, outside the setting of specific cases. In this large gray area of nonpublic communications, at business and social gatherings, the boundaries of propriety are poorly marked and consumers cannot know the ultimate consequences.

Regulators uniformly and consistently attend the national and regional conventions of the industries they regulate, addressing the business sessions and mingling during the social hours. The chairman of the SEC traditionally addresses the annual December get-together in Florida of the Investment Bankers Association. The chairman of the Federal Communications Commission speaks before the National Association of Broadcasters and sometimes all seven FCC commissioners attend the NAB convention. A few regulators have attempted to limit their outside, informal contacts with industry people to the open sessions of conventions, where the press if not the public is invited. William Cary, the straight-backed professor President Kennedy named as chairman of the SEC, refused, for instance, to attend some of the cocktail parties thrown by securities industry people in Washington. The great majority of regulators, however, are unable or unwilling to follow Chairman Cary's example. Most would be unrealistic to try. Their opportunities for contact with industry are too frequent and their responsibilities to industry are too large for the regulators to limit their contacts to public forums. Therefore, they also see and hear industry representatives in private. A regulator's office door normally is open to industry folk for private chats. Some of the regulators frequently take trips out of Washington to visit a factory or home office of a regulated company. Frequent business contacts lead to occasional social contacts. It is as common for a member of the Securities and Exchange Commission to show up at the cocktail parties as it is for members of the Civil Aeronautics Board to be guests on the gala inaugural flights with which airlines begin service on a new route they've been awarded by the board. And it is not unusual for members of the Interstate Commerce Commission to go fishing with railroaders.

A regulated company can hardly be blamed for using every opportunity for attempting to influence a regulator. It legitimately fears that if it doesn't a competitor will. Indeed, considering what's at stake a company would be remiss in its duty to its stockholders if it didn't try to exert influence. A piece of paper from the CAB awarding a major route can be worth more than $50 million in annual revenue to the winning airline. A license won from the FCC to operate a television station in a medium-size city can be worth $20 million, in terms of what the station will bring on the open market, and a big station in a very large city like New York may be worth close to $100 million. Approval of a railroad merger by the ICC is worth more than $100 million in terms of annual cost reductions the applying railroads eventually can achieve. Many, many millions of dollars hang on FPC regulation of gas rates, on SEC regulation (or lack thereof) of stockbrokers' commissions and on FCC regulation of long-distance telephone rates.

Big government as a whole has attracted to Washington armies of corporate, industry association and union emissaries, but regulated industries long have been the best represented. Consider the airline industry. The Air Transport Association, long headed by former CAB staff lawyer Stuart

Tipton, has a large Washington staff of lawyers, public relations men and lobbyists, though the ATA is not as influential a behind-the-scenes force as are the officers of individual airlines who reside in Washington. Almost every major airline is represented by a corporate vice president. Some smaller lines have resident vice presidents as well, and others are represented by lesser corporate officials or by hired hands who usually are Washington lawyers representing several clients in regulated industries. Each vice president is backed up by a staff that usually includes public relations men and lawyers, and each invariably outranks CAB members, so far as salary is concerned.

Other industries are almost as well represented. All three of the radio and television broadcasting networks, ABC, CBS, and NBC, have vice presidents in Washington, and the National Association of Broadcasters is a Federal City resident. American Telephone & Telegraph and Western Union, both of which are regulated by the FCC, have vice presidents too. The railroads, truckers, and barge lines each have their trade-association headquarters and some companies have officers in Washington. The Pharmaceutical Manufacturers Association is there to represent the drug makers who are regulated by the Food and Drug Administration. Gas companies regulated by the Federal Power Commission are represented by corporate officers or by law firms. Tommy Corcoran, a prominent Washington lawyer who was a government official in New Deal days, testified before a House subcommittee in 1960 that the law firm of which he was a member was on a retainer of $60,000 a year from Tennessee Gas Transmission Corporation.

Industry has sent many ambassadors to Washington, they invariably have large expense accounts and they engage the regulators in frequent nonpublic communication. But the net result is not as sinister as the people—the consumers—may imagine. Bribery of a public official is not often proved nowadays and in fact probably is rare. The growth of the industry establishment in Washington poses a number of more subtle problems, like jobs and salaries.

Many of those bright young men who resign as regulators long before their terms expire leave to take higher-paying jobs in industry or to join Washington law firms that represent industry before the regulatory agencies. Assuming that the job seeks the man, rather than the man in government using his position to seek a job, the departures would seem to raise no ethical problems. But the distinction normally is difficult to draw. The ethical problem is potentially always present, as a high-ranking staff official of the Securities and Exchange Commission acknowledged when he said, privately, that the interest in industry job opportunities "does get bad when it's blatant and open."

The ethical question aside, the agency-to-industry movement unquestionably aggravates the government's loss of genuine talent and therefore undercuts the theory that the regulators would become experts by reason of many years of service. Certainly the cumulative loss of talent has been great and many of the industry ambassadors are able men who certainly did not have to beg for jobs but who were sought after by industry. One such was Everett Hutchinson, a Texan who was appointed to the Interstate Commerce Commission by President Eisenhower and who handed his resignation to President Johnson in order to become president of the National Association of Motor Bus Operators. Frederick W. Ford, who had been on the Federal Communications Commission since 1957, in 1964 resigned the FCC job, which at that time paid about $20,000 a year, to become president of the National Community Antenna Television Association, reportedly at $50,000 a year.

Big-name law firms in New York and in Washington are filled with men who once were with the SEC, as commissioners or staff members. Some SEC folk have departed for brokerage concerns and mutual funds like the giant Investors Diversified Services. Some moved to seats in corporate executive suites. Donald C. Cook, once on the staff of the SEC's Public Utilities Division and then a commissioner, became president of American Electric Power Company. Ralph T. McElvenny, once on the staff of the same division, became president of American Natural Gas

Company. The other agencies' talent losses perhaps haven't been as great, but they have lost too. Washington law offices that specialize in broadcast matters are as full of former FCC commissioners and staff members as law firms specializing in securities law are crowded with SEC alumni.

The conclusion suggested is that, in general, industry has sought out the more capable people in the regulatory agencies and paid them for their talents.

Large, expensive, black-tie dinners that bring together government officials and industry executives are of course commonplace in Washington. The social intercourse among Defense Department officials and defense contractors no doubt was an element of President Eisenhower's expressed concern about the "military-industrial complex." The permanent presence in Washington of registered lobbyists for all sorts of industry, labor and other special-interest groups makes possible the frequent fund-raising dinners held there in honor of individual senators or representatives who need cash to wage reelection campaigns back home. Dinner at the White House was one reward for corporate executives who gained membership to the President's Clubs of John Kennedy and Lyndon Johnson by contributing at least $1,000 yearly to the Democratic party's war chest.

Businessmen don't give their hard-earned dollars expecting no return. What they normally expect, in buying twenty-dollar tickets to dinners for lawmakers or in contributing through the President's Club, is political recognition and friendship. They don't buy commitments of members of Congress or Presidents any more than they buy votes of regulators. They buy, or hope to buy, a government official's willingness to lend a sympathetic ear, at luncheon someday or in the official's private office, on pertinent matters of legislation, administrative action or procurement.

Regulated businessmen do more and expect more because they have more at stake in Washington. They are among the most prominent members of the President's Club. They are the dependable mainstays of fund-raising dinners for members of Congress, and particularly those members who sit on the commerce committees. In addition, they entertain the regulators with whom normal businessmen are not concerned. The Washington vice presidents of regulated companies normally are registered with Congress as lobbyists. Their work is almost entirely in the area of informal, off-the-record contacts. They scout Capitol Hill, dropping in to see members of Congress in their offices; they frequent the agencies, visiting with regulators in their private offices, and sometimes they go to the White House. They also entertain legislators, regulators and White House personalities at lunch and in their Washington homes. The best of them receive selected regulators, legislators and White House aides in their homes for an evening of convivial mixing. These Washington vice presidents usually are lawyers. But formal, on-the-record appearances at public hearings before congressional committees and regulatory agencies normally are left to a separate staff of corporate lawyers located in Washington or at the company's home office. On the other hand, corporate presidents and board chairmen frequently come to Washington to mix in the informal gatherings and often they also hold membership in the President's Club.

What regulated businesses expect in return for their considerable hospitality and contributions is an appropriately large opportunity to be heard. Specific expectations must be considered in terms of the interrelations of the regulatory agencies, Congress and the White House. From the regulators, a lobbyist can hope to purchase, if not a vote for his company, then sympathy for the interests of the industry of which his company is a part. From members of Congress he hopes for committee and floor votes that someday may be necessary to pass or block a regulator's confirmation, a piece of regulatory legislation or some part of an agency's appropriation. From the White House, he hopes to be included among industrialists who are consulted before regulators' nominations are sent to Congress.

The interrelationships of the regulated, the regulator, Congress and the White House are known to all concerned and the lobbyists' hospitality and contributions are part of the mortar of the politics of regulation. Indeed, regulated industry has no real power over the regulators, except for the power to offer jobs, and industry's influence thus comes in large part from the power that can be brought to bear indirectly, through Congress and the White House.

No one, including the Washington vice presidents, knows precisely how much influence the hospitality and contributions purchase. Pressures from various sources are brought to bear on larger issues of regulation and some cancel out others. A President or member of Congress may side with an industry most of the time but not always and lobbyists can't know all the reasons for an official's action on every issue. They do know that Presidents usually consult regulated industry before they nominate regulators, that White House aides have intervened at the agencies, that the Senate has refused to confirm some nominees and that regulated industries generally have been quite successful in taking their cases to members of Congress.

So knowing, regulated industry in recent years has invested ever more heavily in Washington hospitality and campaign contributions. Some companies are more politically-minded than others. But their total investments certainly amount to some millions of dollars, at least in a presidential campaign year.

No one need lose all the time, except the public. The politics of regulation is a merry-go-round on which there is a place for all, except consumers. The merry-go-round is propelled by the self-interests of industry that must ride for the preservation of revenues and profits; of the regulators who want to keep their jobs; of members of Congress who need campaign cash and of White House figures who want business' confidence and use the regulatory agencies for political ends. The interrelationships of self-interests leave no room for consideration of the public interest. The agencies tend to become umpires not of consumer versus industry interests but of industry versus industry. Taken together, regulation tends to perpetuate the protection of industry and the disregard of consumer interests, including the consumer interest in industrial competition.

When Howard Morgan, an Oregon Democrat, in 1963 told President Kennedy he didn't want to be reappointed to the Federal Power Commission, he inserted in his letter this rather purple prose:

> Ordinary men cannot administer [the regulatory] laws today in the face of pressures generated by huge industries. . . . The big problem in the regulatory field is not influence peddling and corruption as that word is commonly understood. In my experience as a regulatory official I have been approached only once with a veiled intimation that money or stock was available in return for a favorable decision, and that was at the state level, not here in Washington.
>
> But abandonment of the public interest can be caused by many things, of which timidity and a desire for personal security are the most insidious. This commission, for example, must make hundreds and even thousands of decisions each year, a good many of which involve literally scores and hundreds of millions of dollars in a single case. A commissioner can find it very easy to consider whether his vote might arouse an industry campaign against his reconfirmation by the Senate.

ECONOMIC ANALYSIS AND REGULATORY DECISIONS

NICHOLAS JOHNSON

During the administrations of Presidents Kennedy and Johnson there was a greatly increased use of tools of economic analysis in the determination of government programs. Program evaluation and the planning-programing-budgeting system, often called PPBS, rely heavily on economic techniques for the specification of alternatives for decision-makers—alternatives in programs, expenditure levels, and the long-range effects of government decisions.

Such techniques can be complex, their use may occasionally lead us astray, but it also seems clear these efforts at rational analysis have produced a general improvement in the decision-making process of government.

PPBS and economic analysis have typically been applied when there are significant government expenditures to be made—the buying of weapons systems, the expenditures of subsidies, or the encouragement of research.

Regulatory agencies have typically been ignored in this context. They are low-budget operations, and this fact understandably tends to mask their importance to the Bureau of the Budget and the Congress. The Federal Communications Commission $20 million annual appropriation is roughly one one-hundredth of 1 percent of the federal budget—the cost of operating the Defense Department for about 2 hours, on a 24-hour-a-day, 365-day-a-year schedule.

However, a regulatory commission's budget is not a very useful measure of its impact upon the national economy and lives of our people.

The FCC is a resource-managing and planning agency—or ought to be. It functions in what I will treat today as three major areas:

1. It manages the use of a publicly owned resource—the radio spectrum—used by private interests.
2. It regulates in detail the industrial organization and functioning of the broadcasting industry.

Reprinted from statement of Nicholas Johnson in U.S. Congress, Joint Economic Committee, *Economic Analysis and the Efficiency of Government,* Part 1, Hearings of the Subcommittee on Economy in Government, September 1969.

Nicholas Johnson is a Federal Communications Commissioner.

3. It regulates, as common carriers or public utilities, the interstate telephone system, and the international communications industry.

Each of these three prime regulatory responsibilities overlaps. Broadcasters and communications common carriers are both significant users of the radio spectrum; the rates charged by common carriers for network interconnection affect the industrial organization and commission goals for the broadcast industry; new technologies in the broadcast and common carrier industries affect the demand for the radio spectrum.

The magnitude of these regulatory responsibilities is easily illustrated. The use of the radio spectrum by private interests is estimated to add $20 billion to the Gross National Product; the broadcasting industry grosses $3 billion annually; and the commission is presently—indeed this very morning—considering interstate telephone rates that could have a $500 million effect on user rates paid for interstate service alone, not to mention the impact upon state regulatory commissions in their rate-setting procedures.

Thus, this little $20-million agency has a profound effect on the functioning of our entire society: The efficient use of a valuable natural resource, the quality and cost of our telephone network, and the ability of broadcasters to provide the information crucial to self-government by the people.

A commission failure to manage the radio spectrum efficiently can seriously affect economic development and lead to resource misallocations throughout the economy; inadequate utility regulation of the telephone companies could lead to rates that are too high and impair the use of communications by users; the failure to assert public-interest control over the broadcast industry may result in serious imbalances of power throughout the society or in particular communities where media concentrations can threaten the democratic processes.

To illustrate, I have chosen three case studies: Management of the radio spectrum; concentration problems in broadcasting; and new telephone technology.

Let me first mention a general problem that pervades much of my subsequent discussion. One would think that an agency whose planning responsibilities are so great would make a substantial commitment of time and resources to research and policy planning. Such is not the case. There is no central policy planning unit in the commission's organization.

In the almost 3½ years I have been on the commission, I have repeatedly urged, with only limited success, that such a unit be created. There are now plans to establish a very small staff. But the time when the commission can truly be said to possess an "institutional cerebral cortex" is, I am afraid, still far off.

In many ways, the establishment of the Communications Policy Task Force by President Johnson in August 1967 was an implicit criticism of the commission's inability to do policy planning.

In part, this aversion to the policy planning is a function of the commission's conception of self. The commission tends to think of itself as a court, reacting to those matters that are placed before it only in terms of the information from interested parties pursuing their own economic interests. There is at best only limited recognition of the desirability of specifying *all* alternatives—and little capacity to evaluate them when presented to the agency from outside.

The commission's consideration of the domestic satellite question provides ample illustration of this principle. The possibility of domestic satellites for the United States was first raised not by the FCC, but by ABC. The Ford Foundation subsequently filed a proposal that radically changed the frame of reference in which the question was being discussed—including the concept of a "peoples dividend" from the public's massive investment in the space program.

But for the Ford Foundation's proposal, I do not believe the commission would have considered these policy alternatives—or that alternative proposals for adequate funding and interconnection of the Public Broadcasting Corporation would have received the impetus they have.

The problems surrounding spectrum management raise comparable issues. The commission serves as a replacement of the free market in allocating this resource.

Most other resources in our society are allocated by those market forces, and the role of economics in our understanding of efficient resource allocation is paramount. One would, therefore, expect that economic analysis would be a major tool in the commission's undertaking of this task. But so far as I know there is not one economist on the commissions' staff who is at all concerned with the spectrum allocation and management function.

It is not a question of there not being *enough* resources in this area—it is that there are no resources being devoted to it at all. When one realizes that most new developments in communications technology, such as satellites, depend upon the availability of radio spectrum, one can understand the handicap that is placed on efficient commission decisions throughout the entire range of policy matters it must decide.

There are some efforts being made to rectify this situation. The office most concerned with spectrum management at the commission is moving to add a couple of economists to its staff. But, once again, the time when the commission will be able to make consistently intelligent decisions about spectrum utilization is simply not in the foreseeable future.

The magnitude of the problem can perhaps be seen from the Department of Commerce advisory panel recommendation of a couple of years ago which suggested that a governmental effort of perhaps $50 million a year would probably be necessary for this task alone—2.5 times the FCC's current entire budget. The panel believed such expenditures justifiable in terms of more efficient use of the spectrum and its attendant contribution to the functioning of the economy.

In many ways, the commission's actions are of the nature of crisis management—a crisis that would be unnecessary with adequate attention to policy planning and analysis. The commission has made almost no use of market-simulating techniques, such as user fees, in its allocation process.

Let me insert a little detail to make this clearer. What I am talking about with regard to spectrum management is the allocation of radio frequencies to business and other private users, that is, users other than the federal government: police departments, taxicabs, hand-held two-way communications that may be used in a warehouse or as part of a construction project, or whatnot.

We estimate, for example, that any operation in our economy that requires the use of mobile equipment—delivery trucks or something of that sort—can be operated with about 60 percent of the equipment with mobile radio communications as is required without it. The demand for radio frequencies far exceeds the supply, and the system has never really been very effectively managed.

We have simply made frequencies available to those who asked, when they asked, and some get unduly congested and others are really underutilized. We don't really have a very good data base as to where the transmitters are and what geographic areas are now covered.

That is the kind of use I am talking about here and the nature of the economic impact.

One of the commission's primary responsibilities in promoting the public interest in broadcasting is the determination of the industrial structure of the industry. The commission must approve the competitive interrelationships and business practices of the industry. It is elementary economic theory that the structure of an industry and its competitive practices profoundly affect the performance of that industry, its capacity to serve consumer tastes and respond to market forces or other forms of social control.

This area of commission activity has been of great concern to me, as I have detailed in many opinions and articles during my tenure. The commission's failure to exercise its responsibilities in this area has reulted in the already overtaxed Antitrust Division of the Department of Justice becoming the primary force for enforcement of competition where one would expect the commission to play the dominant role.

Thus, we have the Department of Justice successfully opposing the ITT-ABC merger—in a case appropriately titled, "The United States versus the FCC"; successfully obtaining a consent decree divestiture of a television station from newspaper owners after the commission had expressly approved the relationship in a recent renewal action; successfully opposing a proposed TV station-newspaper merger in another community; and filing a request for hearing and divestiture in another community where the commission has regularly approved the concentration situation.

The department has also taken strong procompetitive positions in numerous other commissions proceedings. The department has not only felt the need to intervene to promote competition, it has done so with spectacular success—often in opposition to the commission's natural tendencies. And it was the Department of Justice's intervention—not action by the FCC—that resulted in aborting of the proposed mergers between Transamerica and Metromedia as well as that of Westinghouse and MCA, Inc.

There are two conclusions with regard to efficiency in government that can be drawn from this description of the manner in which competition is promoted in the broadcast industry. First, one government agency, already overtaxed, must undertake the responsibilities of the agency charged with primary responsibility.

Secondly, the performance of the industry in question necessarily suffers from the neglect of the useful effect of competitive forces. Competition is often a superior substitute for government regulation. Unfortunately, the commission devotes very little analytical resources to problems of industrial organization in the broadcast field. What little resources the commission possesses have deteriorated in the last 5 years, and have been generally downgraded in the commission's decision-making process.

There is a footnote to the problem of media concentration which illustrates the commission's handicaps. For some 10 years the commission has been considering the appropriate role for cable television—sometimes called CATV. CATV could affect concentration and user access. It presents an alternative to the present method of program distribution.

It is the commission's responsibility to choose the most appropriate mix of over-the-air and cable technologies in achieving the nation's goals for its mass communications system. This has been an extremely difficult decision for the commission. Almost no resources of an analytic, systems evaluation, or policy planning nature are now being employed by the commission in this problem.

By contrast, the Ford Foundation is sufficiently concerned that it has funded a roughly $150,000 study at the RAND Corp. to evaluate the policy alternatives in CATV. The commission, on the other hand, suggested some policy alternatives in December 1968 and solicited outside response.

I think it fair to say that the commission views solicitation of the views of outside economic interests as a substitute for internal research and analysis. For whatever reasons, it certainly is not doing even as much as the Ford Foundation in trying to determine the most efficient and wisest national policy in this crucial area.

Again the commission is willing to wait to see what accumulates in the "in-box" while it hopes that policy resolution is made elsewhere. And Congress meanwhile is unable to rely on its expert agency for effective policy determination—or even some assistance.

In common carrier regulation the commission has roughly 100 professionals who are responsible for regulation of the interstate telephone system dominated by the multibillion-dollar Bell Co., satellites—including Comsat, international cable communications, and private microwave systems.

In many ways it is remarkable that the commission has achieved as much as it has with such limited resources. But the commission has not yet, for example, evaluated the rate of introduction of new technology in the telephone industry. The commission is simply without the capacity to review the technological decisions that are made in that industry, and this is especially critical when one realizes that the industry is vertically integrated from research through production to service.

I do not now reach the question whether this is the most appropriate organization of the industry. But even if it is, the planning for introduction of new technologies is made almost exclusively by the Bell System, without any public review at all. The commission may affect Bell's decisions through a variety of regulatory policies, but it is almost completely unaware of their impact.

Apparently the assumption is that what is good for Bell is good for the country. That may be so. But there is no theoretical reason why it should be. I am not so confident that the decisions of a monopolist are always the correct ones.

The thrust of my remarks is simply that the use of economic analysis to judge the efficiency of regulatory agencies involves much more than the allocation of their relatively meager budgets. The PPBS system must be modified to relate goals of regulatory policy to the expenditure of the agency's funds on decision-making.

The economic analysis of government turns on the relationship of alternative actions to goals. But regulatory goals are typically specified in only the most general statements and neither the measurement of achievement or the evaluation of alternatives is possible. Yet the impact of this sector of governmental activities on the functioning of the economy and the efficiency of government is almost impossible to overestimate.

Some have argued that the regulatory commissions serve little purpose in our society save as a device to serve big business, at the taxpayers' expense, by permitting industry to do with impunity what would otherwise send its corporate officials to jail. Some economists and commentators argue that many regulatory commissions are a diseconomy—that prices are higher and service worse with them than it would be without them.

I am not prepared to go so far. If such charges could be documented fully, I would agree that the agencies should be abolished. Until then, however, I would prefer to make every effort to attempt to improve their performance, through means such as this very inquiry by the subcommittee.

I cannot close a statement about economic performance without a comment about human performance. There is a growing malaise in this country about the quality of life. It relates not so much to facts as to feel. People do not need scientific indicators to tell them that New York City's air doesn't feel good in their lungs. An economist's analysis is not much help to someone whose personal emptiness and frustrations increase in direct proportion to his material possessions. It doesn't feel good to talk to tape-recorded messages over the telephone and get mail written and addressed by computers.

I saw a bag of popcorn from the A&P store. It came in a clear, plastic bag and a machine had written on it "artificial color and imitation flavor." This sums up, in my judgment, a great deal of what may be wrong in our country today.

This is not a matter of a "generation gap"—although it does seem harder to keep one's sensitivity with age. Our society doesn't make its older people feel any better than its young—if anything, worse. It is middle-aged, middle-class housewives who are picketing the supermarkets' prices—not their teenage daughters. People are tired of everything breaking down and having to take it back to the store. Someday somebody is going to get up from his three-martini lunch to discover that this is the day the world wouldn't work. Everything will break down at once.

People are tired of seeing millionaires go tax-free while their own taxes increase; sick at seeing agricultural subsidies averaging $200,000 a year for the larger beneficiaries while the Department of Agriculture is unable to find enough money to feed the hungry; cynical at road signs warning of $100 fines for littering, while corporations back their factories up to the river where they squat and dump corporate effluent by the ton into the city's water supply.

Television is not the only sick influence in our society, but it is one of the most significant ones. It leaves half of the American people dead in the water each evening. It force-feeds external additives like hair color, deodorant, mouthwash, headache and sleeping pills, coffee, cigarettes, and beer to a bewildered people in search of "more"—instead of the stimulation to live the kind of life that can only bring the satisfactions they seek.

If the regulatory commissions—which believe themselves to be servants of the industries they are supposed to regulate—don't even do a good job of serving industry, one can be sure they do an even worse job of serving human life. As Mason Williams says, "Government makes better deals with business than it does with people."

EFFICIENCY AND REGULATORY POLICY: ISSUES OF COMPLIANCE, DISCLOSURE, AND ACCOUNTABILITY

RALPH NADER

The concept of efficiency is customarily thought of in economic terms. However narrow the concept may be, it is useful to limit it in some sense just so we can handle the variables and not go off in 16 different directions. Indeed, the discipline of economics has offered new tools in the methodology and measurement of efficient performance. Very often its concepts and tools have suffered severe limitation in practice by an inhospitable political environment. One has just to stretch the analytic framework of cost-benefit to include such questions of distribution in time, space, and economic class of these cost-benefits to illustrate how infrequently they are asked in policy forums due to political realities. For example, not until this week have we had a no-holds-barred hearing on some of the sequential costs of automotive design in terms of repair costs before the Senate Antitrust Committee. This is at least 50 years too late, but it is a definite and determinative consequential cost, involving billions of dollars every year. This is also true for the decades-long deferral of analysis of the tax expenditure budget and for the 3-year-long aversion to analyze the cost-benefit of administering organizations (such as insurance companies) in medicare.

At this time, I should like to present three areas of needed analysis that could markedly improve both the efficient use of government resources which in turn are allegedly devoted to advancing the efficiency of those sectors of our society they are regulating. I am speaking not just in terms of economic efficiency, but also efficiency in meeting public needs. I am also not questioning at this time the regulatory scheme and whether it is appropriate, but rather, what the approaches should be to maximize its efficiency given the appropriateness for the time being. As a matter of fact, many of these points, which I am going to

Adapted and reprinted from statement of Ralph Nader in U.S. Congress, Joint Economic Committee, *Economic Analysis and the Efficiency of Government*, Part 3, Hearings of the Subcommittee on Economy in Government, September 1969.

Ralph Nader is associated with the Center for the Study of Responsive Law in Washington, D.C.

make very briefly, could point toward a change in the regulatory process.

It could point toward, in some areas, a deregulation and a different type of proposed overview such as engaging government in independent research and development to put before the market prototype systems, such as nonpolluting vehicles or new kinds of antipollution controls, coupled with a vigorous antitrust enforcement. That is, if you push the analysis of an agency to its limits, you will not only discover ways of being more efficient or inefficient, you may even, of course, begin to challenge the very assumptions under which the agency is operating.

It is realized that the concept of efficiency in these environments inevitably has a heavy information input—stemming from the enabling legislation—but that the rigorous tools still are required to evaluate the statutory and more detailed regulatory missions. These three areas are (1) compliance and sanctions policy; (2) disclosure policy; and (3) a new kind of public servant accountability.

COMPLIANCE AND SANCTIONS POLICY

An efficient compliance and sanctions policy maximizes regulatee observance of the laws and regulations that represent the articulate impact of the agency. Such a policy also makes the more efficient use of existing agency manpower dealing with compliance. Yet there is probably no area in regulatory government that has received less analysis and change than compliance and sanction. Compliance surveys by regulatory agencies are not made regularly; indeed in most cases they are not made at all. Instead, limited compliance manpower has been used as the basis for an anti-analysis, for an obstinate reiteration of inaction and a shallow justification for a noncompliance policy for many activities under regulation.

The need for regular compliance surveys is obvious. They help assess and locate the extent of violations. They help evaluate the cost-benefit effectiveness of available sanctions which the agency is empowered to apply. What are the respective deterrent effects of different applications of sanctions to various regulatees having been charged with different violations? What is the spillover effect for deterrence, coverup strategies and the like of alternative compliance policies? How can limited enforcement resources be optimally distributed? What additional tools (from computers to permitting private remedies to the utilization of focused disclosure) can supplement such enforcement efforts?

I might add to what extent can a large company, by a conscious strategy of delay, tie up an enormous portion of the enforcement personnel of a particular agency, knowing that it would have to divert its attention from other sanctions under its regulatory responsibility? General Motors is doing this quite successfully in the National Highway Safety Bureau, stretching out over 13 months a particular defective wheel hazard, involving 200,000 Chevrolet trucks between 1960 and 1965 models. They have tied up an enormous proportion of the enforcement manpower of that small agency, which of course, has its costs in delaying or postponing other enforcement efforts that should be underway. A compliance survey would address itself to sound treatment of such questions.

At the present time, there is every indication that most regulatory agencies consciously avoid making such compliance surveys. Such surveys may be confidential. But so far as publicly available documents are concerned, I am aware of very few such analyses. I think I would be aware of some of these analyses even if they were confidential.

In 1965 the Wage and Hours and Public Contracts Division of the Department of Labor, charged with enforcing the Fair Labor Standards Act, conducted a public study. The Division's Compliance Survey 1965, as it was called, provided the kind of data that enable analysts to construct a cost-benefit framework that would permit more precise calculations of future compliance benefits of a particular investigation pattern.

Realistically, the reason for such lack of agency interest in conducting compliance surveys of its enforcement activity is the massive amount of illegality which it would have to recognize under its jurisidiction. Most agencies are not willing to reveal the extent to which their regulations are not being enforced or the extent to which these agencies are condoning, and often ignoring, the most blatant violations. Perhaps it is easier to understand why civil servants, who are keen on enforcing the law against economic crimes or safety and health violations, are considered troublemakers and boat rockers and eventually replaced, by briefly viewing the congressional oversight performance of compliance with regulatory laws.

Most citizens in this country know how concerned members of Congress are with law and order—a certain type of law and order associated with the absence of property and corporate status on the part of the alleged violator. Innumerable speeches on the hustings and in the Congress attest to such concern. What about the mockery of law and order displayed, to select a few examples, by (*a*) the systematic violation of the motor carrier safety regulations by interestate bus and truck companies; (*b*) the widespread violations of the already weak railroad safety regulations; (*c*) the dozens of violations of the 1968 and 1969 motor vehicle safety standards by the automobile companies; (*d*) the dozens of tire failures to meet federal standards uncovered but not moved against by the National Highway Safety Bureau; (*e*) the tragically shocking fraud that has permitted false claims and gross violations of the federal motor vehicle pollution standards; (*f*) and the rampant violations of wholesome meat and poultry standards. With few exceptions, the Congress maintains an unsuitably indentured silence. Oversight hearings of the regulatory agencies that are informed and arms-length continue to have a very rare incidence.

Endemic nonenforcement over time builds up a corruption of the politicolegal process that is difficult to overestimate. The regulators begin having a stake in nonenforcement in numerous ways. The distortion, if not repudiation, of the regulatory process reflects the mistaken belief that the regulatory process is generically defective on the part of well-meaning citizens.

To give an illustration, the judgment section in the Antitrust Division of the Justice Department is composed of 12 lawyers, including the head of the section. Six of these lawyers are allocated to insuring compliance with consent decrees. There are literally hundreds of consent decrees affecting all kinds of corporations and trade associations and industries. It is totally unrealistic to expect even a one-percentile compliance overview with that amount of staff.

DISCLOSURE POLICY

A generous disclosure policy contributes to regulatory in-house efficiency and to the firmer performance of the regulatory mission in several ways. First, disclosure of the agencies' activities by the agencies permits more external evaluation by the public of how well the agency is doing. Assuming the process of agency intransigence and complicity with the regulatees not to have hardened irrevocably, such disclosure can have reformist impact. At least, such disclosure reduces the pretense of public interest that is radiated by the agency's brochures and public relations. Second, disclosure distributes and decentralizes participation in the agency's objectives among more groups and more citizens throughout the country. The force of public opinion, citizen intervention, editorial comment and more formal countervailing pressures tend to increase with greater disclosure. The power which special interests have over government and the citizenry is very substantially a function of their power over information and the rate and locus of its distribution.

I have found time and again that agencies not only fail to develop improved systems of information-giving but also spend an inordinate amount of energy to develop ways and excuses to withhold information or make sure that it never is developed so as to be distributed.

From the General Services Administration to the Department of Transportation, there is a great deal of product test information and service information that could be of use to consumers, which in turn would help the efficiency of the free market system to critically feedback the desires and objectives of knowledgeable consumers. There, of course, are strong economic schools of thought in this country that still believe in the effectiveness of the invisible hand. The invisible hand, of course, has to have facts if it is going to be effective. The original theory of the market system was posited on the buyer having facts and on a very, very high degree of competition. It seems to be extremely superficial to talk about the market system without rigorously analyzing the quality of the disclosure to the buyer and the quality of the competition in the marketplace.

One of the most important domestic information policies deals with freeing the multiple sources of information which could assist consumers in their purchasing decisions, counter much deceptive or false advertising, and improve overall the efficiency of the market system. Federal agencies have resisted in the past years the disclosure of brand and nonbrand information developed in the course of procurement or other governmental testing functions.

A dramatic change began to occur within the federal establishment in the latter half of 1968 over the refinement and release to the public of brand and other product information accumulated by various agencies with this same public's funds. The Veterans Administration indicated it would release brand information from future tests on products such as hearing aids and wheelchairs. The Federal Trade Commission was in full swing in its disclosure of nicotine levels by brand of cigarette. But above all, the most optimistic evidence was contained in the still restricted "Report of the Task Force on Product Test Information," (dated December 9, 1968) requested by the White House under the Johnson administration. I consider this report the most encouraging policy document in the consumer affairs area prepared by the previous administration. A flavor of its contents, which will now be released, suggests how bright was the promise in December and how dim the follow-through since that date.

The task force surveyed six agencies—the General Services Administration, the Department of Defense, the National Bureau of Standards, the Veterans Administration, and the Departments of Agriculture and Health, Education and Welfare. These agencies perform the bulk of government product testing. One of them, HEW, announced through Secretary Cohen that it would initiate a broad, new program for releasing product information regarding the "cost, safety, merit or comparative value of goods and services." The Department of Defense, the task force noted, "may possibly be able to release some brand information relating to drugs"; GSA could release 98 product types including tests of antifreeze, flashlights and hand files and HEW might be able to disclose tests of contraceptive devices and drugs. Perhaps most remarkable was the task force's report that the Commerce Department—"and specifically the National Bureau of Standards—is enthusiastic about taking on the program, believing that during the first year general information on perhaps a dozen products (including paints, roofing materials, floor coverings, and textiles) could be prepared for release." "As to nonbrand product information," the task force continued, "since GSA tests a great many unbranded or specially branded products that consumers use in other branded forms, it possesses large amounts of general information about consumer products. Of the federal specifications and standards used in the procurement of items for government agencies, GSA estimates that approximately 900 pertain to items of possible use to the general public. Except for clothing, this generic information includes almost the entire range of products purchased by the average family." At the present time only the manufacturer of the specific product tested is informed of the results of the tests. The task force noted that the army possesses "considerable information" on drugs and added that "a substantial portion of the drugs sold through commercial pharmacies do not meet the exacting specifications set by the army. The task force strongly believes that every effort should be made to include some of this information within any release program."

A strong reminder of the forces working against disclosure is contained in the report's mention of the Department of Agriculture's research program in household appliances that was discontinued without explanation in 1965. "Tests were conducted regularly on commercial refrigerators, stoves, water heaters, irons, washers and dryers for the purpose of evaluating performance in use," said the report; "much brand data were amassed, but department policy precluded reference to brand names in departmental releases."

The task force recommended, in a draft Presidential memorandum, that the President request that "all federal departments and agencies review existing programs to determine what information they have about the properties and performance of products purchased by consumers and to consider the means they can employ to make available to the public information not now released." The draft memorandum suggested by the task force would name the President's Committee on Consumer Interests to serve as coordinator of the program on the following timetable—all federal agencies would report to the task force by April 1, 1969 on what they can release to the public, and by July 1, 1969 "on the steps they have taken to carry out the directions" in the proposed memorandum by the President, and by August 1, 1969 the committee would report to the President on its findings and recommendations.

Since the present administration took office, the recommendations of the Task Force on Product Test Information have either been ignored or actively opposed. Led by the Bureau of the Budget and a highly unsympathetic Presidential staff, this incipient breakthrough in consumer autonomy has been squelched as a practical matter. Lip-service attention remains in Mrs. Virginia Knauer's office, but even in that last repository of consumer concern, there is little anticipation that anything will be done. Of course none of the timetables suggested in the report have been met and the entire operation is on the shelf. It is important to note that the task force's recommendations center on assisting the consumer to help himself in the marketplace, with little need for added government manpower and funds.

Perhaps an indication of how hostile modern industry is to an efficiently functioning market system and an intelligent consumer body is that the recommendations contained in the task force report are strongly opposed by industry and commerce. During the past decade, this is the reaction to any governmental official or member of Congress who proposed such disclosure. The auto industry, for example, has wielded strong representations to keep the National Highway Safety Bureau from releasing the results of compliance testing of automobiles, even though motorists have a right to know at what levels their seat belts tear out or their fuel tanks rupture or what vehicles fail to meet the government's safety standards (by the Bureau's own admission between 15 and 20 percent of the vehicles or equipment tested failed one or more standards.)

If the objective of many regulatory agencies is to improve the efficiency of the regulated industry such as competitive efficiency so they are more responsive to the needs of the people, such information helps consumers provide a similar spur or feedback.

One illustration is particularly instructive. Congress has been concerned about waste in governmental expenditures. Since it is being asked to support more and more state and local activities, Congress is presumably interested in state and local purchasing practices. A few months ago, the General Services Administrator, Robert L. Kunzig, took note publicly of GSA's intention to apply a provision of the Intergovernmental Cooperation Act that would enable states and political subdivisions to make their purchases through GSA and its storage facilities. Mr. Kunzig estimated at least 25-percent savings, adding, "We know in many of the commodities purchased by the states that we buy them from 25- to 35-percent less at the federal level." The reason is that GSA buys in volume from the manufacturer, while states and localities purchase from wholesalers-distributors. When it is considered that state and local purchasing amounts to about $35 million a year from these wholesalers-distributors, a saving of at least 25 percent amounts to a vast resource for financially pressed state and local governments. It also may amount to a cleansing of the state and local political process.

Just last week, in only one example, one of the purchasing officials for the city of Indianapolis was also given the duty by the political party of soliciting political contributions. So here he was on the one hand in the role of negotiating contracts for purchases and on the other hand, trying to dun various contributors for contributions to the political party. The entire local-state purchasing or procurement picture is heavily related to a level of political corruption or political waste that is characteristic.

Soon after Mr. Kunzig made this statement in late May, the National Association of Wholesalers began a most sizable effort to persuade the Congress and the administration of the unwise nature of GSA's impending policy. The Bureau of the Budget, with its customary declaratory but not explanatory fiat, overruled GSA. What members of Congress spoke out, spoke out in favor of the wholesalers' groups. The claim was made that GSA was misinterpreting the law. That may be. But the advisability of such a purchasing policy and what was needed to institute it was never discussed rationally in terms of the economic and political benefits. The proposed move by GSA was shouted and pressured down in a typical power play. In the meantime all levels of government are wondering where their billions of dollars are to come from to meet mounting demands for public services.

Had GSA followed an early and full disclosure policy on the differences in purchasing prices between it and state and local purchasers over the last 10 or 15 years, say, a substantial public constituency would have developed to make the subject at least one for balanced public inquiry and debate. Instead, this recent dustup involving a potential of saving billions of dollars annually received little attention outside of the restricted circle mentioned above.

PUBLIC SERVANT ACCOUNTABILITY

Public servant accountability involves one of the most vexing problems of any bureaucratic structure. As such, little thinking has been done about the subject except by operational lobbyists and other pressure groups. Consequently, there is an overdevelopment of public servant accountability to politicobusiness pressures and an underdevelopment of such accountability to aggrieved citizens or other groups with much cause and little power. Many observers of government have lamented over how immovable, unreachable, unresponsible, government officials can be when they wish to be. The syndrome has become a favorite cartoon subject. But it is not humorous at all. The quality of justice dispensed by an organization of government is tied to the degree of accountability of its higher leadership levels. The present system enhances the kind of accountability to interest groups as a matter of power, not as a matter of right for all citizens. This is the antithesis of basic principles of due process.

What is needed is an access system to invoke accountability as a matter of procedural right so that any citizen can have access no matter how unpolitically connected or poor he may be. Such a system would serve to protect civil servants from the one-sided pressures from groups who apply them as a matter of their power. Or to put it another way, civil servants can better resist, if they wish, these one-sided pressures, or their potential application, if the people had certain rights vis-a-vis the agency and its officials. These officials take an oath of office and all agency employees are expected to adhere to an employee standard of conduct of some length, which is printed in the Federal Register. There has been little development of what these principles mean for individual civil servant accountability toward citizens for their policies or refusals to act. In the next few years, there will probably be a more extensive testing of some of these principles in the form of mandamus and injunctive actions against agency officials. Unless there is a basis in law for the presently unrepresented interests in society to invoke individual agency official accountability and responsibility, the inefficiences of agency performance as a result of being captured by the regulated industries will continue unabated. Piercing the bureaucratic veil and reaching the responsible agency officials will assist significantly in connecting men's decisions with their consequences and inducing the kind of administrative behavior that is more consonant with the statutory and regulatory framework.

GOVERNMENT SECRECY AND THE PEOPLE'S RIGHT TO KNOW

RALPH NADER, GARY SELLERS, REUBEN ROBERTSON, JOHN ESPOSITO, HARRISON WELLFORD, JAMES TURNER, AND ROBERT FELLMETH

A well-informed citizenry is the lifeblood of democracy, for in all arenas of government, information, particularly timely information, is the currency of power. The criticality of information is illustrated in the reply of the Washington lawyer to one who asked him how he prevailed on behalf of his clients: "I get my information a few hours ahead of the rest."

In this nation, where the ultimate power is said to rest with the people, it is clear that a free and prompt flow of information from government to the people is essential to replace the myth of democratic pretense with the reality of citizen access to a just governmental process. It was with these truths in mind that Congress passed, after a decade of temporizing, the Freedom of Information Act (FOIA) in 1966. The act became effective on July 4, 1967. When President Johnson signed the bill into law on July 4, 1966 he stated: "I have always believed that freedom of information is so vital that only the national security, not the desire of public officials or private citizens, should determine when it must be restricted."

The term "citizens" is used in this context to refer to any person or persons who are not regulated by the agency and who do not constitute an organized, special interest group. The distinction is important because most agencies have a two-pronged information policy—one toward citizens and one toward the special interest groups that form the agency's regulatory constituency. For the latter, a pattern has emerged of preferential access and treatment over the years. The lobbyists, the trade associations, and the corporations have made the contacts, have developed the insti-

Reprinted from Ralph Nader, Gary Sellers, Reuben Robertson, John Esposito, Harrison Wellford, James Turner, and Robert Fellmeth, "A Status Report on the Responsiveness of Some Federal Agencies to the People's Right to Know About Their Government," in U.S. Congress, Joint Economic Committee, *Economic Analysis and the Efficiency of Government,* Part 3, Hearings of the Subcommittee on Economy in Government, September 1969.

Ralph Nader and his coauthors are associated with the Center for the Study of Responsive Law in Washington, D.C.

tutions (e.g., industry advisory councils) and have generally compromised or intimidated the agency personnel into affording them entry into the early decisional process prior to public surfacing of rule-making, advanced rule-making, policy speeches, and the like. And it is during the inner council discussion stage, the draft-report or draft-standard stage that most of the decisions are made. The options for public impact at later, public stages narrow very rapidly when there is an established system of preferential access to industry or commercial groups. As is well known to the Washington press corps, this process occurs in the Department of Interior with the oil and coal industries, and with the federal banking agencies and the banking industry—to name two of the more egregious wedlocks.

The relationship between free access to information and responsible government is very direct. All of the agencies we have studied enjoy large discretionary power over the programs they administer. Under the agency's legal structure, they can go one way or another; they can delay action, decide what portions of the law to enforce or not enforce, and even adamantly refuse to carry out programs mandated by Congress. These agencies are more agencies of discretion than they are of law. Within limits, this is often necessarily the case, but without free and fast information to the public, discretion more easily becomes an absolutism or tyranny for the common citizen.

Professor Kenneth C. Davis defined discretion in this way:

> "A public officer has discretion whenever the effective limits on his power leave him free to make a choice among possible courses of action or inaction. /D/iscretion is not limited to what is authorized or what is legal but includes all that is within 'the *effective* limits' on the officer's power. This phraseology is necessary because a good deal of discretion is illegal or of questionable legality. Another facet of the definition is that a choice to do nothing—or to do nothing now—is definitely included; perhaps inaction decisions are ten or twenty times as frequent as action decisions. Discretion is exercised not merely in final dispositions of cases or problems but in each interim step; and interim choices are far more numerous than the final ones. Discretion is not limited to substantive choices but extends to procedures, methods, forms, timing, degrees of emphasis, and many other subsidiary factors."

The Freedom of Information Act which came in on a wave of liberating rhetoric is being undermined by a riptide of bureaucratic ingenuity.

"The law was initiated by Congress and signed by the President with several key concerns," says a 1967 attorney general's memorandum. These are: "that disclosure be the general rule, not the exception; that all individuals have equal rights of access; that the burden be on the government to justify the withholding of a document, not on the person who requests it; that individuals improperly denied access to documents have a right to seek injunctive relief in the courts; that there be a change in government policy and attitude."

The act then explicitly provides for nine exemptions which offer a vast amount of discretion—so vast that to call these exemptions loopholes would be to indulge in the grossest kind of understatement. Exemptions for "internal communications," for material deemed to be compiled for investigatory purposes, for information "given in confidence," are agency favorites. Federal Trade Commission officials have discovered that merely instructing a secretary to open an investigatory file and dropping the item in it serves to take care of the FOIA. And as more people are learning, FTC investigational files have every potential of lying fossil-like, undisturbed by the concern of bureaucratic man.

The broad ambit of discretion, worked upon by agencies which differ in their degree of commitment to public and special interests, is also leading to differing and inconsistent proliferation of practices and interpretations. Each agency has created its unique "common law" in interpreting the act and in developing a maze of confusing regulations. Information which is claimed to be exempt from disclosure in one agency is freely given in another agency. (For example, records of advisory council meetings—United States Department of Agriculture—No. National Highway Safety Bureau—Yes. The Federal Extension Service (USDA) gave the students permission to ask the inspector general to see the audits; the Farmers Home Administration did not.)

Agencies also differ in the depth of the "appeals tier" within the agency which a petitioner must exhaust before he can go to the courts for relief. Each appeals point on the tier increases the probability of exhausting the petitioner and mooting the quest, especially when each internal appeal takes three weeks or months. Consumers Union's experience with the Veterans Administration is a good example of how much stamina and resources a petitioner requires to obtain test results of so mundane a product as hearing aids.

There is little doubt that if government officials display as much imagination and initiative in administering their programs as they do in denying information about them, many national problems now in the grip of bureaucratic blight might become vulnerable to resolution.

The particular intransigence characterizing refusals to provide requested information by various agencies studied this summer is noteworthy. These are not agencies in the "sensitive category." They do not deal with military or foreign affairs. They are entrusted with the most sympathetic missions in the governmental arena—health, safety, food purity and distribution and transportation. Yet even under daily approach and reasoned requests, these agencies refused to provide information, some of which is described below. One can imagine the chances of a citizen writing in from Kansas or Oregon.

What follows is a focus on those agency acts which violate or misinterpret the FOIA. However, it is encouraging to take note of the many public servants in the federal government who have respect for the purpose of the FOIA and who frequently bridle under restrictions by their superiors that they believe wholly unjustified. The benefits of the openness of these civil servants, who have provided accurate information to the students as well as to any other interested persons, have been to further the interest in citizen involvement. Not only have the students been able to obtain a more comprehensive picture of the workings of their government, but agency personnel have in many cases received important insights and feedback from the dialogue they have established with the students. By a significant margin, the National Air Pollution Control Administration (HEW) has displayed the most open position on information access. Against this standard of performance, other agency restrictions become even more outrageous as to their ulterior purposes in protecting incompetence and cloaking regulatory surrenders to special interests—e.g., nonenforcement of the laws governing the behavior of corporations.

It is now appropriate to describe some of the concrete instances of governmental secrecy and the techniques used to exhaust petitioners from persisting in their quest.

1. The FOIA provides a specific exemption from mandatory disclosure for material which is an "investigative file." The text says: "[no disclosure is required of] investigative files compiled for law enforcement purposes, except to the extent available by law to a private party."

The intent of this exemption was to protect that kind of investigative material which if revealed would undermine law enforcement. Thus, in order for material to qualify as an "investigatory file," it must be both investigatory in nature and capable of being used in a law enforcement proceeding. That is, even "investigatory" parts of the file are only exempt for so long as they can be used in a law enforcement proceeding, i.e., if law enforcement is still possible, those investigative parts of the file which relate to that enforcement may also still be privileged. When any prosecution proceedings are completed or precluded by other factors, then the entire file should be open—unless other investigative files would be directly impaired by its disclosure. The foregoing is the broadest possible interpretation that can be taken of that provision in the act.

Several agencies have not been satisfied, however, with these broad limits on the "investigative file" principle, so they have expanded and transmuted its character by changing the definition of what is an investigatory file. For example, the Department of Labor has denied public access to their records of past (5-, 10-, and 15-year-old) violations of the Walsh Healy Act which sets minimum wages and safety standards for businesses which have more than $10,000 worth of sales to the federal government. The only sanction for violators is a 3-year bar from further contracts. Thus the Department of Labor keeps secret the nature of past violations which have ceased and are two decades old on the theory that the Labor Department might still get around to using these violations in some future law enforcement proceeding. The Department of Labor also restricts even their *record* of corporate violations of these Walsh Healey standards (rather than the investigative reports within the files). These records and the records of violations filed by inspectors are analogous to records of traffic tickets and were denied to students. In the selected industry reports (showing what companies had been inspected) the Labor Department blocked out the names of all companies inspected before allowing the students access. These denials were then followed with a request for the students to sign a pledge of nonrevelation in order to receive the documents.

Another illegal broadening of the "investigative file" exemption is invoked when other excuses fail. This is when the agency places public information in an investigatory file and then refuses to separate the two. For example, the Department of Labor has claimed that all material in all Walsh Healey files is "investigative" even when the requested material is noninvestigative in nature. Thus, the department secures secrecy by its own commingling and subsequent refusal to separate. The department then completes its denial to the records of their enforcement of that act.

2. The FOIA provides a specific exemption for internal governmental papers in order to preserve and encourage the freedom of internal communication within government and to prohibit premature disclosure. The text of that exemption says: "(no disclosure is required of) inter-agency or intra-agency memorandums or letters which would not be available by law to a private party in litigation with the agency."

The legislative history of this exemption makes it clear that, in judging whether nondisclosure was to be allowed, the prime criterion was to be the relative finality of resolution of the issue in any such document. The evil to be prevented by the exemption was, in the words of the House report "premature disclosure."

In practice, several agencies have illegally broadened this exemption to deny access to matters relating to *past* decisions within the executive branch. The Department of Agriculture has gone further and denied access to the minutes of the National Food Inspection Advisory Committee and the Poultry Advisory Committee. Those committees are made up of nonfederal personnel, including private members, and their alleged purpose is to suggest policy and discuss new hazards to the public interest. The department wants to prevent the public from realizing what an impact privtae interest groups and their state satellites have on meat and poultry inspection policy and what conditions and new hazards exist.

The Interstate Commerce Commission has also invoked this exemption to deny public access in specific areas to records of congressional correspondence with the ICC. Also the ICC has declined to release a six-year-old study of the ICC made for it by the Civil Service Commission. The ICC has also refused to make public the past evaluations of ICC performance which were prepared by ICC personnel. Thus, no information is released as to how the agency assesses its performance. The public usefulness of a contrary policy was seen a few weeks ago when an internal FDA evaluation report was made public. The Department of Labor has misused this exemption to deny public disclosure of their interpretations of the Walsh Healey Act—made in 1936—even though that act has been amended several times since and the public need for this information is essential if any determination of how the law has been administered over the last 33 years is to be made.

Other illustrations reflect the variety of excuses for denials. The Department of Defense has denied access to information on the quantity of oil being pumped from the bilges of naval ships on the grounds that this data will be included in a report which contains operational data relative to military characteristics and will therefore be classified. The water pollution study group wanted information about oil dumping. The Defense Department makes no claim that the specific information requested is itself classified or in any way exempt from the FOIA. The Defense Department is a past master of the "contamination technique" —take several doses of unclassified material that may prove embarrassing and mix them with other doses of classified information and, lo and behold, the sum is entirely classified. Civilian agencies have been quick to deploy this method.

The Federal Water Pollution Control Administration has denied access to copies of research proposals made to but not accepted by FWPCA. The study group wanted this information to assess the research priorities at the agency, to determine whether there was any unfair preference by FWPCA and to see what reasons were given for denial of such proposals.

Only under pressure from the study group and *The New York Times* did the ICC finally release information pertaining to the expense accounts of ICC commissioners which were assumed by industry groups when the commissioners visited trade meetings.

Before continuing on to discuss even more flexible techniques for information suppression, the point must be made that most of the exemptions in the FOIA are discretionary—that is, with the exception of other statutory restrictions and Executive Orders, the agency does not have to invoke the exemption. It is still expected to produce the information and not take advantage of the exemption without a strict shouldering of the burden. Instead, agencies are simply offering the particular exemption as a reason for denial and not producing the underlying facts which are entitled to invoke the exemption.

Agencies are developing ever-refined ways to handle requests under FOIA. Here are some:

The typical tactic is to delay replying for several weeks and then state that the request for information was not specific enough. This tactic has enormous potential and agencies like it. First, if the agency does not permit the inquirer initial access to learn what specifics the agency has, he has no choice but to make a more general request. Any agency knows that one level of secrecy can lead to more requisite levels of secrecy. So the organization or filing of the information possessed by the agency is not revealed. Consequently, the citizen is exposed to a charge of nonspecificity. The more knowledgeable and fraternally received lobbyists, on the other hand, have no such problems. The Department of Agriculture, especially its Pesticide Regulation Division, has perfected this dismal science to a degree that it may uproot itself by the excess of its success.

The Department of the Interior used the delay technique with all the arrogant presumption of the new Assistant Secretary of Interior, Carl Klein. He developed a hamstringing system of centralized appointments and a centralized room for interviews to be conducted under the watchful eye of his monitors. In the initial three weeks of the study, the department repeatedly denied information by cancellation or delay of scheduled meetings and by this monitoring device. An appeal to Herbert Klein, Director of Communications and Secretary Hickel was necessary to instruct Mr. Carl Klein in his duties to the public. He withdrew his edicts promptly. But other delays emerged. For example, the memo of FWPCA's assistant commissioner for enforcement (which outlined the enforceability of water quality standards) was released only after a 10- to 14-day delay after the initial request and an appeal to the Department of the Interior's information officer. The reason given for the delay was the assertion that this document was still in the working-paper stage; however, the paper had already been completed and circulated. Since any work of man can always be perfected, the designation of "working paper" can have no discretionary limits which is another way of saying that the agency who exploits this technique becomes a law unto itself.

A closely related response to the "working-paper" one is that the information is still not verified or is in incomplete form. The FWPCA gave the latter as the reason for refusing, following a 10-day delay, a student permission to see reports on the status of water pollution abatement programs at 20 federal installations. There is a written demand pending to see the information in whatever form it exists since we have taken the position that the agency's laxity in compiling this information is a self-serving and illegal basis for denial of access.

This request for the status reports on 20 installations was made after FWPCA denied more detailed information about the entire problem on the ground that this general information would give the researcher a "warped impression." (At another time this same researcher was told that release of information would endanger the Department of Interior's relationship with the Defense Department "because DOD is finicky about releasing figures on total sewage." Presumably, the enemy could then rush back to its abacus and calculate the manpower strength of the base.) Sewage from domestic military bases is a national security matter, according to FWPCA. It could coincidentally be a national pollution matter that is the basis of the reluctance.

More primitive responses come forth as an agency loses its last reedy rationalizing props for withholding information. Relevant materials on pesticides in the Department of Agriculture[1] disappeared, on the action of a high official, after the students began researching them with permission at the Pesticides Regulatory Library. Outright lies are not unknown as shown by the attached Appendix II describing in greater detail the Civil Aeronautics Board experience. The National Highway Safety Bureau has denied any knowledge of preferential release to General Motors in late June of an army medical team report on off-base accidents involving servicemen in Europe. But it was sent to GM privately. Since the company has recalled several million cars for a carbon monoxide hazard, GM can be forgiven its urgent interest in a medical report showing high carbon monoxide levels in the automobile crash victims' blood. But why not let all the people know at the same time? The report is being released today.

The Food and Drug Administration, which has been more cooperative than some of the other agencies in releasing information to the study group about food purity regulations (perhaps because it has so little to reveal) claimed through an official spokesman that it maintained no brand name list of beverages containing cyclamate. Such a list, however, had been used repeatedly to answer specific inquiries about specific brand names. On learning that the inquirer was part of the summer study group, the agency made the list available. This illustrates that whatever difficulty we may be having, the lone citizen making inquiry by mail from afar or even by visiting the agency is subjected to more government secrecy.

Another generic technique of preferential treatment is to compile the kinds of information that industry desires but decline to compile the information that a consumer or laborer could use. The Department of Interior compiles much information of use for the minerals industry but very little benefits consumers or workers. The Interior Department had to be pushed and prodded to develop a report on environmental depredations of the coal industry, after half a century, and then was reluctant to make it public. Consumer-related information about federal oil policy—from quotas to offshore leases—have been most hard to elicit from the Interior Department. The same imbalance prevailed for hazards in off-shore drilling.

Search costs and reproduction costs can daunt a citizen after he has secured access to agency information. Copying fees range from no charge in some agencies to $1.00 a page in other agencies. Similarly, some agencies charge no search fees, others charge up to $7.20 an hour. Why the difference?

In conclusion, what are some lessons to be learned? First, the FOIA is not being used by the public to secure relief in the courts. Since the effective date of the FOIA on July 4, 1967, court records reveal that 40 cases were brought under the FOIA (to March 1969). Thirty-seven of these cases involved actions by corporations or private parties seeking information relating to personal claims or benefit. In only three cases did the suits involve a clear challenge by or for the right of the public at large to information. Even more significant, no records have come to our attention of any court actions initiated by the news media who should be the prime public guardians and litigators under the FOIA. Patently,

[1] See Appendix I for additional USDA denial.

the effect of the FOIA cannot be measured by court cases. But just as patently, a mere 40 cases in the first 20 months of the act's history are shocking. There need to be institutions, be they public interest law firms, universities, law school law reviews, newspapers, magazines of the electronic media, who systematically follow through to the courts on denials of agency information. The individual citizen just does not have the resources.

The FOIA will remain putty in the hands of narrow-minded government personnel unless its provisions are given authoritative and concrete interpretation by the courts. Such litigation then feeds back a deterrence that radiates throughout an agency. Many general counsels of agencies are straining the act to its utmost and beyond because of the improbability of judicial review. The new general counsel of the Federal Highway Administration, David Wells, has already begun to apply the Byzantine secrecy that he learned from his former railroad and trucker employers. He now wants to prevent disclosure of violations of automotive safety standards to the public. Yet these violations are relayed quickly to the manufacturer involved. The corporation has the right to receive them but not the motorist who may become a casualty because of not knowing about the safety violations in his car or tires. David Wells will have much to learn and like his mentor, Francis Turner will probably have to learn it all in public.

Second, Congress is not exercising adequate oversight over the way the FOIA is being observed. There have been no congressional hearings since the act was passed, although there is abundant material for a most worthwhile public hearing series. Two reports, one from the House and one from the Senate, have been published compiling the regulations and containing responses to some inquiries from the respective committees. Comprehensive congressional hearings are a must.

Third, a Presidential review group should be constituted to eliminate the inconsistencies which now exist, and are increasing, among the FOIA compliance regulations of the various federal agencies. This group should also establish uniform ground rules which will make it exceedingly difficult to achieve devious and illegal circumventions of the FOIA. For example, there should be a clear-cut injunction against the commingling tactic and agencies should be required to separate or segregate the public information from what information may be legitimately withheld. For another example, there should be a one-stop appeal in the agency before judicial review. Stacking layers of appeals within the agency is a strategy of attrition and facilitates divergent policies within the department or agency.

Fourth, each agency should be specifically required to (a) respond in some manner to all information requests within 7 days of receipt of such request or a specific reason given to justify further delay; (b) have available in the Washington office, and elsewhere as needed, a public information reading room with access to copying machines; (c) prepare in advance and have available in the public reading room that data most typically requested of the agency and all relevant data showing workload, productivity, law enforcement activities and similar agency evaluation information, as well as agency-Congress and agency-public records. Such a system will not only encourage more citizen interest—which should be a frontline policy of all agencies—but also will improve the efficiency of response to citizen requests.

Fifth, specific procedures should be developed for taking corrective actions when federal officials resort to harassment techniques or other actions contrary to the FOIA. The establishment of a director of communications earlier this year offers the opportunity to develop effective sanctions on agency leaders who generate or condone such secrecy. Without such review and sanctions from the White House, agencies will continue to thwart or violate the act with impunity. The most important distinction between agency responses toward information requests is the distinction between the agency's leadership. Clearly then, the most important factor in the executive branch for freedom of information is the President himself. And it is up to you, ladies and gentlemen of the fourth estate, to remind him continually of this first imperative.

APPENDIX I: SOME INFORMATION EXPERIENCES WITH THE U.S. DEPARTMENT OF AGRICULTURE

1. Racial hiring charts for individual electric cooperatives financed by REA loans: although the REA's information office decided to give the information, the Department's Office of General Counsel removed it without telling REA. On appeal to the REA administrator, the charts were made available.
2. Information on the fat content of various brand-name frankfurters tested by the department since 1955. Denied.
3. The Farm Credit Administration's record on the recipients of FCA-approved loans. The FCA must approve loans of more than $100,000 made by federal land banks, and other large loans made by the production credit boards. The FCA has refused several times to reveal the names or locations of the recipients, or the sizes of terms of the loans.
4. Results of the Federal Extension Service's study of its program operations in 60 counties, done in 1965 and 1966. Denied.
5. Lists of specific pieces of information that agencies consider exempt from disclosure under the Freedom of Information Act. Denied.
6. Minutes of meetings of the National Food Inspections Advisory Committee and the Poultry Advisory Committee. Denied.
7. Minutes of meetings of the Citizens Advisory Committee on Civil Rights, whose members were private citizens. Denied.
8. Records of any civil rights complaint—concerning either hiring problems or program discrimination —made against the department. Each one of the agencies, as well as the department's civil rights staff, has refused to tell us who has complained, how the complaints were investigated, and what the department has done to correct any violations it found. Denied.
9. Audits done by the department's inspector general on various agencies. After all our requests for audits were routinely turned down, we asked to see summaries of some of the audit findings. This was refused. In one case, both the audited agency (the Federal Extension Service) and the state director whose program was under study (Dr. Marshall Hahn of VPI) gave us permission to see the OIG audit of extension programs in Virginia. Even so, the OIG refused.
10. Copies of memoranda or directives circulated in the department to tell employees how to handle information requests in general and our summer study in specific. Denied.
11. The Pesticide Regulation Division's registration records for specific pesticide products, for instance the Shell Vapona No-Pest Strip. Denied.
12. Copies of a proposal by the department's Program Review and Evaluation Committee for a new system to keep track of civil rights progress. After the Department refused to give us the chart, we informally asked an administrator and got the chart immediately.
13. Copies of civil rights compliance plans that state universities and land-grant colleges have sent to the Federal Extension Service. FES regulations required the state colleges to prepare adequate plans in order to keep getting federal money for state extension programs. The FES has refused to reveal any details of the plans it has approved.
14. Records of any action the department has taken to correct problems pointed out by a number of groups—the U.S. Civil Rights Commission, the Department of Justice, private citizens, and the department's own inspector general and Citizens Advisory Committee on Civil Rights. Denied.
15. All records of action the Pesticide Regulation Division has taken in a number of areas: seizing unsafe pesticide products; recalling products from the market; issuing citations to manufacturers of unsafe pesticides; and recommending prosecution of pesticide manufacturers. Denied.
16. Information about the Pesticide Regulation Division accident-reporting system. The PRD refused to tell us how it evaluates accident reports and what action it has taken in response to the information.
17. Data that manufacturers submit to PRD when they have their products registered. The PRD claimed that all the information in the registration file is covered by the "trade secret" option, even though the specific product formula is contained in a brown envelope marked "confidential" and can be easily separated from the rest of the file.

18. Records of PRD's pesticide-sampling program, which analyzes samples of pesticides from the market. We asked only for those files where no enforcement was planned, but PRD denied all the files, claiming they were exempt under the clause protecting enforcement records.
19. A Department of Agriculture report revealing health hazards in Talmadge-Aiken Act meat plants has been denied Congressmen Thomas Foley and Benjamin Rosenthal and United Press International. This denial has no time limit, as USDA admits that their investigation is closed in this matter.

APPENDIX II: THE CIVIL AERONAUTICS BOARD, A CASE STUDY OF INFORMATION POLICY AND THE PUBLIC INTEREST

The study of the CAB took as one of its primary areas of concern the ways in which the board and the airlines industry deal with or fail to deal with complaints from members of the public. At the outset, statistical information was requested (in writing) as to the total number of complaints received by the CAB, the volume of complaints lodged against the various airlines, and the major categories and sources of complaints. The CAB refused to give this information on the grounds that it had inadequate personnel to keep any records of this sort. Not until the very end of the summer did we learn, from another source, that the board had made detailed studies of precisely the kind of information requested. The CAB lied.

Similarly, data was requested on the CAB's backlog of consumer complaints. The board took four weeks to respond to this single request for the most basic kind of information as to how well it is performing its duties. When that information was finally provided, we learned that the backlog—number of complaints on which the CAB has taken no action—has risen by over 600 percent over the last five years!

Frustrated by this inability to get the basic statistical information from the CAB, we requested an opportunity to inspect the complaints filed by citizens with the CAB against the airlines. This request under the FOIA was arbitrarily denied on the astonishing theory—articulated and repeated by Charles Kiefer, executive director of the CAB—that if the public's complaints were made available for inspection, the airlines would find out the complainants' identities and retaliate against them. Finally, after weeks of delay, the board agreed to permit inspection of a few complaints, *but only if the student agreed not to write down the names or sources of the complaints.* This meant, for practical purposes, that we could not correspond with citizens filing serious complaints to see whether they were disposed of satisfactorily by the airlines or the CAB.

Late in the summer, we learned of a recent report by the CAB of the causes and handling of customer complaints received by the airlines industry. This important study, made at substantial public expense, demonstrated that citizen discontent with the airlines industry has hit a critical level, and cited specified airlines for their apparent complete lack of interest in the problems of inconvenienced air travelers.

Nevertheless, the CAB has suppressed this report from the public, which has every right to know which airlines are concerned with resolving legitimate complaints—and which ones are not. The report was denied to us on the specious reasoning that it "mentions names of airlines," gives numbers of complaints received by some of the airlines, and was compiled from the records of the airlines regulated by the CAB. For these reasons, and because the CAB feared that the findings might be competitively detrimental to the deficient airlines, the CAB officials concluded—apparently without the benefit of legal advice from the CAB legal staff, it should be noted—that release of the survey to us, or even the names of the airlines considered to be deficient, was precluded by a statutory section prohibiting the board from divulging certain classes of confidential financial and commercial data obtained in CAB audits of the airlines' books. This argument, however, utterly ignores the fact that much of the information requested had already been released to several of the airlines as well as to their trade association. The legitimacy of the CAB's rationale is further shattered by the fact that detailed information on the number and types of complaints is readily exchanged among the airlines themselves, which destroys the shibboleth of pretended confidentiality.

The fact of the matter is that the CAB officials have been regularly providing business management and public relations advice, at public expense, to private interests in the airline industry, and have been withholding critical information on the industry which is needed by the public. The dangers of governmental secrecy are manifest in this episode of patent disregard by an important regulatory agency for its responsibilities to the public. For while the CAB is busy providing services for special corporate interests, it has no time or resources for its basic mission of regulations. For example, during the summer numerous requests for basic statistical data which we requested were denied by the CAB on the grounds that it has inadequate staff and accordingly could not assemble such information or provide it for our study. Some of the records the CAB told us it does not bother to keep include the following statistics:

Speeches and personal appearances made by members of the CAB.

Records of the costs of investigations conducted by the CAB.

Travel allowances and budgetary allocations for individual board members, the executive director and the director of community and congressional relations of the CAB.

Enforcement actions by the CAB's Bureau of Enforcement against air carriers for violations of the law.

Complaints charging racial discrimination by the airlines.

The number of initial decisions of CAB hearing examiners appealed to the board in accordance with its regulations.

The number of interested parties seeking to intervene in CAB proceedings pursuant to its rules of practice.

We frankly find it beyond belief that an agency can effectively protect or advance the public interest without establishing for itself basic priorities and keeping certain basic records of its work. In the atmosphere of openness and public scrutiny contemplated in the freedom of information philosophy we submit, such contempt for the rights and needs of citizens and such patronizing solicitude for the business interest and image of private industry cannot thrive.

CORPORATE SECRECY AND THE NEED FOR FINANCIAL DISCLOSURE

WILLARD F. MUELLER

It is fundamental that a market economy functions properly only in an atmosphere of extensive knowledge concerning financial and other aspects of corporate behavior. Contrary to the assertions of many corporate spokesmen, corporate secrecy —not corporate disclosure—is the great enemy of a market economy in a free society.

A market-directed economy is premised on intelligent responses of businessmen and investors to profit opportunities. Investors direct the flow of capital funds into the most efficient enterprises. But as a firm becomes increasingly conglomerated, its public financial reports become less and less useful to investors.

Additionally, a market economy places heavy reliance on the self-corrective mechanism of the marketplace to keep competition alive. When a firm holds a strong market position resulting in high profits, this acts as a magnet inducing new entry. Or, conversely, when a firm has higher than necessary costs which result in unprofitable operations, this too attracts entry and spurs on competitors to better the inefficient company. But again the published financial statements of the large conglomerate enterprise mask both the high profits and the losses of its various operations.

Ironically, American businessmen today operate under two sets of rules with respect to the disclosure of corporate financial information—one set for large corporations and another for smaller ones. We know a great deal about small and medium-sized corporations because, almost invariably, they are quite specialized. One need only glance at the annual report of almost any industrial company with annual sales under $50 million to learn its strengths and weaknesses in a line of business. But not so with a large conglomerate corporation whose annual report masks more than it reveals. Not surprisingly, therefore,

Adapted and reprinted from statement of Willard F. Mueller before the Monopoly Subcommittee of the Select Committee on Small Business, U.S. Congress, November 1971.

Willard F. Mueller is Vilas Professor of Agricultural Economics and Economics at the University of Wisconsin, Madison, Wisconsin.

it is the large corporation that invariably resists steps to strengthen disclosure requirements—steps that in practice would, at most, place it on a par with small corporations. This is yet another example where allegedly equal treatment under the law results in grossly unequal treatment among those covered by the law. One is reminded of Anatole France's bitter characterization of this anomaly: "The law with majestic impartiality forbids the rich and poor alike from stealing bread and sleeping under bridges."

Although proponents of greater disclosure generally have rested their case on variations of the above arguments, I believe there are even more compelling reasons for more public access to corporate affairs. These arguments do not rest on the needs of the investor or the proper functioning of a competitive market, but on the needs for knowledge in a democratic society by the public at large: by consumers, by public regulatory agencies and other governmental bodies, by the press, and by social scientists and others involved in the essential task of probing and interpreting the changing nature of corporate organization and behavior. For only when important corporate affairs are exposed to public inspection can the social legitimacy of the corporation be determined.

In a free society, no institution vital to the public interest can maintain a claim to legitimacy if its affairs are shrouded in secrecy. Significant steps have been taken in recent years in opening to public view many more governmental affairs, though much more needs to be done on this score. The time is long overdue that similar steps be taken to open the large private corporation to public view. This is especially imperative because of our diminishing knowledge of the operations of the few hundred corporations that control most economic activity in the private sector of the economy.

THE DECLINE IN PUBLIC KNOWLEDGE OF CORPORATE AFFAIRS

The need for more adequate disclosure of corporate financial affairs grows as American corporations grow in size and complexity. Our economic intelligence about many aspects of business organization is worse today than it was around 1900, when Roosevelt made his plea for opening to public view the "mammoth" corporations of his day. It was self-evident to Roosevelt that, "Great corporations exist only because they are created and safeguarded by our institutions; and it is therefore our right and our duty to see that they work in harmony with these institutions."[1] He therefore argued that, "The first requisite [of corporate accountability] is knowledge, full and complete; knowledge which may be made public to the world."

There actually were very few really big businesses in Roosevelt's time. The great trust movement of the period created only two industrial corporations with assets exceeding $500 million by 1909, and both of these, U.S. Steel and Standard Oil (N.J.), were specialized to a particular industry. In contrast, by the first quarter of 1971, there were 111 industrial corporations with assets of $1 billion or more. Although there are about 200,000 corporations and nearly 200,000 partnerships and proprietorships engaged in manufacturing, by the beginning of 1971 the 111 largest of these held at least 51 percent of the assets and 56 percent of the profits of all corporations engaged primarily in manufacturing;[2] the 333 industrial corporations with assets of $500 million or more accounted for fully 70 percent of all industrial assets, excluding their unconsolidated holdings. Indeed, by 1970 the two largest industrial corporations, alone, had combined sales of nearly $40 billion, which is about as great (in constant dollars) as those of the over 200,000 manufacturing establishments operating in 1899.

Thus, there exists an extremely asymmetrical industrial structure, with the bulk of economic activity controlled by an elite of a few hundred enormous corporations and the remainder divided

[1] Roosevelt's first annual message to the Congress, December 1901.

[2] This is a minimum estimate of these corporations' share of industrial assets because it includes only their consolidated assets. These corporations control huge amounts of unconsolidated assets, perhaps another $50 billion or so. Federal Trade Commission, *Economic Report on Corporate Mergers,* 1969, p. 175.

among 400,000 small and medium-sized businesses. And what is true of the industrial sector is increasingly true of the nonindustrial sectors as well.

But much more is involved than an increase in the absolute size of some American corporations and the growing share of industrial activity controlled by a relatively few large businesses.[3] Many large contemporary corporations operate across an increasing number of industries[4] and across many national boundaries. Such multiproduct, multinational corporations enjoy much greater flexibility and discretion in deploying their resources than do their smaller, more specialized rivals.

The new dimensions of corporate control extend beyond the economic into the political. Corporate annual reports increasingly read like a state of the nation address, and in some cases like a state of the world address. Indeed, the tone and scope of a recent ITT annual report are not unlike what one might expect of a prime minister's characterization of the British Empire in its days of glory. ITT proudly proclaimed to its stockholders that its vast international organization "is constantly at work around the clock—in 67 nations on six continents, in activities extending from the Arctic to the Antarctic and quite literally from the bottom of the sea to the moon. . . ."[5] It might appropriately have added that its officers and directors have included such international men of affairs as former U.N. Secretary-General Trygve Lie, Director of ITT-Norway; former Belgium Premier Paul-Henry Spaak, a director of ITT-Belgium; two members of the British House of Lords; a member of the French National Assembly; and, at home, John A. McCone, former director of the CIA and Eugene R. Black, who is widely known in international economic and political circles, where he has held such important posts as president of the International Bank for Reconstruction, special financial advisor to the Secretary-General of the U.N., and financial advisor to the Sheik of Kuwait, as well as board member of dozens of large corporations.

As perhaps the outstanding example—and success story—of the modern multinational conglomerate corporation, ITT is a useful subject of an inquiry into the adequacy of existing corporate-disclosure requirements.

ITT—A Case Study in Inadequate Disclosure

Although ITT is still not a household word, during the last decade it grew nearly eightfold to become one of the world's largest international corporations; its assets grew from $1.1 billion in 1961 to $8.3 billion in 1970. The latter figure excludes properties valued at $527 million that are owned by National Aeronautics and Space Agency and the Department of Defense but operated by ITT.[6]

ITT was already a very large company before it became a highly conglomerated organization. In the four decades following its founding in 1920, it became a large international manufacturer of telecommunications equipment and an operator of telecommunications systems.

In the early 1960s ITT embarked on a major diversification-through-merger program in order to change its image from what its chairman and president characterized as "primarily a one-product company." During 1961–1968 it acquired 52 domestic and 55 foreign corporations, with the acquired domestic companies alone holding combined assets of about $1.5 billion. During 1969 ITT's board of directors approved 22 domestic and 11 foreign acquisitions. The three largest—Hartford Fire Insurance Co., Grinnell Corp., and Canteen Corp.—added over $2 billion. Since 1969 it has acquired another 30 companies, making it

[3] Between 1950 and 1970, the 200 largest industrial corporations increased from 47.7 percent to 61.4 percent their share of the assets of corporations engaged primarily in manufacturing. The 1950 figure is based on *FTC Economic Report on Corporate Mergers*, 1969, p. 173; the 1970 figure is my estimate. The FTC figure for 1968 was 60.9 percent.

[4] *Ibid.*, pp. 213–225. Whereas in 1960 each of the 200 largest industrial corporations operated in an average of 13 industries (four-digit SEC industries), by 1968 each of the 200 largest industrial corporations operated in an average of 20 industries. *Ibid.*, p. 221.

[5] ITT Annual Report, 1966, p. 7.

[6] Prepared statement of Willard F. Mueller in *United States versus International Telephone and Telegraph Corp. and Grinnell Corp.*, United States District Court of Connecticut, p. 22, and Appendix 5.

the most acquisitive corporation of the current merger movement.

Before engaging in this massive merger program in 1960, ITT ranked 34th among America's manufacturing companies and 43rd among the industrials of the world. In 1970 it ranked eighth among America's industrial companies and, with 392,000 employees, it ranked as the fourth largest private industrial employer of the world.

ITT has retained its telecommunications leadership, ranking as the world's second largest manufacturer of such products and the largest outside the United States. But as a result of its acquisition effort, by 1970 its traditional line of telecommunications and electronics manufacturing accounted for only 15 percent of its net income. Much of the rest was derived from the operations of leading firms acquired in such diverse businesses as industrial and consumer electrical, electronic, and other industrial products, life insurance, consumer finance, car rentals, hotels, baking, chemical cellulose and lumber, and residential construction.

Although ITT is primarily a manufacturing corporation, selling to and buying from thousands of other businesses, it also touches directly the lives of millions.

As a consumer you can buy a home and live in ITT-Levitt's planned communities; buy furnishings for your home with personal loans from one of ITT's finance subsidiaries; fertilize your lawn with ITT's Scott fertilizer; insure your home at ITT-Hartford Fire Insurance; buy your life insurance from one of ITT's life insurance subsidiaries; invest your savings in ITT-Hamilton Management mutual funds; munch on ITT-Continental bakery products; savor an ITT-Smithfield ham; buy cigarettes and coffee from ITT-Canteen vending machines; stay at hotels or motels owned by ITT-Sheraton; rent a car from ITT-Avis; buy books from ITT's Bobbs-Merrill publishing division; or attend one of ITT's technical and business schools. Finally, had the ABC-ITT merger not been blocked by the Justice Department, you could have been ITT's guest for an evening of TV viewing.

Moreover, part of each of your tax dollars spent on defense and space programs goes to ITT, which is one of the nation's leading prime defense contractors. ITT maintains Washington's "hot line" to Moscow, mans the air force Distant Early Warning (DEW) system and the giant Ballistic Missile Early Warning System (BMEWS) sites in Greenland and Alaska, the large NASA facility at Cocoa Beach, Florida, and the Defense Department's Western Test Range in California.

With its numerous foreign operations, ITT is an important force in international economic affairs. Since 1960 ITT has acquired over 50 foreign companies and now has about one-third of Europe's telecommunications business.

So the story for Europeans is much the same as for Americans: They can rent ITT-Avis cars, holiday at ITT-Sheraton hotels, buy ITT-Levitt homes, eat ITT-Continental foods and buy ITT mutual funds and insurance.

Massive multinational corporations like ITT have dimensions of economic and political power extending beyond that held by the traditional large corporations. As President Wilson observed in 1919, "These great corporations are economic states. They are no longer private corporations." Clearly, large international corporations of today are much larger "economic states" than those troubling Wilson five decades ago.

Despite the enormous growth of ITT over the last decade we really know less about its constituent parts than we did in 1960, when it was still quite specialized. Each time ITT acquires a public corporation, it further diminishes our economic intelligence of American industrial organization, as the operating statements and balance sheets of the acquired companies are subsumed in ITT's consolidated statements. In 1970, ITT provided the public precious little financial information on its operations. Although it manufactured numerous products, it broke down its net assets into only four broad categories: "manufacturing," "consumer and business services," "telecommunications utilities," and "consolidated," with the largest share (49 percent) in the "consolidated" category.[7] It did little better with respect

[7] ITT, 1970 *Annual Report,* p. 34.

TABLE 1. Principal ITT Product Groups, 1970

	Sales and revenues		Net income	
	In millions	%	In millions	%
MANUFACTURING				
Telecommunications equipment	$1,244	19	$ 52	15
Industrial and consumer products	1,849	29	71	20
Natural resources	287	5	30	8
Defense and space programs	316	5	8	2
Subtotal	$3,696	58%	$161	45%
CONSUMER AND BUSINESS SERVICES				
Food processing and services	$1,241	19	30	8
Consumer services	808	13	19	8
Business and financial services	386	6	21	6
Hartford fire	—	—	88	25
Subtotal	$2,435	38%	$158	45%
UTILITY OPERATIONS	233	4	34	10
Total	$6.364	100%	$353	100%

Source: ITT, 1970 *Annual Report*, p. 34.

to sales and income information, which are detailed in Table 1.

Except for Hartford Fire Insurance Company, it is impossible to determine the financial contribution of the over 100 operations acquired by ITT since 1960. Even such leading acquired companies as Grinnell are lost to public view. With annual sales of near $350 million when acquired in 1969, in 1970 Grinnell was submerged in ITT's "Industrial and Consumer Products Group" which had reported sales of $1,849 million. Similarly, such important and diverse acquisitions as Avis-Rent-A-Car, Canteen, Levitt & Sons, Sheraton Hotels, and Bobbs-Merrill Publishing, were included in ITT's "Consumer and Business Services Group," along with divisions manufacturing frozen foods, providing technical education, parking lots, and other industry or service categories. The product categories used in ITT's 1970 annual report obviously are far too broad for intelligent decision-making by investors, quite apart from their use for the other purposes discussed below.

Lest you assume ITT's financial reporting practices are below par for large corporations, let me remind you that for four consecutive years ITT received the top award of the Financial Analysts Federation for "excellence in corporate reporting." Obviously, ITT has much company when it comes to inadequate reporting.

Let us now turn to SEC's recent efforts to improve the quality of corporate reporting.

THE SEC'S FAILURE TO REQUIRE ADEQUATE DISCLOSURE

For many years the SEC had a rule that corporations subject to its jurisdiction disclose insofar as practicable the relative importance of each product, service or class of similar products that contributed 15 percent or more to gross sales.[8] This rule had long been criticized as being excessively broad. However, the SEC remained unmoved to change until after Sen. Philip Hart's Senate Subcommittee on Antitrust and Monopoly held hearings in 1965 on the subject, and threatened to introduce legislation directing the SEC to require divisional or some other more definitive form of segmented sales and profit reporting. SEC Chair-

[8] This information was required on its Forms S-1, S-7, and 10.

man, Manuel F. Cohen, subsequently informed Senator Hart the SEC already had the authority to require adequate disclosure and that it was considering doing so.

During the next 4 years there was considerable discussion and controversy in the business community, particularly among public accountants, a number of whom had long been critical of this and other SEC reporting requirements.[9] But the greater part of the accounting fraternity opposed stricter rules. Finally, on September 4, 1968, the SEC issued a proposed rule that would have required, among other things, corporations to report the sales and net income of each class of related or similar products which contribute 10 percent or more to sales or net income.

Although the SEC made no systematic, independent analysis of the proposed rule, evidence was presented demonstrating that the proposed rule required little meaningful data from the largest corporations. The SEC, evidently not wishing to be confused by any facts, apparently was much impressed that practically all industry sources objected to even the proposed rule. The result was passage of a watered-down version of the original proposal.

Not only did the SEC permit large corporations to report financial details of only their very largest product lines, but it failed to adopt rules guaranteeing comparability in reporting. Rather than establish reporting criteria of its own, SEC gave management discretion in deciding what constituted meaningful product categories. It did so on the premise that "Management, because of its familiarity with company structure, is in the most informed position to separate the company into components on a reasonable basis for reporting purposes. Accordingly, discretion is left to the management to devise a reporting pattern appropriate to the particular company's operations and responsive to its organizational concepts."[10]

As already noted, SEC's reporting rule has a strong bias requiring much more detailed reporting by small companies than by large companies. An example will illustrate the point. Suppose you wished to obtain financial information concerning the nature and scope of electrical components manufactured by various manufacturing firms. From ITT's financial reports you would learn that it is an important manufacturer of various electrical components, TV sets, radios, phonographs, and tape recorders. However, ITT combines sales and earnings from its electronic and electrical equipment with those from home freezers and household appliances, air conditioning, disc brakes, and industrial pumps. As a result, ITT electrical products are lumped in a broad category of industrial and consumer products with combined sales of $1.8 billion.

The failure of the SEC to require adequate reporting argues forcefully for adopting a more direct approach to the question of corporate secrecy. Because the SEC has repeatedly demonstrated an inability to perform responsibly in this area, I think a new legislative mandate is required. Additionally, even were the agency to perform more responsibly in the future than in the past, new legislation is required because the SEC's authority is restricted mainly to financial disclosure relevant to protecting the investor.

THE FTC'S QUARTERLY FINANCIAL REPORT PROGRAM

Nor are the SEC's shortcomings unique. Every effort to obtain more meaningful information about large corporations meets vigorous opposition, even when the information is not made public. Currently, powerful business interests are trying to prevent the FTC from requiring more detailed financial information for its quarterly financial reports on manufacturing, which provide profit and financial information on manufacturing corporations.[11] The statistical information gen-

[9] Alfred Rappaport and Eugene M. Lerner, *A Framework for Financial Reporting by Diversified Companies,* National Association of Accountants, New York, 1969, pp. 45–55.

[10] Letter accompanied the release of the statement explaining the SEC disclosure rules, August 14, 1969.

[11] Federal Trade Commission, *Quarterly Financial Report on Manufacturing,* U.S. Government Printing Office.

erated by this program is used widely by governmental agencies, especially for national income accounting purposes, and by thousands of corporations. The report has over 10,000 paying subscribers. Although this is the most reliable and timely source of such information, its quality has deteriorated sharply since the program's inception in 1947. Information on many individual "industry" categories is becoming all but meaningless as large corporations spread their operations over more and more lines. To eliminate this defect, the FTC requested permission of the Office of Management and Budget (OMB)[12] to obtain from large corporations reports by line of business rather than consolidated reports for the entire corporation. To date, OMB has rejected the proposal because the information requested was of a confidential nature and corporations would have difficulty providing it.[13] Additionally, leading industrial critics of the proposed improvement in the program argued that the SEC's recently promulgated line-of-business reporting program would give the FTC much of what it needed.[14]

Recently I attended a conference at which a senior official of the Financial Executives Institute took credit for having "squelched" this FTC effort. In subsequent discussion he clarified his statement by adding that he did not take sole credit for this accomplishment. Indeed, he reported that when the Business Advisory Council on Federal Reports met with OMB officials on the FTC proposal, over 30 of the businessmen present objected to the FTC program. This is hardly surprising, however, since only big industrial interests were represented at the OMB meeting; there were no representatives of small business, no representatives of the investment community or other business users of these data, nor any representatives of the public at large.[15] This official also reported that he and other members of the Business Advisory Council had had discussions with OMB officials concerning the transfer of the FTC–QFR program elsewhere in government to insure confidential treatment of the data; by confidential treatment he means that the data should not be used for regulatory purposes. Incidentally, these discussions apparently were held in secret since OMB has not commented publicly on the subject. This illustrates the insidious manner in which the Business Advisory Council on Federal Reports often influences indirectly, through its privileged position as advisor to the Executive Office of the President, that which it cannot control directly.

This most recent episode in preventing adequate corporate disclosure smacks of a repeat of tactics used to frustrate the FTC's 1963 intercorporate relations inquiry. Too often OMB has been the errand boy of the advocates of corporate secrecy. To correct this situation, the Executive Office of the President should not be permitted to interfere with the investigative or information-gathering responsibilities of the independent agencies. The Congress created the FTC as an independent agency to insure that the commission not become a creature of the President. This action was taken because of the fear—for which the Congress had foundation in fact—that the bureau would become a captive of the Office of the President.

12 Under the Federal Reports Act of 1942, the data requests of governmental agencies must be approved by OMB (previously called the Bureau of the Budget).

13 "FTC Proposal on Corporate Data is Tabled," *Washington Sunday Star*, April 25, 1971.

14 In a prepared statement opposing the proposed FTC program, the Financial Executives Institute urged that the FTC utilize the data to be reported to the SEC under its new requirements, arguing that "It is inconsistent and unreasonable to require companies to report detailed profit data on more than one basis." FEI statement on proposed FTC Report Form LB-Annual Receipts and Income by Line of Business, January 21, 1971—OMB Panel Meeting, p. 6. It is difficult to take this argument seriously since the FEI previously had played a leading role in opposing adequate SEC disclosure requirements. See A. Rappaport and E. M. Lerner, *Public Reporting by Conglomerates* (Englewood Cliffs, N.J.: Prentice-Hall, 1968) p. 53.

15 Of the 29 corporate officials attending this meeting, 20 were from the top 50 industrial corporations, six were from the 51st through the 100th largest industrial corporations and three were from the 101st to the 150th largest industrial corporations. The remaining 11 officials represented such big business-dominated trade associations as NAM, Automobile Manufacturers Association, and Financial Executives Institute. "Minutes, BACFR Panel on Proposed FTC Survey Form LB," Office of Management and Budget, Executive Office of the President, January 21, 1971.

Until such time as the OMB is stripped of its present control over the independent agencies, steps should be taken to reform OMB's existing operating procedures. To begin with, the OMB should invite interested members of the public to participate in meetings at which OMB reviews independent agencies' budgets and investigations. This would represent a significant step in eliminating secrecy in government which so often has been the handmaiden of corporate secrecy.

FEDERAL CHARTERING AND CORPORATE SECRECY

In the nearly 100 years since New Jersey amended its constitution in 1875 to liberalize greatly the incorporation process, state chartering statutes have become increasingly framed to suit the interests of corporate enterprise. The whole thrust of this development has been to confer upon the corporation the rights and privileges of private citizens. Yet over the period, as more and more of the economy became the domain of enormous corporate enterprises, they increasingly have taken on the characteristics of public enterprises, as they influence directly and indirectly the livelihood of all Americans. Justice William O. Douglas put it well when he observed: "Enterprises . . . which command tremendous resources, which hold the fate of whole communities of workers in their hands, which have a virtual or actual monopoly, which dominate markets and control vast resources tip the scales on the side of prosperity or on the side of depression, depending on the decisions of the men at the top. This is tremendous power, tremendous responsibility. Such men become virtual governments in the power at their disposal. In fact, if not in law, they become affected with a public interest."[16]

Because of this changed character of the American business scene, it is appropriate that large corporations be recognized and treated as quasi-public institutions. Federal chartering is an appropriate first step in the public transformation of the large corporation from a purely private enterprise to a quasi-public enterprise.

This will necessarily involve a great public policy debate on the future role and responsibility of the large corporation. In my view, such a debate is imperative to the continued social legitimacy of big business, for out of the debate will come a new consensus of what it is reasonable and appropriate to expect from the large corporation.

One is tempted to settle for piecemeal reform, as witness the SEC compromise in setting disclosure standards. The politician's slogan, "a half a loaf is better than none," has great popular appeal. But this siren call of pragmatism serves only to frustrate adequate reform. For half a loaf is not better than none if it only dulls the appetite and the legitimate demand for a full meal.

Elsewhere I have set out in some detail the justification and disclosure requirements of a comprehensive chartering statute.[17] Briefly, such a statute, which probably should be restricted to only the largest corporations, should include the following disclosure provisions:

- The chartering agency should have extensive visitation privileges to insure it ready access to relevant corporate information
- Much more extensive public reporting of the sources of investment, revenues and profits than is now required by the SEC
- Extensive public disclosure of the volumes of all products manufactured and sold, including such information corporations currently supply the Bureau of the Census under strict rules of confidentiality
- Public disclosure of corporate federal income tax returns
- Disclosure of certain social costs
- Disclosure of intercorporate financial ties
- Disclosure of publicly owned facilities operated or leased by private corporations
- Disclosure of various details of the corporation's foreign operations

[16] William O. Douglas, *Democracy and Finance* (New Haven, Conn.: Yale University Press, 1940) p. 15.

[17] "Corporate Disclosure: The Public's Right to Know." Conference on Formulating Financial Reporting Standards, Northwestern University, October 18–19, 1971.

- ○ Public representation on the board of directors where necessary to obtain information on corporate affairs

This, then, in skeletal form is my program for providing greater public disclosure of corporate affairs. It clearly is not an attack on our market economy but an effort to perfect it. Although federal chartering is not a panacea, it is an essential first step in recognizing the large modern corporation for what it is—an essentially public institution.

Nor is this proposal a substitute for a vigorous program to make competition more effective wherever possible. On the contrary, it complements efforts to improve competition by opening new opportunities for the operation of "natural" market forces. But though the program recognizes that competition is not dead as an important disciplining influence in most American industries, it also recognizes that giant corporations enjoy great discretion in making numerous decisions that affect our social, cultural, political, and economic welfare. More complete disclosure by large corporations therefore serves the dual objective of aiding natural market forces and of providing the broader benefits to society flowing from more complete information of corporate affairs.

INDEX

Accident injury industry, 34
Adams, Walter, 12 n., 13, 43–46
Adelman, M., 213 n.
ADR system, 38
Advanced manned strategic aircraft, 118
Advanced weapons, appropriations for, 101–102
Aerojet-General Corp., 138
Aerospace Industry Association, 168
AFL-CIO, 131
Agency for International Development, 216–217
Aggregate consumer spending, 34
Agricultural Conservation Program, 186
Agriculture Department, 38, 49, 216, 270, 274, 277; information experiences with 280–281
Aiken, George, 223
Air Force Association, 113, 140
Airlines, federal subsidies to, 51
Airline terminals, delays at, 18
Air Transport Association, 257
Allen, William M., 57
American Association of State Highway Officials, 229
American Automobile Association, 228
American Broadcasting Company, 262
American Economic Association, 164
American National Gas Company, 258–259
American Paper & Pulp Corp., 56
American political power, economic origin of, 26–32
American Road Builders' Association, 228–229
American Telephone & Telegraph Company, 128, 258
American Trucking Association, 228
American wars, cost of, 110
Anderson, Jack, 31
Anthony, Robert, 168
Antiballistic Missile System (ABM), 101, 120, 162, 167
Antitrust regulation, 36, 263, 269
Arkansas Basin Development Association, Inc., 225
Armed services, peacetime strength of, 123–124
Armed Services Procurement Regulations, 151
Arms race, 58–59; defense expenditures and, 45, 114–128; escalation in, 119
Arms sale, international, 133–134
Ashland Oil Company, 31
Atlantic Richfield Oil Company, 36
Atomic Energy Commission, 20, 128, 131, 136, 148
Automobile, faulty design of, 34–35
Automobile insurance, premiums for, 35–36
Automobile Manufacturers Association, 288, 289 n.
Automobile repairs, 34
Avco, Inc., 138
Avis Rent-A-Car, Inc., 287

Banking lobby, 31
Bank loans, corporate vs. private, 41

Banks, time deposits and, 41
Baran, Paul, 28
Bates, Timothy, 26–32
Bell Telephone Laboratories, 130, 162, 264
Benoit, Emile, 128
Berle, A. A., Jr., 28 n.
Bethlehem Steel Company, 225
Big business: fear of, 3; government capture by, 13
Black, Eugene R., 285
Blackie, William, 173
Boeing Company, 51, 57, 128, 138
Booz, Allen & Hamilton Company, 39
Broadcasting, federal regulation of, 258, 262
Brown, George, 161
Budget Bureau, 83, 179, 261
Budgetary programs, review of, 89
Budgets: efficiency in, 20; military. *See* Military budget
Buesking, Col. A. W., 154, 156
Bureau of Public Roads, 226, 228–229
Bureaucracy: military budget and, 114; welfare and, 25
Burke, Adm. Arleigh, 140
Business, tax subsidy to, 38, 83–88. *See also* Taxes
Business Advisory Council on Federal Reports, 289
Bus lines, subsidies for, 51
Butterbrodt, John, 180
Buzhardt, J. Fred, 174
Bywater, George P., 66

Cabotage Laws, 217
Califano, Joseph, 243–244, 247–248
Campaign contributions, 31; corruption and, 30; special interest groups and, 7
Canteen Corp., 285
Capital gains tax, 77–78
Cargo Preference Acts (1954), 215–217
Cargo thefts, 35
Car insurance, premiums for, 35–36. *See also* Automobile
Cary, William, 257
CATV (cable television), 264
Census Bureau, 290
Central Intelligence Agency, 128, 131
C-5A cargo plane, cost overruns on, 39, 48, 97, 99, 122, 147, 156–157, 159–162, 167–172
Chamber of Commerce, U.S., 64
Champion, George, 173
Charitable institutions, tax exemption for, 79
Charles, Robert H., 145–146, 152
Chase Manhattan Bank, 50, 53, 173
Cheyenne helicopter, 160, 171
China, military budget and, 113, 122
Christiana Securities, Inc., 28
Civil Aeronautics Board, 51, 53, 256, 278; information policy and public interest in, 281–282
Civil war: cost of, 110; veterans' benefits in, 108–109
Clark, John M., 109
Clark, Joseph S., 32 n.
Clawson, Del, 31
Clayton, James L., 107–111
Clear Water Restoration Act (1966), 198
Clements, William, Jr., 173
Cohen, Jerry S., 30 n.
Cohen, Manuel F., 288
Colorado River Compact, 197
Commerce Department, U.S., 51, 54, 58, 194, 263
Commodity Credit Corporation, 49, 184–185
Common Market, 162
Communications Policy Task Force, 262
Competition: in defense industry, 146–147; inventions and, 36; power decentralization and, 46
Compliance surveys, federal regulation and, 268–269
Compulsory consumption as sub-economy, 39–40
Comsat, 264
Congressional appropriations, 178–179
Congressional Subcommittee on Economy in Government, 181
Connally, John B., 48
Consumer information system, 36
Consumers, "involuntary" buying by, 34–35
Controlled market sub-economy, 36–37
Cook, Donald C., 258
Coolidge, Calvin, 184
Corcoran, Tommy, 258
Corporate economy, impact of, 33–34
Corporate secrecy: federal chartering and, 290–291; financial disclosure and, 283–291
Corporate sector, growing power of, 3
Corporate socialism sub-economy, 37–39
Corporation: as "new industrial state," 43–44; ownership vs. control of, 28; secrecy of, 283–291; zoning by, 37
Corporation income tax, 70–71
Corps of Engineers, U.S., 16, 131, 195, 197, 202, 253; U.S. waterways and, 220–223, 226
Cost analysis, problems of, 153–154
Cost overruns, 39, 48, 97, 99, 122, 147, 156–165, 167–172; causes of, 160–163; decision-making and, 162–165; in defense contracting, 38–39; examples of, 160–162
Cost-plus-fixed-fee contract, 152

Council of Defense and Space Industry Associates, 141, 168
Council of Economic Advisers, 72, 92, 180, 225
Council on Environmental Quality, 54, 198
Countervailing power, concept of, 5
Cross, Bert S., 53
Crude oil: exports and imports of, 212; U.S. and world prices of, 207. *See also* Oil

Dairy products, support of, 186
Davis, Kenneth C., 274
Davis, Gen. W. Austin, 139
Defense Budget, 127; inflated, 146; and Joint Economic Commission, 104–106; for 1950, 127; profile of, 100–103. *See also* Military budget
Defense Contract Audit Agency, 151
Defense contracts, largest holders of, 129–130, 136
Defense Department, U.S., 20, 52–53, 58, 98, 113, 115, 118, 127, 216–217, 270, 285; absence of accounting standards in, 150–151; advanced weaponry and, 101–102; arms sale by, 133–134; cost analysis in, 153–154; data processing equipment leased by, 130; economic authority of, 128; incentive contracting and, 152; inefficiency and waste in, 145–146; ITT case and, 285–287; manpower requirements of, 130–131; Merchant Marine and, 217–218; outlays of (1969), 100; patent policy and, 146; posture statement of, 125–126; program budget for, 102; reform of procurement in, 166–174; R & D expenditures by, 131–132; reports to Congress by, 154
Defense expenditures, arms race and, 45. *See also* Defense Department
Defense industry: beneficiaries of, 135–137; concentration and entrenchment of, 137–138; cost overruns in, 38–39, 48, 156–165, 167–172; high profits in, 154–156; informal polity in, 138–142. *See also* Military-industrial complex
Defense Industry Advisory Committee, 57
Defense posture statement, annual, 125
Defense production, geographic distribution of, 137
Democratic party, war chest of, 259
Dennenberg, Herbert S., 39
Depletion allowances in oil industry, 6, 44, 208–209
Depreciation allowance, 76–79
Dewey, D. R., 109
Dillon, Douglas, 75
Distant Early Warning System, 286
Dodd, Thomas, 31
Douglas, Paul H., 74–81, 140, 243–244, 246–247, 249
Douglas, William O., 290
Douglas Aircraft, 161
Douglas amendment, 76–77
Douglas Commission, 243
Downs, Anthony, 231–237
Dresser, John, 58
Dresser Industries, 58
Drug products, excessive profits in, 30
Drugs, worthless, 34
Drumm, Thomas, 51
Dulles, John Foster, 102
Du Pont de Nemours, E. I., Company, Inc., 28 n.

Economic analysis, regulatory decisions and, 261–266
Economic Opportunity Bank, 24
Economic power: political power from, 29–32; strongholds of, 26–29
Edmondson, Ed, 223, 225
Education: bureaucracy in, 19–20; government failures in, 24
Edwards, Richard C., 5 n.
Efficiency: budgets and, 20; in public spending, 15–16
Eisenhower, Dwight D., 30, 45–46, 102, 132–133, 211, 258–259
Elementary and Secondary Education Act, 19, 21
Elliott, Carl, 132
Employment, in industrial-military complex, 130–131
England, Skybolt program for, 160–162
Environmental Education Act (1970), 55
Environmental Protection Agency, 52, 199, 253
Esposito, John, 273–282
Estate tax, 71
Expendable sub-economy, 40–42
Export-Import Bank, 217
Exporting, income treatment in, 82

Family fortunes, distribution and inheritance tax factors in, 27–29
Farmers Home Administration, 274
Farm income, 188
Farm policy, benefits in, 182–190
Farm price support and subsidy program, 182–184, 187–188
Farm programs, cost of, 186–189
Fear, military budget and, 113
Fechteler, William M., 139–140
Federal agencies, appeals tier of, 275
Federal-Aid Act (1916), 227
Federal Barge Lines, 225
Federal budget: for 1950 and 1969, 127. *See also* Military budget

Federal Bureau of Investigation, 58
Federal chartering, corporate secrecy and, 290–291
Federal Communications Commission, 56–57, 254, 258, 261, 264
Federal Corrupt Practices Act, 30
Federal Drug Administration, 201
Federal Extension Service, 274
Federal Farm Board, 184
Federal farm programs, 184–190
Federal government: malaise toward, 3–4; "tax expenditures" by, 37. *See also* Government
Federal grant-in-aid programs, 21
Federal highway programs, 226–230
Federal Housing Administration, 247
Federal housing policy, HUD and, 243–249
Federal housing programs, welfare and, 234–237
Federal policy vs. private sector, 33–42
Federal Power Commission, 55, 201, 253, 260
Federal regulation: agencies and personnel in, 256–260; information policy and, 253–260; objective of, 271
Federal Reports Act (1942), 55
Federal Reserve System, 28, 41
Federal subsidies: to farmers, 182–188; to industry, 38, 48, 83–88; merchant marine and, 216
Federal taxation policy, 63, 72–73, 82
Federal Trade Commission, 34, 36, 41 n., 257, 270, 274, 284 n.; Quarterly Financial Report Program of, 288–290
Federal urban programs, problems of, 231–233. *See also* Urban development
Federal Water Pollution Control Administration, 277–278
Feed grains, direct payments for, 185
Fellmeth, Robert, 273–282
Financial disclosure, corporate secrecy and, 283–291
First National City Bank of New York, 31, 41
Fisher, Irving, 153
Fitzgerald, A. Ernest, 154, 166–174
Fitzhugh, Gilbert W., 166–174
Fitzhugh Report, 166–169
Flood protection, 16
Florida Waterways Association, 225
Fluke, John Maurice, 173
Fly-before-you-buy policy, 169–171
F-111 plans, 122, 139, 154, 159–160
Food and Drug Administration, 34, 258, 278
Ford, Benson, 28 n.
Ford, Frederick W., 258
Ford, Henry, Sr., 28, 229
Ford, Henry, II, 28 n.
Ford Foundation, 28, 262, 264
Ford Motor Company, 28
Fortune, 40
Foster, John S., Jr., 120
Foundations, 65–66, 79
Fox, Ron, 58
France, Anatole, 284
Franchise chains, government loans to, 50
Freedom of Information Act, 273–280
Freeman, A. Myrick, 198–206
Friedman, Milton, 12, 23–25

Gaffney, Mason, 191–197
Galbraith, John Kenneth, 28 n., 43, 45, 112–116
Gates, Thomas L., 140
Gatt, Rene A., 66
Gaulle, Charles de, 161
General Accounting Office, 150, 155
General Dynamics Corp., 57, 113, 116, 128–129, 136–137, 140, 159
General Electric Company, 128–130, 137–138
General Motors Corp., 40, 43, 112, 128, 137
General Services Administration, 39, 269–270
Ghost foundations, 65, 262–264
Gift tax, 71
Gore, Albert, 30
Government: in American economy, 13: dissatisfaction with performance of, 11; flood-control policy of, 16–17; inefficiency of, 11–12, 15–22; omnipresence of, 8; perverse incentives of, 15–22; as promoter of private enterprise, 47–51; reduction in size of, 23–25; regulation of, by industry, 52–59; size of, 12, 23–25; unresponsiveness of, 11–12; water pollution control and, 17, 198–206. *See also* Federal government
Government functions, pluralist viewpoint in, 4–5
Government policy, as vested power, 43–46
Government Printing Office, 52, 54
Government secrecy vs. right to know, 273–282
Government spending, taxpayers and, 6–7, 32, 104–106
Government subsidies: information on, 179; taxpayers and, 32, 38, 48, 83–88. *See also* Tax
Gray, Kenneth, 223
Great Depression, 68, 227
Great Lakes shipping fleet, 218
Greyhound Bus Lines, 31
Grinnell Corp., 285, 287
Gross national product, 33, 42, 127; military expenditures and, 128; quality of, 39; radio broadcasting and, 262

Grymes, Douglas, 48
Gwinn, W. P., 58

Hahn, Marshall, 280
Haig-Simons income definition, 192
Halpern, Seymour, 31
Hardin, Clifford M., 180
Harris, C. Lowell, 49
Harsha, William, 31
Hart, Philip, 34–35, 42, 287
Hartford Fire Insurance Company, 285, 287
Hatcher, R. G., 37
Haveman, Robert H., 3–8, 178 n., 198–206, 220–225
Hawk missile, 171
Headstart program, 19
Health, federal role in, 239
Health, Education and Welfare Department, 55, 88, 242, 270
Health hazards, 39–40
Hercules Powder Company, 138
Highway Trust Fund, 228
Highways, congestion charges for, 19
Hoag, Malcolm, 122 n.
Holding companies, 27–28
Homan, P., 209 n., 211 n.
Hospital costs, increase in, 17
"Hot line," 286
House Appropriations Committee, 121, 178
House Banking and Currency Committee, 31
Household earnings, percentage distribution of, 29
House Ways and Means Committee, 75
Housing Act (1949), 244, 246
Housing codes, enforcement of, 235
Housing policy, HUD bureaucracy and, 243–249
Housing subsidies, 21
Housing and Urban Development Department, 87, 243–249
Houthakker, Hendrik S., 180
Hughes, Howard, 51
Hughes Aircraft Company, 173
Hutchinson, Everette, 258

ICBMs, 138, 161
Ichord, Richard H., 139
Incentive contracting, failure of, 152
Incentives, for public officials, 19–21
Income distribution, taxation and, 67–69
Income tax, 69–70; corporation, 70–71; negative, 25. *See also* Tax
Independent Petroleum Association of America, 211
Industrial concentration, 43–44
Industrial-military complex, 98–99. *See also* Military-industrial complex
Industry: defense contracts to, 1950–1967, 128–130; government regulation by, 52–59
Industry Advisory Committee, 52–59
Industry Advisory Council, 141, 173
Industry advisory groups, 52–59
Inheritance taxes, 27–28
Institute for Defense Analysis, 143, 163
Intergovernmental Cooperation Act, 271
Interior Department, 278
Internal combustion engine, 36, 40
Internal Revenue Service, 68
International arms sale, 133–134
International Bank for Reconstruction and Development, 283
International Telephone & Telegraph Company, 285–288
Interstate Commerce Act, 228
Interstate Commerce Commission, 36, 46, 201, 221, 224, 257, 276
Interstate Highway System, 230
Interstate Oil Compact, 210
Inventions, competition and, 36–37
Investment Bankers Association, 257
Involuntary sub-economy, 34–35

Jackson, Henry, 224
Jackson, Robert C., 173
Javits, Jacob K., 38
JOBS program, 48
Joelson, Charles S., 178 n.
Johnson, Jeh, 245–246, 248
Johnson, Lyndon B., 118, 198, 227, 229, 259, 262, 273
Johnson, Nicholas, 254, 261–269
Johnson, Samuel, 46
Joint Economic Committee, 14 n., 38, 47, 75, 104–106, 126, 171
Justice Department, regulatory decisions by, 263–264, 269

Kahn, A., 209 n., 213 n.
Kaiser Health Plan, 238, 241
Kaufman, Richard F., 100–103, 135–144
Keegan, Capt. Patrick, 139
Kennedy, John F., 53, 75, 102, 140 n., 161, 259, 261
Keynesian economics, 114
Kiefer, Charles, 281
Killian, James R., Jr., 143

Kimble, Stevens & Harsha, 31
Kirkemo, Harold, 51
Kirkland, Joseph, 174
Knauer, Virginia, 271
Kohlmeier, Louis M., 226–230, 256–260
Kolko, Gabriel, 31 n.
Koppers Company, Inc., 48
Korean War, 74, 107–109, 184, 192
Kunzig, Robert L., 271–272
Kuss, Henry J., Jr., 58, 134

Labor Department, U.S., 130, 268, 275–276
Laird, Melvin R., 119, 170
Land retirement programs, 186
Legislators, selling of votes by, 31–32
Lerner, Eugene M., 288 n. 289 n.
Lever Brothers, 55
Levinson, Larry, 244–245
Lewis, Hobart, 174
Lewis, Roger, 141
Lie, Trygve, 285
Ling-Temco-Vought, Inc., 128
Little, Arthur D., & Company, 39
Loans, federal guarantee of, 47
Lobbying in oil industry, 7
Lockheed Aircraft Corp., 39, 48, 64 n. 99, 113, 128–129, 136, 147, 156–160, 172
Logistics Management Institute, 156
Long, Russell, 7, 30
Longwood Foundation, 28 n.
Look magazine, 138
Lovejoy, W., 209 n., 211 n.
Low-income housing subsidies, 21
Lumb, H. C., 204
Lundberg, Ferdinand, 31 n., 32
Lynde, Gen. Nelson M., 139

McClellan, John, 224–225
McCone, John A., 285
McDonald, S., 209 n.
McDonnell-Douglas Corp., 51, 128–130
McElvenny, Ralph T., 258
Macmillan, Harold, 161
McNamara, Robert S., 57, 102, 159
McNary-Haugen bills (1927–1928), 184
McNeil, Wilfred, 173
Mahon, George, 121, 167
Manatos, Mike, 54
Manned Orbiting Laboratory, 115, 118
Manvel, Allen, 249
Maritime Administration, 217
Maritime policy, 215–219
Maritime subsidies, 17–18, 216
Maritime Subsidy Board, 217
Marx, Karl, 26
Massachusetts Institute of Technology, 142–144
Mass Transportation Act, 31
Mead, Walter J., 207–214
Means, Gardner C., 28 n.
Medicaid: influence of, 239–240; reimbursements in, 242
Medicare, 39, 111; inefficiency in, 238–242; influence of, 239–240; reimbursements in, 242
Melman, Seymour, 127–134
MER (maximum efficient rate) prorationing in oil industry, 209–210
Merchant marine: efficiency of, 17-18; foreign competition in, 219; subsidy to, 17–18, 216
Merchant Marine Act (1936), 215
Metcalf, Lee, 14, 52–59
Metropolitan Life Insurance Company, 166, 173
Mettler, Ruben E., 141, 173
Mexico, conquest of, 80
Military aircraft, budget for, 119–122
Military Audit Commission, 115
Military budget: attacks on, 97; bureaucracy and, 114; cost escalation in, 118–120; cost overruns and. *See* Cost overruns; factors behind, 117–126; improving decisions in, 125–126; military power and, 112–116; for 1950–1969, 127–128; planning and, 120; policy decisions and, 177–78; U.S. commitments and, 122–123. *See also* Defense Department
Military contractors, subsidy to, 146. *See also* Defense contracts
Military-industrial complex, 44–45, 127–129, 135–144, 259; beginnings of, 132; economic impact of, 127–134; manpower requirements and, 130–131
Military pay increases, 117
Military planning, budget and, 120
Military power, budget and, 112–116
Military procurement: inefficiency and waste in, 145–146; profits and cost overruns in, 154–158
Military strength, peacetime, 123–124
Minnesota Mining and Manufacturing Company (3M Company), 53
Mintz, Morton, 30 n.
Minuteman missiles program, 119–120, 138, 151, 161
MIRV warhead, 113, 119–120, 138
Mississippi Valley Association, 225
Mitchell, James P., 53
Morgan, Howard, 260

Morris, Thomas, 141
Motion Picture Association, 31
Motorola Corp., 130
M–16 rifle, 139
Mueller, Willard F., 283–291
Mundt, Karl, 224
Murphy, Henry C., 109
Musgrave, Richard, 192
Muskie, bill, 202–203

Nader, Ralph, 13, 33–42, 56, 267–272, 273–282
National Academy of Sciences, 34
National Advisory Commission on Health Manpower, 241
National Aeronautics and Space Administration (NASA), 128, 131, 136, 285
National Association of Broadcasters, 257
National Association of Manufacturers, 64, 289 n.
National Association of Wholesalers, 272
National Bureau of Standards, 270
National Coal Association, 211
National defense, Joint Economic Committee budget for, 104–106. *See also* Defense Department
National Highway Safety Bureau, 269, 271, 274
National Industrial Pollution Control Council, 53, 55
National Inter-regional Highway Committee, 227–228
National Railroad Passenger Corp., 55
National Rivers and Harbors Congress, 225
National Security Budget, Joint Economic Committee and, 104–106
National Security Program, 105–106
NATO (North Atlantic Treaty Organization), military budget and, 123
Natural resources, environmental policy and, 191–197
Navy League, 140
Negative income tax, 25
Negro housing, Baltimore, 233
Nelson, Gaylord, 179
Nemours Foundation, 28 n.
New Deal, 49, 227
Newport News Shipbuilding and Drydock Company, 138
New York City, rent control in, 25–26
New York Herald Tribune, 30
New York Times, 131, 139, 248, 277
Nike Hercules program, 162
Nike-X antiballistic missile system, 130
Nixon, Richard M., 48, 53, 64, 180, 186 n.
Nolan, John, 49
North American Aviation, 128, 133, 139
North American Rockwell Company, 58, 113, 138
Northwestern Transportation Center Study, 216
Nossiter, Bernard, 170
NTA chemical, 55
Nuclear forces and warheads, 20, 120; Defense Budget and, 102–103

Office of Education, 55
Office of Management and Budget, 53, 55–57, 91
Office of Road Inquiry, 227
Office of the Secretary of Defense, 163
Offshore oil rights, 191
Ohio Valley Improvement Association, 225
Oil: rationing of, 25; U.S. and world prices of, 207
Oil depletion allowance, 6 n., 37, 44, 76, 208–209
Oil import quotas, 25, 42, 211–212
Oil industry: "excess capacity" in, 210; government subsidies to, 207–214; income tax credits in, 212; market-demand prorationing in, 209–211; resource misallocation in, 213–214; "spillover costs" in, 213
O'Neill, Richard, 246

Packard, David, 58, 141
Patman, Wright, 28 n., 31, 79
Pay increases, military and civilian, 117
Payroll tax, Social Security and, 71–72
Peabody Coal Company, 225
Peacetime army, 123–124
Peanuts, support for, 185
Pearson, Drew, 31
Pechman, Joseph, A., 67–73, 92–94, 192
Peck, M. J., 159 n.
Penn Central Railroad, 47, 50
Pentagon. *See* Defense Department
Percy, Charles H., 38, 243
Peru, conquest of, 80
Petkas, Peter, 56–57
Petroleum industry, 44. *See also* Oil
Pharmaceutical Manufacturers Association, 258
Phillips Petroleum Company, 31
Planning-programming-budgeting system (PPBS), 261
Polaris submarines, 138
Political power, economic origins of, 26–32
Pollution, industry councils on, 54–56
Poseidon missile, 119–120
Posner, Richard A., 8 n.
Post Office Department, reform of, 24–25
Posture statement, annual, 125
Powell, Lewis Franklin, Jr., 173
Power, technology and, 44

PPBS (planning-programming-budgeting system), 261, 265
Pratt and Whitney engines, 139
Prescott, William H., 80
Price fixing, 36
Private enterprise, government subsidy of, 47–51
Private power, government performance and, 9 ff.
Private sector, federal policy and, 33–42
Private wealth, distribution of, 27
Procter & Gamble Company, 55
Procurement reform, Defense Department, 166–174
Profits in defense contracts, 154–156
Progressive federal tax system, 92–94
Progress payments, 147
Projector, Dorothy, 27 n.
Proxmire, William, 38, 47–48, 140, 157, 169, 174, 179 n., 224
Public Health Service, 56
Public incentives for private decision-makers, 16–19
Public knowledge of corporate affairs, 284–287
Public officials, incentives for, 19–21
Public programs, efficiency in, 15–16
Public servant accountability, 272
Public Works Administration, 227
Public works committees, 7

Radio-television networks, regulation of, 258, 262
Railroads, federal subsidy of, 50
Ramsey, Maj. Gen. Lloyd B., 58
RAND Corporation, 154, 160, 163, 264
Rappaport, Alfred, 288 n.
Rapping, Leonard A., 215–219
Raymond, Jack, 139
Raytheon Corp., 130
RCA Corporation, 130
Reagan, Ronald, 195
Refuse Act (1899), 202
Regulatory agencies, objectives of, 271
Regulatory decisions, economic analysis and, 261–269
Regulatory policy: compliance and sanctions in, 268–269; efficiency and, 267–272
Reich, Michael, 5 n.
Rent control, New ork City, 25–26
Republic Steel Corp., 204
Research and development: expenditures on, 131–133; management of, 253
Rice, Berkeley, 138 n.
Rice, government support for, 185–186
Richardson, Elliot, 55
Rickover, Adm. Hyman George, 148, 150, 155
Ridgeway, James, 143
Right to know vs. government secrecy, 273–282
Rivers, L. Mendel, 167
Robertson, Reuben, 273–282
Rockwell, W. F., Jr., 58
Roosevelt, Franklin Delano, 26
Roosevelt, Theodore, 284
"Ruml plan," 75
Rural Electrification Administration, 49–50

Safety hazards, 39–40
St. Charles, Inc., 66
Scherer, Frederic M., 159–165
Schlesinger, Arthur M., Jr., 161 n.
Schnittker, John A., 185 n.
Scholarships, 24
Schooling: compulsory, 24; government failures in, 24. *See also* Education
Schultze, Charles L., 12, 15–22, 115, 117–126, 182–190
Schumpter, Joseph, 40, 44
Secondary consumer expenditures, 34
Secrecy: in corporate affairs, 283–291; vs. right to know, 8, 273–282
Securities and Exchange Commission, 75, 257–258, 287–290
Selected Acquisition Reports, 171
Self-Interested Policy-Maker Model, 29
Sellers, Gary, 273–282
Senate Antitrust Committee, 207, 267, 287
Senate Defense Preparedness Subcommittee, 121
Senate Finance Committee, 30, 75–76
Shaw, Gaylord, 14, 47–51
Shell Oil Company, 37
Shepherd, Mark, Jr., 58
Shillito, Barry J., 141
Short-weighting, 34
Sierra Club, 195
Singer Company, 173
Skybolt program, 160–162
Slum clearance, 18
Slum landlords, 41
Small Business Administration, 50, 135
Smith, Adam, 4, 46
Social Security payroll tax, 71–73
Soil Conservation Service, 193
Soviet Union: cost overruns and, 164–165; defense budget and, 113, 116, 122; strategic arms race and, 119; supersonic bomber of, 121; TALLINN system of, 120
Soybeans, support for, 185–186
Spaak, Paul-Henri, 285

Spaniards, conquest of Mexico and Peru by, 80
Special interest legislation, 6–7
Standard Oil Company of N.J., 225, 284
State Department, U.S., 58
State taxes, 72
Stennis, John, 167, 170
Stephan, Paula, 220–225
Stern, Philip, 77, 79
Strategic arms race, escalation in, 45, 58–59, 119
Stubbing, Richard A., 145 n.
Sub-economies, categories of, 34–42
Subsidies. *See* Federal subsidies; Tax subsidies
Sugar, support for, 186
Supersonic bomber, threat of, 121
Surrey, Stanley S., 82–91
Swezy, Paul, 28
Sylvania Electric Company, 138
Symington, Stuart, 133
Systems Management Contracting, 128

Task Force on Product Test Information, 271
Tax(es): avoidance of by wealthy, 27–28; capital gains, 77–78; corporation, 70–71; estate, 71, gift, 71; government policy in, 63; income, 25, 69–71; income distribution and, 67–69; inheritance, 27–28; level and structure of, 64; major sources of, 64; payroll, 71–72; as percentage of income, 93; progressive, proportional, and regressive, 69 n., 92–94; rich vs. poor in, 67–73; state and local, 72
Tax Act (1971), 83
Tax aids as subsidies, 49
Tax burden, redistributing of, 93
Tax-exempt foundations, 65–66
Tax-exempt holding companies, 28
Tax Expenditure Budget, 38, 83–91
Tax expenditures: direct governmental assistance and, 88–91; for fiscal 1971, 84–85; tax reform and, 82–91; total, 38
Tax loopholes, 37, 74–81, 265
Taxpayers: economic power and, 29; government spending and, 6–7; government subsidies and, 32
Tax reform, 82–91
Tax Reform Act (1969), 199
"Tax revolt," 72 n.
Tax subsidies, nature and extent of, 83–88
Tax system, federal, 73, 82
Technology, corporation and, 43
Teledyne, Inc., 41
Television as "sick influence," 265
Television networks, regulation of, 258
Tennessee Gas Transmission Corp., 258
Texaco, Inc., 37
Texas Instruments Inc., 58, 130
TF–30 and TFX jets, 122, 160
Theft, government failure in protection against, 23
Thiokol Chemical Corp., 138
Thompson, Ernest O., 211 n.
Thurmond, Strom, 174
Tipton, Stuart, 257–258
Tobacco, government support for, 185–186
Total package procurement concept, 156
Train, Russell, 54
Transfer sub-economy, 35–36
Transportation Act of 1966, 220–225
Transportation Department, U.S., 55, 253
Transportation policy, 215 ff.
Treasury Department, U.S., 74, 77, 82, 87, 91
Trinity Improvement Association, 225
Truman, Harry S., 74
Truth in Negotiations Act, 146, 149–150
TRW, Inc., 173
Turner, James, 273–282
Tyrrell, Merton, 139

Underwater strategic missile systems, 119
United Aircraft Corp., 128
United States Steel Corp., 38, 56, 284
Universities as military contractors, 142–143
Urban development: basic problems of, 231–233; efficiency and equity in, 18, 231–237; social policy and, 231 ff.; zoning and, 18
Urban Mass Transportation Administration, 50
U.S. Export-Import Bank, 51

Vested interests, rivalry among, 5
Vested power, government policy as, 43–46
Veterans Administration, 270
Veterans' benefits, increase in, 1776–1970, 108
Vickrey, William, 19, 192
Vietnam War, 3, 23, 97, 114, 133, 137, 217; ultimate cost of, 107–111
Vinci, Leonardo da, 133
Violence, government failure in protection against, 23

Wages and Hours Public Contracts Division, Labor Department, 268
Wall Street Journal, 30, 34
Walsh-Healy Act, 275
War loans, war costs and, 109
Warren, Col. Joe., 168

Washington Metropolitan Highway Users Conference, 229
Washington Naval Disarmament Treaty (1921), 123
Washington Post, 248
Water development, income tax and, 192
Water institutions, reform of, 195
Water policy: "giveaway" in, 191–197; wastefulness in, 191–192; wealthy beneficiaries of, 194
Water pollution: conventional objections in, 204–205; "enforcement" in, 201–202; federal failure in, 17, 198–206; pluralism in, 205–206
Water Pollution Control Act (1956), 198–199, 277–278
Water Quality Act (1965), 198–199
Water treatment facilities, 201
Wealth: concentration of, 26; distribution of, 27; taxes and, 67–73
Weapons procurement, 145–146
Weapons systems, future expenditures on, 20, 102–103, 117–118, 120
Weaver, Robert C., 244, 246, 248–249
Weidenbaum, Murray L., 49, 113, 137, 148, 155
Weiskopf, Thomas, 5 n.
Weiss, Gertrude, 27 n.
Welfare programs: government improvements in, 25; for special interest groups, 6
Wellford, Harrison, 273–282
Western Electric Company, 130, 162
Westinghouse Electric Corp., 138, 151
Wheat, direct payments for, 185
White, Thomas, 161
Williams, Mason, 266
Wilson, Desmond P., 123 n.
Wilson, Woodrow, 26
Winterthur Foundation, 28 n.
Wood, Robert C., 244–245, 248
Wool, support of, 186
Work incentive programs, 82
World War I: cost of, 110–111; veterans' benefits in, 108
World War II: corporation tax and, 70; cost of, 107, 110–111; farm programs and, 184; highway programs after, 227; income distribution in, 68; veterans' benefits in, 108

Xerox Corp., 40

Zoning boards, land control and, 37

73 74 75 76 9 8 7 6 5 4 3 2 1